Also by David Dreman

The New Contrarian Investment Strategy

Contrarian Investment Strategy

Psychology and the Stock Market

CONTRARIAN INVESTMENT STRATEGIES: THE NEXT GENERATION

Beat the Market by Going Against the Crowd

DAVID DREMAN

SIMON & SCHUSTER

SIMON & SCHUSTER
Rockefeller Center
1230 Avenue of the Americas
New York, NY 10020

SIMON & SCHUSTER and colophon are registered trademarks
of Simon & Schuster Inc.

Designed by Pagesetters/IPA

Manufactured in the United States of America
20 19 18 17 16 15 14 13 12

Library of Congress Cataloging-in-Publication Data

Dreman, David N.
    Contrarian investment strategies : the next generation : beat the
market by going against the crowd / David Dreman.
        p.   cm.
    Includes index.
    1. Speculation.   2. Stocks.   3. Investments.   I. Title.
HG6041.D658   1998
332.63'228—dc21   98-14660
                                                           CIP
ISBN-13: 978-0-684-81350-9
ISBN-10:   0-684-81350-5

ACKNOWLEDGMENTS

Most ideas do not originate in a vacuum, and this is certainly true of this work. I have been fortunate to have been able to exchange views with some excellent thinkers on the Street. In particular, I'd like to thank Jim Michaels, the editor-in-chief of *Forbes,* who I regard as the original contrarian, for being an invaluable mentor to me as a columnist for that magazine for almost twenty years. Jeff Schuss, John Dorfman, and the late Ted Halligan and Vartanig G. Vartan also constantly challenged and developed my thinking.

I am privileged to be acquainted with some of the pioneers studying the psychology of markets. I've known Paul Slovic, one of the fathers of cognitive psychology, for over two decades, and am indebted to him for both his research and ideas. The same is true of the late Amos Tversky, one of the leading figures in this valuable discipline. Dr. Peter Neubauer, an internationally recognized psychiatrist, has also been important in influencing my thinking over the years. I would also like to thank members of the Board of the Institute of Psychology and Markets: Professor Vernon Smith, a pioneer in conducting experiments on investor behavior in markets; Professor Fred Renwick, a respected and original investment thinker; Arnie Wood, the President of Martingale Asset Management, and Professors John Schott and Richard Geist of the Harvard Medical School, all dedicated to helping investors understand the important influences of psychology in markets.

I owe an enormous debt to Dr. Eric Lufkin, the Director of Research of the Dreman Foundation, for his scrupulous statistical studies documenting many of the major findings presented here, as well as the extensive time he spent in supervising the research for this work. Drs. Nelson Woodard and Mitch Stern, both trained in quantitative economics, also played a major role in developing and documenting the research, as did Dr. Michael Berry, with whom I collaborated on a number of articles. Peter Seligman, Rock Albers, and Mike Hemberger provided hundreds of hours of indispensable research assistance.

The exchange of views with Professors Robert Shiller, Meir Statman, Richard Thaler, Russell Fuller, and Richard Zeckhauser—all behavioral economists—has also been important to the work presented here.

My relationship with Simon and Schuster has been both pleasant and constructive. In particular, I would like to thank my editor, Fred Hills, for his many important contributions in shaping this work both on the conceptual and editorial levels. I also very much appreciate the efforts of Hilary Black, an associate editor there.

Needless to say, the statement that any errors in the work are my sole responsibility certainly applies here.

For Holly, Ditto, and Meredith,
without whose love, support—and pleasant diversions—
this book might have been completed many months earlier.

CONTENTS

INTRODUCTION

THROUGH the summer of 1997 the Dow Jones Industrial Average hit new high after new high, continuing the breathtaking advance it began seven years earlier. It took ninety years for the Average to make its first thousand-point gain. Now it hurdled each new barrier in a matter of months. Since the beginning of 1996 the Dow had risen a staggering 3,000 points, and from the autumn of 1990 it had almost quadrupled.

The rise had caught virtually every expert flat-footed. Back in 1990, most firmly declared that the Great Bull Market that had begun in 1982 was over. A level to moderately down market was the best that could be expected. For years the forecasters were confounded by the rise—although they were loath to admit it. But as the averages exploded, so did their confidence.

By the fall of 1997, the market has become increasingly volatile, plunging hundreds of points in a single session only to more than recoup the loss in the next few trading days. Then on October 27, it plummeted 554 points, the largest daily point drop on record, before again approaching an all-time high in January, 1998. The high volatility continued through the end of 1997 and into the new year. What was going on? In the future, there will, of course, be retrospective answers, or at least you will know what the market did next. But hindsight, in and of itself, has never made an investor money.

Some things were clear to me as I wrote this introduction in the first weeks of 1998. We were in a raging Bull Market, one so powerful that it eclipsed any other of this century. Never before in the 101-year history of the Dow had it risen over 20% for three consecutive years, or quadrupled in seven. Never in my recollection or in my study of previous markets have I seen such widespread investor enthusiasm for stocks—even including the run-up prior to the 1929 Crash. The price of stocks, relative to what we call "fundamentals," is higher than in 1929 or in 1987, the years of the two great market crashes of the twentieth century.

This market is different, said many experts who called it a "new era." The last time this consensus was prevalent was just prior to the 1929 Crash. Some have gained international reputations for calling the shots to date. Abby Joseph Cohen, of Goldman Sachs, a gracious and intelligent professional, is the most acclaimed market strategist of our day. Abby towers over all the other forecasters because of her accurate calls on the skyrocketing market for the past few years. Ed Yardini, the chief economist of Deutsche Morgan Grenfell, is another "Wall Street Wizard," as he was recently dubbed by a national financial periodical, for being right on the course of the market and heralding a Dow of 15,000 by the year 2005. Or as yet another money manager put it, "With fundamentals like these, what valuation do you put on this market?" Whee!

I've been here before. I came to Wall Street from my native Canada back in the mid-sixties. I'd hardly unpacked my bags and got my first job on the Street when, along with everyone else I knew, I was swept up by the "go-go" market of the time. Back then the rage was exciting concept companies. We were all making many times our salaries buying them. In fact, a Street job was only the ticket to stay close to the game; our salaries seemed inconsequential—or so we naively thought. After all, the stocks we owned, like University Computing, Lesco-Data Processing, or National Student Marketing didn't just double. No indeed. They shot up five, ten, even twentyfold, all in a couple of years. In our eyes, investors who bought the staid old blue chips were fossils. They simply ignored the enormous money to be made in these fast-track stocks. Experts and average investors all agreed this market was unique.

It wasn't. Within months many of these sizzlers were down as much as 80% or 90%. Many of my colleagues not only lost their tenfold gains, but also their initial capital. I was luckier. Having studied market manias, I came out alive, but still left the better part of my gains on the table.

This humbling experience increased my curiosity about markets. In researching one of my earlier books, I logged a lot of library hours reading the daily financial pages from the years before 1929 to try and get a feel for the prevailing mood of the time. How could those silly investors in the era of flappers and speakeasies really think stocks could go up forever? It was hard to believe they did not realize the enormous folly they were swept up in. Of course, they could not see the future, but it was easy for me to smile, knowing the ending.

But as wild as the prevailing enthusiasm was in these periods, what's out there today seems to be in a different league. A historian reading about this market, at the turn of the twenty-second century, might chuckle at the obvious aberrations taking place now, just as I was amused looking back at 1929. Perhaps he or she will wonder, what were those late-twentieth-century investors smoking?

Once again the experts state, "nothing can stop this market," and the public believes. The public backs that belief with a good part of its hard-earned savings. As a result, the number of American households owning stocks and the size of their holdings dwarf any period in the past.

Yes, many of us have heard it all before. But even hearing it and going through the gut-wrenching experience of portfolios literally melting away, as investor perceptions change suddenly and sharply, does not prevent most of us from continuing on a course that almost certainly will end in disaster.

But it doesn't have to be this way. There are methods to determine whether individual stocks or markets really are too high or too low, as well as how to consistently benefit from this knowledge. As this book will explain, in a period of ebullience, you should have a method to know that it is time to dive into the nearest bomb shelter, or better yet, evacuate from the market in an orderly fashion. One thing I can predict: it is almost axiomatic that the wild enthusiasm of today will be met with the equally unwarranted pessimism of tomorrow.

Yes, the times are very different from when I published *The New Contrarian Investment Strategy* in September of 1982. Back then the market had gone nowhere in seventeen years, and, adjusted for inflation, the Dow was almost back to its prices of the depressed thirties. People were buying art, collectibles, diamonds, precious metals—anything but stocks. All this, as hindsight tells us, just before the greatest bull market of the century began in the late summer of 1982.

I wondered back then if the American Stock Market was not one of the last truly undervalued investments left. I stated that the rally that had begun in August of that year might be only the opening salvo of a major bull market, possibly one that would go as far or even farther than any we have seen in this century. I asked, "If this is true, why is it so little recognized?"

Both my conclusion and the question come from a method of investment analysis I had first developed in the mid-seventies. I called it then—and it is now generally known as—"contrarian strategy." I thought I had made a revolutionary discovery. The evidence overwhelmingly demonstrated that the original contrarian strategy—the low P/E approach—had worked flawlessly for decades. What's more, it was relatively simple to use.

It seemed so obvious. Like a miner who had struck gold, I believed the "claim jumpers" would arrive in droves. The contrarian ideas would be scooped up immediately, soon outdistancing my years of work, perhaps even before my first book was published. Today I know nothing is further from the truth.

Is it because contrarian strategies have proved to be a bust? No, they work far better than I would have hoped twenty years ago. This completely new work, in fact, represents a major expansion of contrarian methods from my original books in the late seventies and early eighties, a result of important new findings in the past few years. Back then, the low P/E method was the only contrarian strategy that had been proven over decades. In this work, I will introduce four new strategies. These substantially expand the contrarian tools available to you. These new strategies can often be used in conjunction with the original low P/E strategy of my earlier books, or in many cases enhance your returns on their own. All have the same rigorous empirical backing as low P/E. These methods have been tested with large numbers of stocks for periods up to fifty years, and display outstanding records. A number of recent academic studies corroborate this exciting work.

The book is written for both the individual and the professional investor, in what I hope is a nontechnical and easily readable style. There are a variety of strategies, some simple, others requiring more experience, but all should allow you to handily outperform the market—no small feat, as we shall see in the opening chapter. Even the detractors of contrarian methods concede this much.

These strategies have succeeded for me personally, but more important they have provided returns well above the market (as well as those of all but a small percentage of investors) for almost two decades for the hundreds of clients of our firm, Dreman Value Management L.L.C., and the hundreds of thousands of clients in the Kemper–Dreman High Return Fund. This Fund, which I have managed since it started, has been ranked, by Lipper Analytical Services, the major mutual fund ranking organization, as the top fund out of 255 in its peer group for the ten years of its existence. It has also been ranked number one in more time periods than any of the 3,175 funds in the Lipper database.

Yet a perplexing question remains: If contrarian strategies work so well, why aren't they more widely followed? This is the second important part of the work. *It is not enough to have winning methods, we must be able to use them.* It sounds almost simplistic, but it isn't. Sure, the methods are easy to understand and initiate. But most investors, whether professional or individual, even with the best of intentions, *cannot follow through.*

There is an enormous but little recognized barrier in the way—investor psychology. A barrier so formidable that it bars all but a few, who intellectually or intuitively understand its workings, from using the strategies consistently. The success of contrarian strategies *requires* you at times to go against gut reactions, the prevailing beliefs in the marketplace, and the experts you respect. All of us pride ourselves to some extent on our individualism and ability to tough it out using our own thinking. In practice, as the investor psychology we will examine demonstrates (and as my experience bears out), it's a nightmare. I kid you not, nor do I exaggerate. That is the bottom line of why contrarian strategies are so rarely followed.

In the process of developing these strategies, I have had the privilege of talking to some of the leading psychologists studying market decision-making. Although they have provided outstanding research identifying many behavioral errors, they have not as yet fully recognized just how lethal these psychological pitfalls are for investors.

It is one thing to have a powerful strategy; it's another to execute it. In 1862, George McClellan, the Union general who built and commanded the powerful Army of the Potomac, was considered a brilliant strategist. Not only did he have superior numbers when Lee and Stonewall Jackson invaded the North in the early fall of that year, but McClellan had an amazing stroke of luck.

The Union army had captured a set of plans that outlined the Confederates' routes of march, their strength, and their dispositions. McClellan had the information that would allow him to annihilate the Rebel forces, and, possibly, end the war. But he dithered, throwing away his powerful advantage, and then froze at the battle of Antietam, where the Confederates could have been mauled. The Confederate battle plans should have given him an enormous victory, but the contradictory information flowing in from his intelligence—about enemy lines of march, strength, and objectives—paralyzed him. The winning strategy was in the General's hands, but he was psychologically incapable of executing it.

An important aspect of this book, then, is investor psychology. The strategies by themselves are not dissimilar to McClellan's situation after capturing the Confederate battle plans. In the marketplace, we too face anxiety, an enormous amount of uncertainty, market noise, and severe consequences from bad decisions. The strategies do not look nearly as clear-cut under these circumstances. If they don't work for a while, most people, even those with strong convictions, quickly discard them.

Without understanding investor psychology and how it affects us all, contrarian strategies, like Lee's captured marching plans, are unlikely to be successfully utilized. This is the reason why most people cannot use these strategies even though they are known to have provided superior results for years.

What I hope to show is that, although the study of investor psychology is still in its early stages, there is a body of research conducted by outstanding psychologists in recent decades, that provides us with patterns of predictable investor errors. These errors are so systematic that the knowledgeable investor can take advantage of them. It is upon this behavior that my contrarian strategies are founded.

The major thesis of this book is that investors overreact to events. Overreaction occurs in most areas of our behavior, from the booing and catcalls of hometown fans if the Chicago Bulls or any other good team loses a few consecutive games, to the loss of China and the subsequent outbreak of McCarthyism. But nowhere can it be demonstrated as clearly as in the marketplace. Under certain well-defined circumstances, investors overreact predictably and systematically. This well-documented discovery has sweeping implications within the fields of finance and economics, as well as in many other areas. It is also the key to improving your investment performance.

The research demonstrates conclusively that people consistently overprice the "best investments," be they growth stocks, initial public offerings, or companies involved in telecommunications. Just as consistently, they underprice the "worst." The "best" investments are not always exciting domestic stocks. They have been precious metals and collectibles in the 1970s, real estate in the 1980s, or investing in the emerging Asian markets in the past few years.

Similarly, "worst" investments change with investor perceptions. In late 1993, investors disdained pharmaceutical and other health-care stocks. They believed these industries would lose most of their value if the Clinton administration passed its health-care plan. As a result, they dived to lower relative levels than at any time since World War II. Yet over the next few years, they became leading market performers. In 1991 and 1992, many computer issues were thought to be poor investments. Subsequently, they led the market for years, many doubling, tripling, even tenfolding.

What our new work shows is that the overvaluation of "best" and the undervaluation of "worst" stocks often goes to extremes—so much so that earnings and other surprises affect "best" and "worst" stocks in a diametrically different way. Chapter 6 will show you the new, well-documented conclusions that all surprises, both good and bad, bode well for out-of-favor stocks, but bode ill for favorites. Since surprises are a way of life in the marketplace, this knowledge will be a potent tool in our new investment strategies.

The overreaction theory, although revolutionary, is elegant in its simplicity. People, as chapter 11 demonstrates conclusively, are consistently too optimistic about stocks that appear to have good prospects and too pessimistic about those having so-so outlooks. Investor overreaction underlies and supports the new investment methods that will be outlined in this book. The strategies we will examine based on this theory can dramatically increase your odds in the marketplace.

My approach will try to accomplish two major functions. Before all else, a successful strategy requires a strong defense: it must preserve your capital. The strategies herein are designed to protect investors from powerful emotional pitfalls. After defense, we need a powerful offense. We achieve this by taking advantage of consistent mistakes made in markets because of predictable behavior patterns. Both parts of the strategies rely on an understanding of investor psychology.

The new work in psychology explains why people in markets often behave like crowds at a theater fire. In one age the rage was tulips, in another collectibles, in another stocks or real estate—but at any moment, most investors rush for the same door at once, and many get trampled.

The bottom line of these methods is, of course, to make money. The strategies we will study are down-to-earth, disciplined, and—most important—have proven successful. Using the approach and the new tools I will outline, you should be able to enhance your investment performance.

No investment strategy should be followed blindly, and a good part of this work is devoted to explaining why my methods work. The ideas, although not complicated, require an understanding of investor psychology and the discipline to carry it through. When you understand them, you can avoid the mistakes of both the market's pros and its "patent medicine men." Both the theory and the methods, then, are simple. But you will still have to avoid some tricky psychological pitfalls, especially in crisis. Knowing these principles won't make it a cakewalk. It is hard to stay unaffected by psychological pressures, as I've too often found in free-falling markets. No matter how often you've been there or how much you've read, you can't escape the fear. But as chapter 12 will demonstrate, you can still act on and profit from the situation.

A number of key chapters cover other important aspects of investor psychology that are essential to successfully utilizing these strategies. Chapters 4 and 5 look at the advice of the investment expert in contemporary markets, and how it almost inevitably works against the investor. Chapter 10 examines the cognitive errors we all make as investors, and how we can avoid many of them, while chapter 16 analyzes the powerful influence of group and peer pressures on people. These often shape incorrect views on the outlook for the market or individual stocks.

The psychology is well documented and leads to a number of decisional safeguards, which I have listed as Rules, that if followed, can both prevent you from falling into the predictable errors that most investors make, and in many circumstances actually help you take advantage of them. Psychology is the necessary link required to activate the contrarian strategies we will examine. Armed with this knowledge, you have a good chance of beating the market. In fact, the awareness you can develop may prove one of your strongest assets in the years ahead.

However, you should close this work or any other if the author says you can harness market psychology easily. Even the state-of-the-art research findings in the field—which I will present—will not accomplish this objective by itself. No, even knowing the strong odds a strategy will work, you will be faced with immense psychological pressures to follow exactly the opposite course. Only by understanding how powerful the tug of these forces can be will you be able to harness them. Without this understanding, I'm afraid no book is going to improve your investment results all that much.

The final aspect of the book is the influence on the reader of widely accepted but spurious investment thinking. Our inherent psychological makeup is not the only danger to our investment health. Not only do we need usable strategies, and the ability to execute them, we must also avoid the all-permeating influence of powerful but fallacious investment mores of our time. There are a number of seductive theories that have dominated the mainstream of Wall Street thinking for years, which can beckon you away from the proven approaches we'll examine. We will also look at the major intellectual fads of the day to see how they hold up in practice, as well as some of the torpedoes hidden within the current framework of "smart" investing.

Much of contemporary practice is tied to this mistaken lore. The concepts are similar to mass-media advertising—you accept the brand names well before you know what's in the package. While this work is not a tract on investment theories, to successfully implement contrarian strategies you must understand why some methods work while others consistently fail.

In particular, the book will deal with the efficient market hypothesis, the most powerful investment theory of the twentieth century, which states that nobody can beat the market over time. This theory permeates virtually every aspect of investment practice today. Whether we are making decisions on the riskiness of portfolios, what mutual funds to buy, whether to buy smaller companies, or to put our savings into index funds, or foreign securities, we are, knowingly or not, following efficient market teachings—almost all of which have been discredited. For this reason, it is important to address this issue to clearly understand where these ideas originate, and where they go wrong.

What we shall find is a theory built on air. Many of the things most of us accept as gospel, such as how to measure risk precisely, the need to diversify into foreign stocks, or that small stocks will provide us with better returns, simply are not true. Knowing why and structuring your portfolio accordingly can be of enormous benefit to you.

As you can see, the successful implementation of contrarian strategies, which at first glance appears to be a snap, really depends on three different but interlinking components. That is why I have laid out not only the contrarian methods, but the essential psychological guidelines necessary to use them, and the problems with the popular teachings of the day.

Some of the work will be controversial, since it goes against popular beliefs and gores sacred cows. Recent work on analysts' earnings forecasts, for instance, points to an enormous and sustained error rate, which is easily documented but cuts to the heart of analysts' raison d'être: providing accurate forecasts. I also challenge the popular belief that small companies have outperformed the S&P 500 over time. The work further demonstrates that measures of risk used to evaluate mutual funds and money managers are seriously flawed, and can actually harm the investor. In the course of this discussion, in chapter sixteen we will examine what the real risks are of investing in today's markets, and I will introduce what I believe to be a more realistic and accessible method to measure risk.

I have fielded criticism from academic and professional experts for close to twenty years, some of it containing sharp personal attacks. Nevertheless, though the fusillades may have sent a few of my feathers flying—not to mention on occasion raising my blood pressure—they have never undermined the work.

The book will also look at a number of important issues not related to contrarian strategies. The most important of these is how to invest for the long term. As we will see in chapter 13, the rules of prudent investing have been turned upside down in the postwar decades, yet your investment advisor, your banker or your broker, probably has little awareness of the fact. If you follow their advice, as well-meaning as it is, you will often come up short in your savings goals. The work will also examine how to create tax-efficient portfolios, which are only now starting to get the attention they deserve. The subject deals with methods to protect yourself from taking inordinate long- or short-term capital gains, whether by managing your own portfolio or by placing it in the hands of an investment advisor or mutual fund.

Another important topic that builds out of contrarian strategies how to react to a crisis. Though millions of words have been written about crisis and panic, a systematic approach to profiting from them has to this time never been presented. Crisis, as I hope to show you in chapter 12, provides enormous opportunity for those who can follow the guidelines that will be laid down.

Finally, the book will provide a number of insights that my clients or I discovered the hard way, from being wary of "guaranteed" performance records of money managers and mutual funds, to staying clear of the hottest initial public offerings.

I should note that on occasion I refer to important research studies both in psychology and in investing that I had presented in my earlier works, as a foundation for some of the new research. This material, however, comprises a small part of the work presented here. To improve the flow I have attempted to relegate footnotes, particularly those providing further detail on research findings, to the back of the work. At times however, I have retained footnotes at the bottom of the page where I thought they would be especially useful to the general reader.

When I published *Psychology and the Stock Market* in 1977, I was half sure I would be drummed out of Wall Street, or at least ostracized, for some of the radical ideas the book presented. To my delight it was well received on the Street, with a number of professionals telling me it was the book they, too, had been thinking of writing. So popular has the original contrarian thinking become in the past two decades, that the academic establishment has adopted it, after years of opposition, and proclaimed it their own.

This book, like its predecessors, presents a very different approach to investing, one that is likely to be challenging—if not anathema—to many of the widely accepted ideas of the day. Whether it is attacked or not, the bottom line is that the methods not only work in theory, they also have been very successful in practice. I think I can promise you an interesting and rewarding trip, as well as a little fun along the way.

So, sit back; enjoy. Nobody beats the market, they say.

Except for those of us who do.

David Dreman
Aspen, Colorado
January 21, 1998

PART I

WHY CURRENT METHODS DON'T WORK

1

The Sure Thing Almost Nobody Plays

IMAGINE you are entering a deluxe, well-appointed casino. Off the lavish entry foyer, there are two ample gambling wings, one hued in reds, the other in muted greens. The red wing looks enticing, but if I may insist, let's first enter the less crowded green rooms to watch the action.

The atmosphere is unhurried, the blackjack tables are sparsely attended, and every player sits behind a mound of green and black chips. You think at first you've come to the wrong place. You see the ordinary table limits, the ordinary clothes, the ordinary games. But then how did these ordinary people get such piles of money?

Then it comes to you. They're all winning. In fact, as you walk around the green wing, you hardly can find a losing player. You know, of course, that the average house take on table games is 5%, but as you count winning and losing hands, you realize these players are getting a better break. They seem to be gaining at a rate of 60% to 40%. You start fresh and take another count. The results are the same.

A pit boss appears at your shoulder.

"Excuse me," you say, "but can this be right? The odds favor the players?"

"Yes, indeed. The odds in the green room usually run 60 to 40. It's been that way since we opened."

"But . . . most of the players must go away winners."

"They sure do. At those odds, we calculate that 9,999 out of 10,000 make money. At our high-stakes tables in the back, they do even better, with winners running about 20,000 to 1. It's a good thing we get so few players, or they'd break the house."

Somewhat amazed, you thank him and shake your head. There's no time to lose, you decide, but you'll need more than the few dollars you have in your pocket. You hatch a plan to gather your life savings, come back to the casino, and win the bundle you've been dreaming of.

On your way out, you glance into the red wing. The action level is much, much higher. The room is crowded and fairly roars with excitement. Can it be even better here, you wonder? Curious, you go in. Players bet multiple table positions, wave frantically for change, entreat the gods for luck. You see few green and black chips, fewer winning players. The piles of chips in front of them are dwindling with each hand. In fact, the odds are worse than normal. Again, you start to count. Although the players continue to excitedly toss in their chips, the odds appear to be maybe 60 to 40 in favor of the house. Once more, your curiosity whetted, you walk over to a pit boss and ask her the odds at these tables.

She tells you what you suspected. They are 60 to 40 in favor of the casino. Warming up to the subject, she chuckles and says, "This room coins gold for the casino, the chances are 9,999 in 10,000 rounds that we wind up winners." You don't have to be a genius to see that this is obviously not the place you want to be.

You go home and get your stash. You return to the casino with your fistful of money, excited, eager for action, all the time figuring how you'll do even better at the game. But then a strange thing happens. You walk into the red wing and start to play.

On Markets and Odds

Sounds like a pleasant dream rapidly degenerating into nightmare. Yet it happens daily in the market. Moreover, the odds in the green and red rooms are not just attention grabbers. They're very real. In the marketplace, in fact, some investments steadily make money, while others lose consistently at these identical odds. Like the casino, most people want investments that have a good chance of beating the market. Yet, despite considerable time and effort devoted to the mission, they gravitate toward investments where swarms of enthusiastic players are endangering their savings at odds similar to those in the red room.

It seems surrealistic, but it isn't. Generations of investors have passed up sure things to buy losing investments. We all know, for instance, that for safety we should invest in treasury bills and government bonds. The investment environment has changed radically in the postwar period, however, as we'll see in detail in chapter 13. Treasury bills and government bonds, gilt-edged securities for centuries, are now surefire ways to destroy your nest egg. Conversely, investments always viewed as more speculative, such as common stocks, have become outstanding vehicles to protect and enhance your capital.

Yes, all the prudent rules of saving we learned at our fathers' knees are out the window. Since the Second World War there has been a revolution every bit as violent to the old order of investing as the French Revolution was to the old order of Europe.

Revolution does not have to mean the destruction of your savings. As the Industrial Revolution shifted fortunes from the titled nobility to entrepreneurs, as the railroad revolution enriched the Vanderbilts and Goulds, as the information revolution enriched the Gateses and Jobses, so this investment revolution, if you know what causes the changing structure, can enrich you. In each of these revolutions, the odds strongly favored those who found the new road and disfavored those stuck in the same old path.

This book is about odds or probabilities in markets, and how to use them to your advantage. There are probabilities of success or failure in the marketplace as surely as in gambling, business, or warfare.

Napoleon was the greatest probability player of modern warfare. Most often outnumbered, he won by moving fast and concentrating his forces on the battlefield on the enemy's weak points. Yes, there was brilliance in his strategies, but a good part of his military genius lay in his knowledge of the odds in any situation. On the first Italian campaign, for instance, he gambled on the perilous dash through Genoese territory rather than throw his ragged, demoralized men against the fortified Alpine passes, and was able to defeat the numerically superior but divided Austrians by keeping his forces unified. While poised precariously before the gates of Vienna, however, he gave the Viennese a generous treaty rather than take a chance on being cut off from his supplies.

The story is told of Napoleon playing cards with his generals and staff to pass the time en route to Egypt with his invasion fleet. He heard one of his aides whispering in the background and asked him to speak up. The aide, fearing for his life, stammered, "I said, General, you are not playing fairly." Napoleon said, "That's true, but I always give the money back at the end of the game."

General Murat, who was to become one of his legendary Marshals, spoke up with trepidation, though he had always been fearless in battle. "General, if I may be so bold, can I ask a question? " Napoleon nodded and he continued, "If you give the money back, why then do you cheat?" Napoleon replied, "Because I want to leave nothing to chance."

"Interesting story," you might say, "but how does it apply to the marketplace?" Believe it or not, despite appearances, the market does not run on chance or luck. Like the battlefield, it runs on probabilities and odds. These control markets every bit as strongly as they do roulette, blackjack, craps, or any other game in a casino. Unlike Napoleon at cards, we don't have to cheat, though our survival does depend on staying ahead of the opposition. As this book will show you, the odds in the marketplace can be turned decisively in your favor.

What is behind the probabilities in markets? Is it a new system to divine the future, or differential equations critical to the development of physics and now used extensively in economics? Millions of dollars' worth of the best research money can buy? No. Our probabilities are not built on any of these techniques or on foreseeing the direction of markets, or on any other conventional approach. Rather they are embedded in investor behavior in the marketplace.

I know it sounds strange. "Psychology," some people might snicker, "is the last place in the world to find any sort of reliable odds." It's true all the same. Betting on well-defined patterns of investor behavior will give you higher probabilities—strongly backed by statistics—than any other method of investing in use today. These are the odds available in the green wing of my imaginary casino. But how do you arrive at them?

That is what this book will try to show you. But the last thing I want to do is ask you to take my advice or anybody else's on faith. Too many systems and faith healers already clutter the marketplace. None that I know of do what they claim—beat the market. And most cost. We will carefully look at the odds of which investment methods work and which don't, forgetting the popularity of one technique or another.

To start, we'll look at the two methods heavily favored by knowledgeable investors: the use of professional money managers and the efficient market hypothesis. The first relies on the "edge" the professional investor can give you by banking on his or her knowledge, skill, and experience to turn the odds in your favor. Do these professionals understand the new market dynamics that I have discussed briefly? Do they win big in this dramatically changed environment? To find out, let's look at the expert record.

Great Expectations

Professional investors manage large pools of money for mutual funds, pension funds, bank trust departments, money management firms, insurance companies, and similar financial institutions. The assets under their management are growing phenomenally, surpassing $14.8 trillion[1] by the end of 1997, and expanding faster than the GDP (gross domestic product). They control over 70% of the trading and 50% of the stock holdings on the New York Stock Exchange. Their buying power staggers the imagination. By 1997 they were estimated to be buying and selling $2 trillion of stocks annually, generating $10 billion of commissions in the process. They claim the crown as the elite of their profession.

The professional money manager is believed to bring a new depth of knowledge to securities markets. Armed with the best research money can buy, and legions of well-trained, battle-hardened colleagues, they were said to have turned the odds decisively in their favor. The change was welcomed by knowledgeable observers of the financial scene. They urged the uninformed and emotional small investor to realize that he was ill equipped to deal with the complex modern market and to turn his money over to one of these seasoned pros. Some writers on the subject have gone so far as to state that the average investor is "obsolete" today. So, with some knowledge of the role these professionals play in the nation's finances, we should now ask whether they have indeed brought the Age of Camelot to markets.

Unfortunately, in a word the answer is no. The great majority of money managers have consistently lagged behind the market averages. John Bogle, chairman of the Vanguard Group, one of the largest mutual fund organizations in the country, stated that 90% of money managers underperformed the market in every ten-year period since their performance began to be measured in the early sixties. Burton Malkiel, a professor of finance at Princeton and author of the widely read *A Random Walk Down Wall Street*, studied all domestic equity mutual funds and found that they underperformed their market benchmarks from 1971 to 1991.[2] Information taken from Morningstar and Lipper Analytical Services, two of the largest services tracking the performance of mutual funds, measured the results for 3-, 5-, and 10-year periods to the third quarter of 1997 for the six major classes of stock funds. The results appear in Figure 1–1. As you can see, the market (as measured by the S&P 500) outperformed all categories of mutual funds for all periods (the one exception was small companies, which provided nominally better returns for five years). Numerous studies by pension-fund consultants, who monitor the results of hundreds, and in some cases thousands, of money managers, have come up with similar findings.

What conclusions can we draw from the tepid performance of professional investors? The rational and unemotional professional, according to financial lore, coolly gauges value and buys securities at bargain

Figure 1-1

The Dart Board Beats The Pros
How Mutual Funds Fared 1987 - 1997*

		Aggressive Growth	Asset Allocation	Equity-Income	Growth	Growth & Income	Small Company
3 year Average	Total Return	23.5%	17.5%	23.5%	25.2%	26.0%	25.4%
	Amount over / under the S&P 500	−6.4%	−12.4%	−6.4%	−4.7%	−3.9%	−4.5%
5 year Average	Total Return	20.4%	13.9%	17.5%	18.9%	18.9%	21.1%
	Amount over / under the S&P 500	−0.4%	−6.9%	−3.3%	−1.9%	−1.9%	0.3%
10 year Average	Total Return	13.8%	11.3%	12.4%	13.3%	13.3%	14.0%
	Amount over / under the S&P 500	−1.0%	−3.5%	−2.4%	−1.5%	−1.5%	−0.8%

*Returns measured to September 30, 1997

Sources of data: Lipper Analytical Services and Morningstar

prices in periods of panic, when the public sells them with no regard to value. The portfolio manager, the legend continues, sells stocks in periods when the public is enamored with them, pushing prices to mania levels.

Evidence compiled by the Securities and Exchange Commission suggests otherwise. The much abused and supposedly emotional individual investor sold securities near the 1968 market top and bought at the market bottoms of both 1970 and 1974. The institutional investor, on the other hand, bought near market tops and sold at the bottoms. In the 1987 crash, the individual investor was scarcely involved. According to SEC records of the crash, almost all of the selling was done by professionals. The market panic in the third quarter of 1990, following the Iraqi invasion of Kuwait, demonstrated once again that professional, not individual, investors were the largest, and often most desperate, sellers.

The same pattern shows clearly with mutual funds. These funds should be fully invested near market bottoms—with low cash reserves—after snapping up bargains dumped on the market by panicky individual investors. Conversely, near market tops, they should sell heavily, accumulating large cash reserves by taking advantage of the speculative whims of an excited public. Again, theory and practice diverge widely. Rather than supporting stocks when prices plummet, they get trampled at the exit. When prices soar, they buy aggressively. The pros seem to judge market direction poorly.[3]

Are investment advisory services that sell advice to the public by subscription any better? Many of these services, as they readily advertise, aim to get you in near the market bottom and out near the top. Would you have profited by subscribing to such services? Again no. For years, pundits, myself included, have publicly charted an almost perfect correlation between the investment advice given and the future direction of the market.

Unfortunately, it is almost perfectly wrong. When advisors go one way, markets go the other. As the averages approach their highs, larger and larger numbers of advisors become bullish, and as they move toward their lows, an increasing number stampede for the exits. The fact is so well known on Wall Street that many of us now use the advisory services as a contrarian indicator. If over 70% of services wax bullish—look out—markets are approaching a high. Conversely, if 70% are terrified of the bear, it's time to buy. This was true at the market high in 1972, when 71% of the services were bullish, at the bottom of the worst market break since the war in late 1974, when 70% thought the market was heading south, and just before the Great Bull Market began in the spring of 1982.[4] Instead of the market following the advisors, the advisors seem to unerringly follow the market.[5]

What then do we make of these statistics? Some skeptics and financial writers (the two being often difficult to distinguish) believe the figures indicate professional money management is inept. The most important service investment management could perform for clients, they might say, would be to walk their dogs or perhaps advise them on their business attire. Other skeptics have cheerfully suggested that blindfolded chimpanzees heavily fortified with margaritas could outperform the experts by throwing darts at the stock pages.

But humor aside, the knowledge that professionals do not outperform the market has been widely known for a generation. This is before considering the effects of the investment revolution. Adjusting for the new financial order, the results only get worse, putting the investor even further behind the eight ball. No, the odds of winning big do not appear to lie with this group, regardless of how much media attention they get or advertising they churn out.

I opened this chapter by assuring you that investors have an excellent chance of beating the market. Now we see even the experts cannot keep up with it. Something obviously is out of whack here, as financial academics began to realize several decades back.

A new world has since been discovered and mapped. The ivory tower explorers went sailing over seas of data, rather than uncharted oceans, but the attitude was similar. They were conquering new intellectual realms for the greater glory of academe, making sweeping pronouncements in the process, and coming up with unbeatable odds—or so they said. Natives—money managers, analysts, investors—beware. You are about to be conquered.

The New Conquistadors

Some of the country's best academic minds looked at this problem soon after it was recognized in the early sixties. The financial professors found a radical new explanation of why professionals do not perform better. For a while, at least, this seemed to be the stock market's equivalent of the theory of relativity, the smashing of the atom, or maybe even the fountain of youth.

Using enormous computer power, by the standard of the day, they put forward an all-encompassing theory. Markets, they said, are efficient. That meant that stock prices are determined by the thorough and diligent work of the brightest analysts, money managers, and other investors. The combined knowledge of thousands of these experts kept prices exactly where they should be. No one can beat the market consistently. It might be hard to accept what the professors said, but they had proven this truth overwhelmingly. Besides, there were benefits. You no longer had to waste endless time and energy trying to outguess the market. No reason to get stressed out; it just couldn't be done. But you could still get higher returns. All you had to do was to take more risk.*

So there it was. Forget the sweating, studying, and tossing and turning you used to do at night trying to buy the right stocks. It didn't help a hoot. Investing had been promoted to a science with the mathematical precision of quantum physics. Just sit back and enjoy the ride.

---

* As they defined it, which we'll look at in chapter 3.

This major new creed has pervaded our academic institutions for three decades. Today, it affects almost every aspect of Wall Street thinking from the proper makeup of your retirement funds, to how to select an investment advisor. It also plays an important role in the decision-making of many large corporations, and influences the SEC and government policymakers. The hypothesis has been so widely accepted in academic circles and on Wall Street that several of its leading proponents—Franco Modigliani, Harry Markowitz, William Sharpe, Merton Miller, Myron Scholes—have received Nobel Prizes for their contributions.[6,7]

The new theory came at a time when there was little to oppose it. The old market methods were dying. None of the ancient rituals seemed to work, no matter how rigorously they were applied, or how extensive the training, experience, or intelligence of the practitioner.

Into this vacuum came the seductive idea of efficient markets, offering a plausible explanation of the professionals' failure, absolving investors of blame (for it preached it was not in their power to change things). Order replaced chaos. Converts flocked to the new gospel by the millions.

The spread of the new faith was not unlike the conquest of the vast Inca empire by Francisco Pizarro and his 180 conquistadors. Like the conquistadors, the scholars used both the faith and the sword to annihilate the pagans' beliefs in the marketplace. If the true faith was not accepted, why then there was the sword—the unleashing of volleys of awesome statistics disproving everything the professionals believed. The frightening new weapon of statistical analysis awed the Wall Street heathen more than Pizarro's cavalry did the Incas, who had never before seen a horse. What amazes, in looking back, is that the leaders of the new faith subdued millions of investors with a smaller troop than the original conquistadors.

But the golden age of efficient markets was not destined to last. Smash, boom, bang, along came the 1987 crash and the pillars of the new paradise crumbled. In retrospect, the elegant hypothesis had a minor hitch. The professors assumed investors were as emotionless and as efficient as the computers they used to build their theory. The October 19, 1987, crash, 80% worse than 1929 in percentage terms and over a thousand times larger in actual dollars, showed it just wasn't so. Like a bizarre Rube Goldberg machine, the theoretically flawless trading systems the professors had introduced turned into a monster unleashing massive panic. The market ended 508 points lower that day. In five trading days ending on October 19, the market had lost one-third of its value—about one trillion dollars.

When the New York Stock Exchange (NYSE) opened on the morning of October 20, the professors' supposedly foolproof trading mechanisms sent stocks into another devastating free fall. To end the rout,[8] the NYSE was forced to ban the new academic tools that were supposed to create Eden on Wall Street. The entire financial system came within a hair's breadth of disintegration, according to the Brady task force and SEC reports commissioned to study the crash. The worst crash in modern history was caused by a theory devoid of any understanding of investor psychology.

The academic dogma that investor psychology played absolutely no role in markets justified the new trading mechanisms responsible for the debacle. This was not something to be faulted only with 20/20 hindsight. Numerous market observers warned of the impending calamity. Eighteen months before the crash, the new academic trading strategies caused Representative John Dingle of Michigan, then-chairman of the House of Representatives Committee on Energy and Commerce, which oversees the SEC, to fear a panic. John Phelan, then-president of the New York Stock Exchange, had also warned that the interaction of the new academic programs could cause a market meltdown. "When I first started talking about this in late 1986," Phelan was quoted as saying after the crash, "people would do almost anything but physically attack you."[9]

I was also worried about the dangers inherent in the academic trading systems. Writing about them in a Forbes column six months before the crash, I noted that the enormous volume in computerized trading programs, portfolio insurance, and numbers of other such strategies all based on financial index futures at low margins, amounted to a potential doomsday machine.[10] The column concluded that if uncontrolled, these aberrations set up the possibility of a sharp correction, if not a crash, not far down the road.

Even though the most destructive of the low-margined trading systems created by efficient market believers were all but completely dismantled in the next several years, the academics who sponsored them, like the faithful of other disproved scientific theories, hung on tenaciously. Everything was blamed but the actual reasons as determined by the commissions set up to study the causes of the crash. To do otherwise would be no less than admitting that the theory was as useful as the eighteenth-century medical belief that bleeding the patient balanced the body's humors.

No, the revolutionary new ideas that sprouted from ivory towers across the country won't give you the odds I've discussed earlier, or for that matter even keep you afloat. But though the theory began to disintegrate with the crash, it left an enormous void among investors. Many of the basic teachings of the efficient market hypothesis (EMH) have now have been conclusively refuted by advanced forms of the same statistical analysis that devastated the investment heathen. Yet contemporary investment practice is built around the belief in efficient markets. Large numbers of investors, though they believe the theory bankrupt, don't know where else to turn.

Where then do the odds of market success lie? Or are there any real odds at all?

A Titanic Clash

We find ourselves in the midst of a sea change of thinking in the investment world, one whose ramifications extend far beyond the stock market, and even beyond economics. Scientists call such changes paradigm shifts. A paradigm encompasses the working beliefs underlying all theory and research in a particular science. Paradigms shift rarely, and the shifts are always resisted by the creators of the old system of beliefs. Bitter polemics and enormous rancor are usually spilled before the change prevails. Still, it is within this paradigm shift that we will find the key to the winning odds in the marketplace.

It is never easy to give up your most basic beliefs. As we all know from our school days, the Ptolemaic system, which held that the earth was the center of the universe, resisted change for centuries. With improved telescopes and more accurate observation, sighting after sighting over the years found planets where the theory stated they shouldn't be. The model became increasingly complex in order to incorporate each new piece of information. The planets and stars moved around the earth in a combination of circles, epicycles, and deferents (points moving on large circles around which the epicycles simultaneously revolved). The result of this hodgepodge was a mind-boggling whirl.

Still, it took generations for scientists to accept the radically different heliocentric paradigm of planetary motion. As Paul Samuelson once phrased it, "Scientific progress advances funeral by funeral."

Markets whirl along in a similar state today. Each new statistical finding throws the efficient market hypothesis into further disarray and requires additional explanations for the sighting of "anomalies" ruled impossible by the theory.

That said, this book is not a scientific treatise. But it is important for the reader to have some understanding of the intellectual clashes in investments and economics today, because the winning odds we will examine, and the advice that stems from them, comes from a radically different paradigm than efficient markets, or for that matter conventional Wall Street thinking. In many ways, it is as different as Copernicus from Ptolemy.

What then do these other methods lack? On paper, at least, they have a high probability of success. The key principle of this book is that people are not the rational, omniscient decision-makers that the efficient market believers claim, and most investment practitioners believe. Rather, we are constantly pushed or pulled by psychological influences.

To be fair, it is not only these groups who do not understand investor psychology and make major mistakes as a result.

All of us are affected by these powerful but unrecognized influences.

All of us have heard of how investor psychology has turned positive or negative on an industry or company, or on the market as a whole.

All experienced investors have no doubt pondered the extreme psychological variations that markets display over time.

The problem we face is that, although we know much of the cause of success or failure lies largely within the realm of psychology, we really do not understand how and where psychology meshes with investment decisions. As a result, we make costly and sometimes disastrous errors time and again. Learning the principles underlying investment behavior will allow us to develop successful market strategies. The methods have worked well over long periods and should continue to succeed, because they are based on predictable patterns of investor behavior. These are the odds available in the green wing.

The psychology of market success that I'll describe is anything but "will-o'-the-wisp." Its bedrock is consistent and predictable investor errors in the marketplace. This bedrock will support a new theory of markets and investing. As you will see, the assumptions underlying the methods are well documented, both empirically and psychologically. At every stage of the development of our new strategies, I'll demonstrate the strong statistical proof the probabilities are built upon.

What we will see is that not only do investors go wrong, they go wrong in a systematic and predictable manner. So predictable, in fact, that consistent investment strategies can be built on their mistakes. More than that we can calculate odds on how well our strategies will work over varying periods, in a similar manner to the gambling casino. These strategies, as I'll demonstrate, have worked for generations, and I suspect since the dawn of markets. That is, if human behavior hasn't changed.

How and why these probabilities work is what this book is about. In examining them we will go far beyond markets, to some seemingly universal laws of human behavior. People encountering the same situation will act the same, within the marketplace or outside of it. Our new investment approach stands on market history, on the latest psychological research, and on thorough statistical analysis.

I hope to demonstrate that we can harness psychology and use it systematically to attain our investment goals. But before we attempt it, we must understand just how powerful these forces are, and why they lead most of us into the red rather than the green rooms. This is the reason why most investors, including the experts, underperform the market averages over time.

The Journey Ahead

The journey will be wide-ranging both in time and breadth. We will examine markets, psychology, finance, economics, statistics, even politics. Part of the text will naturally be somber, but it will have its lighter moments. I wrote in *Psychology and the Stock Market* over twenty years ago that "the integration of financial and psychological understanding is a new and basically uncharted field." To my amazement, the whole new field of behavioral finance has sprung up since. Psychologists, economists, and investment academics are now beginning to study markets and are finding anything but rational behavior. Their major new research can be of profound benefit to you. Once you understand the principles, there is nothing magical or mysterious about the work.

To return to that great probability player of warfare again, Napoleon once asked, "Is it because they are lucky that [great men] become great? No, but being great they have been able to master luck."

While no book can teach you how to make a "great" fortune, I believe this one can give you a much better chance of mastering your luck in markets. Once you see the odds, all you need is an open mind and the courage of your convictions. I am convinced that today the individual investor has an exceptional opportunity to beat both the market and the experts. If you are a serious investor, I think our journey will prove rewarding.

2

From Technical Analysis to Astrology

The Walls Come Tumbling Down

Investing today is not a little like politics in the former Eastern Bloc. The poverty, the corruption, the misery finally overwhelmed the shaky old edifice—in Poland, in East Germany, in the Soviet Union itself. The citizens rejoiced, and the world rejoiced with them. But the reformers could not deliver the progress they had promised. The situation continued to deteriorate. The world went about its business. Then a strange thing happened. The citizens began voting communist bureaucrats back into power. The slogans were different, but the people were the same. Aleksander Kwasniewski, a former communist official, was elected President of Poland over Lech Walesa, one of the activists who had brought the old system down.

Likewise on Wall Street, a new, supposedly scientific approach attacked the methods of generations. Young activists called the old ways bankrupt and undertook to eradicate them. The new science spilled out of academe and welled up on Wall Street. But then, with the battle seemingly won, it too came under withering fire.

Neither school fulfilled its promise—a system that could beat the market.

Like communist bureaucrats, bereft of viable ideas, many Wall Streeters have blended the new theory with the old, creating a muddle similar to the chaos in Eastern Europe. To sidestep the morass, we will look at old and new alike to find out why they cannot achieve the results they promise.

This chapter and the next will examine the investment methods experts have followed for generations. Many investors still believe that these are winning approaches. All they need is the time and diligence to practice them properly. However, the methods, like the pro's performance record, do not stand tall under scrutiny.

Still, almost all current investment methods and practice are based on either the old or the new. But is either really suited to your needs? We'll look at that question now.

The First Victory

The efficient market hypothesis states that stock prices reflect everything known about a company, an industry, or the economy as a whole. This simple academic proposition has some staggering implications when you think about it. It implies that stock prices cannot be predicted, that everything known about a stock is already reflected in its price. Prices will only be moved by events that can't be foreseen. The first conclusion the academics drew was that technical analysis is thus useless in predicting future price movements. Bingo. This statement, if accepted, takes out a major part of Wall Street research with one hard swat.

Technicians are survivors. They have been part of the scene almost since securities were first traded. They believe that by studying a myriad of charts, trading figures, and similar indicators they can do precisely what the professors say they cannot—project the past pattern of stock prices into the future to make major profits.

Investors believe them. The public, and even some pros, will treat a well-known technician who makes one or two major calls with an adulation at times approaching reverence. Tens of thousands treated Joseph Granville like an oracle for making several major market calls in the late 1970s.

Granville modestly acknowledged the acclaim by dressing in the flowing white robes of an Old Testament prophet, and when the spirit moved him, walking on water. (He crossed swimming pools on a glass plank he brought especially for such occasions.) He claimed to be the first person to have "cracked the secret of markets," and could never make a serious error again. Naturally, he believed he would "win a Nobel Prize for this feat." Unfortunately, the gods of the marketplace changed the secret shortly thereafter. Joe dropped to the bottom of the heap over the next fifteen years, according to the Hulbert Service, a watchdog of market letters. Granville was rated last of 20 market timers with a −27.4% average annual return.[1] In this case the professors proved right.

To the pragmatic technician, analysis of price and volume statistics is the key to the direction of price movements. "[The technician's] central thesis is 'the past is prologue,' " wrote my good friend, the late Vartanig G. Vartan, senior financial columnist of *The New York Times*. "A pure chartist is almost monk-like in dedication, believing the essential truth about the market is to be found in squiggles and figures on graph paper. He is unmoved by a plant explosion or a profit explosion."[2]

Technicians believe stocks and the general market move in discernible trends that continue until they clearly signal a change in course. Because stocks never move in a straight line, but invariably retrace a portion of each advance or decline, the analyst must be able to filter the useful information from the vast amount of static. A technician usually has a favorite method, but will use a number of others to confirm or reject a conclusion.

Hail the All-Powerful Chart

The technician's single most important tool is the chart. The most common form of chart is the bar chart or vertical line chart, illustrated in Figure 2–1. These are normally plotted daily or weekly, though monthly movements are tracked for longer-term perspective. The thin vertical lines in the upper graph indicate the weekly trading range, with the small horizontal tick showing the closing price. The series of vertical lines at the bottom of the chart represents weekly volume. Through the recognition of dozens of different patterns, the all-important trends can be pinpointed.

Trend lines are essential to the chartist, because of the paramount principle that a trend once started does not easily change course. A change in trend, or a reversal, the technicians believe, can be recognized by diligent study of the charts. Spotting a change quickly allows them to protect their positions and to benefit from the new market course. This belief is fundamental to the technical method. Technicians have identified large numbers of patterns that clearly indicate, they think, a reversal of course of either the averages or individual stocks. The jargon of the technician is liberally sprinkled with names for the various trend and reversal patterns such as the "head and shoulders" formation, the "reverse head and shoulders" pattern, along with many intricate variations, some with monikers more appropriate to a side show: deformed heads, two heads with one shoulder, and multiple heads and shoulders, to cite a few.

Figure 2-1
Intel Corp
9/30/94 - 9/30/96

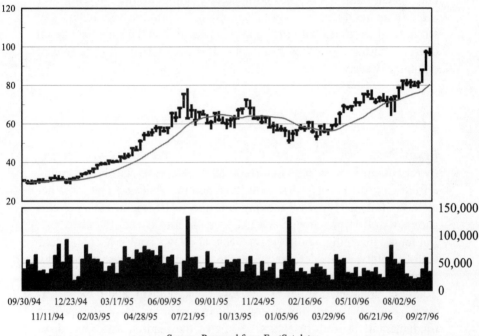

Source: Prepared from FactSet data

Numerous backup indicators are relied on by sophisticated technicians to confirm their favorite method. Support and resistance levels are
two widely used tools. A support level indicates a valley a stock has
climbed out of; a resistance zone is usually a previous peak. At a support level, sufficient demand is available to halt a further decline, at least
for a time. A resistance zone, on the other hand, prevents further upward
movement because enough stock will be sold at that price to halt the
rise.

The Star Wars Technicians

The computer has exponentially increased the information available to
technical analysts. "Star wars" technology has collected quite a following in the last few years. Neural networks and genetic algorithms, for

example, are now used by technical "quants." These tools are cobbled together from the sciences of biology, physics, computer sciences, and statistics to pursue the technician's dream of a system that works consistently. Computer consultants, such as the Santa Fe Institute, a think tank specializing in complex computer systems,[3] hold conferences for Wall Street quantitative analysts. Computers, claim the researchers, can sift through complex patterns light-years faster than the smartest human chartist. Furthermore they can apply objective statistical tests, free of emotional biases.

And There's the Fringe

Beyond "star wars," there is a fringe of technical analysts who primarily rely on the tools of a good fortune-teller. Astrology has been gaining a following in recent years, with its adherents claiming that, as other methods fail, it is rapidly moving into the mainstream. Henry Weingarten, a well-known financial astrologer, organized a conference on astrological investing some years back at New York's Vista Hotel.[4] Unfortunately, he had to relocate the conference; the stars had not warned him that the Trade Center bombing would close the Vista. Astrologers, undaunted either by setbacks or skepticism, claim their "science" predicts price movements much more regularly than either fundamental research or charts.[5] Some of the leading astrological researchers confidently predict the dates and times of these moves. However, they state with perfect candor that they do have problems with market direction—not being sure if it will be up or down.

A budding astrological superstar is Archibald A. H. Crawford, a former technical analyst under Bob Farrell, one of the deans of the field at Merrill Lynch. Crawford, who writes an astrological financial letter, told *The New York Times* that he cashed in on the 1995 bull market "by deciding to go 200% long on December 20, 1994, because of Saturn's 45 degree angle to Neptune." However, by March 12, 1995, the planets apparently had walked out of their orbits, because Crawford now stated to the *Times* that "1995 was going to be a grim, untidy year, with plenty of earthquakes and a market heading South. . . . Prices will top in the first week of April," he stated firmly, "with the Dow ending the year 1,000 points lower at about 3,200."[6]

He missed it by a hair. The Dow rose 36% for the year, ending at 5,100, a mere 62% above where the declension of Saturn indicated. An astrologer should be able to remember that Saturn is two-faced.

Slight miss or no, Crawford ranked second among 42 market timers monitored by Hulbert's Financial Digest in 1994.[7]

If astrology is attempting to become mainstream, what might we find on the outer fringe? Sunspots have their followers. Others read tree stumps. Frederick N. Goldsmith, an unfortunate investment advisor of the 1940s, went to trial when the fuzz found out he got his market signals from a comic strip, put there, he felt, by a famous 19th-century mogul, James R. Keane.

Although technical information has increased exponentially with the advent of computers, and the methods range from charting in the mainstream, to the occult at the fringe, the basic problems remain the same. To quote our friend Joe Granville again: "While the indicators may be crystal clear in definition and theory, they often break down and render false signals." Often, patterns are so complex that even leading chartists disagree on their meaning. Too, the "noise" around the market movements is usually so extreme that the indicators can flash red, yellow, and green—all at the same time.

"There is nothing wrong with the charts, only the chartists," runs another old Wall Street maxim. Maybe, but charting requires a very high degree of interpretive capability.

I learned this myself as a teenager when I visited my father's small commodities trading firm. His chief trader, although excellent at executing orders, was a passionate chartist. He was convinced that, if given the capital, he would make zillions. He kept the office covered with every conceivable type of chart. My father, not wanting to lose the man's skills, gave him a small amount to trade by the charts at the beginning of each year. The money was always gone by the end of January. This meant more intensive study and many more charts before the next yearly stipend came around. When I visited the office many years later, the cycle yet revolved.

The Technician's Moment of Truth

Technical analysis is widespread on Wall Street. The daily comments in market columns of *The Wall Street Journal, The New York Times,* and the financial sections of most newspapers are liberally sprinkled with its jargon. In fact no major or regional brokerage firm could long survive without a troop, or at least one or two, of these distinguished gurus. So there was considerable astonishment in the sixties when academic research began to demonstrate that no trends, tides, or waves could be shown to exist. Technical analysis, the academic findings stated, was useless.

The first findings that price movements were random emerged at the turn of the century. Louis Bachelier, a brilliant French math student, presented such evidence in his doctoral dissertation, written under the supervision of the internationally famous mathematician Jules Henri Poincaré. Bachelier's work, which dealt with commodity prices and government bonds, concluded that past price movements could not predict future changes. His work rested peacefully for sixty years, until financial researchers rediscovered it in 1960.

About the same time, other academicians embarked on the same course. One early study showed that randomly chosen numbers, when plotted, closely resembled actual price patterns of stocks.[8] Another found that price fluctuations resembled Brownian motion, the random movements of microscopic particles suspended in fluids.[9]

A good many researchers tested the proposition that stocks move in discernible trends. Arnold Moore conducted important work in the field in 1964,[10] Clive Granger and Oskar Morgenstern in 1963,[11] and Eugene Fama in 1965.[12] Granger and Morgenstern used the advanced new statistical technique of spectral analysis. Their database included 700 weeks of price information for various industries in the 1939 to 1961 period, as well as the Standard & Poor's and Dow-Jones indices between 1915 and 1961. Eugene Fama analyzed the price movements of the 30 stocks in the Dow-Jones Industrial Average for intervals of 1 to 14 days over 5 years.

All the studies demonstrated that future price movements cannot be predicted from past changes. Without exception, the findings indicated randomness in price—day to day, week to week, even month to month. The efficient market hypothesis originated from this work.[13]

No matter how convinced the technician is about the market's or a stock's next move, he has no more chance of being right than by tossing a coin. When a coin is tossed, even if it comes up heads ten times in a row, there is still a 50–50 chance that it will come up tails on the next throw. Or, in market terms, if a stock closes higher for ten consecutive days, the next day the stock has a 50–50 chance of closing down. That markets display identifiable trends, the central thesis of the technical school, had been overwhelmingly dismissed by academic research.

Destroying the Faith

Every technician I know naturally claims that his particular system works, his case is different. It is his judgment, he will say, that is the final determinant of which of the dozens of available tools to use, and what emphasis to put on each. To examine this claim would take an infinite number of tests. Still, the technicians have offered nothing to date, either in theory or in practice, which disputes the academic evidence. In the end a supposedly systematic and dependable method of beating the market is reduced to faith.

And this is the time to introduce our first investment rule:

RULE 1

Do not use market-timing or technical analysis. *These techniques can only cost you money.*

Curiously, considering that technical analysis has been continuously refuted for three decades, chartists continue to flourish, boasting of their successes and forgetting their bad calls, as though their doctrines had never been challenged. In fact, their status hasn't changed on Wall Street. But they should not be singled out, as the next chapter will demonstrate.

3

Bigger Game Ahead

THERE you sit, browsing through the *Alchemical Street Journal,* over your morning ale, reading in Latin some of the current articles and trying to understand the reasoning. (I suppose this puts us somewhere in the Middle Ages of Europe.) Ah, this is interesting; there've been some promising claims about turning lead into gold. Here are some charts showing how similar the two elements are, in weight, malleability, and other characteristics. Here is an analyst's projections of the breakthroughs to come, although he concedes there may be a few minor problems that, as yet, lack solutions. But progress is clear. Perhaps it's time to buy some more lead mining stock.

In that case, careful perusal of the astrology pages is in order. No serious investor would want to make a move without checking the stars, or, perhaps better, consulting with a licensed professional. Things have gotten so technical these days that the top astrologers are commanding enormous fees. It's come to the point where the individual investor will soon be pretty much left in the dust, at least until the personal computer is invented some five centuries from now.

Which brings us to fundamental analysis, the mainstay of investment techniques in the last years of the twentieth century. In chapter 2, we saw how the academic juggernaut rolled over the ideas, if not the hearts and minds, of the technicians. More formidable opposition lay ahead. Technical analysis, for all its wide following, is dwarfed by fundamental analysis. This method is considered more sophisticated, and is preferred by pension funds, bank trust departments, mutual funds, money managers, and brokers. It is also used by much of corporate America to make decisions from purchasing other companies or divisions, to investing in plant and equipment, to opening new markets.[1]

In essence, the fundamentalist holds that a company's value can be determined through rigorous analysis of its sales, its earnings and dividends, its financial strength, and a host of related measures. To value a stock, the analyst tries to evaluate all relevant information, often supplementing his or her work with visits to the companies to meet with senior management.

The fundamentalist believes that stock prices can diverge sharply from their real worth. His methods allow him to search out the true value, buying solid companies that are underpriced and selling those that are overpriced. The market, he is convinced, must eventually recognize the error of its ways and correct them. Fundamental analysis is considered to be more advanced than its technical cohort, because it draws on sophisticated accounting, investment, business, and economics techniques.

As with technical analysis, there are numerous branches of fundamental analysis. And as with religion, the bitterest disputes are not between contrasting beliefs, but among the various sects of the same faith.

Value Investing

Let's look briefly at the principles and failings of the two major schools of fundamental (or security) analysis: value investing and growth investing.

The most systematic work on value investing is the 658-page epic, *Security Analysis,* by Benjamin Graham and David Dodd, first published in 1934 and revised four times subsequently.[2] The book has been called the bible of value analysis, and for decades Graham has been regarded by Wall Streeters and academics as the father of modern value analysis.

Graham's investment technique stresses the preservation of capital. He defines risk as the possibility of losing your savings. Because of the difficulty of pinpointing real worth, Graham always insisted on an "adequate" margin of safety. Stocks should be purchased by applying stringent valuation formulas, which normally eliminates new issues, concept, and growth stocks. *Security Analysis* lays out rigorous procedures for determining intrinsic value. Graham's rules, based on the lessons of the Great Depression, were so strict that following the ones he devised in the thirties and forties, which he subsequently revised, would have kept investors out of much of the bull market that started in 1947, and almost completely out of the Great Bull Market which began in 1982.

Assessing Earning Power

The principal method of appraising a stock, according to Graham and Dodd, is to determine its earning power. The investor should gauge a company's profitability by tracking it over a long period, usually seven to ten years. He or she should carefully analyze its earnings and dividend trends, financial strength, backlogs, capital spending plans, and other pertinent information. Qualitative factors, such as growth prospects, management, position in its industry, and product development should also be assessed. After thorough analysis, the investor should be in a position to work out conservative projections of earnings.

Cash Flow Analysis

Many value analysts today place more emphasis on cash flow than on earnings. Cash flow is normally defined as after-tax earnings, adding back depreciation and other noncash charges. If we take two companies with similar outlooks, markets, products, and management talent, the one with the higher cash flow will usually be the more rewarding stock. In investing, as in your personal finances, cash is king. The company with good cash flow can capitalize on market opportunities that a firm with weaker cash flow sadly must let slip by. Firms with strong cash flow can also better ride out economic storms than their weaker competitors.

These analysts regard cash flow as more important than earnings because management can reduce earnings by setting up reserves or taking write-offs, or increase them by not taking adequate depreciation or other necessary charges. Although these entries do not show in earnings, they read loud and clear in the statement of cash flow, which the Federal Accounting Standards Board (FASB) has required companies to issue since mid-1988. But cash flow is only one of a number of accounting statements that is important to the value analyst.

Accounting

The fundamentalist attaches high importance to understanding accounting conventions. To get an accurate picture of earnings, adjustments must be made for each accounting item that could distort them.*

Nor is the analyst's emphasis on accounting principles merely an obsession. "Creative" accounting has always been a facile tool in the hands of the adroit corporate manipulator. In the latter half of the eighties, Michael Milken and other junk bond impresarios sold huge amounts of marginal bonds to the public, frequently with little in the way of assets, or even a profitable business to back them. All too often, these bonds were backed by smoke and mirrors and the allure of dazzling interest rates that could be paid only if a minor miracle occurred. The collapse of this market in 1990 caused the loss of hundreds of billions of dollars as well as the insolvency of a number of major financial institutions, including Columbia Savings and Loan and Charles Keating's Lincoln Savings and Loan. More recently, the bankruptcy of Crazy Eddie and the imprisonment of its chairman, Eddie Antar; of Leslie Fay, a medium-size public apparel manufacturer listed on the New York Stock Exchange; and the 1997 decimation of Mercury Finance underscored the need to sift carefully for signs of financial manipulation.

Graham and Dodd and succeeding value analysts recommend that security analysts use an extensive list of financial ratios to evaluate a company. One of the more important is the return on equity—the after-tax profit divided by net worth, which is to say the value of all common stock and retained earnings. This is an important ratio to determine how profitable the business is. Another is pretax return on sales, the income earned before taxes as a percentage of sales. While there are naturally variations from industry to industry, the higher and more stable these ratios, the better regarded the firm. The two ratios will range from 10 or 12% for the average company to as high as 20 or 30% for the more spectacular growth stocks.

Other ratios show whether a company can meet its debts, since a high debt load can lead to default or bankruptcy. A common rule of thumb for an industrial company is that the common stock should represent at least 40 percent of the capital structure.[3]

The no-nonsense approach of Graham and Dodd stated that the ana-

---

* For example, a one-time gain from the sale of a plant or land must be excluded from that year's operating income, as should a large number of extraordinary or one-time charges. (These items will show up in the statement of cash flow.)

lyst should focus on whether the record of earnings could continue, rather than whether a company could expand rapidly. Today most fundamental analysts start here, but put more emphasis on recent developments and future prospects.

Graham laid out four components of stock evaluation: expected earnings, expected dividends, a method for valuing expected earnings, and asset value. All are still widely used. He repeatedly cautions the practitioner to tie the four firmly to the record of the past.

Once future earnings are estimated, an evaluative measure establishes what the price should be. The most commonly used value yardstick is the price/earnings (P/E) ratio—price divided by earnings per share. If a stock trading at $10 earned $1.00 last year, and is expected to earn $1.25 this year, it is said to be trading at a price/earnings ratio of 10 on the latest full year's earnings and at 8 on anticipated earnings for the current year. The higher the P/E ratio, the more favorable the company's prospects; the lower the multiple, the more lackluster they appear.

A cardinal conviction of Graham and Dodd is that investors overemphasize near-term prospects, overpricing companies for which they are favorable and underpricing those for which they are poorer. They thus recommended upper limits on the P/E ratio the investor should pay for a stock with excellent prospects and lower limits on the P/E ratios of companies with so-so outlooks. If a company fell below the lower limit, it was probably undervalued and worth a look.

Price-to-Book Value

A second method of picking stocks is to buy companies trading at a significant discount to their book, or net asset, value (the value of the common stock after deducting all liabilities and preferred shares). Usually, this is calculated per common share by dividing the total by the number of common shares outstanding.

Again, to do this the investor must be familiar with accounting. Book value is often crucial in evaluating a private company, noted Graham and Dodd, but once the firm goes public the market turns its focus almost exclusively to earnings. Formulas were given for taking advantage of companies selling under book, or for valuing other assets priced nominally on the balance sheet. Many of these techniques have become central to merger and acquisition evaluation today.

Contemporary asset players, however, increasingly use relative book value—the book value of the company relative to the market—rather than absolute value. The reason is that the average company in the S&P

500 currently trades at over five times book. Companies priced under book, though common up to the seventies, are sighted about as frequently as unicorns in contemporary markets. Although debate rages as to whether this means markets are overvalued, a good part of the increase appears to result from absolute book value being far too conservative. With inflation putting prices up manyfold since the war, the replacement value of land, buildings, and other corporate assets is often far more than shown on its books.

Contemporary Value Techniques

Although most value analysts use methods outlined by Graham and Dodd, they usually emphasize one set over another. According to *Institutional Investor Magazine*, most pension-fund consultants group value managers into four categories, by the criteria they use to determine cheap stocks.[4]

The first category is the low P/E manager, who buys stocks with multiples below the market average. This manager normally owns out-of-favor stocks. The second is the high-yield investor, who buys stocks with higher-than-market dividend yields and future dividend potential. The third category buys low market valuation relative to book value, which often leads him to depressed cyclicals. This manager is sometimes considered the most contrarian, as he or she will buy companies with no current earnings. The last group focuses on the private or going concern value, measuring underlying assets or cash flow much the way takeover specialists do. Though the tributaries can diverge widely, all spring from methods described above.

Visions of Sugar Plums

Although all fundamental analysis sprouts from the same tree, one branch, the growth school, has dominated for considerable periods. This branch has perplexed value analysts back to the time of Graham and Dodd, because followers of this school often seem to turn the traditional valuation principles upside down. And, the growth analyst would say, for good reason.

Had someone put $10,000 into Microsoft, with its Windows software for PCs, on March 13, 1986, when it went public at $1.55 a share, he could have sold it for $1,750,000 in the third quarter of 1997. Wal-Mart's earnings increased 23 times in the 1970–1980 period, and 40 times by

1993. Anyone astute enough to buy $10,000 worth of Wal-Mart's stock in 1970, when it went public, could have pocketed $10,000,000 by 1993. An investor who plunked $2,750 on Thomas J. Watson's Computing and Tabulating Company in 1914 was rolling in $20 million in IBM stock by the beginning of the 1970s. It hardly surprises, then, with our economic growth depending on invention and technological change, that the growth school has so often ruled fundamental analysis.

American history is full of stories of investors who seized opportunities and made fortunes. The tradition of Microsoft, McDonald's, IBM, Compaq, and Wal-Mart is deeply rooted Americana. Participating in new, potentially vast enterprises gives us an exciting sense of communion with the Bill Gateses, the Warren Buffetts, and the John Kluges.

The growth analyst attempts to zero in on companies that can expect rapid and stable expansion. Like his more conservative value counterparts, he starts with the past, but his emphasis is on the future. He seeks companies that will continue to have superior profit margins and earn above-average returns on equity. A growth company should be less affected by economic uncertainties and should produce rising earnings through both inflationary and recessionary conditions, when many firms falter.

The analyst must successfully pinpoint trends: how well a new line of computers will do for Compaq or Hewlett Packard, how many customers America Online will put on the Internet this year, or how big a market exists for Merck's newest blockbuster drug. Extensive digging goes into determining product growth, market share, development of competition, maintenance of profit margins, and dozens of other factors. Growth stocks traditionally have traded at lofty multiples—two, three, four, or more times the P/E ratios of their more pedestrian compeers—which makes an error in projections fatal.

A growth company is believed to have remarkable control over its destiny. It normally has an entrenched position in a rapidly expanding market. Often its edge comes from exciting new technology that holds out the prospect of gigantic markets, as in the case of CompuServe, Netscape, and other Internet access companies. At times it comes from patent protection, as with the large ethical drug companies, and sometimes from an imaginative adaptation of manufacturing, production, and marketing techniques to a service industry, such as McDonald's.

Growth companies reputedly have excellent management with the vision to create entirely new markets. Microsoft's management foresaw the importance of internal software for PCs and correctly predicted a multi-billion-dollar market. On the other hand, IBM, for which Microsoft was originally only a tiny subcontractor, believed this software would be a small, commodity-like business with lackluster profit margins that it did not want to bother with. There are no billionaires at IBM.

As with basic fundamental analysis, growth stock investing has many rules. But once again, a system that appears sensible in theory has proved difficult in practice.

Why Don't They Work?

To judge from the record of professional investors presented in chapter 1, fundamental research has been no more successful than technical analysis. This seems strange, because the fundamental school appears to build on a much more solid foundation. Graham and Dodd, always skeptical of growth techniques, gave good reasons why this branch of analysis may not work. The first problem lies in the nature of the analysis itself. They believe that a forecast based on the measurable earnings power of the past is more secure than one built on extrapolated trends of growth. Such projections can be chancy, they repeatedly warn, even for prime growth companies. Then, too, for every real growth stock, dozens will fade in the stretch, if not at the gate.

The second problem with growth investing is that, even with accurate analysis, the question remains of what the proper P/E should be. It didn't take a genius in the 1920s to realize that the automobile would be a growth industry for decades. If anything, investors underestimated the industry's expansion. But that didn't help the analyst pick the three or four survivors from the hundreds of promising companies. Packard, Nash, Stutz-Bearcat, Duesenberg, Studebaker, and dozens of others were formidable competitors in their day. Internet companies now present a similar jungle of possibilities. Scores of companies contend for this rapidly growing market, many with state-of-the-art technology. Which will survive? What price shall we pay for their prospects?

The third problem is: a rapidly growing company can trade at a P/E ratio of 40 or 50, then drop to 25 or even 15 as investors change their minds about its value. This happened to biotech stocks in 1993 and 1994. It also happened to Ascend Communications and 3Com in July of 1996. These stocks fell 45% or 50%, as perceptions went negative. In little more than a heartbeat, they turned positive again and the stocks regained most of their losses within six weeks.* Evaluation, then, is just as difficult as forecasting.

---

* But not for long. Ascend dropped over 70% again by late 1997 on disappointing prospects.

An even more troublesome question: Why have the conservative proponents of the Graham and Dodd model not outperformed, or even kept up with, the market as a whole? First, standard analysis increasingly emphasizes near-term outlooks while downplaying other key fundamentals, thus abandoning one of Graham's key principles. Forecasting is the most important factor in contemporary securities analysis. As we shall see in chapter 5, research analysts forecast poorly. Chapter 5 also demonstrates that even a moderate miss can devastate a stock's price.

Second, although certain issues may be substantially undervalued, there is no guarantee that the market will recognize it. The stocks may linger in the dumps for years.

Warren Buffett gave a third reason. He said he consistently applied fundamentals that "others cavalierly disregarded." But were they disregarded? Or were their adherents forced by weaknesses in the methods to abandon them, most often involuntarily? Part II will examine this question in some detail. Meanwhile, let's look at methods born of mixed fundamental and technical lineage: market timing, tactical asset allocation, and momentum.

Market Timing and Tactical Asset Allocation

Market timing, as the name implies, tries to time purchases and sales to the phases of the market. If this could actually be done, money would grow on trees. In the past ten years, catching the major swings would have more than tripled the results of simply buying and holding the S&P 500.

Market timing is a hybrid of fundamental and technical ingredients. Market timers watch the trend and level of interest rates, the degree and direction of business activity, corporate profits, industrial production, etc. If, for example, inflation is decelerating, interest rates have peaked and are edging down, and employment is beginning to pick up after a decline, economic factors are considered favorable. If technical patterns are also encouraging, a strong buy signal has been given. On the other hand, if inflation is creeping ominously higher, accompanied by rising interest rates, while profitability and employment are beginning to slip, and technical patterns look menacing, we know it's time to sell. What could be simpler?

Unfortunately, real market movements give dozens of signals, madly flashing buy, sell, and hold all at once. To further complicate the situation, institutions watch the same leading technicians (Robert Farrell, Bob Prechter, Elaine Garzarelli, and a handful of others) and the same indicators, as well as each other. Thus, the major money managers will all react to the same information at the same time. Since they currently control a large percentage of stock trading, market timing may create a self-fulfilling prophecy that exacerbates market swings.

Various academic and institutional studies, as well as the long-term performance of money managers who practice this method, indicate that market timing doesn't work. To time markets profitably, Nobel laureate William Sharpe finds that a money manager must call three moves out of four, after commissions and transaction costs.[5]

In light of these and similar findings, increasing numbers of investors have turned to tactical asset allocation (TAA), particularly after the 1987 crash and the 1990 free fall, which caught most market timers napping.[6] Like its less sophisticated sibling, TAA promises to move the investor into and out of the market at the right time. It also states it will shift the portfolio mix (normally stocks, bonds, and cash) as conditions change. Most TAA signals are based on both economic and market indicators. In the end, TAA, in spite of its more respectable title, still depends on some kind of fixed formula or on technical analysis.

While many professionals regard TAA as simply another form of market timing, adherents violently disagree. Does it work? The figures are not encouraging. Figure 3–1, taken from Lipper and Morningstar data, shows the returns of 186 asset allocators for the 12 years to September 1997 compared to the S&P 500 and the average of all domestic equity funds.[7] The period covers a good part of the bull market, as well as the 1987 crash, and the sharp downturn in 1990. This was the ideal time for market timers or asset allocators to prove their mettle. They should have got you out before the 1987 and 1990 debacles and back in on time to ride the resurgent bull. Had they succeeded, you would have outperformed the market handily.

As the chart shows, heroes they ain't. While the market surged 734% over the entire period, and the average equity fund moved up 589%, the asset allocators increased only 384%, about half the gain of the averages (all figures are dividend adjusted). Tactical asset allocation has obviously not set the world on fire. In fact, it's downright awful, even in the periods where asset allocators claimed they swept the field.

The prosecution rests.

Momentum

The final fundamental-technical hybrid, which has gained major popularity in the last few years, is momentum investing. Managers of value

Figure 3-1

MISTIMING

Compounded returns of asset allocation funds versus all
domestic equity funds and the S&P 500

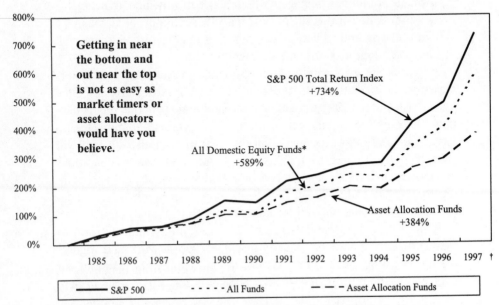

Sources of data: Lipper Analytical Services and Morningstar

* "All Funds" is an asset-weighted index of the compounded returns all equity mutual fund categories
followed by Morningstar.

† Returns measured through September 30, 1997.

and growth funds alike use this method. A momentum investor buys
stocks that are outperforming their industries or the market, and sells
them when they lag. Although earnings momentum is the most common
method, this technique can be used in other ways. Investors can purchase stocks that are outperforming and liquidate underperforming issues (not unlike conventional technical analysis), or they can look at
sales momentum. A momentum analyst can also follow various fundamental yardsticks, but emphasizes accelerating earnings growth quarter
by quarter. And so on.

Trouble is, with the increasing popularity of this method, many managers are playing the same game. So much so that they jump on the same
figures at the same time, jerking the price sharply. Thus, as momentum
slows for a favored stock, everyone scrambles for the exit simultaneously, and the price tumbles. Which is precisely what happened to momentum players in technology stocks in late 1997. Momentum had been

positive for these stocks for several years and buyers jumped on the bandwagon in ever-increasing numbers. When technology stocks turned sour that fall, scores of major players all sold at once, often driving prices down as much as 50%. A sure way to buy high and sell low you say? Maybe, but popular all the same.

There is little documentation from the schools or from the Street that momentum beats the market.[8] But why bother with facts? Evidence or no, it is one of the trendiest concepts in investing today. Once again, theory has little to do with reality.

A Purposeful Random Walk

If fundamentalists were perplexed by why their results weren't better, the academics certainly were not. Starting in the 1970s, they shifted their research firepower from the technical to the fundamental front. They made extensive studies of mutual funds, the great majority of which subscribe to security analysis. The professors demonstrated that the funds did no better than the market.[9]

Academic analysis proved as unsparing of the fundamental practitioner's sensibilities as of the technician's. Other prevailing beliefs were treated as harshly. No link was found between portfolio turnover and subsequent performance. Rapid turnover does not improve results, but seems to damage them slightly. No relationship was found between performance and sales charges.[10] In sum, the reports firmly concluded that mutual funds do not outperform the market.

The results hardly comforted fund managers, who like to represent superior performance. The mutual fund manager not only underperformed the market, but adjusting for risk as the academics defined it, often fared even worse. Other researchers roughed up the poor manager just as harshly. At the time, the money managers appeared to be routed as badly as the Inca armies who fled from Pizarro and his terrifying cavalry. But, as we'll see, much of the seemingly awesome academic firepower was problematic or just plain wrong. In the 1960s, however, and for years afterward, it overwhelmed all opposition.

The Three Faces of EMH

To explain their discoveries, academic investigators, as we saw in the first chapter, proposed a revolutionary hypothesis. Today called "the semi-strong form" of the efficient market hypothesis, it holds that competition between sophisticated and knowledgeable investors keeps stock prices about where they should be. This happens because all facts that determine stock prices are analyzed by large numbers of interested investors. New information, such as a change in a company's earnings outlook or a dividend cut, is quickly digested and immediately reflected in the stock price. Like it or not, competition by so many investors, all seeking hidden values, makes stock prices reflect the best estimates of their real worth. Prices may not always be right, but they are unbiased, so if they are wrong, they are just as likely to be too high as too low.

Because the market is efficient, the theorists continue, investors should expect only a fair return commensurate with the risk of purchasing a particular stock. Risk, as the theorists have defined it, is volatility. The greater the volatility of the security or portfolio, as measured against the market, the greater the risk. Securities or portfolios with greater risk should provide larger rewards.*

Since meaningful information enters the marketplace unpredictably, prices react in a random manner. This is the real reason that charting and technical analysis do not work. Nobody knows what new data will enter the market, whether it will be positive or negative, or whether it will affect the market as a whole, or only a single company.

The key premise of the semi-strong form of EMH is that the market reacts almost instantaneously and correctly to new information, so investors cannot benefit from it. To prove this thesis, researchers conducted a number of studies that they claimed validated it.

One important study explored the market's understanding of stock splits. In effect, when a stock is split, there is no free lunch—the shareholder still has the same proportionate ownership as before. If naive traders run up the price, said the academics, knowledgeable investors will sell until it's back in line, and market efficiency will be proved. And, said the researchers, this was indeed the case. Tests confirmed that stock prices after a split was distributed maintained about the same long-term relationship to market movements as before.[11]

Another study measuring the earnings of 261 large corporations between 1946 and 1966 concluded that all but 10 to 15% of the data in the earnings reports was anticipated by the reporting month, indicating the market's awareness of information.[12] Other tests came up with similar results, demonstrating, the professors said, that the market quickly adjusts to inputs.

Did these tests actually prove what they claim and cinch the case that

---

* For more detail on the academic definition of risk see chapter 14 and Appendix A.

markets react quickly to new information? They did not, as we will see.

The semi-strong form of EMH is intuitively appealing, because it explains the single most obvious mystery about investing: How can thousands of intelligent and hard-working professional stock-pickers be endlessly outwitted by the market and embarrassed by their selections? It also provides a rational explanation for the often inexplicable behavior of markets.

This form of EMH has much wider implications than the weak form, which said only that investors would not benefit from technical analysis. The new argument, if correct, tears the heart out of fundamental research. No amount of fundamental analysis, including the exhaustive high-priced studies done by major Wall Street brokerage houses, will give investors an edge. If enough buyers and sellers have correctly evaluated new information, under- and overvalued stocks will be rare indeed.[13]

The implications are sweeping. If you're in the market, the theory tells you to buy and hold rather than trade a lot. Trading increases your commissions without increasing your return. It also tells you to assume that investors who have outperformed the market in the past were just plain lucky and that you have no reason to believe they will continue to do so.[14]

The semi-strong form also contends that no mutual fund, money manager, or individual investor, no matter how sophisticated, can beat the market using public information. If one does, it's pure chance.

Finally, there is the strong form of the efficient market hypothesis. This form claims that no information, including that known by corporate insiders or by specialists trading the company's stock (who have confidential material about unexecuted orders on their "books"), can help you outperform the market. In the few studies done to date, some evidence has surfaced that both insiders and specialists display an ability to beat the market.[15,16] However, the strong form of EMH is generally considered too extreme, and is not widely accepted.

EMH was also supported by studies that indicated mutual funds and other monies managed by professionals did not outperform the market. Eugene Fama, the leading advocate of EMH (*Fortune* magazine referred to him as the Solomon of stocks), reviewed the literature and development of EMH in December 1991.[17] Fama's report was thorough, covering hundreds of papers published since his last major review twenty years earlier.

Despite the thousands of papers in the last two decades, relatively little new research supporting the efficient market hypothesis has been produced, with two exceptions. Some new studies show daily and weekly predictability in price movements from past movements. But after transaction costs there is nothing much left.

A second area of new support for efficient markets, according to Fama, comes from event studies, the study of specific events and how they affect a stock or the market. In the past twenty years, hundreds of such studies have been undertaken. Fama concludes that "on average stock prices adjust quickly to information about investment decisions, dividend changes, changes in capital structure, and corporate-control transactions."[18] He also refers to another large body of research from event studies that shows the opposite conclusion: rather than adjusting rapidly to new information, prices adjust slowly and thus inefficiently. Nevertheless, he concludes his review article with the statement: "The cleanest evidence of market-efficiency comes from event studies, especially from event studies on daily returns." We will return to Professor Fama and his assertions in the final chapter.

A discussion of the efficient market's classic, albeit almost completely refuted, master creation, modern portfolio theory (MPT), is found in Appendix A. MPT details how the rational marketplace supposedly works, and is widely used to make investment decisions by some of the largest banks, pension funds, brokerage houses, and perhaps by a mutual fund you own.

The Power of an Idea

Whether EMH and MPT do a good job of describing markets or are pure blather, they have fired the imagination not only of academe, but also of Wall Street. Prior to these theories, investment managers and mutual funds were measured on the rates of return their portfolios generated,[19] usually compared to the S&P 500 or the Dow Jones, with no adjustments made for risk. The development of modern portfolio theory resulted in academics and consultants putting risk measurements into the formula to determine how well a portfolio performed. If a portfolio earned the market return with higher risk, it was deemed on a risk-adjusted basis to have underperformed the market.[20]

Risk measurement has grown into a multi-billion-dollar industry and influences the decisions of countless investors, either directly or through their pension funds. If you buy a mutual fund from Charles Schwab, as millions do, you might take your cue from its recommended list. To rank funds, Schwab and most other mass marketers calculate risk as well as performance. Risk is measured according to academic principles which, as we shall see in chapter 14, have now been discredited by leading academic researchers themselves, and are probably money-losers.

Similar risk measurements are used by consultants who recommend money managers to large pension funds and to other clients, and to the wrap-fee programs of the large brokerage houses, which recommend money managers for millions of smaller customers.

On the theory that you cannot beat the market over time, hundreds of billions of dollars have gone into various forms of index funds, from the S&P 500 to the Russell 2000.* Leaders in the indexing business, such as Vanguard's Index 500 fund, Wells Fargo, and Bankers Trust, have attracted large portions of these flows. Finally, a myriad of other products has come out of EMH and MPT, ranging from small cap stocks to MPT strategies for money management firms.

In the last few dozen pages, we have reviewed the academic dismantlement of the two most important market theories of our day, and their replacement, at least intellectually, by a third. The new theory has swept through the universities, and then progressively through the financial press, individual and corporate investors, and among professionals themselves. On the assumption that it is impossible to outdo the market, many professionals have radically altered their techniques and their concept of risk—a fitting tribute to the power of an idea conceived little more than three decades earlier.

The theory so pervades professional investing and academia that Michael Jensen, one of the important contributors to its development, stated some years back, "It's dangerously close to the point where no graduate student would dare to submit a paper criticizing the hypothesis."[21] At the same time, it is sad, for in accepting the new way, the money manager acknowledges that his or her prime raison d'être—to earn superior returns for the client—is beyond reach.

But it's not time to throw in the towel yet. Although the efficient market hypothesis seems to unravel some of the investment knots we have seen, it fails to untie many others. How, for instance, could professional investors as a group underperform the market for decades? How could the bulk of professional opinion prove so consistently and dramatically wrong at crucial market turning points? Or, if investors are so unfailingly rational, how could euphoria and panic prevail so often? More to the point, if the market were so efficient, how could the 1987 crash have happened? Particularly when thousands of investment professionals were not only trained in, but carefully followed, efficient market

---

* The Russell 2000 is the most widely followed small-company index.

teachings? Their numbers included prominent academics who developed advanced theories built on EMH and MPT that were obliterated in the crash. These professionals backed their decisions with hundreds of billions of dollars.

None of these things could happen, according to the theory. One nonacademic observer noted that Compaq Computer fell 65% between 1991 and 1993, with its price declining from $9 to $3, before soaring to $79 in late 1997. Fundamentals varied little during this time. "When was the market efficient?" he asked. "When it took Compaq down to 3 or drove it up to 79?" Efficient markets should not behave this way.

Thus, before accepting the academic theory that ours is the best of all possible financial worlds—that our advanced analytical methods result in highly efficient markets—let's move back to the questions posed a few pages earlier. Are there flaws in the analytical methods themselves—flaws so serious that even trained professionals cannot avoid them—that lead to consistent investment errors? We will find the surprising answers in the next section.

PART II

THE EXPERT WAY TO LOSE YOUR SAVINGS

4

Dangerous Forecasts

IN OSCAR WILDE's classic novel, *The Picture of Dorian Gray,* the protagonist enjoys all the dissipations late-nineteenth-century London can offer without showing the slightest sign of wear or tear. Today you might suspect a skillful plastic surgeon was lurking in the background, but Dorian Gray had discovered a simpler method. He had a portrait, carefully hidden away, that showed all the results of his debauchery, while his own visage remained youthful and pure to the world.

Unfortunately, that picture would eventually be his undoing, as is often the case in an adult morality tale. Yet, with a little stretch of the imagination, I think we can find another portrait that reflects the same division between outer appearance and inner truth. It will not be of a particular person, but rather of the class of people generically best known as experts. In particular, we'll want to recognize the portraiture of the experts who forecast the performance of stocks or markets. They, too, seem to pass through life unblemished by inaccurate predictions or poor stock choices, even though the true picture drawn from the latest research will accurately show every statistical wrinkle, scar, wart, and sagging chin.

As a society, we have always had a schizophrenic attitude toward experts. On the one hand, when we want their help, we rush to them, and breathlessly await their utterances. But if we don't need them and look objectively at their performance, our attitude is often less reverential and more colored with amusement, or even downright skepticism. With good reason. Experts are often wrong—sometimes remarkably so.

The stock market, for the reasons demonstrated in this chapter and the next, is a prime place for major expert errors—mistakes that cost many investors a good part of their savings. It is important for you to know just how insidious these errors can be, and how difficult they are to avoid. To succeed in the marketplace you'll have to go back and "unlearn" many of the bad habits in which we have all been schooled. Just as a good golfer may have to unlearn a bad swing, forgetting much of what he relied on in the past, or a good tennis player her serve, so it is in markets. Here we must learn to live without our dependence on experts, taught us from our earliest days as investors. For the reasons I'll discuss, it will prove tougher than overcoming that slice in golf or that blah serve in tennis. But when you see how dramatically it improves your odds in the market, I'm sure you'll want to give it a try.

What we shall see first is that it is not only the poor stock market forecaster who is off the mark repeatedly. No, the problem of expert error is universal, as the following examples illustrate.

A Portrait of Dorian Guru

Americans have always believed technology is the key element in advancing our standard of living and quality of life. Well, not quite always. The commissioner of the U.S. Office of Patents, in urging President William McKinley in 1899 to close down the patent office, said, "Everything that can be invented has been invented."[1] In 1901, Wilbur told Orville, "Man will not fly for fifty years." The Wright brothers flew on December 17, 1903.

Military history has its share of experts who missed the mark by more than a little. "The army is the Indian's best friend," said one well-known American brigadier-general. His name—General George Custer. Unfortunately, the Indians didn't share his belief, as they attested at the Little Big Horn River in 1876. Other American military experts have proven as savvy. In August 1941, Captain William T. Pulleston, the former chief of U.S. Naval Intelligence, stated, "The Hawaiian Islands are over-protected; the entire Japanese Fleet and Air Force could not seriously threaten Oahu." Said Secretary of the Navy Frank Knox on December 4, 1941, "No matter what happens the U.S. Navy is not going to be caught napping."[2] Three days later the officer in charge of radar at Pearl Harbor was told by a subordinate that a radar signal indicated at least 50 planes, possibly far more, were approaching Oahu at almost 180 miles an hour. His reply, "Well don't worry about it . . . it's nothing." The military experts, after all, were assured by some of the keenest diplomatic minds America has ever produced. John Foster Dulles, the Secretary of State who was influential in shaping American postwar foreign policy, said in 1941, "Only hysteria entertains the idea that . . . Japan contemplates war upon us."[3]

But let's be fair. The "competence" of military experts goes far beyond the United States. Major George Elliot, a respected writer on military affairs, wrote in May 1939, only months before Germany attacked Poland, that, "although Germany is tremendously stronger in armored divisions . . . Poland's superior cavalry is ideally suited to the terrain of Eastern Europe." Poland's vaunted cavalry, superb lancers or no, were almost immediately crushed by the German tanks.

Experts have risen to the occasion in many other fields. An 1865 review of *Alice's Adventures in Wonderland* in *Children's Books* said of Lewis Carroll's work, "We fancy that any real child might be more puzzled than enchanted by this stiff overwrought story."[4] The prestigious *Saturday Review of London* on May 8, 1858, wrote of Charles Dickens, "We do not believe in the permanence of his reputation. . . . Our children will wonder what their ancestors meant by putting Mr. Dickens at the head of the novelists of his day."[5] William Winstanley, who compiled the *Lives of the Most Famous English Poets*, wrote in 1687 of John Milton, "His fame is gone out like a candle in a sniff and his memory will always stink."[6] *The Southern Quarterly Review* was a little more courtly in its review of Herman Melville's classic in 1851: "*Moby Dick* is sad stuff, dull and dreary, or ridiculous. Mr. Melville's Quakers are the wretchedest dolts and drivellers, and his Mad Captain . . . is a monstrous bore."[7] Well, to be fair, they were writing about Yankees.

The London Critic wrote in 1855, "Walt Whitman is as unacquainted with art as a hog is with mathematics."[8] But U.S. reviewers gave the Brits as good as they received. "I'm sorry Mr. Kipling, but you just don't know how to use the English language," wrote the editor of the *San Francisco Examiner* in 1889, informing Kipling that he should not send in further articles.[9] In rejecting the thriller *The Day of the Jackal* in April 1970, a publisher wrote author Frederick Forsyth, "[Your] book has no reader interest." By 1983, uninterested readers had bought 8 million copies.

The experts have proven equally astute in Hollywood. Louis B. Mayer, cofounder of MGM, was told by one of his senior executives not to bid for the rights for *Gone With the Wind*: "Forget it, Louis, no Civil War picture ever made a nickel." Louis replied, "Irving knows what's right." Another expert observed, "*Gone With the Wind* is going to be the biggest flop in Hollywood history. I'm glad it will be Clark Gable falling flat on his face and not Gary Cooper." The observer—Gary Cooper. Marilyn Monroe was told early in her career, "You'd better learn secretarial work, or else get married."[10] A Universal Studio executive dismissed two actors at the same meeting, telling the first, "You have no talent," and the second, "You have a chip on your tooth, your Adam's apple sticks out too far, and you talk too slow."[11] The first actor was Burt Reynolds and the second was Clint Eastwood, the movies' two biggest box-office draws in the 1970s.

Experts have proved as insightful in the other arts. Samuel Pepys, a noted British author, wrote after seeing Shakespeare's *A Midsummer Night's Dream*, "It's the most insipid, ridiculous play I ever saw in my life."[12] A theater critic wrote after watching *Annie Get Your Gun*, "Irving Berlin's score is musically not exciting—of the real songs only one or two are tuneful." *Annie Get Your Gun* was the greatest stage success of Irving Berlin's career, with at least eight songs that were among the top hits of the time. Michael Todd, a major Broadway producer and impresario, told Walter Winchell after seeing a new Broadway show, "No legs, no jokes, no chance." The show was *Oklahoma!*, one of the greatest musicals of all time. The head of the advertising agency in charge of another new Broadway show advised, "I don't think we can do anything with these reviews. It's a disaster. Close it." The producers of *Grease* decided not to listen to the advice. It was the longest-running show in Broadway history.[13]

Music and painting are not much different. The manager of the Grand Ole Opry told one young singer, "You ain't going nowhere . . . son. You ought to go back to drivin' a truck." The singer was Elvis Presley.[14] "We don't like their sound. Groups of guitars are on their way out," said a Decca Recording Company executive in 1962 in turning down the Beatles.[15] "The biggest no-talent I ever worked with," said a senior executive in firing Buddy Holly from the Decca label in 1956.

A review of Impressionist painter Edgar Degas in *The New York Times* in 1904 said, "Degas is repulsive." Degas's masterpieces sell for $10 million and above today. Emile Zola, one of the great French novelists of his day and a leading defender of Impressionist artists, said in 1900 of Paul Cézanne, "Paul may have had the genius of a great painter, but he never had the persistence to become one."[16] Cézanne's best works regularly fetch $10 million to $20 million. Edouard Manet, one of the earliest Impressionists, said to Claude Monet of Pierre-Auguste Renoir, "He has no talent at all, that boy. . . . Tell him to please give up painting." Renoir is one of the acknowledged masters of Impressionism, whose masterpieces have sold above $60 million. A well-known American art critic said of Picasso in 1934: "[Picasso's] prestige is rapidly waning and the custodians of his fame and his pictures are fighting a losing battle to elevate him to a position among the immortals."[17] Picasso painted many of his important works in the next forty years.

Perhaps you're thinking, "But the arts and the military are different from the more scientific areas, like medicine, economics, science, and finance." Are they? Experts seem to make their share of bloopers in these disciplines too. A parliamentary commission in Great Britain set up to investigate the value of the incandescent lightbulb concluded in 1878 that "[Edison's ideas are] good enough for our transatlantic friends . . . but unworthy of the attention of practical or scientific men."[18] President Rutherford B. Hayes said in 1876 after participating in a telephone conversation between Washington and Philadelphia, "That's an amazing invention, but who would ever want to use one of them?"[19] Alexander Graham Bell patented the telephone in 1876 and tried to sell it to Western Union, but the company was not interested. Lord Kelvin, one of the preeminent British scientists of the nineteenth century said that "Radio has no future."[20]

A potential initial investor in the Ford Motor Company was told by his banker, "The horse is here to stay, but the automobile is only a novelty—a fad."[21] The investor bought $5,000 worth of Ford stock anyway and sold his shares several years later for $12.5 million. The editor of the *London Daily Express*, when told in 1922 that the inventor of television wanted to see him, said, "For God's sake go down to reception and get rid of the lunatic who's down there. He says he's got a machine for seeing by wireless! Watch him—he may have a razor on him."[22]

Newer technology seems to have been greeted no better. Thomas J. Watson, the founder of IBM, said in 1943, "I think there is a world market for about five computers."[23] Ken Olson, the founder of Digital Equipment, stated in 1977 just before the PC revolution began, "There is no reason for any individual to have a computer in their home."

Expert opinion in other technical areas: Albert Einstein, whose theory of relativity was instrumental in creating the nuclear bomb, said in 1932, "There is not the slightest indication that [nuclear energy] will ever be obtainable. It would mean the atom would have to be shattered at will."[24] On June 3, 1979, the American Institute of Architects held its annual convention at the Crosby Kemper arena in Kansas City and named it the winner of its coveted AIA honor award for design excellence. The next day the arena's roof collapsed.[25]

Unfortunately, the history of expert predictions in the world of economics and finance is not much different. Many of us have heard of how wrong the experts were after the 1929 Crash. Bernard Baruch, the most distinguished financier of his time and the advisor to a number of presidents, cabled Winston Churchill in mid-November 1929: "FINANCIAL STORM DEFINITELY PASSED." The prestigious Harvard Economic Society wrote in its weekly letter on November 16, 1929,

"[A] severe depression like that of 1920–21 is outside the range of probability." On September 20, 1930, it wrote, "[R]ecovery will soon be evident," adding on November 15, 1930, that "[the] outlook is for the end of the decline in business in the early part of 1931, and steady . . . revival for the remainder of the year."[26] In 1931, hard-pressed for funds because of the Depression, the Society was forced to discontinue publication.

Fast-forwarding a few decades, the managing director of the International Monetary Fund said in 1959, "In all likelihood world inflation is over." Prices have more than quintupled since then, a bigger rise than in the previous thousand years. In 1968, *Business Week* wrote, "With over 50 foreign cars already on sale here, the Japanese auto industry isn't likely to carve out a big share of the market for itself."

Economic forecasting has proven to be anything but an exact science. A survey of 32 major economic forecasters in December 1973 discovered that only one had projected any decline in economic activity in 1974, which saw the worst recession of the entire postwar period. What about the one man who proved correct in late 1973 and actually did see the recession coming? An article reported: "[Mr. X] stopped issuing stock market forecasts several years ago after being wide of the mark time after time."

Was this instance, striking as it is, simply the exception that proves the rule? Apparently not. Other evidence indicates that the forecasting record of the "dismal science" is dismal indeed. In 1947, a group of well-known forecasters predicted that U.S. economic activity would decline approximately 6%. The economy that year was one of the strongest on record, showing an increase of 11%. A survey of many dozens of economists and business analysts in late 1969, with business already in a downturn, disclosed that few believed a recession would occur in 1970.[27] The Blue Chip Economic Indicators, a service based in Sedona, Arizona, collected the forecasts of GNP by the 52 most important economic research firms in the country, for which clients paid up to $50,000 annually. For the six years to the end of 1982, the average forecast was off by a remarkable 43 percent. More recent evidence indicates economic forecasting is still wide of the mark with regularity.

In 1995, the Bank Credit Analyst, a respected economic and interest rate advisory firm, analyzed the interest rate forecasts of the 50 largest economic forecasting firms. As Figure 4–1 shows, forecasters were consistently wrong in the 1988–1994 period, thereby missing the major bond market moves. In each case, as the dotted line on the chart indicates, they projected a continuation of the present trend: the bond market in actuality swung sharply higher and lower.

Figure 4–1

Blue Chip Economic Indicators
Forecast of Long Treasury Yields
1988–1995

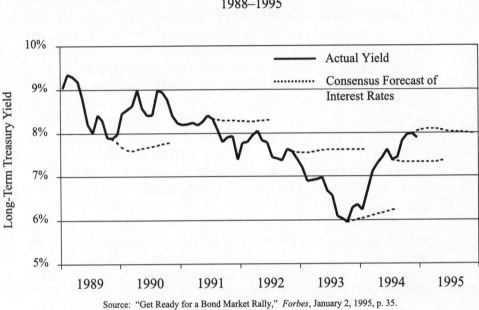

Source: "Get Ready for a Bond Market Rally," *Forbes*, January 2, 1995, p. 35.
Reprinted by Permission of FORBES Magazine © Forbes Inc., 1995.

Unfortunately, the Federal Reserve's own rating as an economic seer is questionable at best. In July 1990, with a recession already underway, Fed Chairman Alan Greenspan told Congress that "the likelihood of a near-term recession seems low." The Fed did not cut interest rates to bolster the economy until December of that year. In the recessions beginning in 1973 and 1980, the Fed actually raised interest rates as business began to fall, in the belief it had been allowing the economy to expand too quickly. And the Fed raised the discount rate just two months before the 1981–1982 recession began.[28]

The Difficulties of Forecasting

Although we may chuckle at how far off the track experts can be, their task is anything but easy. Sometimes the statements are just plain silly, like that of the commissioner of the U.S. Office of Patents. But keep in mind that when we ask an expert for a forecast, we're asking him or her to read the future. Screening tens of thousands of actors, actresses, singers, or other artists is a judgment call; the only advantage the cast-ing director has over the rest of us is his experience in the business. For every brilliant success, thousands of hopefuls are destined to fail. Find-ing the few exceptional talents is difficult, if not impossible. This is also the reason why many revolutionary new technologies are not recognized immediately. In their embryonic stages they are not much better, and perhaps worse, than what is already out there.

The banker who counseled his client against investing in the Ford Motor Company was giving sage advice. The automobile was an unre-liable and costly machine. Hundreds of manufacturers had already tried to introduce a car for the average man and failed. This included Henry Ford, who had already gone bankrupt twice, with The Detroit Automo-bile Company in 1900 and The Henry Ford Company in 1901. Viewed with the luxury of hindsight, many of the economic and financial fore-casts look ridiculous, but the outcomes were far more difficult to project at the time. The information processing necessary to making forecasts in complicated fields such as economics, investments, politics, or the military arts is enormous, often involving overwhelming amounts of data.

Let us look at just how good people are at digging through mounds of data to come up with the right answer.

Predictable Expert Errors

Although most of us tossed aside the illusion of expert invincibility long ago, it is only in the past few decades that we have discovered that, un-der certain conditions, *experts err predictably and often.* Experts in fields as far apart as psychology, engineering, publishing, even soil sam-pling, all make the same kinds of mistakes. As we shall see, the condi-tions for such errors are as fertile in the stock market as anywhere.

The problem of expert failure can be traced to man's weakness as an information processor. Just how much information a person can handle effectively has come under intense scrutiny in recent years, with strik-ing results. One is that the investor's comprehension of vast storehouses of data about companies, industries, or the economy mandated by cur-rent methods may not always give him or her the extra "edge." In fact, ingesting large amounts of investment information can lead to worse rather than better decisions. Impossible? In the next chapter, you'll see that analyst forecasting, the heart of security analysis, which selects stocks precisely by the methods we are questioning, misses the mark time and again. We'll also see shortly that the favorite stocks and industries of large groups of professional investors have fared worse than the averages for over sixty years. This is the primary reason for the sub-par performance of professionals over time that we witnessed in chapter 1.

To outdo the market, then, we must first have a good idea of the forces that victimize even the pros. Once these forces are understood, the investor can build defenses and find routes to skirt the pitfalls.

The Floor Becomes the Ceiling

Nobel Laureate Herbert Simon, one of the pioneers in the field, has studied man's capabilities as an information processor for four decades. According to Simon, we react to only a minute portion of the information thrown at us. But Simon states that even the filtering process is not a passive activity that provides a reasonable representation of the world. Rather we actively exclude any data "that is not within the scope of our attention,"[29] and can end up with a dangerously inaccurate representation of the world.

People, when swamped by information, may select only a small portion of the total, and reach a dramatically different conclusion than what the entire data set would suggest. Says Simon, "The capacity of the human mind for formulating and solving complex problems is very small compared with the size of the problems whose solution is required."[30]

Researchers in many fields began to ponder cognitive limitations. Could they actually prevent the professional from carrying out his responsibilities?

Some of the first experiments were conducted on clinical psychologists, who, like psychiatrists, make complex diagnostic decisions in arriving at the proper treatment. In the late 1940s and early 1950s, Paul Meehl, one of the pioneer investigators, made 20 separate surveys of groups of clinical psychologists. He required them to thoroughly examine psychotic and schizophrenic patients, to recommend treatment, then to predict how the patients would respond to the prescribed treatment.[31] He then compared the predictions to the average recovery rates for the standard treatments.

Meehl expected the psychologists' diagnoses to improve on the standard treatment and to result in higher recovery rates. The averages from standard treatment would be the floor from which the effectiveness of the diagnoses could be gauged. But, in the words of one researcher, "This floor turned out to be the ceiling." The predictions of the groups of clinicians were inferior to the simple averages in 18 out of 20 studies and as good only twice! Further studies showed no correlation between a clinical psychologist's training and experience and his or her accuracy. One study found, surprisingly, that psychologists were no better at interpersonal judgments than individuals with no training, and sometimes worse.[32]

Do such findings extend beyond the couch? Yes. Radiologists failed to diagnose lung disease from X-rays 30% of the time, although the symptoms were clearly evident.[33]

And, in a classic study of tonsillectomies in the mid-1930s (a fashionable operation at the time), a group of doctors examined 1,000 New York City schoolchildren. The doctors recommended 61% have their tonsils removed. The remaining children were examined by a second group of physicians, who diagnosed that 45% needed tonsillectomies. A third set of physicians, examining the remaining children, recommended the removal of 46% of the rapidly dwindling stock of tonsils. A final examination was carried out on the survivors and, sure enough, 45% needed their tonsils out. At this point, only 65 children remained. Fortunately, the doctors decided to call off further testing before tonsils became an endangered species in the New York City school system.[34]

A Multibillion-Dollar Slip in Investment Theory

Scores of studies have made it clear that expert failure extends far beyond the investment scene and that the problem often resides in man's information-processing capabilities. Current work indicates he is a serial or sequential processor of data, who can handle information reliably in a linear manner—that is, he can move from one point to the next in a logical sequence. In building a model ship or a space shuttle, there is a defined sequence of procedures. Each step, no matter how complex the technology, advances from the preceding step to the next step until completion.

The type of problem that proved so difficult to professionals is quite different, however; here configural (or interactive) reasoning, rather than linear, was required. In a configural problem, the decision-maker's interpretation of a piece of information changes depending on how he evaluates other inputs. Take the case of the security analyst: where two companies have the same trend of earnings, the emphasis placed on growth rates will be weighed quite differently depending on the outlooks for their industries, revenue growth, profit margins, returns on capital, and the host of analytical criteria we looked at previously. His evaluation will also be tempered by changes in the state of the economy, the level of interest rates, and the companies' competitive environments. Thus, a successful analyst must be adept at configural processing; he must integrate many diverse factors, and if one changes, he must reweigh the whole assessment.

Not unlike juggling, each factor is another ball in the air, increasing the difficulty of the process. Are professionals, in or out of the investment field, capable of the intricate analysis their methods demand?

A special technique has been designed, using a statistical test called ANOVA (Analysis of Variance), to evaluate the configural capabilities of experts. In one such study, nine radiologists were given a highly configural problem: deciding whether a gastric ulcer was malignant.[35] To make a proper diagnosis, the radiologist must work from seven major cues either present or absent in an X-ray. These can combine to form 57 possible combinations. Experienced gastroenterologists indicated that a completely accurate diagnosis can be made only by configurally examining the combinations formed from the seven original cues.[36]

Although the diagnosis requires a high level of configural processing, the researchers found that in actual practice, it accounted for a small part of all decisions—some 3%. Over 90% came from serially adding the individual symptoms.

A similar problem is deciding whether a psychiatric patient is to be allowed to leave the hospital for short periods. The hospital staff has to consider six primary cues that can be present or absent (for example, does the patient have a drinking problem?) and 64 possible interactions. Nurses, social workers, and psychologists showed little evidence of configural thinking, although it was essential for the optimum solution.[37] In another test, 13 clinical psychologists and 16 advanced graduate students attempted to determine whether the symptoms of 861 patients were neurotic or psychotic, a highly configural task. The nonconfigural results were in line with the first two examples.[38]

Curious what he would find in the stock market, Paul Slovic, an internationally respected cognitive psychologist, tested the importance of configural (or interactive) reasoning in the decisions of market professionals. In one study he provided thirteen stockbrokers and five graduate students in finance with eight important financial inputs—trend of earnings per share, profit margins, outlook for near-term profits, etc.—inputs they considered significant in analyzing companies. They had to think configurally to find the optimum solution. As it turned out, however, configural reasoning, on average, accounted for only 4% of the decisions made—results roughly equivalent to those of the radiologists and psychologists.

Moreover, what the brokers said about how they analyzed the various inputs differed significantly from what they did.[39] For example, a broker who said the trend of earnings per share was most important might actually place greater emphasis on near-term prospects. Finally, the more experienced the brokers, the less accurate their assessment of their own scales of weighting appeared to be. All in all, the evidence indicates that most people are weak configural processors, in or out of the marketplace.

Security Analysis—A Mission Impossible?

In light of what we have just seen, you might be wondering if you can depend on current investment methods. Before jumping to any conclusions, let's watch an analyst evaluate a company using fundamental analysis. Suppose our analyst decides to examine Hewlett Packard. How will he or she go about it?

Hewlett designs and manufactures precision electronic products and systems for measurement and computation. Examining the company's financial statements, one sees a gigantic operation. In 1996, it had revenues of over $38 billion and net profit of $2.675 billion, and employed 102,300 people domestically and abroad. Foreign sales in 75 countries account for 56 percent of total revenues.

The analyst will probably start with earnings power, that most important determinant of value. To do his job properly, he'll have to look at dozens or hundreds of inputs. He will review in detail the recent history and prospects of each major product line.

If the analyst is the thorough type—and he said he was on his résumé—he will go further, possibly getting breakdowns from management of how each of these groups is doing in every major market.

But we're not finished with our friend yet. In fact, his most difficult innings lie ahead. Multiplying this information by many other HP products extends the length and perhaps tediousness of the analysis manyfold. If tediousness were his only concern, however, the analyst might happily accept it. A far more serious problem is that much of the information he is able to ferret out is highly uncertain.

Facts provided to him by management as the basis for his various estimates are partial or incomplete, and sometimes incorrect. A company officer may tell him that a new laser printer is up nicely in revenues but that sales of fax machines are so-so year-to-date. If he asks how to translate a "so-so" or an "up nicely" into a reasonable earnings estimate, as often as not the officer may shrug and say, "Company policy does not permit me to divulge the information." Or, "That's your problem."

In any case, our friend is left on his own. He must rely on his own judgment, deciding whether "nicely" means up 10% or 30%, or "so-so" means flat or down sharply. He can check with trade sources and the competition, but the information provided will also be qualitative and sometimes misleading. Thus, the analyst's judgment is taxed at every stage of the analysis.

Whatever the company or industry, the analyst is bombarded with vast amounts of difficult-to-quantify information on competitive conditions, capacity utilization rates, and pricing. What will be the effect on IBM or Compaq of a fast new laptop computer from Toshiba? How badly will Chrysler, GM, or Toyota be hurt by a price cut in a popular model by Ford? All pertinent information must somehow be synthesized and evaluated in order to arrive at an earnings estimate.

On top of the forecasting problems, the harried analyst must also assess management, expansion plans, finances, probable dividends, accounting, and dozens of other vital factors. All estimates are contingent on general economic conditions, which means correctly gauging interest rates, unemployment, inflation, industrial production, and other economic variables here and abroad. Economists themselves are often wrong in these estimates, as we've already seen. Earnings forecasting, then, depends on large numbers of underlying assumptions, many of which are rapidly changing and hard to quantify—which means their accuracy is always in doubt.

The theory is anything but undemanding of its poor adherents. The amount of information they are expected to process is staggering. Even if our poor analyst has won his spurs in the super-computer category, the demands on him do not end here. Contemporary investment theory's final requirement is the most difficult of all. It requires him to correctly weigh all these factors against each other.

We've already seen that man is simply not a good configural processor of information. The reach of conventional investment theory may very well exceed the grasp of many of us to use it properly. What it will do is bring us well into the range of information overload.

How Much Is Too Much?

Under conditions of complexity and uncertainty, experts demand as much information as possible to assist them in their decision-making.

Seems logical. Naturally, there is tremendous demand for such incremental information on the Street, because investors believe the increased dosage gives them a shot at the big money. But as I have indicated earlier, that information "edge" may not help you. A large number of studies show rather conclusively that giving an expert more information doesn't do much to improve his judgment.[40]

In a study of what appears to be a favored class of guinea pigs, clinical psychologists were given background information on a large number of cases and asked what they thought their chances were of being right on each one. As information increased, the diagnosticians' confidence rose dramatically, but their accuracy continued to be low. At low information, psychologists estimated they would be correct 33% of the time; their accuracy was actually 26%. When the information was increased fourfold, they expected to be correct in 53% of the cases; in fact they were right 28% of the time, an increase of only 2%.

Interestingly, the finding seems universal—no improvement with more information. The same results were obtained using track handicappers. Eight veterans of the racing form were progressively given 5 to 40 pieces of the information they considered important in picking

Figure 4-2

Bad News for the Handicappers

Average changes in confidence and accuracy with increasing amounts of information

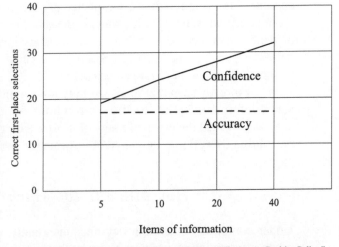

Source: Adapted from Paul Slovic, "Behavioral Problems Adhering to a Decision Policy," IGRF speech, May, 1973.

winners. As Figure 4–2 shows, their confidence rose directly with the amount of information, but the number of winners, alas, did not.[41]

As the above studies demonstrate, people in situations of uncertainty are generally overconfident based on the information available to them, believing they are right much more often than they are. One of the earliest demonstrations of overconfidence involved the predictive power of interviews. Many people think a short interview is sufficient for making reasonable predictions about a person's behavior. Analysts, for example, frequently gauge company managements through meetings lasting less than an hour. Extensive research indicates that these judgments are often wrong. One interesting example took place at the Harvard Business School. The school thought that by interviewing candidates beforehand, it could recruit students who would garner higher grades. The candidates selected did worse than students accepted on their academic credentials alone. Nevertheless, superficial impressions are hard to shake and often dominate behavior.

Overconfidence, according to cognitive psychologists, has many implications. A number of studies indicate that when a problem is relatively simple to diagnose, people are realistic about their ability to solve it. When the problem becomes more complex, however, and the solution depends on a number of hard-to-quantify factors, they became overconfident of their ability to reach a solution (accuracy 61%). If the task is impossible, for example, deciphering European from American handwriting, they became "super overconfident" (accuracy 51%).[42]

A large number of such studies demonstrate that people are consistently overconfident when forming strong impressions from limited knowledge. Lawyers, for example, tend to overestimate their chances of winning in court. If both sides in a court case are asked who will win, each will say its chances of winning are greater than 50%.[43] Studies of clinical psychologists,[44] physicians,[45] engineers,[46] negotiators,[47] and security analysts[48] showed they were far too confident in the accuracy of their predictions. Clinical psychologists, for example, believed their diagnosis was accurate 90% of the time, when it was correct in only 50% of cases. As one observer said of expert prediction, "[it] is often wrong but rarely in doubt."

The same overconfidence occurs when experienced writers or academics working on books or research papers estimate the time of completion. The estimates are invariably overconfident; the books and papers are completed months or years behind schedule, and, as this writer can attest, are sometimes not completed at all.

Studies in cognitive psychology also indicate people are overconfident that their forecasts will be correct. The typical result is that respondents are correct in only 80% of the cases when they describe themselves as 99% sure.[49]

The question becomes even more interesting when experts are compared to lay people. A number of studies show that when the predictability of the problem is reasonably high, the experts are generally more accurate than lay people. Expert bridge players, for example, proved much more capable of assessing the odds of winning a particular hand than average players.[50] When predictability is very low, however, experts are more prone to overconfidence than novices. When experts predict highly complex situations, such as the future of the Eastern Bloc economies, the impact of religious fundamentalists on foreign policy in the Middle East, or the movement of the stock market, they usually demonstrate overconfidence. Because of the richness of information available to them, they believe they have the advantage in their area of expertise. Lay people with a very limited understanding of the subject, on the other hand, will normally be more conservative in their judgments.[51]

Overconfident experts are legion on the investment scene. Wall Street places immense faith in detailed analysis by its experts. In-depth research houses turn out thousands upon thousands of reports, running to a hundred pages or more, sprinkled with dozens of tables and charts. They set up Washington listening posts to catch the slightest whiff of change in government policy, and call scores of conferences to provide money managers with penetrating understanding.

The more detailed the level of knowledge, the more effective the expert is considered to be. In 1992, for example, several of the most respected analysts following Compaq Computer knew, almost to the unit, the number of new orders and shipments that Compaq and its competitors were making both domestically and abroad. Even so, they wrote bearish reports on the stock, entirely missing the dramatic improvement in Compaq's competitive position. Listing the stock as a sell, they watched it go up over 16-fold in the next five years. As with the clinical psychologists and the handicappers, the information available had little to do with accurately predicting the outcome.

This result is, unfortunately, no exception. The inferior investment performance noted in chapter 1, as well as those that we will look at next, were based on just such detailed research. To quote a disillusioned money manager of the early seventies, "You pick the top [research] house on the Street and the second top house on the Street—they all built tremendous reputations, research-in-depth, but they killed their clients."[52] Nothing much has changed.

I offer a rule for investing that is applicable in almost any other field of endeavor:

RULE 2

Respect the difficulty of working with a mass of information. Few of us can use it successfully. In-depth information does not translate into in-depth profits.

I hope it is becoming apparent that these configural relationships are extremely complex. Stock market investors are not dealing with 24 or 48 relevant interactions, but with an astronomical number. We have already seen how far fewer inputs overtax the configural or interactive judgment of experts. Because Wall Street experts, as those elsewhere, are unaware of these psychological findings, they remain convinced that their problems can be handled if only those few extra facts are available. They overload with information, which doesn't help their thinking but makes them more confident and therefore more vulnerable to serious errors.

Unfortunately, according to the findings of a number of clinical studies, overconfidence seems to be a cognitive bias. In other words, the mind is probably designed to extract as much information as possible from what is available, but does not realize that the available information is only a small part of the total necessary to build an accurate forecast in uncertain conditions. Evaluating stocks is no different.

Under conditions of anxiety and uncertainty, with a vast, interacting web of information, the market becomes a giant Rorschach test. The investor sees any pattern he or she wishes. In fact, investors can find patterns that aren't there, says recent research in configural processing—a phenomenon called illusory correlation.

Trained psychologists, for example, were given background information on psychotics, and were also given drawings allegedly made by them, but actually prepared by the experimenters. With remarkable consistency, the psychologists saw the cues in the drawings that they expected to see—muscular figures "drawn" by men worried about their masculinity, or big eyes by suspicious people. Not only were these characteristics not stressed in the drawings; in many cases they were less pronounced than usual.[53] Because the psychologists focused on the anticipated aberrations, they missed important correlations actually present.[54]

Investors attempt to simplify and rationalize complexity that seems at times impenetrable. Often, they notice facts that are simply coincidental and think they have found correlations. If they buy the stock in the "correlation" and it goes up, they will invest in it through many a loss. The market thus provides an excellent field for illusory correlation. The head and shoulders formation on a chart cuts through thousands of disparate facts that the chartist believes no one can analyze, or buying growth stocks simplifies an otherwise bewildering range of investment alternatives. Such methods, which seemed to work in the past, are pervasive on Wall Street. The problem is that some of the correlations are illusory and others are chance. Trusting in them begets error. A chartist may have summed it up most appropriately: "If I hadn't made money some of the time, I would have acquired market wisdom quicker."

Which brings us to the next rule, one that may at first glance appear simple, but is both important and will prove harder to follow than you may think.

RULE 3

Don't make an investment decision based on correlations. All correlations in the market, whether real or illusory, will shift and soon disappear.

Now, there are people with outstanding gifts for abstract reasoning, who can cut through enormously complex situations. Every field will have its Warren Buffetts or John Templetons. But these people are rare. It seems, then, that the information-processing capabilities and the standards of abstract reasoning required by current investment methods are too complicated for the majority of us, professional or amateur.

A Surefire Way to Lose Money

At this point, you might wonder if I'm exaggerating the problems of decision-making and forecasting in the stock market. The answer, I think, can be found by considering the favorite investments of market professionals over time.

Consider a large international conference of institutional investors held at the New York Hilton in February 1970. The 2,000 delegates were polled for the stock that would show outstanding appreciation that year. The favorite was National Student Marketing—the highest-octane performer of the day. From a price of 120 in February, it dropped 95 percent by July. At the same conference in 1972, the airlines were expected to perform best for the balance of the year. Then within 1% of their highs, the carriers' stocks fell 50% that year in the face of a sharply rising market. The conference the following year voted them a group to avoid.

Are these simply chance results? In an earlier book, *The New Contrarian Investment Strategy* (1982), I included 52 surveys of how the favorite stocks of large numbers of professional investors had subsequently fared over the 51-year period between 1929 and 1980. The number of professionals participating ranged from 25 to several thousand. The median was well over a hundred. Wherever possible, the professional choices were measured against the S&P 500 for the next 12 months.*

Eighteen of the studies measured the performance of five or more stocks the experts picked as their favorites.[55] By diversifying into a number of stocks instead of one or two, the element of chance is reduced. Yet, the eighteen portfolios so chosen underperformed the market on sixteen occasions! This meant, in effect, that, when you received professional advice about stocks, it would be bad advice almost 90% of the time.

Throwing darts at the stock pages, or flipping a coin, would give you a 50–50 chance of beating the market.

The other 34 samples did little better. Overall, the favorite stocks and industries of large groups of money managers and analysts did worse than the market on 40 of 52 occasions, or 77% of the time.

But these surveys, although extending over fifty years, end in 1980. Has expert stock-picking improved since then? More recently, the *Wall Street Journal* conducted a poll on whether the choices of four well-known professionals could outperform the market in each year between 1986 and 1993. At the end of the year, four pros gave their five favorite picks for the next year to John Dorfman, the editor of the financial section, who reviewed them 12 months later, eliminating the two lowest performers and adding two fresh experts. In 16 of 32 cases, the portfolios underperformed the market. Somewhat better than the past, but no better than the toss of a coin.[56],†

---

* Several studies used different averages or time periods.

† I was one of these experts for six years. Over this period, using the contrarian strategies we will look at, my portfolios outperformed the market in five of the six years I participated from 1987 to 1992, with a combined gain of 156% versus 120% for the market.

Table 4–1

EXPERT FORCASTS OF FAVORITE STOCKS AND INDUSTRIES 1929–1993

Time Span	Source of Surveys	Total Surveys	Percent of Surveys Underperforming Market in Next Year
1929–32	Cowles Surveys	3	100%
1953–76	*Trusts and Estates*	21	67
1967–69	*Financial Analysts Journal*	1	100
1967–72	*California Business*	7	71
1969–73	*Institutional Investor*	7	100
1973	*Business Week*	2	50
1974	*Seminar* (Edson Gould)	2	100
1974	Callan Associates	4	100
1974–76	Mueller Surveys	4	75
1980	Financial World "All-Stars"	1	100
1986–93	*Wall Street Journal*	8	50
Total number of surveys		**60**	
Percent of professional surveys *underperforming* market			**75%**

NOTE: DIVIDENDS EXCLUDED IN ALL COMPARISONS.
SOURCE: AS UPDATED FROM *The New Contrarian Investment Strategy*

Table 4–1 gives the results of all such surveys that I found through 1993. As the table shows, only 25% of the surveys of the experts' "best" stocks outperform the market.

The findings startled me. While I knew that experts make mistakes, I didn't know the magnitude of the errors were as striking or as consistent as the results make evident.

In the past fifteen years, the performance of professional investors has been more carefully scrutinized than ever before. As we saw in chapters 1 and 2, money managers as a group have not outperformed the market. In fact, as the figures show, only about 10% have beaten the averages over this period. The studies through the years clearly demonstrate that professional investors in the large majority of cases were tugged toward the popular stocks of the day, usually near their peaks, and like most investors, steered away from unpopular, underpriced issues, as the subsequent year's market action indicated. Also interesting is that although there were dozens of industries to choose from, one industry—technology—was favored so often over the years. And so unsuccessfully! Expert advice, in these surveys at least, clearly led investors to overpriced issues and away from the better values.

What do we make of these results? The number of samples seems far too large for the outcome to be simply chance. No, the evidence indicates a surprisingly high level of error among professionals in choosing stocks and portfolios over six and a half decades.

The failure rate among financial professionals, at times approaching 90%, indicates not only that errors are made, but that under uncertain conditions, there must be systematic and predictable forces working against the unwary investor.

Such evidence is obviously incompatible with the central assumption of the efficient market hypothesis.[57]

Far more important is the practical implication of what we have just seen: a plausible explanation of why fundamental methods often don't work. The theory demands too much from man as a configural reasoner and information processor. Under conditions of information overload, both within and outside of markets, our mental tachometers surge far above the red line. When this happens, we no longer process information reliably. Confidence rises as our input of information increases, but our decisions do not improve. This leads to another rule.

RULE 4

Tread carefully with current investment methods. Our limitations in processing complex information correctly prevent their successful use by most of us.

While it is true that experts do as poorly in other complex circumstances, the market professional unfortunately works in a goldfish bowl. In no other calling I am aware of is the outcome of decisions so easily measurable.

Examining the stock-picking record of money managers and other market professionals, a critical question is how accurate are analysts' earnings estimates, the key element underlying stock selections, and the heart of investing as it is practiced today. That question is examined next. The results of some very thorough studies on the accuracy of the top security analysts on Wall Street will surprise you.

5

Would You Play a 1 in 50 Billion Shot?

THE RED wing of my imaginary casino had some pretty awful odds for the players caught up in the frenzied atmosphere. Yet the poor results, to extend the analogy, were not all the fault of the casino operator. On your stroll through, you may have noticed that players kept asking—and paying—for advice from a collection of well-dressed men and women who seemed to know everything about the game.

In this chapter, we'll examine the advice of this chic group, who happen to be security analysts. Their estimates are the crucial factor the majority of investors look at in deciding what stocks to buy, hold, or sell.

Although they don't agree on many issues, Wall Streeters and financial academics concur that company earnings are the major determinant of stock prices. The heart of modern security analysis centers on predicting stock movements from precise near-term earnings estimates. As a result, major brokerage houses have research budgets in the eight figures, and hire top analysts to provide accurate estimates. The largest bank trust departments, mutual funds, and other institutional clients demand the "best" because of the tens of millions of dollars in commissions they command.

Institutional Investor magazine several decades ago formalized the process of determining the "best" analysts. Each year the magazine selects an "All-Star" team made up of the "top" analysts in all the important industries—biotech, computers, telecommunications, pharmaceuticals, chemicals—after polling hundreds of institutions. There is a first, second, and third team for each industry. The magazine portrays the team on its cover each year, dressed in football uniforms with the brokerage firm's name on each star's jersey. The competition to make the teams is fierce, and many analysts and their sales forces spend a month or two before the selection begins calling or visiting major institutional clients and providing that extra something that shows why they are All Stars. Making the "team" is a tremendous boost to the analyst's career. Being selected to the first team can garner the analyst a salary of seven figures and can net his or her brokerage house several times that in commissions.

If a brokerage firm can boast a number of All Stars, profitability ratchets up accordingly. Some years back, the managing partners and the director of research of a large brokerage house decided to let one of their analysts go. The office executioner was on his way to inform the analyst, when the research director came running down the corridor, grabbed his arm, and gasping for breath said, "Wait . . . we can't do it . . . he just made the second team."

Salary scales, as you may guess, are in the stratosphere. According to *Institutional Investor* in mid-1995, "the bulk of experienced analysts make between $300,000 and $500,000 a year; standouts receive more than $600,000." At Merrill Lynch alone, more than 30 analysts make $500,000. Then there is the million-dollar-a-year club, which includes several dozen of the Street's outstanding oracles. Income-wise, they are in a class with entertainers and professional athletes.

Brokers launch bidding wars to bring top analysts aboard.[1] In one day in early August 1995, Lehman Brothers, Inc., lured back a healthcare analyst from Salomon Brothers before he could even start work, while Merrill Lynch snatched three analysts from Salomon. Two of the three were top insurance analysts who would each receive an annual package of $1.2 million. At the same time as its Salomon coup, Merrill paid $1.2 million to a health-care analyst and $700,000 to a computer analyst. Lehman hooked a top life insurance analyst from Merrill, while earlier in 1995 Morgan Stanley offered Stephen Girsky, a highly regarded auto analyst, a $1.4-million-a-year package to reel him in from Paine Webber. That firm, in turn, offered over $1 million to bring in a health-care analyst from Lehman. Lehman raised its bid even higher, however, and the analyst jumped back. According to *The Wall Street Journal,* "part of the heavy analyst turnover is seasonal. Brokerage firms typically like to hire top analysts before September 1—the cutoff for the annual rankings by *Institutional Investor* magazine for its widely watched All-Star Research Team."[2]

Some analysts now earn over $2 million—exceeding the pay of a number of CEOs of Fortune 500 companies. Jack Grubman, a highly regarded telecommunications analyst, jumped ship from Paine Webber to Salomon. The price was a two-year contract with annual pay of $2.5 million. The salary was so high that his research colleagues jokingly refer to underwritings of the firm being offered to its clients in "Grubman units" of $2.5 million each.

Needless to say, Wall Streeters often give top analysts the same adulation that teenagers reserve for rock stars and film heroes. Also needless to say, *la crème,* selected from over 15,000 analysts across the country, are sensational stock-pickers.

Aren't they?

Financial World measured the analysts' results some years back.[3] The article stated, "It was not an easy task. Most brokerage houses were reluctant to release the batting averages of their superstars." In many cases, the results were gotten from outside sources, such as major clients, and then "only grudgingly." After months of digging, the magazine came up with the recommendations of 20 superstars.

The conclusion: "Heroes were few and far between—during the period in question, the market rose 14.1 percent. If you had purchased or sold 132 stocks they recommended, when they told you to, your gain would have been only 9.3 percent," some 34 percent worse than selecting stocks by throwing darts. The magazine added, "Of the hundred and thirty-two stocks the superstars recommended, only 42, or just over 1/3, beat the S&P 500." A large institutional buyer of research summed it up. "In hot markets the analysts . . . get brave at just the wrong time and cautious just at the wrong time. It's uncanny, when they say one thing, start doing the opposite. Usually you are right."[4]

In addition to superstars, professional investors rely on earnings forecasting services such as I/B/E/S, Zacks, and First Call, who have on-line features to give the pros instant revisions of estimates. First Call provides a service that also gives money managers, as well as competing analysts, all analysts' reports immediately upon their release. Many of these reports deal with forecast changes. Over 1,000 companies are covered. Changes in analysts' estimates are prime items on the financial news networks such as CNBC and CNN-FN. Investors from the managers of multi-billion-dollar pension funds to the average Joe act quickly on changes in analyst forecasts or earnings surprises, which are flashed immediately by the wire services and other financial media. Near-term earnings estimates, as noted, are the major trigger of investment decisions today.

The requirement for precise earnings estimates has been increasing in recent years. Missing the analysts' estimates by pennies can send a stock's price down sharply. Better-than-expected earnings can send prices soaring. How good, then, are these estimates? We've already seen the performance of the Institutional "All Stars." But this was only for a one-year period. Nobody's perfect: Was this a one-time slip? To answer this question, we'll next look at the long-term analyst forecasting record. This will be important to the investment strategies considered in the chapters ahead.

The Forecasting Follies

Should analysts' estimates have the influence on contemporary investors that they do, or are they a guaranteed way of losing money, as some professionals claim? There is a clear-cut answer to this question.

Updating the work in the *New Contrarian Investment Strtegy,* as well as a number of articles in Forbes and elsewhere,[5] I did a study in collaboration with Michael Berry of James Madison University on analysts' forecasts, which was published in *The Financial Analysts Journal* in May/June 1995.[6] It examined brokerage analysts' quarterly forecasts of earnings as compared to earnings actually reported between 1973 and 1991, which has subsequently been updated to 1996. Estimates for the quarter were usually made in the previous three months, and analysts could revise their estimates up to two weeks before the end of the quarter. In all, 94,251 consensus forecasts[7] were used, and we required at least four separate analysts' estimates before including a stock in the study.[8] Larger companies, such as Microsoft or Exxon, might have as many as 30 or 40 estimates. More than 1,500 New York Stock Exchange, Nasdaq, and AMEX companies were included, and on average, there were about 1,000 companies in the sample. The study was, to my knowledge, the most comprehensive on analyst forecasting to date.[9]

How do analysts do at this game, where even slight errors can result in instant wipeouts? A glance at Figure 5–1 tells all. The results are startling—analysts' estimates were sharply and consistently off the mark, even though they were made less than three months before the end of the quarter for which actual earnings were reported. The average error for the sample was a whopping 44% annually. Again, this was no small sample: it included approximately 500,000 individual analysts' estimates.

Interestingly, these large errors are occurring in the midst of the information revolution. In the early 1970s, when I was an analyst, nothing was on-line. Today, the analysts at major brokerage houses have immediate access to the reports of competitors, estimate changes, and volumes of other information. There is exponentially more information available today than in the early 1970s. It's like moving from a hand-cranked telephone to a miniature cellular. Yet in spite of the information revolution, estimates seem to have gotten worse, not better, as the hori-

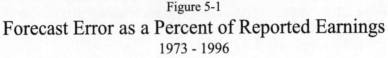

Figure 5-1

Forecast Error as a Percent of Reported Earnings
1973 - 1996

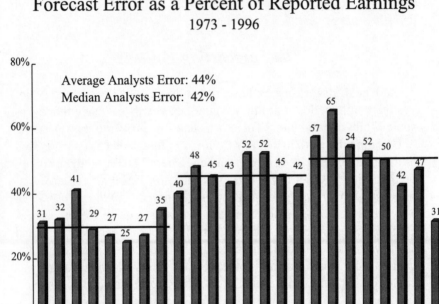

Source of data: A-N Research Corp. (Formerly the research department of Abel Noser Corp.) and I/B/E/S, 1973 - 1996

zontal lines on the chart indicate. In the last eight years of the study, the average error was an astounding 50% and in two of those years, 57% and 65% respectively.

Since many market professionals believe that a forecast error of plus or minus 5% is large enough to trigger a major price movement, what did a miss of 57% in 1989 or one of 65% in 1990 do? When we look at the price drops on sizzling stocks after analyst misses, at times of only a few percent, it becomes apparent that estimate errors even this small are dangerous to your investment health. Yet, this is precisely how the game is played on the Street, by analysts, by the large mutual funds, pension funds, other institutional investors, and by average investors. But before we draw any further conclusions, we'll look at some other results from the study.

You might wonder whether the results are skewed by a few large errors. To check for this kind of skew, we measured earnings surprises

four different ways.[10] In all cases, errors were high. What about surprises from companies that report small or nominal earnings? Wouldn't
a miss here result in a higher percentage error than one from companies
reporting large earnings? If, for example, the estimates were $1.00, and
the company actually reported 90 cents, the miss would be 10%. But if
the estimates were 10 cents and the company reported only 1 cent, the
miss would be 900%.

To measure this effect, we eliminated all companies that reported
earnings in the + or − 10-cent range to prevent large percentage errors
from this group distorting the study. The problem is that many of the
fastest growing small companies report earnings of 30 to 50 cents a
share annually, which translates into 7.5 to 12.5 cents quarterly. Large
companies in this range were also eliminated. Even using this ultraconservative method, the average forecast error was still 23% on average, more than quadruple the size that market pros believe could set off
a major price reaction.

Missing the Barn Door

I'm sure that many readers know only too well what happens when a
stock misses the consensus forecast by much. High flying 3Com tumbled 45% when analysts' forecasts missed reported earnings by a scant
1% in 1997. Sun Microsystems dropped 30% on a 6% shortfall. On May
30, 1997, Intel announced earnings for its June quarter would be sharply
higher than the 1996 quarter; however, they would be somewhat below
the analysts' consensus forecast. (It turned out by 3%.) This caused a
price drop of 26 points or 16% on the opening, which reverberated first
through technology stocks and then through the market as a whole. The
result was the S&P 500 lost $87 billion in minutes. Oak Technology, a
high-flying IPO, dropped from $32 in March to $10¼ in early June
1996, primarily as the result of disappointing earnings. Cascade Communications, then a leading computer networking company, plummeted
from $91 in late 1996 to $24 by March of 1997, or 76%, as a result of
earnings falling short of the analysts' consensus estimate. Merrill Lynch
and Lehman, at the time, cut their estimates by about 8%. Ditto Zoll
Medical, which fell 26% on a 1-cent earnings shortfall to expectations.
People who relied on these estimates got clobbered—to say the least.

But these are horror stories. Again, we must ask if they are exceptions. How good is this dedicated and hardworking group at their voca-
tion? To answer this question, we looked at how close forecasts came to

levels considered acceptable to the pros. We have seen that earnings surprises of even a few percentage points can trigger major price reactions. Current investment practice demands estimates that are very close to—or dead on—reported results. Normally, the higher the valuation of a stock, the more important the precision. Street-smart pros normally expect reported earnings to be within a 5% range of the consensus estimate—and many demand better.

Is it doable? Look at Figure 5–2. This time we examined the number of consensus estimates that fell within the ranges most professional investors believe will have no impact on the stock price. We used our large database of nearly 100,000 analyst consensus estimates for the 24 years to the end of 1996.

The figure summarizes what we found. Again, the results are devastating to believers in precise forecasts. The distribution of estimates clearly refutes their value to investors. Only about one in four was in the ±5% range of reported earnings that a good number of pros deem es-

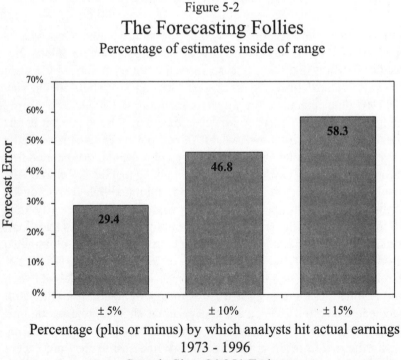

Figure 5-2

The Forecasting Follies

Percentage of estimates inside of range

Percentage (plus or minus) by which analysts hit actual earnings
1973 - 1996
Sample Size: 94,251 Estimates

Source of data: A-N Research Corp. (Formerly the research department of Abel Noser Corp.) and I/B/E/S

sential. Using the plus or minus 10% error band, which many professional investors would argue is too large, we found that only 47% of the consensus forecasts could be called accurate. Almost 55% missed this more lenient minimum range. Worse yet, only 58% of the consensus forecasts were within a plus or minus 15% band—a level that almost all Wall Streeters would call too high.

Of what value are estimates that seriously miss the mark two-thirds or three-quarters of the time? After the horror stories precipitated when forecasts were off even minutely, the answer seems to be . . . not much. We have seen then that estimates carefully prepared only three months in advance, by well-paid and diligent analysts, are notoriously inaccurate. To complicate matters, many stocks sell not on today's earnings, but on expected earnings years into the future. The analysts' chances of being on the money with their forecasts are not much higher than winning a lottery. Current investment practice seems to demand a precision that is impossible to deliver. Putting your money on these estimates means you are making a bet with the odds stacked heavily against you.

"But, maybe, there is a reason for this," believers in their forecasting prowess might argue. "Analysts may not be able to hit the broad side of a barn overall, but that's because there are a lot of volatile industries out there that are impossible to forecast accurately. You can make good estimates where it counts, in stable, growing industries, where appreciation is almost inevitable."

A plausible statement. We fed it to our computer, which digested the database and spit out the answer a few minutes later. We divided the same analysts' consensus estimates into 62 industry groups and then measured accuracy for each. The answer is shown in Table 5–1. Alas, the results were no better. The average error was 50% and the median 43% annually. These errors were a touch larger than forecasting individual companies without considering the industries they are in. We also found that over the entire time period, 90% of all industries had analyst consensus forecast errors larger than 20% annually, while 10% of industries showed surprises larger than 86%. As the chart indicates, analysts' errors occurred indiscriminately across industries. Errors are as high for industries that are supposed to have clearly definable prospects, or "visibility," years into the future, such as computers or pharmaceuticals, as they are for industries where the outlooks are considered murky, such as autos or aluminum.

We also examined the standardized error, a statistical tool that adjusts for the volatility of reported earnings for differing industries. We found that after adjusting for the volatility of various industries, forecasting er-

Table 5–1

ANALYSIS FORECAST ERRORS BY INDUSTRY

1973–1996

62 Subindustry Groupings:

Average Error: 50%

Median Error: 43%

Industry	% Error	Industry	% Error
Capital Goods	49%	Insurance	35%
Chemicals	27%	Metals/Mining	71%
Communications	25%	Oil	73%
Consumer Goods	42%	Publishing	26%
Entertainment	50%	Textiles	41%
Financial	32%	Tobacco	4%
Foods	25%	Transportation	75%
Healthcare	29%		

62 subindustries represented in 15 above industries for simplification.

SOURCE OF DATA: A-N RESEARCH CORP. (FORMERLY THE RESEARCH DEPARTMENT OF ABEL NOSER CORP.) AND I/B/E/S, 1973–1996.

rors continued to be high across almost all industries, with growth industries often showing larger errors than industries considered to be more volatile. This result is so consistent we should call it a rule:

RULE 5

There are no highly predictable industries in which you can count on analysts' forecasts. Relying on these estimates will lead to trouble.

The high-visibility, high-growth industries have as many errors as the others. That analysts miss the mark consistently in supposedly high-visibility industries—and give them much higher valuations—suggests that these industries are often overpriced.

Finally, let's settle one remaining item of business with analysts' forecasts. Are they less accurate in periods of boom or recession, when earnings presumably are more difficult to calculate? Is this a possible reason why their forecasts are not any better?

Analyst Forecasts in Booms and Busts

Our 1973–1996 study covered five periods of business expansion and four periods of recession. If you think about it, you might expect to see analysts' forecasts too high in periods of recession, because earnings are dropping sharply for economic reasons that are impossible for the analyst to predict. Conversely, in periods of expansion, estimates might be too low, as business is actually much better than economists and company managements anticipate. It certainly seems plausible, and at first provides a partial explanation for the battered analyst's record. Unfortunately, it just ain't so, as Table 5–2 indicates.

The table is broken into three columns: All Surprises, which is the average of all positive and negative surprises through the study, Positive Surprises, and Negative Surprises.[11] The surprises are shown for each period of business expansion or recession. The bottom row shows the average of all consensus forecasts for periods of both expansion and recession. The average surprise for all expansions (44.9%) is little different from the average surprise through the entire period (44.3%), or the average surprise in recessions (47.4%). Moreover, the average of positive surprises in expansions and recessions are also very similar (23.2% versus 25.5%), as are negative surprises (–79.1% versus –77.4%).

The statistical analysis demonstrates that economic conditions do not seem to magnify analyst errors. They are about the same in periods of expansion or recession as they are at other times. What did come out clearly is that analysts are always optimistic. Their forecasts are too optimistic in periods of recession, and this optimism doesn't decrease in periods of economic recovery, or in more normal times. This last find-

Table 5–2

ANALYSTS FORECAST ERRORS IN EXPANSIONS AND RECESSIONS 1973–1996

	All Surprises (Absolute Value)	*Positive Surprises*	*Negative Surprises*
Expansions	44.9%	23.2%	–79.1%
Recessions	47.4%	25.5%	–77.4%
Full Sample (1973–1996)	44.3%	23.7%	–76.5%

ALL FIGURES ARE AVERAGE SURPRISES.
SURPRISE = (ACTUAL − FORECAST)/|ACTUAL|, IN PERCENT
SOURCE OF DATA: A-N RESEARCH CORP. (FORMERLY THE RESEARCH DEPARTMENT OF ABEL NOSER CORP.) AND I/B/E/S, 1973–1996.

ing is not new. A number of research papers have been devoted to the subject of analyst optimism, and, with the exception of one that used far too short a period of time, all have come up with the same conclusion.[12]

This is an important finding for the investor: if analysts are generally optimistic, there will be a large number of disappointments created not by events, but by initially seeing the company or industry through rose-colored glasses.

How optimistic are analysts' estimates? Jennifer Francis and Donna Philbrick studied analyst estimates from the Value Line Investment Survey, some 918 stocks for the 1987–1989 period.[13] Value Line is well known on the Street for having near-consensus forecasts. The researchers found that analysts were optimistic in their forecasts by 9% annually, on average. Again, remembering the devastating effect of even a small miss on high-octane stocks, these are very large odds to be stacked against the investor looking for ultra-precise earnings estimates.

The overoptimism of analysts is brought out even more clearly by I/B/E/S, the largest earnings forecasting service, which monitors quarterly consensus forecasts on more than 7,000 domestic companies. In a report to its subscribers, I/B/E/S stated that the average revision for stocks in the S&P 500, which make up approximately 75% of the market value of stocks traded on the New York Stock Exchange, is 12.9% from the beginning to the end of the year in which the forecast is made. Analysts revise their estimates 6.3% in the first half and 19.5% in the second half of the year. Despite these estimate changes, according to I/B/E/S, analysts tend to be optimistic. What seems apparent is that analysts do not sufficiently revise their optimistically biased forecasts in the first half, and then almost triple the size of the revisions, usually downward, in the second half of the year. Even so, their forecasts of earnings are still too high at year-end.

In a recent study, Eric Lufkin[14] and I provided further evidence of analysts' overoptimism. Between 1982 and 1997, analysts overestimated the growth of earnings of companies in the S&P 500 by a startling 188%. The actual growth was 7.8% annually, while the original projected growth at the beginning of each year was 21.9%.[15]

What makes analysts so optimistic? The subject is anything but academic, because it is precisely this undue optimism that induces many people, including large numbers of pros, to buy these stocks. As we have seen in the recent examples, and will see more thoroughly in the chapters ahead, unwarranted optimism exacts a fearful price.

A rule is in order here.

RULE 6

Analysts' forecasts are usually optimistic. Make the appropriate downward adjustment to your earnings estimate.

Next we'll turn briefly to past studies of analyst and management forecasts to see if they were any more helpful to the investor.

Was Forecasting in the Past Any Better?

Let us start by looking at the management record. Because the thorough analyst or money manager carefully interviews senior corporate officials in making his or her projections, a number of past academic studies have measured management forecasts of their own companies' earnings. As Table 5–3, taken from *The New Contrarian Investment*

Table 5–3

FORECASTS, ANALYSTS VERSUS MANAGEMENT
Management Forecasts, One Year or Less[16]

Study	Period Studied	Number of Companies	Mean Error[17]
Green and Segall, 1967[18]	1963–64	7	14.0%
Copeland and Marioni, 1972[19]	1968	50	20.1%
McDonald, 1973[20]	1966–70	151	13.6%
Basi, Carey and Twark, 1976[21]	1970–71	88	10.1%
	Mean error in management studies: 14.5%		

Analysis Forecasts, One Year or Less

Study	Period Studied	Number of Companies	Mean Error[17]
Samuel S. Stewart, Jr., 1973[22]	1960–64	14	10–15%
Barefield and Cominsky, 1975[23]	1967–72	100	16.1%
Basi, Carey and Twark, 1976	1970–71	88	13.8%
Malcolm Richards, 1976[24]	1972	93	8.8%
Richards and Frazer, 1977[25]	1973	213	22.7%
Richards, Benjamin and Strawser, 1977[26]	1972–76	92	24.1%
Richards, Benjamin and Strawser, 1977	1969–72	50	18.1%
	Mean error in analysts studies: 16.6%		

SOURCE: THE NEW CONTRARIAN INVESTMENT STRATEGY.

Strategy, indicates, the average error of four management studies between 1963 and 1971 was 14.5%. The rate of forecasting error by senior corporate officers (presumably in the know, if not to some extent controlling reported earnings) is significantly higher than acceptable to practitioners.

Analysts also struck out from 1960 to 1976, as demonstrated by the seven studies charted in the second part of Table 5–3. As you can see, the mean error of the seven studies was 16.6%, and the studies were for a year or less. Could a couple of major errors or the odd poor forecaster have caused these results? Richards, and Barefield & Cominsky, agreed in previous studies that there was no significant differential among forecasters on any given company. The consensus was far off target, time and again.

Richards and Frazer concluded that a lack of expensive research doesn't put the small investor at a disadvantage. "It is unnecessary to pay large sums for certain services when others are available at low cost." The authors graciously did not add, "Particularly since they were so wide of the mark."

More confirming evidence by Richards, Benjamin, and Strawser indicates the average industry forecasting error made by analysts annually for the 1972–1976 period. Over the entire time, the error ran to 26.2% annually. More significantly, some of the industries supposedly having the "highest visibility," such as computers and retail stores, actually had the worst estimates. The average annual analyst error in the office equipment and computer group was an astonishing 88.8%. Since these two samples were taken from the S&P Earnings Forecaster,* which then carried the largest or most widely followed companies, and since they covered periods from five to nine years, the results can scarcely be considered an aberration.

We see, then, that analysts' forecasts from the sixties through the mid-seventies are still wide of the mark, albeit the errors are smaller than more recently.

What Does It All Mean?

We have found that analyst forecast errors have been unacceptably high for a long time, and they have gone up over the past two decades. An

---

* The S&P Earnings Forecaster was one of the original services that measured earnings estimates in the 1960s and 1970s.

error rate of 44% is frightful—much too high to be used by money managers or individual investors for selecting stocks. Normally, stock-pickers believe they can fine-tune estimates within a 5% range. The studies show the average error is over eight times this size. Error rates of 10 to 15% make it impossible to pick out a growth stock (with earnings increasing at 20% clip) from an average company (with earnings growth of 7%), or even from an also-ran (with earnings expanding at 4%). What then do error rates of over 40% do?

Dropping companies with small earnings per share (to avoid large percentage errors) does not eliminate the problem. The error rate is still over 20%. Worse yet, analysts err often. Figure 5–2 showed that only one in four consensus analysts' estimates fell within the crucial 5% range of reported earnings. Missing this range would spell big trouble for stock-pickers relying on laser-like estimates.

Unfortunately, the problems don't end here. Forecasting by industry was just as bad. Forecast errors averaged over 40%, with error rates almost indistinguishable between those industries with supposedly excellent visibility (for which investors pay top dollar) and those considered to have dull prospects. If earnings estimates are not precise enough to weed out the real growth stocks from the also-rans, the question naturally arises why anyone should pay enormous premiums for "high-visibility" companies.

Finally, we have seen two additional problems with analysts' forecasts. First, the error rates are not due to the business cycle. Analyst forecast errors are high in all stages of the cycle. Second, and more important, analysts have a strong optimistic bias in their forecasts. Not only are the errors high, but there is a consistent tendency to overestimate earnings. This is deadly when you pay a premium price for a stock. The towering forecast errors combined with analysts' optimism result in a high probability of disaster. As we saw, even a slight "miss" for stocks with supposedly excellent visibility has unleashed waves of selling, taking the prices down five or even ten times the percentage miss of the forecasting error itself.

The size and frequency of the forecasting errors call into question many important methods of choosing stocks that rely on finely tuned estimates running years into the future. Yet accurate earnings estimates are essential to most of the stock valuation methods we looked at in chapter 3. The intrinsic value theory, formulated by John Burr Williams, is based on forecasting earnings, cash flow, or dividends, often two decades or more ahead. The growth and momentum schools of investing also require finely calibrated, precise estimates many years into the future to justify the prices they pay for stocks. The higher the multiple, the greater the visibility of earnings demanded.

If the average forecast error is 44% annually, the chance of getting a bull's-eye at a distance of ten years seems extremely slim. Which brings us to another rule.

RULE 7

Most current security analysis requires a precision in analysts' estimates that is impossible to provide. Avoid methods that demand this level of accuracy.

Hey, I'm Special

What do we make of these results? If the evidence is so strong, why aren't more investors, particularly the pros, aware of it, and why do they not incorporate it into their methods, rather than quick-marching into an ambush? Why do Wall Streeters blithely overlook these findings as mere curiosities—simple statistics that affect others but not them? Many pros believe their own analysis is different. They, themselves, will hit the mark time and again with pinpoint accuracy. If they happen to miss, why it was a simple slip, or else the company misled them. More thorough research would have prevented the error. Next time, it won't happen.

Let's examine why this mentality is prevalent in the face of overwhelming evidence to the contrary.

Some Causes of Forecasting Errors

As we just saw, investors either ignore or aren't impressed by the statistical destruction of forecasting, even though the destruction has been thorough and spans decades. There are a number of reasons, some economic, some psychological, why investors depending on finely calibrated forecasts are likely to end up with egg on their face. Cragg and Malkiel did an early analysis of long-term estimates, published in the *Journal of Finance*.[27] They examined earnings projections of groups of security analysts at five highly respected investment organizations, including two New York City bank trust departments, a mutual fund, and an investment advisory firm. These organizations made one- to five-year estimates for 185 companies. The researchers found that most analysts' estimates were simply linear extrapolations of current trends with low correlations between actual and predicted earnings.

Despite the vast amount of additional information now available to analysts, say Cragg and Malkiel, and despite the frequent company visits, estimates are still projected as a continuation of past trends. "The remarkable conclusion of the present study is that the careful estimates of security analysts . . . performed little better than those of (past) company growth rates."

The researchers found that analysts could have done better with their five-year estimates by simply assuming that earnings would continue to expand near the long-term rate of 4% annually.[28]

Yet another important research finding indicates the fallibility of relying on earnings forecasts. Oxford Professor I. M. D. Little, in a paper appropriately titled "Higgledy Piggledy Growth," revealed that the futures of a large number of British companies could not be predicted from recent earnings trends.[29] Little's work proved uncomfortable to theoreticians and practitioners alike, who promptly criticized its methodology. Little accepted the criticism, carefully redid the work, but the outcome was the same. Earnings appeared to follow a random walk of their own, with past and future rates showing virtually no correlation. Recent trends (so important to security analysis in projecting earnings) provided no indication of the future course.[30]

A number of studies reach the same conclusion:[31] changes in the earnings of American companies fluctuate randomly over time.

Richard Brealey, for example, examined the percentage changes of earnings of 711 American industrial companies between 1945 and 1964. He too found that trends were not sustained, but actually demonstrated a slight tendency toward reversal. The only exception was companies with the steadiest rates of earnings growth, and even their correlations were only mildly positive.[32]

Juxtaposing the second set of studies to the first provides part of the explanation of why analyst forecasting errors are so high. If analysts extrapolate past earnings trends into the future, as Cragg and Malkiel have shown, and earnings do follow a random walk, as Little and Brealey have demonstrated, then one would expect sizable errors. *And large forecast errors are what we have found consistently through the chapter.*

Thus, once again and from quite another tack, we see the precariousness of attempting to place major emphasis on earning forecasts.

RULE 8

It is impossible, in a dynamic economy with constantly changing political, economic, industrial, and competitive conditions, to use the past to estimate the future.

There are several other economic reasons that can cause earnings forecasts to be off base. One is what Harvard economist Richard Zeck-hauser calls "the big bath theory." In a paper coauthored with Jay Patel of Boston University and François Degeorge of the HEC School of Management in Paris, the researchers provide evidence that many companies try to manage earnings by trying to show consistent, gradual improvements.[33] Analysts have an appetite for steady growth, and that is what management tries to serve up. When they can't do it, they take the "big bath," writing off everything they can, perhaps even more than is necessary (accounting again), in order to show a steady progression of earnings after the bath. The big bath could be another unpredictable effect that throws analysts' forecasts off.

Reviewing the evidence makes it appear that forecasting is far more art than science and, like the creative fields, has few masters. Excluding the highly talented exceptions, people simply cannot predict the future with any reliability, as the figures starkly tell us.

Career Pressures and Forecasts

There are some substantive factors that affect the analyst directly, the most important being career pressure. These can result in forecasts missing miserably. After surveying the major brokerage houses, John Dorfman, then editor of the market section of *The Wall Street Journal,* whom we met earlier,[34] provided a list of what determines an analyst's bonus, normally a substantial part of his or her salary. In Dorfman's words, "Investors might be surprised by what *doesn't* go into calculating analysts' bonuses. Accuracy of profit estimates? That's almost never a direct factor. . . . Performance of stocks that the analyst likes or hates? . . . It is rarely given major weight." *The ranking of seven factors determining an analyst's compensation places "accuracy of forecasts" dead last.*

What is most important is how the analyst is rated by the brokerage firm's sales force. Many firms conduct a formal poll of the sales force, which ranks the analysts primarily on how much commission business they can drum up. At Raymond James, the sales force's rating accounts for 50 percent of the analyst's bonus. Top executives also review a print-out of how much business is done in the analyst's stocks. The report is called "stock done" for short. Paine Webber keeps careful records of what percentage of trades it handles in every stock, and its market share in stocks it provides research for, compared to market share of competitors. Michael Culp, then director of Prudential Securities, instituted a rule requiring his analysts to make 110 contacts a month, but, he added quickly, most of his analysts were not affected, because they were making 135. Another firm ranks analysts' recommendations when calculating their bonuses. A buy recommendation is worth 130 points, a sell recommendation only 60. Sell recommendations don't generate nearly as much business as buy recommendations. No points are added for accuracy.[35]

Making the *Institutional Investor* All-Star Team, according to *The Wall Street Journal* list, ranks second. "The team," as we've seen, results in big commissions for the analyst's firm. Even as he denied the importance of the Institutional Investor poll, one research director said, "Most of the guys know they'll be visiting for 'I-I' in the spring." That is, the analyst will be making the annual pilgrimage to visit institutional clients, implicitly lobbying for their vote to fame and fortune. "I'm a lonely guy in March and April, shortly before the balloting," the research director continued.

Do you find these remarks disturbing? I do. After all, most investors put their savings in the hands of research experts, whose forecasts are the cornerstones of their recommendations. But the forecasts are a trivial factor, or even a nonevent in determining their compensation. Unfortunately, that's always been the name of the game.

There are other direct pressures on analysts. An important one, well known on the Street, is the fear of issuing sell recommendations. Sell recommendations are only a small fraction of the buys. A company that the analyst issues a sell recommendation on will often ban him or her from further contact. If he issues a sell recommendation on the entire industry, he may receive an industry blackball, which virtually excludes him from talking to any important executives. If the analyst is an expert in the industry, and it represents an important part of his intellectual property, he is facing major career damage by pressing the sell button.

Recommending a sell, even when the analyst proves to be dead-on, can be costly. In the late 1980s, an analyst at Janney Montgomery Scott issued a sell recommendation on one of the Atlantic City casinos owned by Donald Trump. Trump went bananas and insisted the analyst be fired for his lack of knowledge. Shortly thereafter, he was fired, but naturally, said the brokerage firm, "for other reasons." The analyst proved right and the casino went into Chapter 11. Out of a job, he won the equivalent of a few years of salary from an arbitration panel. But the analyst was never rewarded for his excellent call and, in fact, suffered because of it.

Another analyst was banned from an analysts' meeting of then high-flying Boston Chicken. His offense: he had issued a sell recommendation on the company. "We don't want you here," Boston Chicken's CFO told him. "We don't want you to confuse yourself with the facts."[36] A number of studies indicate that analysts issue five or six times as many buy as sell recommendations.[37] Obviously, career pressures have an impact on the buy-sell-hold rating.

Many companies lash out if analysts write negative reports. The retribution can take many forms. One analyst at Prudential Securities wrote a number of negative reports about Citicorp in 1992. Frustrated that Prudential could not become the lead underwriter in some asset-backed bond deals, a Prudential investment banker went to Citicorp and was told the reason was the analyst. The same analyst, a year later, criticized Banc One and its complex derivative holdings, which eventually cost Banc One hundreds of millions of dollars in write-offs. Banc One stopped its bond trading with Prudential. By coincidence, the analyst left the firm shortly thereafter. A Kidder Peabody analyst repeatedly recommended the sale of NationsBank. The bank stopped all stock and bond trading with Kidder for its trust accounts.[38]

For analysts at brokerage firms that are also large underwriters, the pressure is even greater. Negative reports are a major no-no. Bell South officials were unhappy about comments of a Salomon Brothers analyst who stated its management was inefficient and ranked it sixth out of the seven regional Bells. Salomon, a bond powerhouse, was excluded from the lucrative lead-manager role in a large Bell South issue. In late 1994, Conseco fired Merrill Lynch as its lead underwriter in a big bond offering shortly after its analyst downgraded Conseco's stock. Smith Barney, according to sources, believes it lost a chance to be part of the underwriting group of Owens-Corning Fiberglass after one of its analysts wrote a negative report on the company in early 1995.[39]

Just how heavy career pressures can be for analysts working for major underwriting firms if they recommend a sale is shown in an academic study. The work examined 250 analyst reports from investment banking houses, matching them up with 250 from brokerage firms that did not conduct investment banking. The conclusion: investment banking house brokers issued 25% more buy recommendations and a remarkable 46% fewer sell recommendations.[40]

What is apparent from the above is that the most important responsibility of the analyst for the brokerage firm is to be a good marketer. The analyst has to tell a good story, not one that is necessarily right. The bottom line is commissions. A good marketer and a good forecaster are different animals. We have already seen one example of the All Stars significantly underperforming the market with their picks. Another example is that major money managers, to whom the All Stars devote the bulk of their attention, consistently do worse than the averages.

Analysts of necessity use disingenuous gradations that actually mean sell, such as underweight, lighten up, fully-valued, overvalued, source of funds, swap-and-hold, or even strong hold. As Peter Siris, a former analyst at UBS Securities, summed it up, "There's a game out there. Most people aren't fooled by what analysts have to say . . . because they know in a lot of cases they're shills. But those poor [small] investors— somebody ought to tell them."[41]

You've been warned!

Even if brokerage firms don't focus on accurate estimates, however, analysts are not punished for producing them. Although underwriting firms may be pressured by clients or potential clients not to make sell recommendations on their stocks, to my knowledge an analyst has never been reprimanded for a conservative earnings estimate on a client's stock. The question still remains: Why are analysts' forecasts too optimistic?

Psychological Influences on Analysts' Decisions

In the last chapter, we saw that expert forecasts were sharply off the mark in many fields besides the stock market. In publishing, politics, medicine, warfare, or betting the ponies, experts were wrong time and again. We further examined our ability to process large amounts of information, in areas from radiology to psychology, and found that here, too, we often were not up to the task. Specifically, man has proven to be a so-so configural or interactive processor of information. The stock market requires high-level configural reasoning to weigh thousands of market, company, industry, economic, and political inputs at the same time. Most people simply cannot do it.

We also saw that increased information makes experts more confident, but unfortunately not more accurate. For the security analyst, as we considered briefly, the availability of information has gone up almost exponentially in recent years. The analyst traveling with a laptop can run spreadsheets, check stock quotes, receive faxes, or even tap into voluminous databases. At home base, his data input capabilities increase enormously. As a J. P. Morgan technology analyst puts it, "This business will be affected by all the new technology. If I don't use it I'll be at a competitive disadvantage."[42] Technology has produced such a sea of data that analysts are foundering in information. The data glut threatens to swamp, rather than enhance, investment decisions.

As the Morgan analyst continued, extracting useful information from the 49 databases the bank subscribes to is like finding a needle in a haystack. "The more data you get, the less information you have," he groans.[43] His intuition coincides with the psychological findings. One of the effects of dealing with vast amounts of information, which we touched on in chapter 4, is the expert's mistaken belief that he can make accurate forecasts, despite the difficulties we have examined.

Increased information, as was demonstrated, does not lead to increased accuracy. A large number of studies in cognitive psychology indicate that human judgment is often predictably incorrect. Nor is overconfidence unique to analysts. People in situations of uncertainty are generally overconfident based on the information available to them; they usually believe they are right much more often than they are.

Amos Tversky, one of the leading figures in cognitive psychology, researched expert overconfidence in the stock market.* According to Tversky, "In one study, analysts were asked such questions as what is the probability that the price of a given stock will exceed $X by a given date. On average, analysts were 80% confident but only 60% accurate in their assessments."[44] The study was repeated numerous times.

In other studies, analysts were asked for their high and low estimates for the price of a stock. The high estimate was to be a number they were 95% sure the actual price would fall below; the low estimate was the price they were 95% sure the stock would remain above. Thus, the high and low estimates should have included 90% of the cases, which is to say that, if the analysts were realistic and unbiased, the number of price movements above and below this range would be 10%. In fact, the estimates missed the range 35% of the time, or three and a half times as often as the forecasters estimated.

Tversky went on to note that "rather than operating on rational expectations" (with total logic, unaffected by behavior, as efficient market theory assumes investors do), "people are commonly biased in several directions: They are optimistic; they overestimate the chances that they will succeed, and they overestimate their degree of knowledge, in the sense that their confidence far exceeds their 'hit rate.' "[45]

---

* He died prematurely of cancer at 59 in 1996. Tversky was on the board of the Dreman Foundation, which is dedicated to the study of investor and economic decision-making.

Tversky was queried about overconfidence at an investment behavioral conference in 1995. The questioner asked what he thought of the fact that analysts were not very good at forecasting future earnings. He responded, in part, "From the standpoint of the behavioral phenomena . . . analysts should be more skeptical of their ability to predict [earnings] than they usually are. Time and time again, we learn that our confidence is misplaced, and our overconfidence leads to bad decisions, *so recognizing our limited ability to predict the future is an important lesson to learn.*" [Italics mine.][46]

Tversky was asked at the same conference if analysts and other professional investors learn from their experiences. He replied that, "unfortunately cognitive illusions are not easily unlearned. . . . The fact that in the real world people have not learned to eliminate . . . overconfidence speaks for itself."[47] An earlier study by Baruch Fischhoff showed that even when experts are warned about the existence of this problem, forecasters appear unable to adjust for its effects.[48] This explains why neither analysts nor investors benefit from the findings that earnings estimates cannot be made with precision, and therefore continually suffer the consequences of high forecasting errors.

These findings apply to many other fields. A classic analysis of cognitive psychologists found that it was impossible to predict which psychologists would be good diagnosticians. Further, there were no mechanical forecasting models that could be continuously used to improve judgment. It concluded the only way to resolve the problem was to look at the record of the diagnostician over a substantial period of time.

Researchers have also shown that people can maintain a high degree of confidence in their answers, even when they know the "hit rate" is not very high. The phenomenon has been called "the illusion of validity."[49] This also helps to explain the belief that analysts can pinpoint their estimates despite the strong evidence to the contrary. People make confident predictions from incomplete and fallible data. There are excellent lessons here for the stock forecaster.

Mr. Inside and Mr. Outside

We have seen that forecasters in many professions are far too confident of their estimates, and that the forecasts are too optimistic. Both can be deadly in the marketplace. Research indicates some of the psychological reasons these patterns occur so repeatedly.

Daniel Kahneman, who for several decades coauthored many important scholarly pieces with Amos Tversky, wrote on this subject in collaboration with Dan Lovallo.[50]

Forecasters are "excessively prone" to treat each problem as unique, paying no attention to history. Cognitive psychologists note there are two distinct methods of forecasting. The first is called the "inside view." This method is the one overwhelmingly used to forecast earnings estimates and stock prices. The analyst or the stock forecaster focuses entirely on the stock and related aspects such as growth rates, market share, product development, the general market, the economic outlook, and a host of other variables.

The "outside view," on the other hand, ignores the multitude of factors that go into making the individual forecast, and focuses instead on the group of cases believed to be most similar. In the case of earnings estimates, for example, it would zero in on how accurate earnings forecasts have been overall, or how accurate they have been for a specific industry or for the company itself, in deciding how precisely the analyst can estimate and the reliance that can be placed on the forecast.

If the stock market forecaster is to succeed using the inside view, he must capture the critical elements of the future. The outside view, in contrast, is essentially statistical and comparative, and does not attempt to read the future in any detail.

Kahneman relates a story to demonstrate the difference. In the mid-1970s, he was involved with a group of experts in developing a curriculum on judgment and decision-making under uncertainty for high schools in Israel. When the team had been in operation for a year and had made some significant progress, discussion turned to how long it would take to complete the project. Everyone in the group, including Kahneman, gave an estimate. The forecasts ranged from 18 to 30 months. Kahneman then asked one of his colleagues, an expert in curriculum development, to think of similar projects he was familiar with, at a parallel stage in time and development. "How long did it take them from that point to complete their projects?" he asked.

After a long pause, the expert replied with obvious discomfort that, first of all, about 40% of the projects were never completed. Of the balance, he said, "I cannot think of any that was completed in less than seven years, nor any that took more than ten." Kahneman then asked if there were any factors that made this team superior in attempting the task. None, said the expert. "Indeed we are slightly below average in terms of our resources and our potential." As experienced as he was with the outside view, the curriculum development expert was just as susceptible to the inside case.*

As is now apparent, the inside and outside view draw on dramatically different sources of information, and the processes are poles apart. The outside view ignores the innumerable details of the project at hand (the cornerstone of analysis using the inside view) and makes no attempt to forecast the outcome of the project into the future. Instead, it focuses on the statistics of projects similar to the one being undertaken to garner the odds of success or failure. The basic difference is that, with the outside view, the problem is not treated as unique, but as an instance of a number of similar problems. The outside view could be applied to a large number of the problems we've seen in the past two chapters, including curriculum building, medical, psychiatric or legal diagnosis, as well as forecasting earnings or future stock prices.

According to Kahneman, "It should be obvious that when both methods are applied with intelligence and skill the outside view is much more likely to yield a realistic estimate. In general, the future of long and complex undertakings is simply not foreseeable in detail." The number of possible outcomes when dozens or hundreds of factors interact in the marketplace is almost infinite. Even if one could foresee each of the possibilities, the probability of any particular scenario is negligible. Yet this is precisely what the analyst is trying to accomplish with a single, precise prediction.

The Forecasters' Plague

Let's return to our analytical friends and look at their chances of success in terms of the inside view. As Table 5–4 makes clear, the odds of their being correct on their forecasts over any but the shortest periods of time are extremely low, which means the odds of making money consistently using precise forecasts are almost negligible.

As we saw earlier, the Street demands forecasts normally within a range of ±5%. Table 5–4, taken from our previous analysts' forecasting study, shows how slim the probability of getting estimates within this range actually is. Remember, only 29% of forecasts were within this range in any one quarter.

The table shows the odds of an analyst hitting the target for 1 quarter,

---

* Kahneman noted it took eight more years after that discussion to complete the project.

Table 5–4

THE PROBABILITY GAME

The Chances of a Stock Surviving Without an Earnings Surprise

5% Surprise			
	Any Surprise	*Negative Surprise*	*Positive Surprise*
1 quarter	29%	63%	67%
4 quarters	1 / 130	1 / 7	1 / 5
10 quarters	1 / 200,000	1 / 110	1 / 58
20 quarters	1 / 50 billion	1 / 12,000	1 / 3,400

10% Surprise			
	Any Surprise	*Negative Surprise*	*Positive Surprise*
1 quarter	47%	70%	77%
4 quarters	1 / 21	1 / 4	1 / 3
10 quarters	1 / 2,000	1 / 35	1 / 14
20 quarters	1 / 4 million	1 / 1,250	1 / 200

SOURCE OF DATA: A-N RESEARCH CORP. (FORMERLY THE RESEARCH DEPARTMENT OF ABEL NOSER CORP.) AND I/B/E/S, 1973–1996.

4 quarters, 10 quarters, and 20 quarters; for all earnings surprises in column 1, negative surprises in column 2, and positive surprises in column 3. It is not reassuring. The odds are staggering against the investor who relies on fine-tuned earnings estimates. There is only a 1 in 130 chance that the analysts' consensus forecast will be within 5% for any four consecutive quarters. Going longer makes the odds dramatically worse. For any ten consecutive quarters, the odds of fine-tuning the estimates for a company within this range fall to 1 in 200,000, and for 20 consecutive quarters, 1 in 50 billion.

To put this in perspective, *your odds are ten times greater of being the big winner of the New York State Lottery than of pinpointing earnings five years ahead.* Few people would put a couple of bucks in a lottery with odds like these, but thousands of investors will play them in the marketplace.

Some folks will say, "Who cares if earnings come in above estimates. In fact, I'll applaud." Fair enough. So we asked: what are the chances that you will avoid a 5% negative surprise for 10 to 20 consecutive quarters? Terrible. The investor has only a 1 in 7 chance of *not* getting a negative earnings surprise 5% below the consensus forecast after only four quarters. After ten quarters, the chances of not receiving at least one crippling earnings surprise go down to 1 in 110, and for 20 quarters, they are 1 in 12,000. Yet, as we have also seen, forecasts often have to go out a decade or more to justify the high prices at which many companies are trading.

Even if we stretched the acceptable forecast band to 10%, which we saw is too imprecise for many stock-pickers, the chance of consistently having accurate forecasts is still only 1 in 21 for four quarters, 1 in 2,000 for 2½ years, and 1 in 4 million for 5 years. Think about it—should anyone sane want to play against these odds? Yet, as we know, relying on accurate estimates is the way most people play the investment game. Investors who realize the odds will obviously go with them if there is a way to do it, which is exactly what we'll look at in the next section.

What we see here is a classic case of using the inside rather than the outside view. Evidence such as the above strongly supports Kahneman's statement that the outside view is much more likely to yield realistic results. Yet, as Kahneman states, "The inside view is overwhelmingly preferred in forecasting." Looking at the figures above, we might all ask why.

The answer, again, is psychological. The natural way a decision-maker approaches a problem is to focus all of his or her knowledge on the task, concentrating particularly on its unique features. Kahneman noted that a general observation of overconfidence is that, even when forecasters are aware of findings such as the foregoing, they will still use the inside approach, disregarding the outside view, regardless of how strong its statistical documentation.

Often, the relevance of the outside view is explicitly denied. Analysts and money managers I have talked to about high error rates repeatedly shrug them off. Usually, the problem is attributed to unreliable information from company managements, extraordinary circumstances, or not having been thorough enough (by failing to integrate even more complex and elusive variables into an analysis already severely overloaded with information). In sum, they ignore the record of forecasting, because they have been taught and believe that investment theory, when executed properly, will yield the precise results that they require. Analysts and money managers seem unable to recognize the problems inherent in forecasting.

This situation is not unique to Wall Street. Indeed, the relevance of the statistical calculations inherent in the outside view is usually explicitly denied. Doctors and lawyers often argue against allying statistical odds to particular cases. Sometimes their preference for the inside view is couched in almost moral terms. Thus, the professional will say, "My client or patient is not a statistic, his case is truly unique." Many disciplines implicitly teach their practitioners that the inside view is the only professional way to come to grips with the unique problems they will meet. The outside view is rejected as a crude analogy from instances that are only superficially similar.

To not rely on the skyrocketing earnings estimates of a company such as Yahoo, on the cutting edge of Internet technology, many analysts would argue, is vastly unfair to current shareholders and potential buyers. Ironically, rapid technology change, accompanied by rapierlike growth, makes the forecasting process even more difficult than for more mundane companies.

This leads back to the important question of overconfidence.

Analyst Overconfidence

We have observed that analyst forecasts are consistently overoptimistic. This bias in tandem with overconfidence can be extremely dangerous, particularly when stocks are highly valued.

It should be pretty obvious by now that analysts are far from being alone in their overconfidence. We have also seen that overoptimism is bred by overconfidence. Overoptimism shows itself regularly in many fields. In defense procurement, for example, major contracts often come in triple or quadruple the original estimates and the performance is often well below the original specifications. When President Nixon approved the Space Shuttle Program, one of the major goals was to be cost effective by putting a payload into space at a relatively low cost, thus requiring less use of costly rocket systems. In 1972, at the time of its approval, NASA estimated it would cost $200 a pound to put the shuttle and payload into orbit, and the space shuttles would fly 25 times a year. To the end of 1996, the actual costs were slightly higher than projected—$10,000 a pound—while the number of flights averaged four or five a year. In a new submission, NASA is now estimating these costs will drop to $1,000 a pound—perhaps as low as $100.[51] Any believers?

Overoptimism often results from differences in estimates made from the inside rather than the outside view. A clear-cut example was demonstrated in an article in the *Journal of Business Venturing*.[52] The authors asked new entrepreneurs about their chances of success, and also queried them on what they thought the success rate was for similar start-up companies. First, they found the entrepreneurs' estimates of their own chances of hitting it big were completely unrelated to objective measures of success, such as a college education, prior management experience in the business, or the amount of capital they could put into the fledgling firms. Second, the entrepreneurs were strikingly overoptimistic. Over 80% believed their chances of success were 70% or higher. By comparison, the chance they attributed to similar businesses was 59%. They were far too optimistic about both their own and the average survival rate of start-up business. According to Dun & Bradstreet, the survival rate of new firms is 33% after five years.

Overoptimism shows up in many other parts of the corporate world. With capital spending projects, optimistic bias is a familiar fact of life. The typical project finishes late, comes in over budget, and fails to achieve its initial goal. Grossly optimistic errors appear to be very frequent with new technologies or other projects where the firm is in an unfamiliar situation. A Rand Corporation study some years back examined the cost of new types of plants in the energy field.[53] The norm was that actual construction costs doubled initial estimates, while 80% of the projects failed to gain their projected market share.

A psychological study examining the cause of this type of failure concluded that most companies demanded a worst-case scenario for a capital spending project. "But the worst case forecasts are almost always too optimistic. When managers look at the downside, then generally describe a mildly pessimistic future rather than the worst possible future."[54]

A review of the literature on overconfidence turns up three major reasons for a wide-ranging optimistic bias.[55] First, people have unrealistic optimism about future events. Second, they have unrealistically positive self-evaluations. Third, they have unrealistic confidence in their ability to control a situation. Thus, for every positive trait—such as managerial risk-taking, safe driving, or a sense of humor—they rank themselves above the median. People also overestimate the skills and the resources at their disposal to ensure a favorable outcome, while they underestimate the likelihood of problems affecting them personally. A security analyst is well aware that stocks trading in the stratosphere will collapse if earnings come in under target. But he is also confident that he knows everything there is to know about the high-flyer he is recommending, and so strongly believes it won't happen to him. A good rule to train yourself to follow:

RULE 9

Be realistic about the downside of an investment, recognizing our human tendency to be both overly optimistic and overly confident. Expect the worst to be much more severe than your initial projection.

In this chapter, we have looked at the striking errors in analysts' forecasts, errors so high that they render the majority of current investment methods inoperable. We have also seen that in spite of high error rates being recognized for decades, neither analysts nor investors who religiously depend on them have altered their methods in any way.

The problem is not unique to analysts or market forecasters. We have also looked at how pervasive it is in many professions where information is difficult to analyze, as well as how hard the problem is to recognize, let alone change. Finally, we have found overoptimism to be a strong component of expert forecasts, both within and outside of the stock market.

Next, a look at the market reaction to errors in analysts' forecasts. The results, I'm sure, will prove interesting.

6

Nasty Surprises

LIKELY you remember the Gulf War. The massive deployment of American military might in Saudi Arabia, the swift liberation of Kuwait, and the thorough drubbing of the forces of Iraq and its maniacal leader Saddam Hussein. You might also recall the stirring videos that purported to show Iraqi SCUD missiles being blasted out of the sky by American ground-to-air defense missiles. This was considered a pleasant surprise by some military experts who had long questioned the effectiveness of American antimissile weaponry.

If you're a tad practical, you may have thought that the good news coverage would send investors scurrying to buy stock in missile defense contractors. That's what surprises do on Wall Street, they constantly change companies' prospects—i.e., their earnings outlooks—and thus inevitably their stock prices. The market is always adjusting to surprises, or anticipating them, or discounting them—the standard fare of investment news you hear or read every day. The key players, of course, in making a surprise, a market surprise, are the analysts we met in the last chapter, the people who predict what will happen *barring any surprises*.

Incidentally, there are analysts who look at the performance of military hardware. And despite the optimistic field reports, and the stirring videos, the actual success of the antimissiles based on a rigorous statistical study wasn't very high. The failure of the SCUDS to perform was due both to their defects and the unrealistically high performance expected from their firing crews. Time to think twice about that stock purchase? Maybe. But far more important, maybe it's time to reconsider the whole market mechanism of surprises, not simply from an anecdotal perspective, but from a solid statistical basis.

Earnings surprises have a consistent and predictable effect on stock prices. More to the point, their impact on stocks that people like is dramatically different from their impact on stocks they don't like. Understanding the nature of surprises provides a high-probability method of beating the market.

Paying Through the Nose for Growth

At times, no price seems too high for aggressive growth stocks or IPOs (initial public offerings). Investors repeatedly pay through the nose, and just as repeatedly get stung. Nevertheless, as chapters 4 and 5 showed, strong psychological forces compel investors to buy sizzling issues, and then prevent them from even analyzing where they went wrong.

The pattern is, not surprisingly, repeated for larger companies. Investors believe they can forecast the prospects for both exciting and unexciting stocks well into the future. They have high expectations for "best stocks," and high confidence that expectations will be met. Similarly, they have low expectations for stocks that appear to have lackluster or poor prospects, but again high confidence that their estimates will be dead on.

Companies with the best prospects, fastest growth rates, and most exciting concepts normally trade at a high price relative to earnings (P/E), cash flow (P/CF), and book value (P/BV), and invariably provide low or no dividend yields.[1] Conversely, stocks with poor outlooks trade at low P/Es, price-to-cash flow, or price-to-book value, and usually have higher dividend yields. (For information on where to find price-earnings, price-to-book value, price-to-cash flow ratios and dividend yields of companies, please turn to pages 202–203, chapter 9.)

Often, the disparity between what investors will pay for a favored stock and one blacklisted is immense. People in early 1996, for example, were willing to pay 23 times as much for each dollar of earnings of Netscape, the Internet wunderkind, as for Fannie Mae (Federal National Mortgage Association), which incidentally is no slouch in expanding income, having increased it at more than 20% annually over the previous twenty years. But investors will pay these price differentials, which can be enormous, because of their confidence in their ability to pinpoint the future. Let's look at what happens when—surprise!—their forecasts miss the mark.

The Many Faces of Surprise

To find out how stocks react when analysts err, I did a number of studies in collaboration with Nelson Woodard, Eric Lufkin, Michael Berry, and Mitchell Stern for the 24 years ending with 1996.[2] To be consistent, we worked with exactly the same analysts' consensus forecasts that were used to calculate analysts' errors in the last chapter.

We wanted to measure a number of factors important to investors. First, what do analyst forecasting errors do to stock prices? Second—and as important—do earnings surprises have the same impact on favored as on unfavored stocks? Stocks trading in outer space are there because of analysts' confidence in their future—possibly mixed with a wee dose of overoptimism. Did they react the same way to earnings surprises as stocks that are in the investor doghouse? Third, we wished to examine just how accurate investors expect analysts' forecasts to be. To help resolve this, we measured how even tiny surprises affect a stock's price by considering any amount over one penny a share a surprise.

To answer the three questions, we analyzed the stocks strictly according to how exciting or dull investors believed their prospects were, using three different value measures: price-earnings ratio, price-to-cash flow, and price-to-book value. The higher the three ratios, the more enticing the stock is to an investor, and the more he or she is willing to pay. Conversely, the lower the three ratios, the more unpopular the stock. We divided the stocks in all of the quarters in our 1973–1996 study into three groups strictly by how they ranked by each of these three value measures. The 20% of stocks that had the highest P/Es, for example, were placed in the top P/E group (called a quintile in statistical jargon), the next 60% in the middle group, the lowest 20% in the bottom group. We did this the same way for all three value measures. The portfolios were reassembled on this basis for every quarter in the study. We then calculated the effect of surprises on each group of stocks beginning in the second quarter of 1973 and ending in the fourth quarter of 1996.[3]

The study used the 1,500 largest companies in the Compustat database with fiscal years ending in March, June, September, and December.[4] Approximately 750–1,000 large companies were used in each of the 95 quarters of the study.

What the Record Shows

Next we set a yardstick to gauge the result of market surprise. The surprises are measured against the analyst consensus forecast, the average estimate of the group of analysts following each stock as described in the last chapter. A surprise is measured against actual earnings, so it doesn't matter whether the earnings are up or down. If a company reports a loss of 80 cents a share, as an example, and the Street expected a loss of one dollar a share, then it would be considered a positive surprise of 20 cents divided by the 80 cents reported or 25%.

Do surprises impact favored and unfavored stocks in the same way? To find out we'll look at the combined effect of positive and negative surprises—on both groups. The results are shown in the Figures 6–1a, 6–1b, and 6–1c. In each, the 20% of stocks most out of favor by one of the three value measures—price-to-earnings (6–1a), price-to-cash flow (6-1b) and price-to-book value (6-1c)—are depicted by the dark bar, the 60% of stocks in the middle groups by gray, and the most favored 20% in white.[5] The charts calculate the return above or below the market's for each of the 95 quarters of the study.

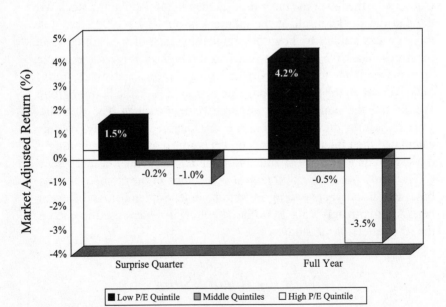

Figure 6-1a
Price/Earnings All Surprises
Compustat 1500 1973 - 1996

0% = Market Return (3.6% quarterly, 15.6% annually)
All figures are market adjusted.

Figure 6-1b
Price/Cash Flow All Surprises
Compustat 1500 1973 - 1996

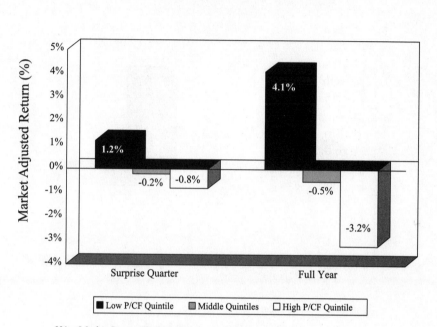

0% = Market Return (3.6% quarterly, 15.6% annually)
All figures are market adjusted.

The figures show the effect of an earnings surprise—measured in the quarter in which earnings were actually reported—which is almost always the quarter following that in which the income was earned. We will call the quarter earnings are announced in the "surprise quarter." The left-hand group of bars shows the effect of the surprise in the quarter it was announced, while the right-hand group represents the effect after one year. The market itself is set at 0 in the center of the vertical scale on the chart. The surprise return must be added to the market return in each period to get the total return. If a bar shows a 3% positive return, for example, it means that it did 3% better than the market over this period of the study. The market provided a 15.6% return on average, annually throughout the entire period. If it was a 3% negative return, it means it did 3% worse than the market. This type of chart lets you easily see how surprise affects each group of stocks.

Each of the charts shows at a glance that surprise helps unpopular stocks and hurts popular ones. Looking first at price/earnings ratios in Figure 6–1a, we see that all surprises to unpopular stocks (positive and

Figure 6-1c

Price/Book Value All Surprises

Compustat 1500 1973 - 1996

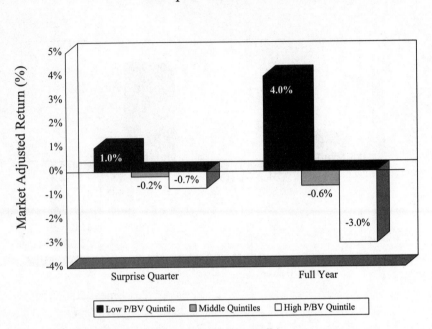

0% = Market Return (3.6% quarterly, 15.6% annually)
All figures are market adjusted.

negative combined) return 1.5% above market in the surprise quarter over the life of the study. If, for example, the market was up 2.5% in the quarter (the average quarterly return of stocks over the past 70 years), the most out-of favor stocks, as measured by the lowest 20% of P/Es, are up 1.5%, or 60% more than the market in the surprise quarter.

Beyond the surprise quarter, what's more, the beneficial or lethal effect of surprise increases. At the end of one year, the most out-of-favor stocks outperform the market by 4.2%. This nearly tripled the outperformance of the market in the surprise quarter itself. Again, looking at the long-term rate of return of stocks, the most out-of favor stocks outperform the market by about 41% annually. Remember, this is with positive and negative surprises combined, indicating that all surprises taken together very much favor stocks investors believe have lackluster prospects.

As Figure 6–1a also shows, surprise works against stocks with the best expectations, in this case the 20% of stocks with the highest P/E multiples. This group underperformed the market by 1% in the surprise quarter, and that differential increases to 3.5% for the full year, some 22% under the market.

Surprise does not have much effect on the 60% of stocks that make up the middle grouping. These stocks are not normally over- or under-valued much. As chart 6–1a shows, the stocks are down by less than one quarter of 1 percent in the surprise quarter. A year after the surprise there is a small negative (–0.5%) effect.

However, the difference in the effects of surprise on "best" and "worst" stocks is large and increasing over time. Worst stocks outper-formed best stocks by 2.5% in the surprise quarter, then steadily rose to 7.7% by the end of the year.

To summarize, Figure 6–1a reveals that earnings surprises do not af-fect the returns of the various P/E groups the same way. Surprise works to the benefit of low P/E stocks and against the high P/E group, while it has a nominal effect on stocks in the middle group. Is there any differ-ence in how surprise affects stocks ranked by the other value measures?

Toute la Différence

Figure 6–1b looks at the effects of surprise on stocks measured by price-to-cash flow. The chart is nearly identical to Figure 6–1a for the surprise quarter and the full year. The lowest price-to-cash flow group again strongly outperforms the market in both cases. Similarly, the favorite stocks, the 20% of highest price-to-cash flow issues, significantly un-derperform the average in both periods, while the middle group is al-most unaffected by surprise. By this value measurement, surprises in analysts' forecasts once again work powerfully in favor of the most un-wanted group and against the most highly regarded stocks.

Figure 6–1c demonstrates the effects of surprise measured by price-to-book value. Remember, the higher the price-to-book value ratio, the more popular a stock is, and vice-versa. Again, the results are similar. Favorite stocks underperform in the surprise quarter (–0.7%) and do even worse for the full year (–3.0%). Stocks that are unpopular outper-form in the quarter (+1.0%) and take off nicely over the full year (+4.0%). Once more, the middle 60% of stocks are minimally affected by earnings surprises.

What is remarkable is not only that out-of-favor stocks outperform by all three measures, but how similar the performance is regardless of the value measure we choose. We thus begin to see a path to making money in the stock market. Earnings surprises, whether positive or negative, af-fect favored and out-of-favor stocks very differently. Surprise consistently results in above-average performance for out-of-favor stocks and below-average performance for favored stocks. Has the lightbulb gone on? We can find illumination in Contrarian Investment Rule 10:

RULE 10

Take advantage of the high rate of analyst forecast error by simply investing in out-of-favor stocks.

Conversely, buying favorites and being exposed to the frequent surprises will cost you money. How much money? A look at the magnitude of this surprise effect is a sobering experience, as I'll demonstrate shortly.

The Effect of Positive Surprises

Examine Figure 6–2. It shows the effects of positive surprises on stocks in our high, low, and middle groupings, by P/E. As you can see, positive surprise galvanizes the lowest 20% of stocks. In the surprise quarter, they outperform the averages by 3.6%, or two and a half times the quarterly return of the market over almost 80 years. For the full year, the lowest P/E quintile charges ahead of the market by a remarkable 8.1%. Think about this for a moment. Since the late 1920s, stocks have returned about 10.5% annually. Owning out-of-favor stocks that have positive surprises will fetch you almost double the market return over time. We'll look at the reasons for this astonishing increase in return shortly.

Positive surprise also has a noticeable, but more subdued effect on stocks in the middle quintiles. The middle group outperforms the market by 2.3% in the quarter. But the above-market return increases by less than 1% for the remaining nine months. They don't continue to steadily appreciate. Their reaction to positive surprise is moderate, probably because they are the least under- or overvalued.

Finally, positive surprises have far less effect on favorite stocks. Stocks that receive positive surprises outperform the market by 1.7% in the surprise quarter. The "best" stocks do not keep improving, however, as with the case of the low P/E group. Rather, they decline slightly over the next nine months.

Although not shown, the lowest 20% of stocks ranked by price-to-cash flow or price-to-book value are remarkably similar. Both sharply outperform the market for surprise quarter and for the full year, and rout the most favored stocks for the two periods. The result for the 60% of

Figure 6-2
Price/Earnings Positive Surprises
Compustat 1500 1973 - 1996

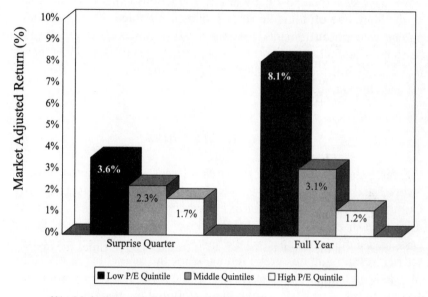

0% = Market Return (3.6% quarterly, 15.6% annually)
All figures are market adjusted.

stocks in middle quintiles is close to that of the middle group of P/Es in Figure 6–2.

Why do positive surprises for "best" stocks cause only a moderate rise in the surprise quarter? Since analysts and investors alike believe they can precisely judge which stocks will be the real winners in the years ahead, a positive surprise does little more than confirm their expectations. It's no great shakes—the top companies *should* have rapidly growing revenues, market share, and earnings. By the end of the year, therefore, the effect of the surprise almost disappears.

Investors react very differently to positive surprises for out-of-favor companies, however, no matter which of the three value yardsticks by which we measure them. Investors put these stocks into the lowest category precisely because they expect them to continue to mope. These are the dogs of the investment world; they deserve minimal valuations. A positive earnings surprise for a stock in this group is an event. Investors sit up and take notice.

Maybe these companies are not as bad as analysts and investors believed. Out-of-favor stocks, therefore, do not just move up in the quarter of the surprise and then drop back again, as do the favorites. Instead, they continue to move steadily higher relative to the market in the year following the surprise.

We have seen three distinctly different reactions to earnings surprise by the high, low, and middle stock groups using three of the most important value measurements. Like the weather, however, all days can't be sunny—and all news can't be good. Negative surprises, which normally send chills down investors' spines, are the other side of the coin we need to examine.

Calling In the Chips

Figures 6–3a and 6–3b show the effect of negative surprise on "best," "worst," and middle groups by price-to-cash flow, and price-to-earnings. Out-of-favor stocks again win in a breeze.* Let's start by looking at price-to-cash flow (Figure 6–3a). Negative surprises in analysts' forecasts have a minimal impact on the lowest 20% of stocks in the surprise quarter, resulting in this group falling below the market by only 8/10th of 1%. Moreover, the market shrugs off the surprise by the end of the year, with the out-of-favor group outperforming the market by 2/10 of 1%. The results for the lowest P/Es (Figure 6–3b) and price-to-book value (not shown) are similar.

Negative surprises are like water off a duck's back for this group. Investors have low expectations for what they consider lackluster or bad stocks, and when they do disappoint, few eyebrows are raised. The bottom line is that a negative surprise is not much of an event in the surprise quarter and is a non-event in the nine months following the news.

Consider the "best" companies, however. Investors expect only glowing prospects for these stocks. After all, they confidently—*over*confidently—believe that they can divine the future of a "good" stock with precision. These stocks are not supposed to disappoint; people pay top dollar for them for exactly this reason. So when the negative surprise arrives, the results are devastating.

Figure 6–3a shows how "best" stocks, by price-to-cash flow, react to negative earnings surprises. In the quarter that investors receive the news, the stocks underperform the market by a startling 4.8%. They do six times as badly as the lowest price-to-cash flow group, when receiv-

---

* Although not shown, the effect to price-to-book value is very similar.

ing "bad" surprises. Worse yet, while the most out-of-favor stocks out-perform the market slightly in the next nine months, the favorites continue to drop. At the end of the year, they are 11.3% under the averages. Favorite stocks with negative surprises underperform the market's return by a shocking 72% annually, on average, over the 24 years of the study. As Figure 6–3a also shows, the lowest price-to-cash flow group outperforms the highest by a remarkable 11.5% in years when both groups suffer negative surprises.

Figure 6–3b, which measures negative surprise by price/earnings ratio, shows similar results. Negative surprises on the highest 20% of stocks drop the stocks sharply in the surprise quarter, followed by a much larger decline in the next nine months.

What do we make of numbers like these? It's apparent that investors are shaken when companies they expect to excel disappoint. The disappointment doesn't have to be large. You may remember that we purposely used a very small analyst forecast error—one cent and over—to

Figure 6-3a

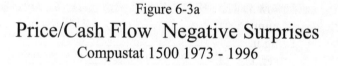

Price/Cash Flow Negative Surprises
Compustat 1500 1973 - 1996

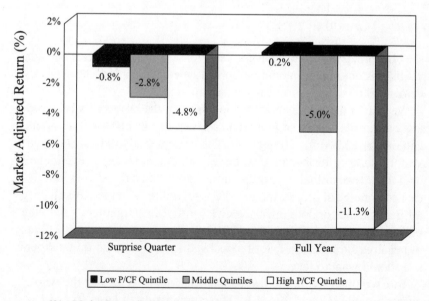

0% = Market Return (3.6% quarterly, 15.6% annually)
All figures are market adjusted.

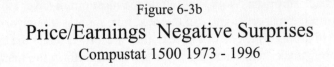

Figure 6-3b
Price/Earnings Negative Surprises
Compustat 1500 1973 - 1996

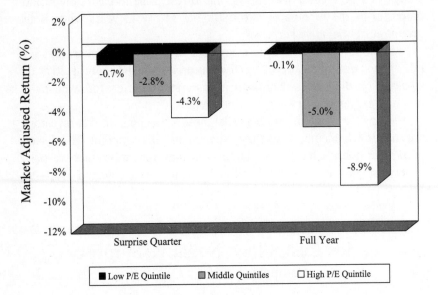

0% = Market Return (3.6% quarterly, 15.6% annually)
All figures are market adjusted.

see how precise estimates have to be. From the major declines of high-visibility stocks on even nominal forecast errors, it appears the accuracy demanded of earnings forecasts is far too high.

We saw in the last chapter (Table 5–4) that the probability of avoiding a negative surprise of more than 5% was one in 110 for 10 quarters, and one in 12,000 for 20 quarters. The current study indicates that investor tolerance for negative surprises on popular stocks is even lower than this. If we blithely overlook these results and believe a wider forecast error range of plus or minus 10% is tolerable, then there is still only a 1 in 35 chance of dodging a negative surprise in 10 quarters—with the odds going up to one in 1,250 for 20. Considering the devastating effects of negative surprises on favorite stocks, these are odds no rational person should want to face.

Too, we observed in the last chapter that analysts are, on the whole, overoptimistic in their forecasts. The combination of large forecast errors by analysts and their noted overoptimism—9% annually in one landmark study—is lethal for buyers of favorite stocks.[6]

Finally, Figure 6–3a shows the expected: negative surprises have more effect on the 60% of stocks in the middle group than on the low price-to-cash flow stocks, but far less than on the high price-to-cash flow group for both the surprise quarter and the year. But this is almost entirely offset by their outperformance with positive surprises. In fact, as Figures 6–1a, 6–1b, and 6–1c, indicate, when positive and negative surprises are put together, they have almost no effect on the middle groupings. Overall, they are a nonevent for this 60% of stocks. All the findings behind the charts in this chapter are statistically significant.[7]

Pulling the Trigger

Regardless of which valuation method was used, when earnings came in above analysts' forecasts on out-of-favor stocks, they shot out the lights. Just as apparent was the sharp underperformance of the winners, the top 20% of stocks as measured by price-to-earnings or price-to-cash flow ratios, when analysts' estimates were too optimistic.

What the study shows, then, is that the overvaluation of "best" stocks and the undervaluation of "worst" stocks is often driven to extremes. That brings us quite naturally to Rule 11:

RULE 11

Positive and negative surprises affect "best" and "worst" stocks in a diametrically opposite manner.

People are far too confident of their ability to predict complex outcomes in the future. This was shown to be true in many fields from medicine and law to mediation. The stock market, with thousands of constantly shifting company, industry, economic, and political events, certainly ranks among the most formidable areas in which to make forecasts.

Good or bad news, which occurs frequently in markets, results in diametrically opposite movements of "best" and "worst" stocks. When we recall that money managers are considered "stars" if they can outperform markets by 2% or 3% annually over a 5-year period, the 4.1% annual outperformance of the "worst" stocks after all surprises, as measured by price-to-cash flow (shown in Figure 6–1b, with similar results in 6–1a and 6–1c), coupled with the 3.2% underperformance of the "best," is an enormous differential. The disparity, of course, is firmly anchored on investor overconfidence of pinpointing future events. We see then that *surprise has an enormous, predictable, and systematic influence on stock prices.*

Looking more carefully at the charts we also can see that earnings surprises cause two distinct categories of price reactions in both "best" and "worst" stocks. The first I'll call an *event trigger,* and the second, which will be discussed shortly, a *reinforcing event.*

I define an event trigger as unexpected negative news on a stock believed to have excellent prospects, or unexpectedly positive news on a stock believed to have a mediocre outlook. The event trigger results in people looking at the two categories of stocks very differently. They take off their dark or rose-colored glasses. They now evaluate the companies more realistically, and the reappraisal results in a major price change to correct the market's previous overreaction.

There are two types of event triggers. The first is a negative surprise for a favored company, which will drive its stock price down. The second is a positive surprise for an unfavored stock, which pushes its price much higher. The event trigger initiates the process of perceptual change among investors, which can continue for a long time. As has been shown, the process goes on beyond the quarter in which the surprise is reported and through the year following the surprise. In the next section, we'll see it continues for much longer periods.

Event triggers can result from surprises other than earnings. A nonearnings surprise might be the approval by the FDA of an important new drug—or its denial of further testing. Winning or losing a landmark tobacco case would be another. New technology that suddenly obsoletes an important semiconductor would be a third. There could be hundreds of such surprises, any one of which could have a sharp and lasting impact on a stock's price. Although not tested as yet, observation suggests that the impact of such surprises on stock prices would be similar to the impact an earnings surprise has had on the best, worst, and middle groups.

Event triggers are most frequently activated by earnings surprises, however. The first type of event trigger is a negative surprise on a highly regarded company. An example is the 1992 earnings surprise that felled high-flying U.S. Surgical. At the time, it was the largest manufacturer of laparoscopic surgical equipment. Laparoscopic surgery, as you probably know, enormously reduces the dangers of surgery and the time of recovery. It was a rapidly growing medical area with exploding earnings and an exciting story. The stock soared, trading as high as $108 late in 1992. It then had a number of disappointing earnings surprises and dropped as low as $17 the following year.

Investors now saw not only disappointing earnings, but also rapidly increasing competition from Johnson & Johnson, a slow-down in anticipated growth in the laparoscopic market, and serious questions about the company's senior management. With the strong market and some recovery in earnings, the company has risen to $29 in late 1997, a little over one-third of its previous high. The event trigger resulted in a major and permanent reassessment of the company by investors.

As we saw, investors systematically overrate the futures of such companies. When a negative earnings surprise occurs, people are stunned by news on "best" stocks. Their reaction is to sell—fast!—sending the prices down, often dramatically.

The second type of event trigger is a positive surprise—or a series of positive surprises—for an out-of-favor stock. Investors do not expect positive surprises from companies they consider to have poor outlooks. When they happen, people begin a process of perceptual change. The stocks are reevaluated more positively, and they outperform the market significantly, largely because of the original undervaluations.

Dell Computer, a manufacturer of desktop and notebook computers, is a good example of an event trigger on an out-of-favor stock. The company traded as low as $1¾ in 1993 on a disappointing outlook. Earnings in 1994 came in above forecast for a number of quarters and the stock reacted strongly. By November of that year it more than tripled, rising to $6¼, and continued to move up to $103 by October of 1997.

Investors' perceptions about a company, an industry, or the market itself often do not change with a single positive or negative surprise. Jeffrey Abarbanell and Victor Bernard of the University of Michigan, for example, have studied analyst estimates and find they have been slow to adjust to earnings surprises. Whether the estimate was too high or too low, analysts do not revise them accurately immediately, but take as long as three quarters after the surprise to do so.[8] When the forecasts are too high, they continue to be high for the next nine months, and when they are too low, they continue to be too low for the next three quarters.

As Abarbanell and Bernard put it, analysts "underreact to recent earnings reports." This underreaction generates new surprises, which reinforce investors' changing opinion of a company. If, for example, investors are taken aback by a negative earnings surprise on a favorite stock, and more negative surprises occur in the following quarters (as a result of analysts not revising earnings down enough), people's increasingly poor reappraisal of the company drops the stock even lower. The event trigger in this case continues over a number of quarters. The same is true for a series of positive surprises on an out-of-favor company.[9]

Reinforcing Events

The second category of earnings surprise is what I call *reinforcing events*. Rather than changing investor perceptions about a stock, these surprises reinforce the current beliefs about the company. Since they confirm the current market opinion, they should have much less impact on stock prices. Reinforcing events are defined as positive surprises on favored stocks or negative surprises on out-of-favor stocks. A positive surprise on a favored stock reinforces the previous perception that this is an excellent company. Good companies should do well. If they have positive surprises, it is only to be expected.

In 1994, Duracell was a highly regarded growth stock. It reported a number of positive earnings surprises that year. Once again, however, investors expected a top company to deliver excellent results, and the stock merely kept pace with the market for the year.

Similarly, investors have low expectations for out-of-favor stocks and negative surprises simply reinforce their perceptions of the company. Negative surprises have relatively little impact on their prices in the surprise quarter, and none in the nine months following.

An example of a reinforcing event on an out-of-favor stock was the announcement in late 1994 by KeyCorp of a large unexpected loss from trading in derivatives on interest rate futures. The losses would cancel much or all of its fourth quarter's earnings. The announcements resulted in this stock declining only moderately. The next year it was up over 50%, and another 100% by late 1997. A reinforcing event has only a minimal impact on stock price movements.

Figure 6-4 shows just how different the impact of earnings surprise is on event triggers and reinforcing events for the surprise quarter (on left), as well as for the full year (on right). The figure uses price-to-book value to measure the surprise effect, but measuring by price-to-cash flow or by price-to-earnings ratios results in very similar numbers. The two types of event triggers (negative surprises on favored stocks and positive surprises on out-of-favor stocks) have substantially more impact on stock prices than reinforcing events (positive surprises on favored and negative surprises on out-of-favor issues).

Look first at event triggers in Figure 6-4, the two adjoining columns on the left side of the chart, for both the quarter and the year. We see that

Figure 6-4

The Impact of Event Triggers & Reinforcing Events
Price/Book Value 1973 - 1996

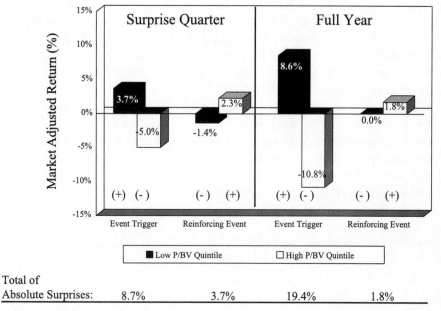

Total of Absolute Surprises:	8.7%	3.7%	19.4%	1.8%

0% = Market Return (3.6% quarterly, 15.6% annually)
All figures are market adjusted.

adding them together, the total price impact is 8.7% (+3.7% and –5.0%) in the surprise quarter. By contrast, adding the reinforcing events together results in a much smaller surprise impact—3.7% (2.3% and –1.4%) for the same quarter. For the full year, we also see that the size of the event triggers more than doubles, resulting in a total impact of 19.4%. Reinforcing events, on the other hand, have a negligible 1.8% impact on prices after one year.

Figure 6–4 demonstrates not only two distinct categories of surprises, event triggers and reinforcing events, but that their response to unanticipated good and bad news is remarkably different. Event triggers result in a perceptual change, which continues through the end of the year, and has a major impact on stock prices.

The effect of reinforcing events on prices, on the other hand, is minor by the end of the 12 months following the surprise. The event trigger moves stock prices about 2½ times as much as the reinforcing events in the quarter of the surprise, and 10 times as much after one year. The chart is statistically significant at the 0.1% level, which means there is only a 1 in 1,000 possibility it could be sheer chance.

The Effects of Surprise Over Time

We have seen the results of surprise on best and worst stocks for up to one year after the surprise is announced. Are there lingering effects beyond that? Figure 6–5, which measures the performance of the best and worst groups of stocks by P/E ratios for five-year periods following an earnings surprise, provides the answer. Let us look first at the two types of event triggers (good news on "worst" stocks and bad news on "best"). The figure indicates that the lowest P/E group showing positive earnings surprises (low P/E positive) outperforms the market in all 20 quarters after the surprises, and records an above-market return of 34.7% for the five-year period. Conversely, the highest P/E group receiving negative surprises (high P/E negative) underperforms in every quarter for the fol-

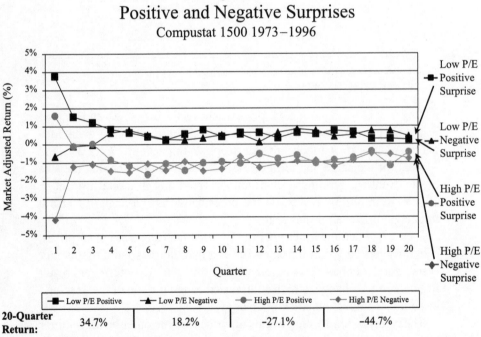

Figure 6–5
Positive and Negative Surprises
Compustat 1500 1973–1996

	Low P/E Positive	Low P/E Negative	High P/E Positive	High P/E Negative
20-Quarter Return:	34.7%	18.2%	-27.1%	-44.7%

0% = Market Return

lowing five years, lagging the market by 44.7% for the full period. As we can see, the differential between these two groups continues to increase significantly through the five years measured.

Is the entire difference in performance between the two types of event triggers caused by earnings surprises? Did the original surprises change investor perceptions permanently? These questions are impossible to answer statistically at this time. We do know that investors were far too confident of their prognostications for both "best" and "worst" stocks, which led to best stocks being significantly overvalued and worst stocks being undervalued. When the dark or rose-colored glasses were removed, perhaps they were swapped for each other. As was also noted earlier, not one but a series of surprises may occur, some in later quarters, including surprises other than analysts' forecast errors, that continue to reinforce the price revaluations.

What we can say, however, is that the enormous market outperformance by the low P/E group,* and the underperformance by the highest quintile, indicate that there certainly had to be an event or a series of events that changed investor perceptions of what were "best" and "worst" stocks.

We also see the effects of reinforcing events. "Worst" stocks with negative surprises (low P/E negative) consistently outperform after the surprise quarter and for the next 19 quarters, while "best" stocks with positive surprises (high P/E positive) just as consistently underperform. Although the differences are not as large as for "best" and "worst" stocks that experienced an event trigger in the surprise quarter, they are still major. "Best" stocks underperformed the market by 27.1% in the full 5-year periods, while "worst" stocks outperformed by 18.2%. (The results for the other two value measures, price-to-cash flow and price-to-book, are again similar.)

The middle group is not shown. However, the long-term findings differ little from those at the end of the first year. Surprise has a major effect only in the quarter the news is announced. After that they perform in line with the market. Overall, positive and negative surprises cancel out, which is pretty much what we should expect, since being in the middle group shows that these stocks are not overvalued or undervalued by much.

---

*As well as similar outperformance by price-to-cash flow and price-to-book value groups, although not shown.

A Surprising Opportunity

Contrarian investment Rule 10 positioned us in out-of-favor stocks to take advantage of analysts' forecast errors and other surprises. We can now go further in delineating the effect of surprises, which will prove an essential tool for the strategies to be outlined shortly. Rule 12 summarizes our findings on surprise:

RULE 12

(A) **Surprises, as a group, improve the performance of out-of-favor stocks, while impairing the performance of favorites.**

(B) **Positive surprises result in major appreciation for out-of-favor stocks, while having minimal impact on favorites.**

(C) **Negative surprises result in major drops in the price of favorites, while having virtually no impact on out-of-favor stocks.**

(D) **The effect of an earnings surprise continues for an extended period of time.**

In this chapter, we have examined the role of surprise and have found that it consistently favors stocks that investors believe have poor outlooks and just as consistently works against those believed to be *la crème*. Because of the frequency of earnings surprises demonstrated in the last chapter, we know it is a powerful force acting to reverse previous over- or undervaluations of stocks.

Just how important surprise and the resulting change in investor expectations are in developing powerful investment strategies will be shown front and center in the next chapter. It's time to roll up our sleeves and sit down at a table in the green wing.

PART III

THE WORLD OF CONTRARIAN INVESTING

7

Contrarian Investment Strategies

WHEN the British marched out to surrender to General Washington and his French allies at Yorktown, scabbards pointed up and rifles pointed down, their military bands played a popular tune of the day, "The World Turned Upside Down." And so it must have seemed to this crisp, smartly dressed army surrendering to a ragtag militia from these insignificant colonies. How could the most powerful nation on Earth be reduced to such an ignoble outcome? Many a money manager and other professional investor immaculately dressed in Armani suits, in their well-appointed offices, flanked by the latest and most powerful market technology of the day, must wonder the same thing. How can they have performed so dismally, when they buy the top research and investment advice, which naturally must lead them to the "best" stocks?

It's a real puzzle.

But . . . are the stocks the experts like really the ones to buy? We have seen that the answer is a strong no. The favorite stocks of analysts and money managers were consistently punished by earnings surprises, while the stocks nobody loved or wanted just as consistently benefited from them. Investor enthusiasm often results in popular stocks becoming overpriced, while the lack of it dumps them into the bargain basement. Earnings and other surprises result in a reevaluation of both groups and more realistic pricing.

This is certainly a large, critical piece of the puzzle, but how do we fit it into a practical investment strategy? After all, we're not just trying to analyze market dynamics, we're seeking to learn how to profit from them. For a change, rather than trying to build a deductive case, I'm going to put the answer right on the table for your inspection. While I'm at it, we should go ahead and make the next contrarian investment rule.

RULE 13

Favored stocks underperform the market, while out-of-favor companies outperform the market, *but the reappraisal often happens slowly, even glacially.*

It is this reevaluation process that is the key to large and consistent profits in the marketplace. For decades, investor reaction to "best" and "worst" stocks has been consistent and predictable. And here we come to the bottom line for the practical reader. Investor behavior is so predictable, in this respect, that the average reader can take advantage of it. There are proven yet uncomplicated contrarian strategies that should allow you to outperform the market handily, with relatively little risk.

Sounds a little heady, doesn't it? Now let's start at the beginning and see exactly what's behind these assertions. A bit of intellectual discussion, if you will, to reveal the elemental structure, function, and statistical justifications of the four variations on the contrarian strategies that have been highly successful to date. Using our "key," you'll see how the pieces of the puzzle rapidly fall into place—although I'm afraid it won't get you a discount on one of those Armani suits.

The World Turned Upside Down

What seemed apparent from our review of expert forecasts is that the companies they liked the best tended to be the wrong ones to buy. Therefore, ask another question: Should you avoid the stocks the experts or the crowd are pursuing and pursue the ones they are avoiding? The answer, as we shall see, is an unqualified yes. We can document the consistent success of these investment strategies going back sixty years—strategies that dramatically oppose conventional wisdom—and the reasons they work.

For the findings show that companies the market expects the best futures for, as measured by the price/earnings, price-to-cash flow, price-to-book value, and price-to-dividend ratios, have consistently done the worst, while the stocks believed to have the most dismal futures have always done the best. The strategy is not without an element of black humor. In fact, to the true believers at the shrines of efficient markets or other contemporary investment methods, the approach may appear to be a form of Satan worship: the best investments turn out "bad," and the bad ones turn out "good."

However, the findings are not in the least magical. Most investors do not recognize the immense difficulty of predicting earnings and economic events, and when forecasting methods fail, a predictable reaction occurs.

Here we confront the main irony: *One of the most obvious and consistent variables that can be harnessed into a workable investment strategy is the continuous overreaction of man himself to companies he considers to have excellent or mundane prospects.* This works just as surely with the investor today as it has with investors in all markets of the past.

In Visibility We Trust

As we have seen, estimating a company's outlook years into the future is an article of faith among Wall Street experts. The clearer the company's prospects and the better they look, the better the "visibility." Companies with the clearest "visibility"—i.e., best earnings prospects and fastest growth rates—are normally accorded high valuations (whether evaluated by price-to-earnings, price-to-cash flow, price-to-book value, or price-to-dividends). Similarly, those companies with poor or lackluster visibility are banished to the lower valuation tiers.

In order to make such evaluations, forecasts extending growth well into the future must be made with extreme accuracy. We know, however, that the reliability of these forecasts is very low. We also know, when earnings of a favorite company fall below the forecast, the surprise, even if it is minute, has a devastating effect on its stock prices. Not surprisingly, investment strategies *based on precise estimates* have performed erratically, to say the least.

There are many reasons why companies show outstanding earnings and sales growth for years and then slow down. Sometimes it is simply accounting gimmickry (which we looked at in chapter 3). Or a company might have a short-term competitive advantage, which the market, enraptured by the high profit margins and earnings, interprets as a long-term trend.

Today, a large percentage of the hundreds of high-flying, aggressive growth stocks—franchising, Internet access, telecommunications—fall into this category. AST Research was a rapidly growing manufacturer of IBM-compatible desk-top and notebook computers. AST's "edge" was its direct marketing to the public, thus avoiding the middleman and providing low-cost products. Rapid technology change and competition

caught up with it within a few years, and its earnings plummeted from a peak of $2.61 a share in 1992 to a loss of $3.00 in 1996, accompanied by a drop in the price from $40 to $5.

The more successful a company becomes, the more difficult it is to continue the record: Competition, governmental controls, and increasing market saturation all play a role in slowing growth. Too, a management team skilled at running a rapidly growing $50 or $100 million corporation may be lost at the $300 to $500 million sales level. Products and markets seemingly invulnerable to competition are suddenly inundated by it. Untouchable patents are circumvented by new discoveries. Costs cannot be controlled and prices cannot be raised, so profit margins are squeezed. Markets that appeared open for years of brisk growth become saturated. Political or economic events occur, such as an oil embargo or a sharp recession, totally beyond the control of even the most astute management, wreaking havoc in the marketplace. History constantly reminds us that in an uncertain world there is no visibility of prospects. Future earnings cannot then be predicted with accuracy. As we have seen with high-expectation companies that have negative surprises, the best companies can be terribly overpriced and can be drastically reappraised.

The term "best," used by so many professional and individual investors, also filters out the inherent risk of the situation. Conversely, the lowest-visibility stocks have been shown to be significantly underpriced and, when they have positive surprises, are subject to sharp upward reappraisals. Just as the inherent risk is understated for high-expectation situations, it is often exaggerated, sometimes dramatically, for low-expectation stocks. This puts the master key of the book in our hands— why the investment strategies that we'll examine work remarkably well over time.

In the Beginning . . .

Beginning in the 1960s, researchers began to wonder if visibility—that crucial pillar of modern security analysis—was actually as solid as generally believed. The original studies were done with price-earnings ratios because of their availability in the early databases. One of the first of these researchers asked: "How accurate is the P/E ratio as a measure of subsequent market performance?"

Francis Nicholson, then with the Provident National Bank, was the interrogator. In one comprehensive study done in 1968, measuring the relative performance of high versus low P/E stocks, he analyzed 189

Figure 7–1

Francis Nicholson's Pioneer Study
Percentage Gains, 1937–62

Average Price Appreciation Percentages Over Total Period

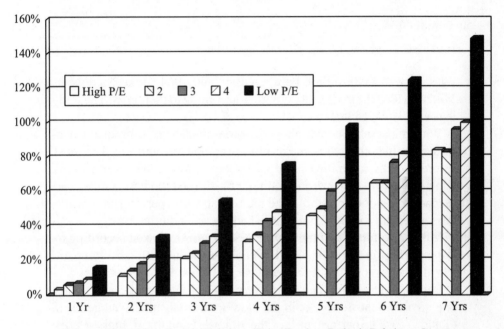

Source: Adapted from Francis Nicholson, "Price-Earnings Ratios in Relation to Investment
Results," *Financial Analysts Journal* (January–February 1968).

companies of trust company quality in 18 industries over the 25 years
between 1937 and 1962.[1] The results are given in Figure 7–1.

Nicholson divided the stocks into five equal groups solely according
to their P/E rankings. These quintiles were rearranged by their P/E rankings for periods of one to seven years. Recasting the quintiles annually
on the basis of new P/E information resulted in the stocks most out of
favor showing a 16% annual rate of appreciation over the total time
span. Conversely, switching in the highest P/Es on the same basis resulted in only 3% annual appreciation over the period. Although the performance discrepancies were reduced with longer holding periods, even
after the original portfolios were held for seven years the lowest 20%
did almost twice as well as the highest.

Similar results were turned up by Paul Miller, Jr., who used as his
database the companies on the Compustat 1800 Industrial Tapes with

Table 7–1
AVERAGE PRICE INCREASE PER YEAR, 1948–1964

P/E Quintile	Price Increase
1st (highest P/E)	7.7%
2nd	9.2%
3rd	12.0%
4th	12.8%
5th (lowest P/E)	18.4%

SOURCE: DREXEL & CO., PHILADELPHIA, MONTHLY REVIEW, 1966.

sales of over $150 million between 1948 and 1964.[2] Like Nicholson, Miller divided the stocks into quintiles according to their P/Es. The findings are displayed in Table 7–1.

With remarkable consistency, investors misjudged subsequent performance. In both studies, the results are completely uniform. The most favored stocks (quintile 1) sharply underperformed the other groups, while the least popular group (quintile 5), showed the best results. The second most popular quintile had the second worst performance, while the second most unpopular quintile had the second best results.

Miller also found that the lowest 20% of stocks, ranked according to P/Es, did best in 12 of the next 17 years. The highest 20%, by comparison, did best in only 1 subsequent year and worst in 8.

Benjamin Graham's *The Intelligent Investor* cites a third study, this one involving the 30 stocks in the Dow Jones Industrial Average itself (Table 7–2). The performance of the 10 lowest and the 10 highest P/Es in the group, and of the combined 30 stocks in the industrial average,

Table 7–2
AVERAGE ANNUAL PERCENTAGE GAIN OR LOSS ON THE DOW JONES INDUSTRIAL AVERAGE
1937–1969

Period	10 Low-Multiple Issues	10 High-Multiple Issues	30 DJIA Stocks
1937–42	– 2.2%	– 10.0%	– 6.3%
1943–47	17.3%	8.3%	14.9%
1948–52	16.4%	4.6%	9.9%
1953–57	20.9%	10.0%	13.7%
1958–62	10.2%	– 3.3%	3.6%
1963–69	8.0%	4.6%	4.0%

SOURCE: BENJAMIN GRAHAM, *THE INTELLIGENT INVESTOR,* 4TH ED., P. 80. COPYRIGHT © 1973 BY HARPER & ROW PUBLISHERS, INC. REPRINTED BY PERMISSION OF HARPERCOLLINS PUBLISHERS, INC.

was measured over set periods between 1937 and 1969. In each time span, the low P/Es did better than the market and the high P/Es did worse.

The study also calculated the results of investing $10,000 in either the high- or low-multiple groups in the Industrial Average in 1937 and switching every 5 years into the highest P/Es (in the first case) and the lowest P/Es (in the latter). Ten thousand dollars invested in the lowest P/Es this way in 1937 would have increased to $66,866 by the end of 1962. Invested in the highest P/Es, the $10,000 would have appreciated to only $25,437. Finally, $10,000 in the Dow Jones Average itself would have grown to $35,600 by 1962. (Graham's findings have recently been recycled into a hot new investment strategy, "The Dogs of the Dow.")

A number of other studies in the 1960s came up with similar findings. The conclusion of these studies, of course, is that low-P/E stocks were distinctly superior investments over an almost 30-year period. But theories, like sacred cows, die hard. The findings created little stir at the time.[3]

More Nasty, Ugly Little Facts

If the low P/E results were analyzed at all, they were criticized. For one thing, the growth school has always had a major following among investors. Many institutional investors could not bring themselves to believe the efficacy of the findings. After all, like the studies that discredited earnings forecasts, these findings did seem cavalierly to toss aside our years of practice (or perhaps brainwashing) to the contrary. When I published a paper in early 1976 summarizing some of the previous research, a number of professionals told me that such information was only history: "Markets of the 1970s are very different."

The evidence, of course, was a transitory enigma to our financial friends in academe who, in the late 1960s, were tightening the final nuts and bolts of the formidable efficient market hypothesis. According to this academic-launched dreadnought, such results simply could not exist. Why? Because rational, profit-seeking investors would not allow them. Clever investors would immediately jump into the better performing, lower P/E stocks, and stay clear of the trickier high P/E multiples until all the extra profits were extracted.

Further EMH criticism asserted that low-P/E stocks were systematically riskier (in the parlance, had higher betas) and therefore ought to provide higher returns. For the coup de grâce, methodological criticisms of the studies were wheeled into action. They were mostly hairsplitting and not convincing—at least to me. But, recalling Einstein's dictum that the theory determines the observations, the evidence could not stand if the dreadnought was to proceed merrily along annihilating traditional investment practice.

Buying low-P/E stocks appeared successful in studies of past performance. As a practical matter, it had worked for me—no small inducement to belief. Consequently, I thought it might be interesting to update the findings, which I did, first in *Psychology and the Stock Market* (1977) and second in *Contrarian Investment Strategy* (in 1980). Watching the collapse of the high-P/E concept stocks through the early 1970s and of the entire two-tier market in 1973–1974, I saw that things had not changed much. The studies again demonstrated the low P/E case, as indicated by the results of the second study, from August 1968 to August of 1977, shown here.

The experimental design tried to deal as thoroughly as possible with the problems of the previous findings.[4] The sample, the largest to that time, was constructed from the Compustat 1800 Industrial Tapes, which contain data on the largest publicly held companies in the country. Included in the sample of 1,251 issues were 70% of the common stocks listed on the New York Stock Exchange, as well as large companies on the AMEX and over-the-counter.[5] The study covered the mid-1968–1977 period. The total return (capital gains or losses and dividends paid) was measured in each quarter of the study.[6]

I used a large number of different holding periods to get as many comparisons as possible of the performance of the various P/E groups. Portfolios were recast according to new P/E information as frequently as every three, six, or nine months, or held unchanged for as long as nine years.

Table 7–3 gives the results for the entire period. Even a glance at the record indicates the superior results of the low-multiple groups over the length of the study. Recasting the quintiles annually according to latest 12-month earnings showed dramatic results. Had an investor put $10,000 evenly in the bottom 20% of P/Es at the end of August 1968 and switched yearly thereafter to keep in the lowest P/Es continuously, he or she would have seen their capital increase $10,326 before commissions through August 31, 1977. These returns occurred during an extremely poor period for the market! (The averages returned only 4.8% annually.) By comparison, had someone switched every 12 months on the same basis into the best stocks, the highest P/Es (quintile 1), his or her $10,000 would have decreased to $9,733. Over the life of the study, the lowest P/E stocks more than doubled, while the most-favored group was still near the starting gate.

Table 7–3

A WORKABLE INVESTMENT STRATEGY
Annualized Compound Rates of Return
August 1968–August 1977 (Full Period Study)

Stocks Ranked by *P/E Multiples*			*Holding* *Original* *Portfolio for*
	Switching After Each		
Quintiles	*1 Year*	*3 Years*	*9 Years*
1st (highest)	−0.3%	−0.9%	0.8%
2nd	2.5%	2.9%	4.3%
3rd	4.8%	4.9%	4.1%
4th	7.7%	6.8%	6.2%
5th (lowest)	8.2%	9.3%	7.2%
		Average return of sample: 4.8%	

Even buying and holding the same stocks over the length of the study distinctly favored the low P/Es. Ten thousand dollars in the bottom 20% of stocks in August 1968 held unchanged to August 1977 would have become $18,618, while $10,000 in the top 20% only grew by $743, or 8/10 of 1% annually. Although the superiority of the bottom over the top group is the most impressive, the second lowest always did far better than the second highest.

The findings once again show the clear-cut advantage of a low P/E strategy. The study covered the two-tier market of 1970–1972, the bear market of 1973–1974 (the worst in the postwar period) and the subsequent recovery. It did not matter whether the investor started near a market top or a market bottom; superior returns were provided in any phase of the market cycle.

The cycle we measured showed the widest fluctuations of any in the postwar period. The average multiple of the S&P varied sharply—from a high of 21 to a low of 7—yet the findings consistently and dramatically supported the strategy of buying and holding out-of-favor stocks. The results were certainly more striking than I had expected. If anything, they indicated that patterns of investor behavior—and error—are far more systematic than one would have believed.

Through the 1980s to the mid-1990s, I completed (with various collaborators) half a dozen separate studies on low P/E strategies, most of which were published in *Forbes*.* One study measured the 1,800 largest

---

* One academic study in the *Financial Analysts Journal* was done in collaboration with Mike Berry.

companies on the Compustat tapes between 1963 and 1985. The lowest P/E quintile returned 20.7% annually against 10.4% for the highest.[7] Another divided the 6,000 stocks on the Compustat tapes into five equal groups according to market size, for 21 years ending in 1989. Each group was then divided again into five subgroups according to P/E rankings. The low P/E groups handily outperformed the high P/E groups for all market sizes, ranging from the smallest at around $50 million in market value to the largest at nearly $6 billion.[8]

Another study measured how low price-to-cash flow performed for the 22 years ending March 31, 1985, using 750 large companies. The results are shown in Table 7–4. The stocks were again separated into five equal groups and ranked each year according to the ratio of price-to-cash flow.[9] As the chart shows, the most out-of-favor stocks—lowest price-to-cash flow—almost doubled the annual performance of the favorites through this extensive period.[10]

But what of some of the past criticisms? Did any of them still have validity?[11] Our experimental design adjusted for these criticisms, and still provided the results shown above.

All this has been reconfirmed by other research in the late 1970s and early 1980s. Three carefully prepared studies by Sanjoy Basu came up with similar results.[12] In his study published in the *Journal of Finance* in June 1977, Basu used a database of 1,400 firms from the New York Stock Exchange between August 1956 and August 1971. He took 750

Table 7–4

CONTRARIAN CASH FLOW

Long term—over the last 22 years, Apr. 1, 1963–Mar. 31, 1985—investors who gauged value by cash flow instead of, say, earnings alone would have fared well.			Over the last seven years—Jan. 1, 1978–Mar. 31, 1985—a particularly strong market period, the practice also would have worked well.		
Price to cash flow by group	*Total return*	*Appreciation*	*Dividend*	*Price to cash flow by group*	*Total return*	*Appreciation*	*Dividend*
Lowest	20.1%	14.6%	5.5%	Lowest	27.4%	21.0%	6.4%
Second-lowest	14.3	8.0	6.3	Second-lowest	20.1	12.2	7.9
Middle	8.7	3.2	5.5	Middle	17.4	11.4	6.0
Second-highest	8.0	3.8	4.2	Second-highest	19.4	15.3	4.1
Highest	10.7	8.2	2.5	Highest	16.5	14.2	2.3

SOURCE: *FORBES,* JUNE 16, 1986.

companies that had year-ends of December 31 and turned over the port-folios annually, using prices on April 1 of the following year. Like most of the previous studies, he divided the stocks into quintiles according to P/E rankings. The results (again using total return) are shown in Table 7–5.

Basu's conclusions were similar to all the others: "The average an-nual rates of return decline (to some extent monotonically) as one moves from low P/E to high P/E portfolios."

Basu found, as we did, that the low P/E stocks provided superior re-turns, and were also somewhat less risky. Again, using his words: "However, contrary to capital market theory, the higher returns on the low P/E portfolios were not associated with higher levels of systematic risk; the systematic risks of portfolios D and E [the lowest] were lower than those for A, A* and B [the highest]."[13]

This and subsequent work, updated and adjusted for previous criti-cisms through the mid-1980s, added many links to a chain extending over 40 years, documenting the superior performance of low P/E issues.

Whatever Took So Long?

Given the weight of the evidence, you'd think that contrarian value ap-proaches would have captured the imagination (and wallets) of investors long ago. By the 1990s, perhaps we should have been looking back at the golden age, when only a handful of pioneers reaped the rewards and

Table 7–5

PERFORMANCE OF STOCKS ACCORDING TO P/E RANKING
APRIL 1957–MARCH 1971

P/E Quintile	Average Annual Return (%)	BETA (systematic risk)
A (highest)	9.3	1.1121
A*	9.6	1.0579
B	9.3	1.0387
C	11.7	0.9678
D	13.6	0.9401
E (lowest)	16.3	0.9866

A = highest P/E quintile
A* = highest P/E quintile, excluding stocks with negative earnings

SOURCE: SANJOY BASU, "INVESTMENT PERFORMANCE OF COMMON STOCKS IN RELATION TO THEIR PRICE/EARNINGS RATIOS: A TEST OF THE EFFICIENT MARKET HYPOTHESIS," *JOURNAL OF FINANCE*, 32 (JUNE 1977) P. 67.

only the favored few knew what a powerful tool these strategies were. But that's not the case. Even today, contrarians are a distinct minority— and, remarkably, are likely to remain so.

One reason for the situation is historical. You'll remember how EMH swept the land and banished the heathen from Wall Street. As the new orthodoxy, EMH had everything to gain from a long and prosperous reign. Not to mention a good deal to lose if competing ideas shouldered their way onto the Street. That, of course, is as much innate human psychology, as any of the other crowd reactions we will examine.

In the late 1970s and through most of the 1980s this work did not stand tall with efficient market advocates, particularly those residing at the high shrine of market fundamentalism, the University of Chicago. As a leading heretic, I often experienced the wrath of the true believers. My work came under sharp attack, and my *Forbes* columns even had the distinction of being assigned to classes of students to hammer apart. On several occasions my unfortunate editors had sets of twenty or more letters attacking the work, which they on occasion good-naturedly published.

With the publication of my books and additional articles the barrage intensified. Letters attacked every part of the findings, saving some choice remarks for the author.

None found any statistical fault with the work, but questioned the Neanderthal beliefs of a writer who couldn't understand the overwhelming sweep and beauty of efficient market thinking.

When I submitted a paper reporting the findings to the *Financial Analysts Journal*, it was not accepted or rejected, but left in some purgatory reserved for ideas that don't fit the prevailing paradigm.

I presented a low P/E paper at a 1984 conference of leading psychologists and economists, only to watch a leading exponent of EMH slam my paper on the table and bark that "these results are impossible." (The slammer is now writing a paper on contrarian strategies.)

The low-P/E anomaly was large enough to continue to attract attention from academe and Wall Street. In academe the work was also dismissed using the old academic standby, risk measurement. Low-P/E stocks might provide higher returns, but they were far more risky, said the critics. Rational investors accepted the higher risk only by demanding higher returns.

The Great Discovery

Through the 1980s, Wall Street became increasingly interested in contrarian investment strategies. With continuing improvements in databases, confirmation that these strategies worked grew stronger. And stronger yet.

In 1983, two researchers wrote a low P/E article, similar to my paper that the journal refused to publish. The academics did not reference my work (possibly to avoid controversy with the efficient market theorists), although they consulted me on numerous occasions in writing their paper. The tide continued to gain strength. Dennis Stattman and Rosenberg, Reid, and Lanstein, for example, found that low price-to-book value outperformed high price-to-book value and the market.[14] At the same time, the evidence mounted that beta had no value as a predictor of stock prices. Though the economic fundamentalists attempted to rationalize away their existence for almost three decades, these exasperating methods just did not have the good manners to disappear. That contrarian strategies worked and beta did not was a death knell for efficient markets.

What was a poor apostle of the new religion to do? Since neither of these results could be denied, the answer of course was to be the first to discover them. That is exactly what Eugene Fama, the apostle of efficient markets, did. In the 1990s, academics firmly planted their own flag on the newfound world of contrarian strategies.

In a revolutionary paper—that boldly thrust thirty years into the past—Professor Fama discovered precisely what Francis Nicholson, other researchers of the 1960s, Sanjoy Basu, Stattman, Rosenberg, et al., and I had found in the seventies and eighties: contrarian strategies worked. Worse yet, beta didn't. The three decades of stating that contrarian strategies provided better returns because they were riskier were swept away by the discovery that beta, the risk measure the apostle and his disciples used, was valueless.

To be fair, Fama and French do reference Basu, Stattman, and Rosenberg, et al., in passing, as well as Ball,[15] who argued low P/E is a catchall for all risk that cannot be explicitly separated or even found. Ball's explanation was widely accepted by efficient marketers for years.

Ball's paper is not unlike the phlogiston theory of heat popular in the eighteenth century. According to the theory, some elements are more combustible than others because they contain more phlogiston, while others are less so because they contain smaller amounts. Phlogiston was weightless, odorless, and could not be detected, but nevertheless it was there. How else could combustion occur (or how could low P/E strategies beat the market if they were not risky, regardless of the fact that said risk could not be detected)? Circular and fallacious reasoning, yes, but Ball, Fama, et al. used precisely this logic to defend EMH. In both cases, the theorists defend themselves against phenomena they cannot explain through the creation of ingenious fudge-factors. (The efficient market hypothesis, as we will see in the final chapter, has a grab bag full of these defenses.)

The landmark 1992 paper by Eugene Fama, coauthored with Kenneth French, showed that the lowest price-to-book value ratios, price-to-earnings ratios, and small capitalization stocks provide the highest returns over time.[16] Figure 7–2 provides Fama and French's price-to-book value results. The sample used an average of 2,300 companies annually from the Compustat tapes. Stock returns are shown in quintiles by price-to-book value (P/BV), which are recast annually. The highest price-to-book value stocks are in column 3 and the lowest or most unpopular in column 1. As the figure indicates, low price-to-book value (20.5%) provides more than double the annual return of high P/BV for the entire

Figure 7-2

Fama & French 1992
CRSP & Compustat Data 1963–1990
Price/Book Value

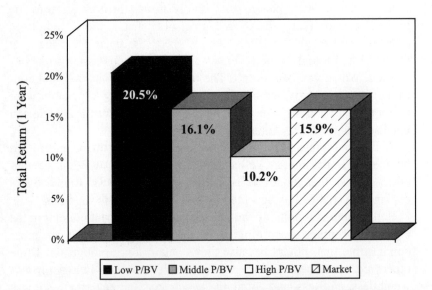

Source of data: E. Fama and K. French, "The Cross-Section of Expected Stock Returns," *Journal of Finance*, 47 (June 1992): pp. 427–465.

sample through the life of the study. Low P/BV outperforms the market by 4.6% annually on average, while high P/BV underperforms by 5.7%.

Fama downplayed the low P/E effect in an interview, saying the reason low P/E stocks do well is that so many of them are the same stocks as are in the price-to-book value sample. One could say precisely the opposite and be just as correct. As *Fortune* concluded, "Some might call that academic hairsplitting."[17] Since Fama had resisted the low-P/E effect for almost thirty years, another not unreasonable conclusion is, it may be a symptom of academic face-saving.

What about beta, the "phlogiston factor" used to discredit the higher returns of low P/E and low price-to-book value? Beta was no longer defensible. Fama and French found no relationship between beta and return. EMH gospel asserted that a stock with a higher beta should provide higher returns; it did not. Nor did lower-risk stocks provide inferior results. According to Fama and French, beta did not account for the disparity in return between favored and unfavored stocks.*

The blessing of contrarian strategies by the high priests at Chicago now allowed the investment world to eat what had been forbidden fruit. Value strategies were looked at with new reverence, and value indexes were introduced by Standard and Poor's, Frank Russell, and scads of other consultants.

Fortified by Professor Fama's findings, other researchers now found the courage to spring boldly into the past. Lakonishok, Shleifer, and Vishny, in late 1994, went a step further and "discovered" contrarian strategies in an article published in the *Journal of Finance*, "Contrarian Investment, Extrapolation, and Risk."[18] The three professors used the thousands of companies on the Compustat tapes (the CRSP tapes were used for pricing) from April 1968 to April 1990, selecting only stocks on the NYSE or the AMEX to help correct for stock selection bias.[19]

Lakonishok et al. measured the performance of the three important value strategies we've looked at and came up with similar results. Figure 7–3 shows the annual performance of stocks as measured by their P/E ratios. The results were calculated by recasting the returns of the large sample annually. Low P/Es significantly outperform high P/Es and the market averages. The same is true for the returns of price-to-cash flow, and price-to-book value (not shown). This all adds up to an overwhelming case for the superior performance of contrarian strategies.

---

* We will look at the question of how to assess risk in more detail in chapter 14.

Figure 7–3

Lakonishok, Shleifer, and Vishny 1994
CRSP and Compustat Data 1968 – 1990
Price/Earnings

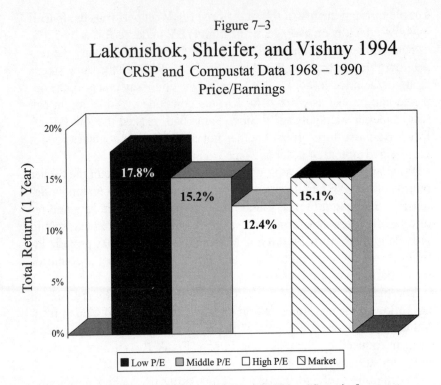

Source: Adapted from J. Lakonishok, A. Shleifer, and R. Vishny, "Contrarian Investment,
Extrapolation and Risk," *Journal of Finance*, 49 (December 1994), pp. 1541–1578.

The Last Nail

These pesky contrarian strategies, then, have proved watertight for a lot
longer than the efficient market hypothesis. In fact, they have been getting stronger with each passing year.

The good news for you is that this wave of discoveries provides
strong evidence that there are consistent, high-odds ways to beat the
market. The methods also protect your capital in a bear market, as I'll
demonstrate shortly. It sounds a little like having your cake and eating
it, too, but there are good reasons why these strategies continue to work
for disciplined investors. (That's why the list of 41 rules—all based on
investor psychological failings—is a critical reminder.)

As we have seen, there are a number of contrarian strategies besides
low P/E that work just fine. Low price-to-cash flow and low price-to-
book value are both potent tools for beating the market. Some of my recent work demonstrates that buying stocks with high dividend yields
has been successful in outperforming the averages. Beating the market

Figure 7-4
Four Flavors of Value
1970 - 1996

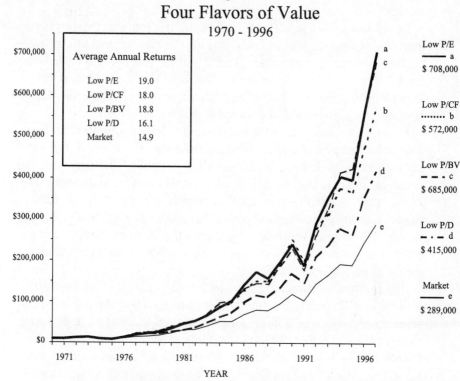

* Initial Investment of Ten Thousand Dollars in 1970 with Annual Rebalancing

isn't easy. Remember, according to Vanguard's John C. Bogle and the performance figures in chapter 1, only about 10% of managers are able to accomplish this in any decade.

Figure 7–4, taken from a study I did in collaboration with Eric Lufkin, shows how effective contrarian value strategies have been for the 27 years ending December 31, 1996. The study measures the Compustat 1500—the 1,500 largest stocks publicly traded. Four separate value measures were used: low P/E, price-to-book value (P/BV), price-to-cash flow (P/CF), and highest yield (lowest price-to-dividend or P/D). For each measure, stocks were divided into quintiles strictly according to P/E, P/BV, P/CF, and price-to-dividend, and the results were calculated annually throughout the study. The chart shows the returns against market using each of these strategies for the 27-year period.

Value strategies work with a vengeance! All four outperform the averages, and the returns of three of the strategies are outstanding. Ten thousand dollars invested in the bottom 20% of P/Es in the Compustat 1500 in 1970 would be worth $708,000 at the end of 1996 (all figures include reinvested dividends), about 2½ times the $289,000 return of the market.

Low price-to-cash flow (P/CF), taken strictly from the statistics available from Compustat (thus excluding all the high octane adjustments claimed to soup up performance), also worked just fine. Low price-to-book value (P/BV), a favorite of Benjamin Graham's, was a hair's breadth behind low P/E, but ahead of the other two strategies for the period and sharply ahead of the market.

Finally, let's move on to the price-to-dividend investment strategy. This value method is a little different from the other three. Normally, high dividend yields are found in utility and other industry groups, which are not expected to have rapid appreciation. On the opposite side of the scale, stocks that pay small dividends or none at all are usually found in rapidly growing industries. Instead of paying dividends, the money is held back to finance rapid growth. There has always been a good deal of controversy about whether stocks with high dividend yields outperform the averages.

The answer is surprising. High-yield stocks out-distanced the market by 44%—or 1.5% per year, although trailing the other three value measures. Ironically, though large numbers of investors buy large dividend payers for income, this method is probably most suitable for tax-free accounts. In a high tax bracket, the performance advantage over the market will decline fairly significantly, because a large part of the return is dividends, which are taxable.

Another reasonable question is, how did the favorite stocks perform by the same yardsticks? Badly. Regardless of which value measure I used, none of the favorites came close to beating the market over the 27-year period. Ten thousand dollars invested in the highest P/E group returned $137,000, only 47% of the $289,000 return of the market. The same amount in the highest price-to-cash flow category and highest price-to-book value returned $99,600 and $117,000, respectively. It was just as bad for the low-yield and no-yield group. Ten thousand dollars invested in this sector returned $102,000, a dismal 35% of the market return.

But the story doesn't end here. Most investors want more than just to increase their nest egg in a rising market. As important, they would like to keep it intact when the bear growls. Morningstar, Lipper, and The Forbes Annual Mutual Funds Survey, among others, for example, rank mutual funds on how they perform through several bear markets.

To find out whether our contrarian strategies worked in down markets, we measured the return of the value stocks in each of the four categories for all down quarters in the study and then averaged them. As

Figure 7-5

When the Bear Growls
Bear Market Returns 1970 - 1996

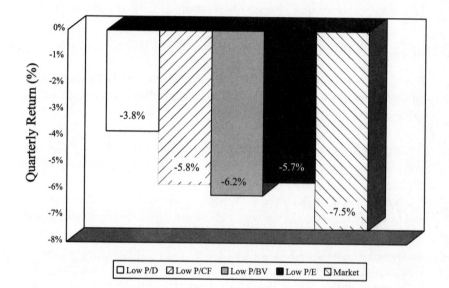

Figure 7–5 shows, the value strategies all did better than the averages in the down markets, through the same period (1970–1996).

While the market dropped 7.5% in the average down quarter, low P/E, price-to-cash flow and price-to-book value all fell less, under 6.2%. The best performers, as you might expect, were the high yield stocks, declining only 3.8%, or half as much as the market.

As you also probably guessed, the high-P/E, high-P/CF, high-P/BV, and low-yield stocks were hit hard. High-P/E, high-P/BV, and high-P/CF were down about 9½%, 2% more than the market averages. The worst returns by far were the stocks paying low or no dividend, which were down 12.2% quarterly, versus 7.5% for the market.

Value stocks, then, not only provide higher returns in a rising market, but also star on the defense. The value strategies, originally presented by Ben Graham and other market pioneers, played out at least as well, and perhaps better, than they would have imagined.

Summing It Up

The consistency of these studies is truly remarkable. Over almost every period measured, the stocks considered to have the best prospects fared significantly worse than the contrarian stocks, using the same criteria. This leads us to another general observation, or rule, if you like:

RULE 14

Buy solid companies currently out of market favor, as measured by their low price-to-earnings, price-to-cash flow or price-to-book value ratios, or by their high yields.

You might wonder: If these strategies do so well, why doesn't everyone use them? This lands us smack in the realm of investor psychology (or Behavioral Finance, as it is now called by economists).

Though the statistics drag us toward the value camp, our emotions just as surely tug us the other way. People are captivated by exciting new concepts. The lure of hitting a home run on a hot new idea overwhelms caution. The sizzle and glitz of an initial public offering like a Planet Hollywood at 140 times earnings and 13 times revenues, or a Spyglass, an Internet search engine designer priced at 175 times estimated earnings, is just too great.[20]

While these are extreme examples of investor evaluation run amok, they show why value strategies have worked so well over the years. People pay for concept, whether in the absurd cases of Planet Hollywood or Spyglass, or in consistently overpricing the trendy industries of the day. Investors just as surely want to stay well away from companies whose outlooks seem poor.

Most investors have a negative reaction to contrarian stocks. Recall that these companies violate just about every idea of proper investment theory. "Do you know what's down there?" a major money manager once asked me, shaking his head in disapproval, "How can any prudent man look at companies like these with such unthinkably poor visibility?"

The favored stocks, on the other hand, present the best visibility money can buy. How, then, can one recommend such a reversal of course?

The psychological consistency of the error is remarkable. There are, of course, excellent stocks that justify their price-to-earnings ratios, and others that deserve the slimmest of multiples. But, as the evidence indicates, these are relatively few, and the chances of recognizing them are very small.

Contrarian strategies succeed because investors do not know their limitations as forecasters. As long as investors believe they can pinpoint the future of favored and out-of-favor stocks, you should be able to make good returns on contrarian strategies. Human nature being what it is, this edge should continue for a few years longer.

We have seen how consistently contrarian strategies have worked for investors over the years. The good news for you is that this wave of discoveries provides strong evidence that there are consistent high-odds ways to beat the market. Next let's turn to how we can use these contrarian strategies to crank up portfolio returns.

8

Boosting Portfolio Profits

IF YOU'VE felt a bit that you've been "hitting the books" in the last chapter or two, then what is next should be the change of pace you need. This is going to be a discussion with a practical and profitable mission: how to use contrarian strategies to boost portfolio results. We are going to put the theory and statistical studies we've looked at to work. It's important to understand the ideas, for as with a good college course, it's not the rote information we cram that does any good, but how we learn to apply critical thinking to the subject matter.

How can you build a portfolio that should easily outdistance the market, while providing better protection when the bear growls? Since a good sell discipline is one of the hardest things to develop, what guidelines should you use to sell? The rules I'll add in this chapter and the next, while certainly not guaranteed to get you out at the top (if you know of any that do, please write) have a high probability of success. But, before figuring out when to sell to protect our profits, let's figure out what to buy. Fortunately, there are four proven ways to do this.

Strategy #1: Low P/E

The low P/E strategy is the oldest and best documented of all the contrarian strategies, and the one most used by market professionals today. Although there are many ways to calculate a P/E ratio, the most common is to take reported earnings for a company (before nonrecurring gains or losses) for the last 12 months and then divide them into price. The strategy has outperformed in both up and down markets since the mid-1930s, and likely will for a good deal longer.

Figure 8–1 shows the returns of the low P/E strategy for the 27 years ending December 31, 1996, using the largest 1,500 companies on the Compustat tapes.[1] The return the investor receives each year is broken down into its two basic components—capital appreciation and dividends.

The stocks are sorted in the usual manner into five equal groups in each quarter of the study, strictly according to their P/E rankings, and the returns are annualized.[2]

Figure 8–1 once again demonstrates the superior performance of the low P/E group. Over the 27 years of the study, the bottom group averaged a return of 19.0% annually, compared to 15.3% for the market (the last set of bars on the right) and 12.3% for the highest P/E group. The lowest P/Es beat the highest P/Es by 6.7% a year. If you're putting money away for your retirement fund, this performance differential becomes enormous over time, as Figure 7–4 indicated.

Looking at the chart again, you'll see that these cheap stocks also provide higher dividend yields. As Figure 8–1 also reveals, the low-P/E

Figure 8-1

Price/Earnings

Dividends, Appreciation & Total Returns
January 1, 1970 - December 31, 1996

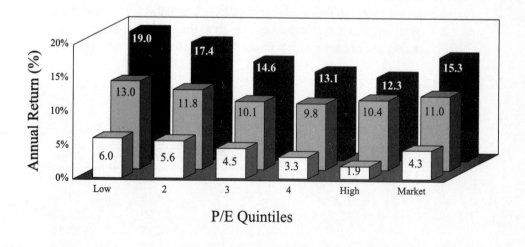

group yields 6.0% over the life of the study compared to 4.3% for the market, and only 1.9% for the highest P/E group. The return advantage of "worst" over "best" stocks is 4.1% annually, which on $10,000 over 27 years is $438,000.

Still, according to conventional investment theory, low P/E stocks *should* provide higher yields. These "uglies" are going nowhere, so their requirements for additional plant and capital equipment to foster expansion are much lower than for the highest P/E group. Therefore, they can afford to pay out more.

What is *not* as it should be is shown in the appreciation column in Figure 8–1. Here we see the low P/E stocks also have far better appreciation than either the high P/E group or the market. All the money that goes into capital expansion for the "best" stocks does not reflect itself in top-gun performance. The "down and outers" outstrip the top tier once again. Low P/E stocks provide the best of both worlds: higher yield and better appreciation, something that conventional wisdom states shouldn't happen.

The higher dividend returns, incidentally, help prop up the prices of cheap stocks in bear markets, one of the important reasons why low P/E and other contrarian strategies outperform in bad times.

Table 8–1 shows how buying the lowest P/E quintile and holding it unchanged for periods of 2 to 8 years over the 1970–1996 period would have done. As a glance at the table shows, the results are rather remarkable. The low P/E portfolios still provide by far the highest annual returns in the second year (18.7%), sharply out-distancing the highest P/E group (11.9%), and the market (15.3%). Low P/E returns stay well above market and high P/E stocks, for both the 3- and the 5-year periods.

It's surprising that the returns stay as high as they do for so long. This indicates that the undervaluation of the low P/E stocks is very marked.

Table 8–1
PRICE/EARNINGS
BUY-AND-HOLD ANNUAL RETURNS
January 1, 1970–December 31, 1996

P/E Quintiles	2 Years	3 Years	5 Years	8 Years
Low P/E	18.7%	18.1%	18.7%	18.4%
2	16.9%	16.5%	17.1%	17.5%
3	15.3%	15.2%	15.5%	16.2%
4	13.5%	13.7%	14.4%	15.3%
High P/E	11.9%	11.3%	11.8%	12.8%
Market	15.3%	15.0%	15.6%	16.2%

For high P/E stocks, the overvaluation is just as significant. Even after 5 years, they continue to display much lower returns than the market. Holding the lowest 20% of stocks for 8 and even 9 years (not shown) still provides well-above-market returns for the low P/E group, with virtually no deterioration of performance from year one.

Another advantage of low P/E and other contrarian strategies is that they don't require a lot of work to be effective. As we just saw, rebalancing low P/E portfolios annually with large-size companies resulted in far above-market returns. However, you could rebalance far less frequently. This is a low intensity strategy with high-intensity results. You don't have to spend much time agonizing over the stocks you pick and constantly monitoring or interpreting every company, industry, or economic squiggle to divine all-important information. No, just select your portfolio (we'll look at how to do this shortly) and put it on automatic pilot. You'll save aggravation, not to mention commission and transaction costs this way.

At the same time, you'll outdistance the market by a comfortable margin, which, as you know, few money managers can do. The point of the chart is not to get you to hold a portfolio intact into eternity, but to show that our normal work ethic of constantly being busy to be successful is not useful but often counterproductive in investing.

While I wouldn't buy a portfolio and hold it sight unseen for eight years, Table 8–1 (a large sample of stocks over the last 27 years) demonstrates you can make big bucks in the market by positioning yourself carefully at the beginning and fine-tuning moderately thereafter.

Strategies #2 and #3: Price-to-Cash Flow and Price-to-Book Value

Let's now look more specifically at two other important contrarian strategies, selecting stocks by price-to-cash flow or by price-to-book value. Cash flow, as you may remember from chapter 3, is normally defined as after-tax earnings, adding back depreciation and other noncash charges. Cash flow is regarded by many analysts as more important than earnings in evaluating a company, for the reasons outlined in that chapter.

As was also discussed in chapter 3, price-to-book value was a favorite tool of Benjamin Graham and other earlier value analysts.[3]

Figures 8–2 and 8–3 give the results of each. The sample, the time period, and the methodology are identical to those used for price-to-earnings. Again, glancing at Figures 8–2 and 8–3, you can see the superior performance of the worst stocks, the lowest 20% of price-to-book value

Figure 8-2

Price/Cash Flow

Dividends, Appreciation & Total Returns
January 1, 1970 - December 31, 1996

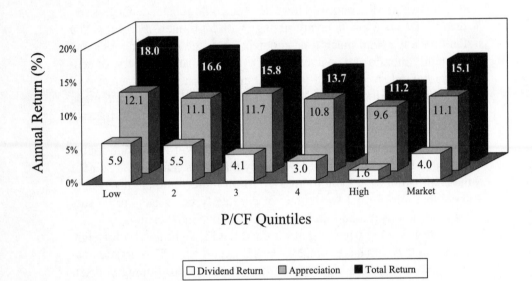

P/CF Quintiles

☐ Dividend Return   ▨ Appreciation   ■ Total Return

or price-to-cash flow, over the top 20% by the same measurements. Secondly, the similarity of results is remarkable. The low-P/E strategy is somewhat more rewarding, returning 19.0% annually for the 27 years of the study vs. 18.8% for low price-to-book value and 18.0% for low price-to-cash flow.

But all three value strategies handily beat the market and sharply outperform the best stocks in each case. Once again, we see the key ingredients of outperformance. Low price-to-cash flow and low price-to-book value have significantly higher dividends than the market and more than triple the dividend of the best stocks in each category, thereby providing a good part of total return. Too, look at the appreciation of the low price-to-cash flow and the low price-to-book value groupings. By this measurement, both groups not only outperform the highest stocks, but also the market handily. The accepted reason for buying "best stocks," much higher appreciation, is shown to be fallacious.

Figures 8–2 and 8–3 again indicate that contrarian stocks give you the best of both worlds—higher appreciation and higher dividends. The

Figure 8-3
Price/Book Value
Dividends, Appreciation & Total Returns
January 1, 1970 - December 31, 1996

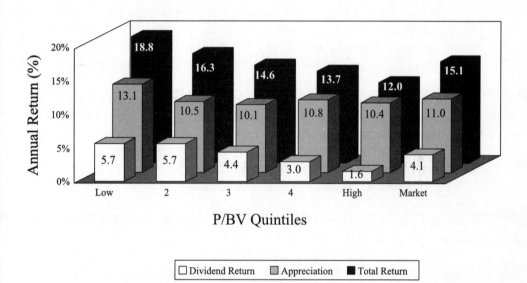

bottom quintile provides dividend returns three times as large as the
highest P/E quintile, another easy win for the out-of-favor stocks. Figures 8–1 to 8–3 demonstrate that the conventional wisdom of setting
radically different investment goals for conservative and aggressive investors is simply one more investment myth. Which brings us to another
important investment rule:

RULE 15

**Don't speculate on highly priced concept stocks to make above-
average returns. The blue-chip stocks that widows and orphans
traditionally choose are equally valuable for the more aggressive
businessman or -woman.**

Stocks classified as a "businessman's risk" by many brokerage firms,
both because of their low dividends and high price-to-value ratios, often

turn out to be "bummers." As a group they consistently underperform the market. A better term might be "businessman's folly." Figures 8–1 to 8–3 go far to reject this concept.

The strategies of buying the lowest 20% of stocks either by price-to-book value, or price-to-cash flow, as we have seen, hold up through both bull and bear markets. Buying and holding portfolios of the lowest price-to-cash flow and price-to-book value without any change in their composition for periods of two, three, five, and eight years (not shown) provide returns very similar to those of buying and holding the lowest P/E portfolio (Table 8–1). Investing in these two groups results in returns well above the market's, and sharply higher than the favorite stocks in each group for every period up to eight years.[4] The "best" stocks continue to underperform for these extended periods.

It again demonstrates that you don't have to watch the market like a gunslinger, ready to slap leather at any new piece of information. Relax, you'll probably make far more money by moving slowly. There is the collateral reward of not shooting yourself in the foot by moving quickly and incorrectly, as is often the case with pros.

The final and one of the most important rewards of the "buy and hold" approach, as indicated with low P/E or the other low price-to-value strategies, is that lower transaction costs can result in a substantial increase in your capital over time.

Transaction costs are often not recognized by investors but can be very expensive.* These are the eighths and quarters it costs you to buy or sell a stock. An example might help to demonstrate why. If a stock is trading at $35–35¼ and you wish to buy it, you would probably pay $35¼. If you want to sell it, you would probably receive $35. Such costs can total 5% or more of capital in a year.

The more commissions and transaction costs can be reduced, of course, the better your overall results. In my experience, the contrarian approach reduces transaction costs and commissions substantially.

If the average transaction cost (the commission plus the difference in the bid/ask spread) is ½ of 1% and the portfolio turnover is 100% a year, it costs you 2½% of your capital in 5 years, over 5% in 10. If you are a heavy trader with turnover say at 200% a year, the costs move up dramatically—10% in 5 years, 20% in 10.

---

* There is always a spread between the bid (the price the buyer is willing to pay) and the offer (the price at which a seller is willing to sell you a stock). The larger the company, normally the smaller the spread. Also, spreads are smaller on the NYSE than on Nasdaq or other markets. A spread on a large NYSE stock like GM or Exxon might be 1/8 or 1/4 of a point; the spread by a Nasdaq dealer on a like-sized company might be 1/4 or 1/2 a point. But more of this in chapter 15.

The average mutual fund manager has a portfolio turnover of 90% a year, with some aggressive growth and momentum funds turning over their entire asset base several times annually. If you wonder why some traders have patches on the elbows of their sport jackets, you can now guess the reason.

What these three low price-to-value strategies can do for you then is to provide high enough returns over time so that only a minimum of trading is required, thereby reducing, perhaps substantially, these costs and enhancing your portfolio returns. This leads us to Rule 16:

RULE 16

Avoid unnecessary trading. The costs can significantly lower your returns over time. Low price-to-value strategies provide well above market returns for years, and are an excellent means of eliminating excessive transaction costs.

The three major strategies show markedly superior returns for "worst" stocks, and painfully lower returns for best, while avoiding high trading costs. Finally, since yield is a very important factor for many readers, let's look at the high dividend strategy.

Strategy # 4: Price-to-Dividend

Figure 8–4 provides the annual returns of price-to-dividend strategies. The method and period used are the same as those for the previous three strategies. As the chart indicates, however, high yielding stocks perform somewhat differently from the previous contrarian strategies. The highest yielding stocks outperform the market by 1.2%, and the stocks with low or no yield by nearly 4% annually.

However, the composition of the returns is different. Almost half of the 16.1% annual return of the highest yielding group comes from the yield itself. Moreover, appreciation, at 8.2% annually over the 27-year period, is lower than for any of the other "worst" groupings or for the market. Buying stocks with high dividend yields beats the market but provides lower total returns than the previous three contrarian strategies.

Once again a "buy-and-hold" strategy works well this time for the lowest price-to-dividend group. Not only do you continue to beat the market over time with this method, but your returns actually increase with a longer holding period.* Remember, the longer you hold your

---

* With dividends reinvested.

Figure 8-4
Price/Dividends
Dividends, Appreciation & Total Returns
January 1, 1970 - December 31, 1996

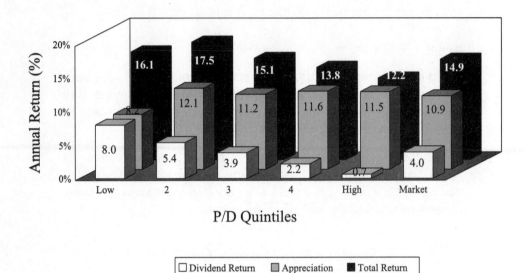

P/D Quintiles

☐ Dividend Return   ▨ Appreciation   ■ Total Return

portfolio, the lower the transaction costs. As important, if you depend on high income, dividends are rising rapidly through the 27-year period. The average yield, as we saw in Figure 8–4, was 8% annually for the 27 years of the study. Also of note is that this high dividend rate is increasing with time. At the end of 8 years, the dividend rate increased 72%. A $10,000 portfolio originally paying $800 a year now would pay $1,503 dollars 8 years later, before their reinvestment, which, of course, would make the overall portfolio return higher. At the end of 8 years, keeping portfolios intact, a $10,000 portfolio would be up 230% versus 203% for the market.

For investors who require income, this appears to be a far better strategy over time than owning bonds. If interest rates spike up, bond prices will go down sharply. A 30-year bond, for example, will drop 12% for every 1% increase in interest rates. With the wide fluctuations of interest rates in the past two decades, the bond market has actually been more volatile than the stock market. Buying high-yielding stocks makes

good sense for the yield-conscious investor. Dividends go up over time—interest payments on bonds do not.

High-yielding stocks also provide you with the best protection in a bear market, as we saw in Figure 7–5 in the previous chapter. These stocks give the dividend-oriented investor more protection of principal on the downside and provide both rising dividend income as well as capital appreciation—the latter occurs only rarely with long bonds.*

Is this a strategy for everyone? I don't think so. It works best for people who need a constant source of income. Naturally, unless you hold the stocks in a tax-free account, the income is taxable. In a tax-free account the investor is far better off using one of the other three contrarian strategies, which as we saw in Figures 8–1, 8–2, and 8–3 provide significantly higher returns than price-to-dividends.

However, what works fine in financial theory often doesn't consider investor psychology. Many investors, particularly the older generation, feel much more secure living on the dividends and keeping their capital intact. Sure they might have substantially more capital in the end using the three other higher-octane value strategies, which would require them to occasionally draw down on the principal for their living expenses. But their comfort level, as I have found, can often go down markedly. Following this strategy will not provide the optimum returns, but it will outperform the market, before deducting dividends, and make a lot of people who depend on income sleep more soundly.

Value, then, in the form of contrarian strategies, is the closest thing there is to a strategy for all seasons. Now some guidelines to help you implement contrarian strategies are in order.

Contrarian Stock Selection: A–B–C Rules

The initial problem confronting any investor is how to select individual stocks and the number of stocks to hold in his portfolio. A few simple rules have proven their worth over the years:

RULE 17

Buy only contrarian stocks because of their superior performance characteristics.

---

* For a more detailed discussion of how stocks fare against bonds over time, please see chapter 13.

RULE 18

Invest equally in 20 to 30 stocks, diversified among 15 or more industries (if your assets are of sufficient size).

Diversification is essential. Returns among individual issues will vary widely, so it is dangerous to rely on only a few companies or industries. By spreading the risk, you have a much better chance of performing in line with the out-of-favor quintiles shown above, rather than substantially above or below this level.[5]

In our 1970–1996 sample, for example, in each of the four contrarian strategies examined, exactly half of the 300 stocks in the lowest quintile performed better than the market over the entire period of the study.

RULE 19

Buy medium- or large-sized stocks listed on the New York Stock Exchange, or only larger companies on Nasdaq or the American Stock Exchange.

Such companies (upon which the studies have been based) are usually subject to less accounting gimmickry than smaller ones, which provides some added measure of protection. Accounting, as we have seen repeatedly, is a devilishly tricky subject and has taken a heavy toll of investors—sophisticates as well as novices.

The larger and medium-sized companies present another advantage to investors: they are more in the public eye. A turnaround in the fortunes of Chrysler (which occurred some years ago) is far more noticeable than a change in the fortunes of some publicly owned five-restaurant steak franchise buried, say, in the sands and winds of Death Valley. Finally, the larger companies have more "staying power." Their failure rate is substantially lower than among smaller or start-up companies.[6]

Should We Abandon Security Analysis Entirely?

As we have seen, selecting stocks by their contrarian characteristics and placing no reliance on security analysis has given better-than-average returns over long periods of time. Should we, then, consider abandoning security analysis entirely? The evidence we've seen certainly shows it doesn't help much. However, I would not go quite this far (and not just because I've been thoroughly steeped in the doctrines of the Old Church).

I believe parts of it can be valuable within a contrarian framework. Contrarian methods eliminate or downgrade those aspects of traditional analysis, such as forecasting, that have been shown to be consistently error-prone. By recognizing the limitations of security analysis, you can, I believe, apply it to achieve even better results within the contrarian approach.

In the next sections, I'll attempt to show you how five fundamental indicators can be used to supplement the three A–B–C rules of contrarian selection we just looked at. Following this analysis, we'll examine other contrarian methods that do not depend on security evaluation at all. These, too, should provide above-average market results. After reviewing the various methods, you can choose which suits you best.

An Eclectic Approach

In my own application of the low P/E approach, I use the bottom 40% of stocks according to P/Es for stock selection. The two lowest quintiles provide plenty of scope for applying the ancillary selection indicators that follow.

If, after what you've seen, you are brave enough to dabble in security analysis, here are the ancillary indicators I believe most helpful:

INDICATOR 1. A STRONG FINANCIAL POSITION

This is easily determinable for a company from information contained within its financial statements. (The definitions of the appropriate ratios—current assets versus current liabilities,* debt as a percentage of capital structure, interest coverage, etc.—can all be found in any textbook on finance, as well as in material provided free of charge by some of the major brokerage houses.)[†]

A strong financial position will enable the company to sail unimpaired through periods of operating difficulties, which contrarian companies sometimes experience. Financial strength is also important in deciding whether a company's dividends can be maintained or increased.

---

* Previously defined in chapter 3, and in glossary.
[†] Martin S. Fridson's book *Financial Statement Analysis* (Wiley Press, 1995) provides a brief introduction to corporate accounting and outlines most of the important financial ratios the average investor would require.

INDICATOR 2. AS MANY FAVORABLE OPERATING AND FINANCIAL RATIOS AS POSSIBLE

This helps to ensure that there are no structural flaws in the company. The definition of such ratios again can be found in standard financial textbooks.

INDICATOR 3. A HIGHER RATE OF EARNINGS GROWTH THAN THE S&P 500 IN THE IMMEDIATE PAST, AND THE LIKELIHOOD THAT IT WILL NOT PLUMMET IN THE NEAR FUTURE

Such future estimates are not an attempt to pinpoint earnings, but only their general direction. Remember that we are dealing with stocks in the bottom quintiles, for which only the worst is expected. Unlike conventional forecasting methods, we do not require precise earnings estimates, but need merely note their direction, and only for short periods, usually about a year or so.

In my initial contrarian work, I was more of a purist on this subject. I thought, since contrarian strategies worked at least in part because of analysts' errors, why bother with forecasting at all? Some rather harsh experiences have caused me to modify this position.

If, for example, the Street estimates that a company's earnings are likely to be down for some time, I would not rush in to buy, no matter how positive my indicators appeared to be. Often, as we've seen, analysts are overoptimistic. All too frequently, an estimated moderate decline in earnings turns into a drop off a cliff. This was the case with Chrysler in the early 1990s when the initial estimates were for relatively small declines. The actual drop in earnings brought the company to the brink of Chapter 11. The stock fell over 80% before rebounding. If earnings are declining, stock prices often follow them down for some time.

The important distinction between forecasting the general direction of earnings and trying to derive precise earnings estimates is that the former method is far simpler and thus more likely to succeed.

INDICATOR 4. EARNINGS ESTIMATES SHOULD ALWAYS LEAN TO THE CONSERVATIVE SIDE

This ties in to Graham and Dodd's "margin of safety" principle. By relying on general directional forecasts and keeping them conservative, you are reducing the chance of error even further. If you do this, and the company still looks as though its earnings will grow more quickly than the S&P for a year or so, you have a potentially rewarding investment.

INDICATOR 5. AN ABOVE-AVERAGE DIVIDEND YIELD, WHICH THE
COMPANY CAN SUSTAIN AND INCREASE

This is an important indicator and depends on indicators 1 through 4 being favorable. Because of its importance to the strategy I'll propose, let's look at it in some detail. As we have seen, conventional investment thinking about dividends is far off the mark. Current wisdom holds that contrarian stocks should provide higher dividend yields but lag in capital gains. According to the good books, the two goals are not compatible. You must go for one or the other.

What shouldn't happen, but does, as we saw clearly in Figures 8–1, 8–2, and 8–3, is that the low price-to-earnings, price-to-cash-flow, and price-to-book-value strategies also provide considerably better appreciation than the most favored stocks by the same yardsticks. Only the highest dividend group lags in appreciation, but still beats the market in total return (dividends and capital appreciation).

In practice, I have found that indicator 5, an above-average and growing dividend yield, improved performance when used in conjunction with the primary rule of buying contrarian stocks.

Now that we have looked at five indicators that should prove helpful regardless of the contrarian strategy we use, I'll turn briefly to another matter. A question I'm frequently asked is "What is the best approach to contrarian investing? Is it better to select one method, such as price-to-earnings or price-to-book value, and focus solely on it?" For me, the answer is no. While you can certainly select one strategy and run with it successfully, once again I favor a more eclectic approach. Our money management firm uses the low-P/E method as its core strategy, but also utilizes the other three contrarian strategies extensively. Investment opportunities vary, and often you can find exceptional value with one method that does not show up as clearly with another.

Low P/E is probably the most accessible of the four contrarian strategies, because the information on P/E ratios is available daily in the financial section of any large newspaper, next to a stock's price. The information is also updated quarterly, while price-to-cash flow or price-to-book value usually aren't, because the underlying information to calculate them often is available only annually. While price-to-dividend information is also near-instantaneous, it is a secondary strategy because of the superior returns of the first three contrarian methods. However, it too has its moments in the sun, as we shall see.

To the Trenches

It's time to move into trenches to see how contrarian decisions are made under fire. I'll draw on past recommendations I've made in my *Forbes* column and to the clients of our investment counseling firm, as well as examples from the Kemper-Dreman High Return Stock mutual fund that I manage. While one can be accused of telling "war stories," remembering only the victories while forgetting the setbacks (not to mention the routs), I think that it is important to present practical examples of how the A–B–C rules and five indicators were often clear-cut—not only with 20/20 hindsight, but at the time. Our first stop will be a couple of examples of how we've selected low-P/E stocks.

Using the Low-P/E Strategy

1. Galen Health Care

I recommended the stock in my *Forbes* column twice in 1993, the first time at a price of $12 in the April 26 issue.[7] Galen, at the time one of the country's largest hospital management companies, operated 71 hospitals in 18 states and 2 foreign countries. It became a public company as a result of Humana's spin-off of Galen stock to its shareholders in March of that year.

Humana has a rapidly growing managed health plan business (HMO), which it believed was buried under a bushel basket because of the sluggish earnings growth and prospects for Galen. Humana's management believed separating the two entities would result in a higher market valuation for its HMO business, thus the spin-off.

Galen's earnings were down over 30% from their peak several years before, and the outlook was for more quarters of lackluster results before an improvement occurred. It was, in short, a blah stock.

So far, so good. On the plus side, it had a number of strong fundamentals. It was cheap measured by all three of our contrarian strategies. It had a P/E multiple of 13 on depressed earnings, which were likely to have a strong rebound in the next year because of cost cutting and more normal revenue growth. Galen was also cheap on a price-to-cash-flow basis. When measured by price-to-book value, it was in the bargain basement, priced at 1.2 times book value against 2.5 for the market at the time.

Secondly, Indicator 1 (financial strength) was solid, if not spectacular, and Indicator 2 (a fair number of respectable operating and financial ratios) was also good. Although the other indicators were mixed and the

Figure 8–5

Galen Health Care / Columbia/HCA Health Care

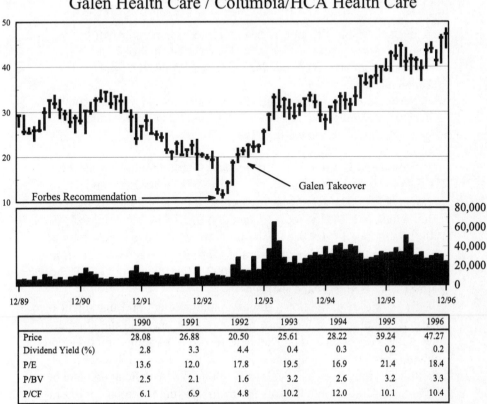

Source: Prepared from FactSet data.

	1990	1991	1992	1993	1994	1995	1996
Price	28.08	26.88	20.50	25.61	28.22	39.24	47.27
Dividend Yield (%)	2.8	3.3	4.4	0.4	0.3	0.2	0.2
P/E	13.6	12.0	17.8	19.5	16.9	21.4	18.4
P/BV	2.5	2.1	1.6	3.2	2.6	3.2	3.3
P/CF	6.1	6.9	4.8	10.2	12.0	10.1	10.4

company at that time paid no dividend, it was plainly underpriced for its industry, that until a year or two earlier had been considered one of the better growth areas. Market perceptions had done a one-eighty on the company, swinging from glowing optimism to extreme pessimism, although its outlook continued to be well above average.

Galen hit the unloved and unwanted list big time. Ignored by the market, it drifted aimlessly. Potential buyers of value had their antennae raised, however. Within months of the spin-off, rapidly growing Columbia/HCA Healthcare Corporation, another major hospital management company, made a stock offer for Galen. The stock moved up 150% within months.*

---

* Please note that the figures quoted in this and subsequent charts are yearly averages. They may differ somewhat from figures quoted in the text, which were taken on specific days during the year.

2. Eli Lilly

As I wrote in my *Forbes* column of March 29, 1993:

> A major oversold situation is beginning to become apparent in the pharmaceutical stocks, which were knocked down sharply last year and have continued their decline since the President's State of the Union message.
>
> No question, the pharmaceuticals are under heavy investor fire and the pressure will probably get worse. I would be surprised if the drug industry didn't trend lower from here.

I recommended a number of drug stocks, continuing, "All have low P/Es, conservative earnings estimates, strong balance sheets and above-average yields." The group sharply outpaced the rapidly rising market.

Let's look at Eli Lilly, recommended at $12.75 in that column.[8] "Eli Lilly," I continued, "has been battered both by negative psychology on drug stocks and by lower-than-average near-term new-product development . . . earnings should be up from 1992. The stock trades at a P/E of 8 times 1992 estimates and yields 4.7%."

Lilly is one of the nation's largest manufacturers and marketers of pharmaceuticals and health-care products. Not only did the company have a low P/E, but it had an excellent record of earnings and dividend growth. They grew at compounded rates of 18% and 17.1% respectively over the previous five years, gaining high marks by indicators 3 and 5.

Moreover, indicator 1 was off the charts. Its debt-to-total-capital ratio was 10%, against 55% for the S&P 500, and its working capital ratio, too, was very high. To continue the checklist, Lilly's return on equity (ROE) was a staggering 28.5% in the previous year, and had averaged 27.1% over the previous five years, almost double the average large company. Its net profit margin, another important financial ratio, averaged 22.5% over the previous five years, again about double the percentage of the average company. Other ratios were also very strong.

Even the worst political scenario for the stock would envision above-average earnings growth, albeit at a lesser rate than in the past. Moreover, the fears of the drug pipeline running dry are as old as the hills for large pharmaceutical companies. Because of their enormous research and development budgets, most, including Lilly, have scads of products in the pipeline.

Analysts looking only at near term blockbuster products frequently forget this. Lilly turned out to be no exception. Prozac, the antidepressant, caught fire, and is continuing to expand its sales, including a mar-

Figure 8-6
Eli Lilly & Co.

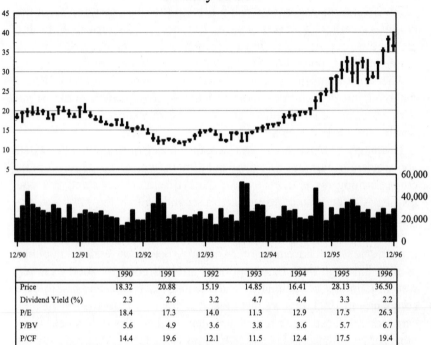

	1990	1991	1992	1993	1994	1995	1996
Price	18.32	20.88	15.19	14.85	16.41	28.13	36.50
Dividend Yield (%)	2.3	2.6	3.2	4.7	4.4	3.3	2.2
P/E	18.4	17.3	14.0	11.3	12.9	17.5	26.3
P/BV	5.6	4.9	3.6	3.8	3.6	5.7	6.7
P/CF	14.4	19.6	12.1	11.5	12.4	17.5	19.4

Source: Prepared from FactSet data

ket for depressed toy poodles, whose quality of life has seemingly been significantly improved by its prescription.

The stock seemed definitely underpriced. As my article warned, it went lower that year, dropping to $11 or another 14%. But as we saw in chapter 3, market timing is difficult if not impossible. It then rallied to $70 by the end of 1997, appreciating 449% from its recommended price. (The total return was 565%.)

Note that, although I used a conservative estimate, as per indicator 4, it turned out too high by 15%. Yet the negative earnings surprise was shrugged off by the market, which, as we saw in chapter 6, is normal for low-P/E stocks.

Here was the classic GARP double play, both above-average earnings growth, and a major expansion of its P/E multiple, as Figure 8–6 indicates. And what is GARP, you ask? This gives me the opportunity for a little aside on a well-kept secret.

The World of GARP

For a value manager, disclosing it is a little like emerging from the closet as an efficient market believer. But, here goes—growth and value are not always poles apart. In fact, sometimes you can fit a tasty growth entrée into your portfolio—if you don't pay too much for it.

The Street terms this strategy GARP—Growth at a Reasonable Price. Although this definition can cover a wide range of growth stocks, some with prices in the stratosphere, it has proven very successful when used within a low-P/E strategy.

If you buy a GARP stock, you have the chance of a double play. First, above-average earnings and dividend growth, which should result in its outperforming the market, even if the P/E remains constant. But you also have a fair chance to make the second half of the play—an expanding P/E ratio, if the above-average growth continues.

How do you find a GARP stock? There are a number of ways. Often growth stocks will have temporary negative news that sends them plummeting, although their basic outlooks are still good. A good example was the Clintons' confrontation with the pharmaceutical and health-care companies in 1993, that we just looked at. Investor fears that the health-care industry faced a dire future sent many of these first-rate stocks tumbling, often collapsing P/Es to half of previous levels. Pharmaceuticals traded at P/Es of 8 to 14, bringing the industry into the low-P/E camp. Here was an excellent case of GARP, ripe for the picking. With low P/Es, yields between 4.5% and 6.5%, and growth, even in a worst case, well above the S&P 500, the stocks proved to be a screaming buy, doubling in less than two years.

GARP opportunities come around more often than you might think because of earnings disappointments, fears that knock down entire growth industries, and many other market overreactions. A good GARP situation allows you the possibility of a home run, while staying safely in the value camp.

Using Low Price-to-Cash Flow

3. Ford

Low price-to-cash flow, as Figure 8–2 demonstrated, had well-above-average returns over time. Price-to-cash flow is often a more useful measure than earnings when a company has large noncash expenses, such as depreciation in bad years.* If you tried to buy normally low-P/E cyclical stocks in a recession, when earnings of these companies tumble, the P/Es can get very high—if not infinite.

Ford, for example, in a bad period for autos, made only 92 cents a share in 1990, down from $4.57 a share the previous year. Because of the large drop in earnings, the P/E rose to 14 from 5 the year before. By price-to-cash flow, however, it was still dirt cheap, trading at a little more than 2 times cash flow at its low of $13 that year. In 1991 earnings crashed; Ford reported a $2.40 a share loss. The P/E was now infinite, so the low-P/E buyer would not touch the stock. Still, it traded at a modest 3.6 times its reported cash flow of $3.62 a share that year. The stock looked undervalued.[†]

Once again the financial pages, and sometimes the front pages, blared out the tale of how the American auto companies would be left in the dust by the Japanese and Europeans, through poor management, insurmountable inefficiency, and lack of vision. Forgotten, apparently, was that Ford was one of the lowest-cost producers in Europe and that auto cycles were almost as old as the automobile itself. Moreover, Ford also had a low price-to-book value, trading at about 60% of its book value in 1991, about one-fifth the market's.

Finally, the company, despite cutting the dividend rate, ranked very high by the price-to-dividend measure, our useful secondary strategy, yielding an average of 7.6% in 1990 and 6.4% in 1991. The dividend is an important indicator of how management sees the future. Although Ford's board of directors cut the dividend from $1.50 a share in 1989 to 80 cents a share in 1992, that they paid any dividend at all indicated their confidence that the company was not in financial difficulty, despite the sometimes shrill comments of analysts and the press. Only in their minds was the company going down for the third time.

I recommended Ford in my *Forbes* column of January 6, 1992.

> Cyclical stocks—airlines, autos, forest products, et al.—are now as cheap relative to the market as at any time in the postwar period. As a

---

* Although these charges are reflected in earnings, they do not show in cash flow. Granted the depreciation must be made up eventually, it gives the company breathing space if it needs it to meet payments in financially difficult years.

[†] Another way of avoiding this problem is to average earnings over a period of time—say five years—for a cyclical company. Doing this for Ford for the five years ending 1992, where it reported a $2.40 a share loss, would have resulted in average earnings of $2.62 a share. Using the same price of 13, the P/E ratio now is under 5, which still makes the stock appear very cheap.

Figure 8-7

Ford Motor Co.

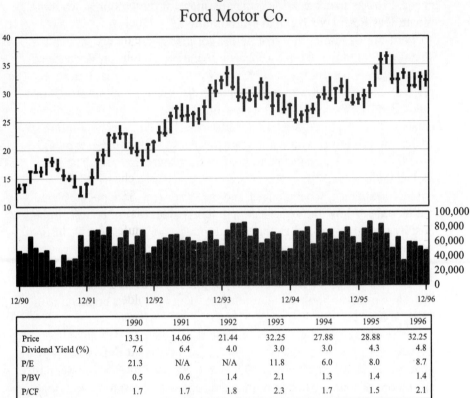

	1990	1991	1992	1993	1994	1995	1996
Price	13.31	14.06	21.44	32.25	27.88	28.88	32.25
Dividend Yield (%)	7.6	6.4	4.0	3.0	3.0	4.3	4.8
P/E	21.3	N/A	N/A	11.8	6.0	8.0	8.7
P/BV	0.5	0.6	1.4	2.1	1.3	1.4	1.4
P/CF	1.7	1.7	1.8	2.3	1.7	1.5	2.1

Source: Prepared from FactSet data

group these stocks are actually selling lower than after the October 1987 crash. . . .

All of which may have created an extraordinary buying opportunity. As the economy recovers, these companies should get a lot of bounce from the cost-cutting in recent years as well as from comparisons with quarters in 1991 that showed large restructuring charges. . . .

GM and Ford have slumped to 12-month lows in recent weeks. Major cost-cutting and a tight rein on inventories should result in a substantial swing in the bottom line when consumers come back to the showrooms. Ford (12½) is currently hurting not only from weak domestic sales but also from the poor results of its normally highly profitable European and financial groups. The company is likely to show modest profits this year, with substantial improvement in 1993. Ford has also recently bolstered its balance sheet with a large $2.3 billion preferred issue.

I was using what I believed to be a conservative earnings forecast for Ford, but the estimate proved far too high. Ford reported a 73-cent-a-share loss for the year. But it didn't matter. The stock was so cheap, it bounced up to $22 by early 1993, appreciating more than 75% from the point I recommended it and kept climbing. In October 1997 it traded over $50.

Time for a Miss

4. Westinghouse

Westinghouse, a blue chip for generations, was a cheap stock in the fourth quarter of 1990 at $25, down from a high of $38, because of the sharp market sell-off accompanying the Gulf Crisis. After GE, it was the nation's second largest electrical equipment manufacturer. Like GE, Westinghouse had a rapidly growing financial group, and in addition, a highly profitable broadcasting sector. Moreover, since the mid-seventies, the company had made amazing progress, with earnings increases in virtually every year. The stock rewarded its shareholders by ten-folding from its low in mid-1974, and management said more of the same type of growth was a-coming.

It also scored high by every contrarian strategy. At the $25 price, its P/E was 7, well under the 13 of the market. It traded at 4.5 times its cash flow and at 1.6 times its book value. All very cheap, even in a depressed stock environment, and for kickers it yielded a well-above-market 5.2%.

It also ranked high by many of the financial indicators. It was rock-solid financially (indicator 1), with debt less than 20% of the capital structure. Also impressive were indicators 2, 3, and 5—a good number of favorable financial and operating ratios, an above-average rate-of-earnings growth, and above-average yield as well as an increasing dividend. Here was the ideal contrarian stock—or so it seemed.

As it turned out, there was only one minor hitch—the company's financial division.

Being heavily involved in financial stocks in 1990, the year of the major financial crisis, I was naturally concerned about Westinghouse's rapidly growing financial division, which had a major stake in real estate. We analyzed it carefully, discussing it with management virtually profit center by profit center. Not to worry, they told us; they didn't do anything foolish like those real estate developers, banks, and other financial institutions. Everything was well in hand.

And so it seemed, until they reported their first billion-plus write-off in 1991.

Figure 8-8

Westinghouse Electric

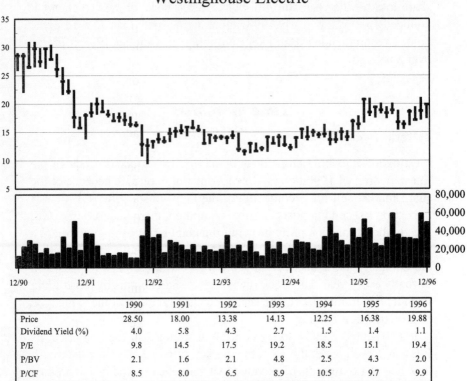

	1990	1991	1992	1993	1994	1995	1996
Price	28.50	18.00	13.38	14.13	12.25	16.38	19.88
Dividend Yield (%)	4.0	5.8	4.3	2.7	1.5	1.4	1.1
P/E	9.8	14.5	17.5	19.2	18.5	15.1	19.4
P/BV	2.1	1.6	2.1	4.8	2.5	4.3	2.0
P/CF	8.5	8.0	6.5	8.9	10.5	9.7	9.9

Source: Prepared from FactSet data

The stock went down to $17, at which point I sold. I no longer had faith in the credibility of Westinghouse's then management. Westinghouse continued to underestimate or refuse to disclose the extent of their real estate problems. It made further write-offs in the next year or two, and the stock drifted under $10 by late 1992. I should have known—on paper it was just too perfect a contrarian stock!

Price-to-Book-Value Strategies

5. Fleet Financial

Price-to-book value, even more than price-to-cash flow, is an excellent contrarian indicator when a company stumbles and earnings crater. A good example were the bank stocks in the financial crisis of 1990. As real estate free-fell, bank stocks plummeted. Savings and loans, even more dependent than banks on real estate loans, were decimated, and the banking industry was severely shaken. In the first nine months of 1990, the Keefe Bruyette's Index of the 100 largest banks dropped an astonishing 50%.[9]

But in crisis, as we'll see in detail in chapter 12, there is also major opportunity, particularly for the contrarian. Thus, when most bank analysts on the Street were exorcising bank shares out of the hands of investors, some of the banks showed remarkably strong fundamentals. Most traded at 60% or less of book value, including many that had already stepped up to the plate and taken all or the greater part of their anticipated real estate losses. Most still had more than adequate capital to meet the requirements of the regulators.

Take the case of Fleet Financial, a large regional bank holding company. The bank took enormous real estate losses in 1990. Earnings plummeted from $3.30 in 1989 to a loss of 51 cents a share the following year. The loss was accompanied by a decline in the stock from $25 to $9. Even after the loss, Fleet had a book value of $17.62 a share, or almost double its market price. A cheap stock even by Benjamin Graham's criteria, back in the depressed thirties.

Although the dividend rate was cut, it was not eliminated. The stock still paid 60% of the previous rate, indicating management's confidence in the future. The stock provided a well-above-average 7–8% yield—on the lower dividend. The dividend was raised in each succeeding year and now is 50% above the rate prior to the cut.

A word of caution: Buying companies that show losses is considerably riskier than simply buying contrarian stocks. The investor must be very sure of the company's financial strength, and should use only a small portion of his portfolio for this purpose, while diversifying into a number of other issues to spread the risk.

To sum up, price-to-book value was an excellent criterion for banks who stepped up and took their medicine early. At the bottom of the banking crisis they traded at the lowest financial ratios since the 1930s. In the case of Fleet, the stock rose from as low as $9 in October of 1990 to over $24 by April of 1991, a gain of 160%. By late December of 1997 it had appreciated 700% to $73.

Price-to-Dividend

6. KeyCorp

Price-to-dividend, as we have seen, also provides above-average returns. At its most effective it can be used with other contrarian methods to ferret out undervalued stocks, providing a combination of above-

Figure 8-9

Fleet Financial

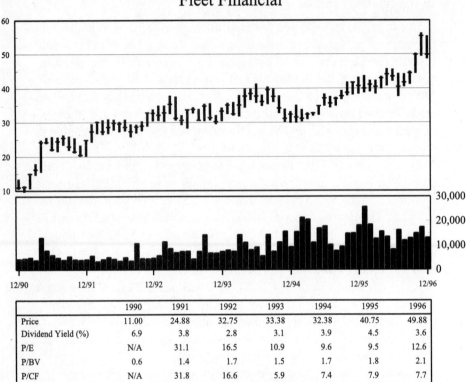

	1990	1991	1992	1993	1994	1995	1996
Price	11.00	24.88	32.75	33.38	32.38	40.75	49.88
Dividend Yield (%)	6.9	3.8	2.8	3.1	3.9	4.5	3.6
P/E	N/A	31.1	16.5	10.9	9.6	9.5	12.6
P/BV	0.6	1.4	1.7	1.5	1.7	1.8	2.1
P/CF	N/A	31.8	16.6	5.9	7.4	7.9	7.7

Source: Prepared from FactSet data

average income and first-rate appreciation. As noted, a high yield, even if earnings are temporarily depressed, indicates management's confidence in the future. How management and the board of directors react to a serious problem is usually worth noting.

The drug stocks were an example of a group where a combination of high yield and low P/E resulted in investors scoring big. High yield also works well in tandem with price-to-book value. Most of the banks that took large losses on real estate in 1990 cut their dividends but did not eliminate them. The careful investor could thus see that this group of banks had confidence in the future. He or she could also observe that even after major charges, the capital was still well above the minimum required. Too, the regulators, having been burnt by the S&Ls, would bring strong pressure on banks to keep dividends conservative or omit them entirely, if they thought they saw problems in the loan portfolios.

Which brings us to KeyCorp, a large and well-managed regional bank holding company. Key's stock plummeted from $20 in mid-1989 to $12 in the fourth quarter of 1990. The bank announced large real estate write-offs, but even so earnings in 1990 did not fall from the $2.32 a share earned in 1989. Key's capital was still 6.7% of assets, well above the minimum required. So strong was its financial position that Key did not cut, but instead increased its dividend in 1990 by 10%. This provided a high 7% yield, with the stock near its lowest price in years. It also traded at only 80% of book value.

Needless to say, it recovered rapidly, more than doubling in price in 12 months and reaching $70 by late 1997. It was also a high dividend fan's dream. Yield increased almost 73% in the next six years.

This was not an isolated instance; literally dozens of large- and medium-sized banks could be picked off by the shrewd buyer in the same manner, which I'll more fully detail in chapter 12.

Figure 8–10

KeyCorp

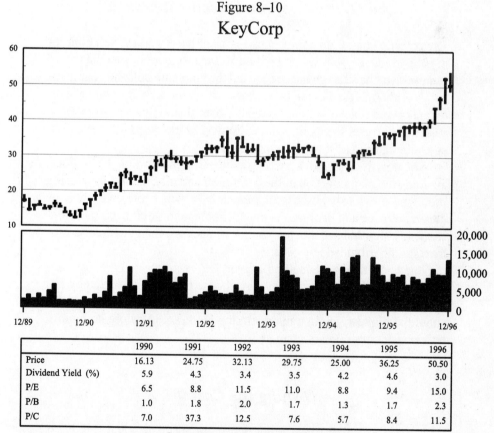

	1990	1991	1992	1993	1994	1995	1996
Price	16.13	24.75	32.13	29.75	25.00	36.25	50.50
Dividend Yield (%)	5.9	4.3	3.4	3.5	4.2	4.6	3.0
P/E	6.5	8.8	11.5	11.0	8.8	9.4	15.0
P/B	1.0	1.8	2.0	1.7	1.3	1.7	2.3
P/C	7.0	37.3	12.5	7.6	5.7	8.4	11.5

Source: Prepared from FactSet data.

A Beneficial Side Effect

All five of the successful examples—Galen, Eli Lilly, Ford, Fleet Financial, and KeyCorp—demonstrate a beneficial side effect of these strategies. Often contrarian stocks can move substantially higher in price and still be good holdings. The reason: Earnings are moving up rapidly enough so that the P/E, price-to-book value, or price-to-cash-flow ratios remain low. This produces a substantially lower turnover rate than most investment strategies. A lower turnover rate means that, if you are in a taxable account, you will have lower capital gains taxes. This is particularly important for capital gains under 18 months that are taxed as ordinary income. You will also have lower commission and transaction costs, as was noted earlier.

An Overview of the Eclectic Approach

The eclectic contrarian approaches I present have worked well both for my clients and myself. While I would be the last to argue that the record is definitive, the strategy has succeeded through both bull and bear quarters.[10] Although the degree of success will certainly vary among individuals—and for the same individual—over differing time periods, the eclectic approach seems to be an extremely workable investment strategy, eliminating most complex judgments.

Indicators 1, 2, 4, and 5 are reasonably straightforward calculations, avoiding the major portion of the configural and information-processing problems previously discussed. Indicator 3, which projects only the general direction of earnings, is much simpler and safer to use, and consequently should have a better chance of success, than the precise estimates ordinarily made by security analysts.

Obviously, this is the method I favor.

As an investor, however, you may choose to follow this strategy as I have laid it down, or look at the other variations in the next chapter that should also allow you to outperform the market. But before doing this, let's revisit our casino of chapter 1.

Owning the Casino

At this point I think I hear a few murmurs out there—and rightly so. There are zillions of "how to" investment books, touting this method or that. Are there any real odds that contrarian strategies will beat the market over time? Indeed there are.

Calculating the returns of our 27-year study of the 1,500 largest stocks on the Compustat database, we find the odds of contrarian strategies outperforming the market are about 60–40 in any single quarter. The casinos in Las Vegas and Atlantic City make a bundle with odds 5–10% in their favor. The probabilities of beating the averages using contrarian strategies, then, are even higher. In chapter 1, these probabilities were described in general terms; now we'll look at them in detail. The results, I think, will surprise you.

First, unlike Vegas, if you only do as well as the market, you walk away with your pockets bulging. You don't just get your cash back, you get it compounded. Ten thousand dollars invested in the market, as Figure 7–4 showed, became $289,000 twenty-seven years later before dividends and capital gain taxes. In the market casino, just breaking even would give you over 28 times your money in 27 years.

However, Figure 7–4 also demonstrated how well we would have done in contrarian strategies over time. Using low price-to-cash flow, you would have doubled the performance of the market, increasing your $10,000 of initial capital 57-fold. With price-to-book value, you would have outperformed price-to-cash flow some, increasing capital a modest 68 times. Investing in stocks produces enormous returns, even if you do only as well as the market. If you adopt a contrarian strategy, the results are spectacular.

You may have some questions at this point. First, is 25 years a realistic time frame? How many people invest for anything near this time? If you are in your twenties or thirties, 25 years is not unreasonable, particularly if you are building your nest egg in an IRA or other retirement plan.

But as Table 8–2 demonstrates, you get some mouth-watering gains for shorter periods. The table indicates the amount that $10,000 would become in periods of 5 to 25 years relative to the market using the four contrarian strategies we have examined.[11] As you can see, all four contrarian strategies whip the market in every period. And the percentage they do it by goes up dramatically with time. Low P/E had the best returns. In five years using the price-to-earnings strategy you outdistance the market by 19%. This rises to 67% in 15 years and 101% in 20. Look at the difference compounding makes. At the end of five years, for example, again using the price-to-earnings measure, the return is $3,727 over the market's, by ten years it's increased to $15,241, and by the end of 25 to $340,437. Remember this is an initial one-time investment of only $10,000.

Table 8–2

THE PAYOFF USING CONTRARIAN STRATEGIES

Return on $10,000 Initial Investment

1970–1996 with Annual Rebalancing*

	5 Years	10 Years	15 Years	20 Years	25 Years
Low P/E	$22,849	$51,461	$114,893	$257,591	$581,787
Low P/CF	$21,914	$47,799	$103,880	$223,978	$488,126
Low P/BV	$21,818	$47,681	$103,488	$223,620	$490,046
Low P/D	$20,276	$40,913	$81,877	$163,517	$327,157
Market	$19,122	$36,220	$68,709	$128,321	$241,350

*THE MEDIAN COMPOUNDED RETURN IN A MONTE CARLO SIMULATION OF 10,000 TRIALS.

"No question contrarian strategies look impressive, if not over-whelming in studies," some readers would ask, "but what are my chances of beating the market in practice? After all, we've all heard the story of the average depth of a river being 4 feet—but the poor hiker with a 50 pound backpack finds it's 2 feet in some places and 8 feet in others."

Again, let's look at our chances of outdistancing the market over time in terms of the odds at a casino. Using our 27-year study,[12] we know that the odds are 60–40 in our favor in any single play. But what are they over a large number of hands? In market terms that would mean playing these strategies over some years.

To determine the answer, we use a statistical calculation, not by co-incidence called the Monte Carlo simulation. We treat each quarter as a single card. Since we have a 27-year study, we have 108 quarters. Using low P/E as our strategy, we randomly pick a quarter from the 108 quarters in the 27 years, calculate the return against the market, whether it is positive or negative. The card is then put back into the 108-quarter deck. We then randomly select another card in the same manner, calculate the return, and again put it back into the deck. This allows any quarter to be drawn more than once, or other quarters to be missed entirely in a random selection.

In effect we are taking any possible combination of market returns over the 108 quarters of the study to determine just what are the probabilities of beating the market. A game would consist of 100 draws for each hand, which would total 25 years.[13] This gives us an almost infinite number of combinations of cards, which provides very accurate odds of how well a strategy will work over time. The Monte Carlo simulation allows us to get billions of possible combinations (actually 3×10^{24}, or more than the number of inches from here to the Andromeda Galaxy, which is two million light-years away).

But most investors don't make a one-time investment in the market. They put away a few thousand dollars or more each year. Not wanting to bore the computer, we asked it to calculate the odds of beating the market for 10,000 plays of each strategy, investing sums from $1,000 to $20,000 annually. The computer did this for the four value strategies, with only a minor whine at the monotony.

Table 8–3 shows the result of investing these amounts using the low-P/E strategy against the market over time. As you can see, the dollars you accumulate using a contrarian strategy are almost mind-boggling. Investing only $1,000 a year over 25 years in a tax-free account would become $392,459 dollars. Investing $20,000 a year in the same way— $7,849,183.

If you used the low P/E strategy and repositioned your portfolio quarterly into the lowest P/E group, what are your odds of beating the market over 25 years? High enough to make the owner of the plushest casino drool. If you play a 100-card series 10,000 times, your probabilities of winning are 9,999 out of 10,000! That's right, you would underperform the market only once in ten thousand 100-card plays.[14] Remember, this casino is different; even underperforming the market doesn't send you away with empty pockets, but with a large stack of chips if you get even a reasonable percentage of the market's return.

But say that 25 years was much too long for you to invest—what would happen if you moved to a 10-year span? Using this strategy for 10 years reduced your chances of beating the market, but not by much.

Table 8–3

BUILDING A NEST EGG THE EASY WAY
Adding to the Investment Each Year 1970–1996*

		5 Years	10 Years	15 Years	20 Years	25 Years
$1,000	Low P/E	$8,538	$27,950	$71,218	$169,145	$392,459
	Market	$7,728	$22,724	$51,504	$107,362	$215,519
$5,000	Low P/E	$42,688	$139,749	$356,092	$845,725	$1,962,296
	Market	$38,639	$113,618	$257,520	$536,812	$1,077,594
$10,000	Low P/E	$85,375	$279,498	$712,183	$1,691,450	$3,924,592
	Market	$77,278	$227,236	$515,040	$1,073,624	$2,155,188
$20,000	Low P/E	$170,751	$558,996	$1,424,367	$3,382,901	$7,849,183
	Market	$154,556	$454,472	$1,030,079	$2,147,248	$4,310,377

*THE MEDIAN COMPOUNDED RETURN IN A MONTE CARLO SIMULATION OF 10,000 TRIALS.

You would still come out a winner 9,917 times out of every 10,000 hands you played, not bad in casinos or markets. If you invested for five years in this manner, your odds of beating the market are still 95.3 out of every hundred hands. The probabilities of winning with this strategy are a gambler's or an investor's fantasy.

But let's stop for a moment. Maybe you don't like to turn over a part of your portfolio each and every quarter. Such a strategy might be too anxiety-producing; it might drive you, along with the toy poodle, to Prozac. How do we do if we opt for a longer holding period, say a year, without changing any part of the portfolio? Once again, this casino pays off like a dream. If you played this strategy for one-year periods, for the full length of the study, thus making modest changes to the portfolio annually, your odds go down. But, I'm sure you'll take them—try winning 9,923 of 10,000 hands. If you wanted to go for shorter periods, your odds of beating the market decrease some, but are still high—94% for ten years and 87% for five years.

The probabilities are nearly identical for price-to-cash flow and price-to-book value. A casino owner would die for these odds rather than the roughly 55–45 the house gets. In fact, some casino owners, including Bugsy Segal, pushed daisies for the lesser odds.

These odds are by far the highest consistently available of any investment strategy of which I am aware. There is nothing closer to a sure thing for millions of investors, yet strangely enough, few play this game.

The green wing has always been sparsely populated, and, despite all the statistics, it's likely to remain so.

Walking Away from the Chips

It's important to realize that investing using contrarian strategies is a long-term game. One roll of the dice or a single hand at blackjack is meaningless to the casino owner. He knows there will be hot streaks that will cost him a night's, a week's, or sometimes even a month's revenues. He may grumble when he loses, but he doesn't shut down the casino. He knows he'll get it back.

As an investor, you should follow the same principles. You won't win every hand. You'll have periods of spectacular returns and others you might diplomatically describe as lousy. But it's important to remember that contrarian strategies, like the odds for the casino owner, put you in the catbird seat. Professional investors, along with everyday folks, normally forget this important principle and demand superior returns from every hand.

Even though a strategy works most of the time and generates excellent returns, *no strategy works consistently*. The fast-track, aggressive growth stocks will, on occasion, knock the stuffing out of low-P/E or other contrarian methods for several years at a clip—sometimes longer. But over time, it's simply no contest. Still, human nature being what it is, our expectations are almost always too high.

Even when we look at the record of these superb returns (which encompass both bull and bear markets over decades), we are still disappointed that a contrarian strategy doesn't win each and every year. The probability is zero that any investment strategy would, just as it is that you'll win a hundred straight hands at blackjack. It's obvious—if we were totally rational data processors. But we are not. We demand the impossible, and repeatedly make poor decisions in pursuit of the unattainable.

Take the following example of how easily a winning strategy can be abandoned. In 1988, growth investing sharply outperformed the value approach. Many value managers trailed the S&P 500 by 14% or 15%—when the market was ahead 33%. These strategies continued to underperform for several years. The chant went up from some consultants and sophisticated clients that value was dead. "Contrarian strategies might have worked well in the past," they said, "but now, with almost everyone using them, they just aren't effective anymore."

Then, contrarian strategies did the unthinkable—they underperformed in the bear market of 1990. How could this happen?

Again, it was simply the laws of probability. Contrarian stocks have an excellent record of doing better in bear markets, but this doesn't mean they will do so every time (they don't have to in order to get the well-above-average returns we saw in bear markets in Figure 7–5). Still, when this happens, consultants and professionals, as well as individual investors, believe the strategies have lost their edge. Large numbers of investors, from giant institutions to individuals, abandoned them at this point, which happened to be right at the bottom of their performance cycle. From then on, these strategies outpaced the market handily for years.

My own experience, as well as that of many other contrarian money managers, is similar. Over the past twenty-five years, I've seen this same syndrome occur virtually every time contrarian styles underperform the market for any length of time. If you can shrug off the few bad periods, you should do very well. However, the psychology to follow through is much more difficult than it may appear.

Though the strategies are simple and easy to use, the influence of immediate events is very powerful. We will look at why most people can't shake off these influences and at some of the principles that can help you to do so in chapter 10. But before we do that, let's look at a new contrarian strategy just off the drawing board, which has some unique advantages for investors, and some additional variations and alternatives you can add to your arsenal.

9

A New, Powerful
Contrarian Approach

WHEN I wrote *Contrarian Investment Strategy* in 1980, I stressed the low-P/E strategy because it was the best documented way to beat the market at the time. As we have seen, there are a number of other contrarian methods that should produce top-notch results. All the strategies we viewed in the last chapters, however, relied on buying companies that investors put at the absolute bottom of their dance cards, by price-to-value measurements. Since the psychological forces that drive people toward the best and away from the worst stocks are predictable,[1] these same influences should work to our advantage in a variety of other situations.

Are there other contrarian strategies that will perform well in investment markets and elsewhere? Yes. In this chapter, we'll examine a new strategy that works on exactly the same behavioral principles, but in a very different way. This method will allow you to participate in virtually every major industry in a manner similar to an index fund. Unlike an index fund, however, it should provide well-above-market returns.

Finally, we'll also look at a number of ways to use contrarian strategies that require little reliance on judgment, the weakest link in the investment decision-making process, yet which will still provide superior performance over time.

These additional methods may not be suitable for every investor, but you should be aware of them, since they represent some of the latest results from new research. Happily, there now is solid support for strategies that are a valid alternative to the contrarian methods we've been looking at. These methods will meet the needs of people who would like a simplified approach.

Contrarian Strategies Within Industries

As we've already documented, investors are entirely too confident of their ability to forecast which stocks will win and which will lose. Trends and fashions in the marketplace play a powerful role in drawing people to popular stocks. Similarly, lack of excitement or lackluster outlooks push investors away from others. Does that extend beyond "best" and "worst" stocks as measured by the contrarian indicators in the last chapter? It should.

If trends and fashions exist in the marketplace as a whole, it is reasonable from a psychological perspective to expect that they exist within specific industries.[2] Analyst research, expert opinion, current prospects, and a host of other variables should work on investor expectations almost identically within industries as in the overall market. The result again will be expectations set too high for favored stocks within an industry and too low for out-of-favor companies. Thus, Merck might be a favorite in the pharmaceutical industry, while Glaxo might be thought of as a laggard. Similarly, the American International Group might be a favorite in the insurance industry, while Ohio Casualty is unloved and unwanted. Overpricing and underpricing of favored and unfavored stocks within value and growth industries would thus appear to be a natural extension of contrarian strategies. Sounds great in theory, but unlike our academic friends, we're going to ask a rude question: does it work?

To get the answer, in collaboration with Eric Lufkin, I examined the 1,500 largest companies on the Compustat tapes by market size between 1970 and 1996.[3] The 1,500 stocks were divided into 44 industries.[4] The most favored stocks consisted of the 20% of companies in each industry with the highest P/Es, price-to-cash flow, or price-to-book value ratios, or lowest yields. The most unpopular were the 20% of stocks in each industry that had the lowest ratios by the first three measurements and the highest yield by the fourth. Returns were calculated in the same way for the remaining 60% of stocks in the middle quintiles.

Using the industry strategy (and taking low P/E as our example), the lowest multiple in one industry, such as banking, might be 10; in another industry, such as biotech, 25. Yet, if we were right, the lowest P/E stocks in both industries should provide well-above-market returns. In this strategy, we speak of relative P/E—the lowest 20% of P/Es (or price-to-cash flow, price-to-book value, or highest yield) within an industry—versus the lowest absolute P/Es in the entire market, the strategy in the past two chapters.

Figures 9–1 and 9–2 give the results of our study for low price-to-

Figure 9-1

Industry-Relative
Price/Earnings

Dividends, Appreciation & Total Returns
January 1, 1970 - December 31, 1996

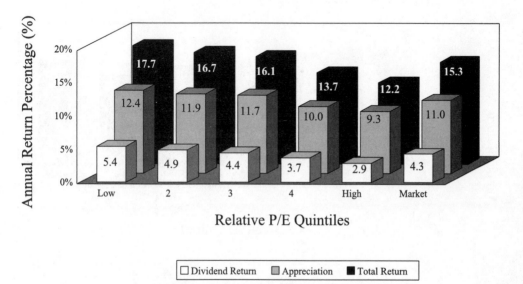

earnings and low price-to-dividend.* Looking at Figure 9–1, for example, we see the lowest 20% of stocks as measured by price-to-earnings
for each of the 44 industries in the first column, the second lowest in the
second, the highest in the fifth, and the market in the last column on the
right. The lowest price-to-earnings group provides an average return of
17.7% annually over the 27 years of the study. The highest 20% returns
12.2%, the market 15.3%. The lowest price-to-earnings group outperforms the highest by 5.5% annually over the life of the study.

I find Figure 9–2 particularly interesting. It shows that the total annual return using the industry-relative high dividend strategy is 17.0%,
which is higher than the absolute price-to-dividend strategy return of
16.1% shown in the last chapter. This is because appreciation is higher
using the industry dividend strategy than it is buying the highest yield-

---

* Results for low price-to-cash flow and low price-to-book value (not shown) are very
similar.

Figure 9-2
Industry-Relative
Price/Dividends
Dividends, Appreciation & Total Returns
January 1, 1970 - December 31, 1996

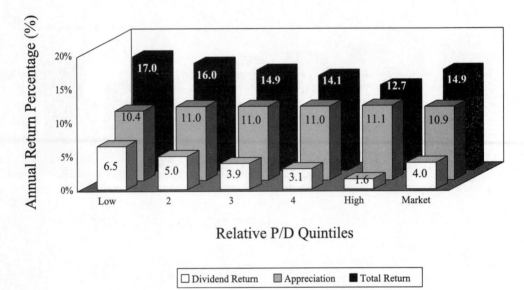

Relative P/D Quintiles

☐ Dividend Return   ▨ Appreciation   ■ Total Return

ing stocks available in the overall market (10.4% vs. 8.2%). Yield itself is somewhat lower than buying the highest absolute dividend payers (6.5% versus 8.0%), because most of the high-priced industries pay small dividends.

Table 9–1 shows the returns of buying low P/E stocks by this method and holding them for periods of 2, 3, 5, and 8 years. Again, the results of investing in the most out-of-favor stocks within industries are similar to buying the most unpopular stocks overall. As Table 9–1 indicates, the returns of the laggards do not decay over longer periods of time. A buy-and-hold strategy, as noted, enhances your capital by avoiding most commissions and other transaction costs, and by minimizing capital gains taxes. The returns of price-to-cash flow and price-to-book value (not shown) are also similar.

Figure 9–3 demonstrates just how soundly the relative (or industry) contrarian strategies beat the averages over the full 27 years of the study. Low price-to-cash flow does the best. Ten thousand dollars invested by

Table 9–1

INDUSTRY-RELATIVE PRICE/EARNINGS BUY-AND-HOLD ANNUAL RETURNS
January 1, 1970–December 31, 1996

P/E Quintiles	2 Years	3 Years	5 Years	8 Years
Low P/E	17.6%	17.4%	18.2%	18.3%
2	16.6%	16.3%	16.8%	17.1%
3	15.8%	15.4%	15.7%	16.3%
4	13.8%	13.5%	13.9%	14.8%
High P/E	12.5%	12.2%	12.9%	13.8%
Market	15.3%	15.0%	15.6%	16.2%

this method at the beginning of the period becomes $626,000* in 27 years. Low relative P/E and low price-to-book value also work well, while low relative price-to-dividend easily outperforms the market and lags behind the other three strategies by much less than on an absolute basis.

Are these returns simply due to the superior performance of industries loaded with unloved stocks? No. The most out-of-favor stocks in an industry, regardless of whether they were dirt cheap or highly priced, outperformed the most popular stocks in each group and the market average 80–90% of the time. The evidence suggests that the relative value has a potent effect in all industries.[5]

So, a new strategy is born. Let's make that Rule 20 to summarize the concept.

RULE 20

Buy the least expensive stocks within an industry, as determined by the four contrarian strategies, regardless of how high or low the general price of the industry group.

This strategy will beat the market handily most of the time. The psychological reasons are identical to those behind the contrarian strategies we looked at previously.

We also tested to see if the relative industry effect is independent of the absolute value effects discussed in the last two chapters, and found that it was. Table 9–2 shows just how different the various contrarian value measurements are for the cheapest and most expensive industries. Price, for example, is only 70% of book value (.7) for the lowest price-to-book value group in the cheapest 20% of industries, and this group

---

* Dividends are reinvested.

Figure 9-3

Another Flavor of Value: Industry-Relative Strategies
1970–1996

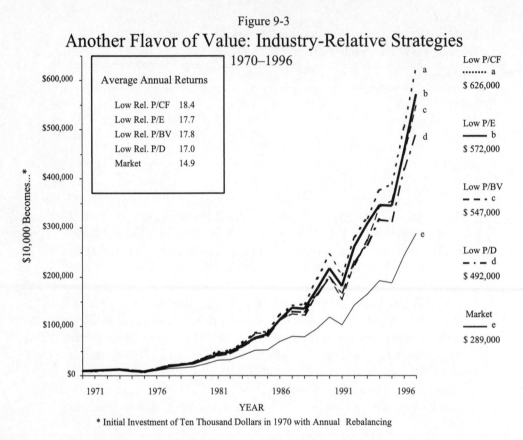

Average Annual Returns	
Low Rel. P/CF	18.4
Low Rel. P/E	17.7
Low Rel. P/BV	17.8
Low Rel. P/D	17.0
Market	14.9

Low P/CF
········ a
$ 626,000

Low P/E
——— b
$ 572,000

Low P/BV
— — · c
$ 547,000

Low P/D
— · — d
$ 492,000

Market
——— e
$ 289,000

$10,000 Becomes...*

YEAR

* Initial Investment of Ten Thousand Dollars in 1970 with Annual Rebalancing

returns 18.4% annually over the length of the study (well above the market's 14.9%). By contrast, the lowest price-to-book value stocks in the highest 20% of industries are 1.4 by this measure, double the price-to-book value ratio of the cheapest 20%. Still, they provide a well-above-average 17.4% return. Thus, the industry effect is very different than that of simply buying the lowest valued stocks in the averages. So we now have two separate and distinct effects that allow you to beat the market, both strongly backed by statistical evidence.

Why Buy the Cheapest Stocks in an Industry?

Perhaps you're wondering, "What is the advantage of buying the cheapest stocks within an industry rather than the cheapest stocks overall?" There are several reasons why it can make good sense. Hundreds of thousands of investors, tired of being battered by bad advice, have moved into index funds, as have large numbers of their institutional counterparts. Index funds now account for several hundred billion dollars.

The exciting development about buying the cheapest stocks in a group of major industries is that it leads to excellent long-term returns, while allowing you the chance to participate in stocks across the board. Our study indicates the returns dwarf those of an index fund. While it's not a strategy for everybody, it will work for investors who can afford to own a 40- or 50-stock portfolio across 30 or 40 major industry groups.

Our research also shows that once the portfolio is in place, as Table 9–1 demonstrated for low P/E, it needs little fine-tuning. Buying a portfolio of the lowest valued stocks in an industry and holding it without any changes—regardless of the contrarian strategy you prefer—results in higher annual returns over five-year holding periods than holding the portfolios for only one year. Returns, in statistician's terms, do not "decay" over five-year periods; they actually improve.

Why this works is speculative, but it appears that company fortunes do change over time. Industry laggards often tighten their belts, improve their management, and find ways of increasing their market share or developing new products, which results in their continued outperformance of the market for long periods. Analysts and investors slowly change their opinions of these laggards. Now when earnings surprise pleasantly, the market applauds and awards higher prices.

For favored-industry stocks, the process is exactly the opposite. Expectations are too optimistic—so high that even a brilliant management cannot meet them. Something has to go wrong. A glitch occurs because of increased competition (which builds rapidly in high-profit businesses) or a slight lag in the introduction of new products. And so it

Table 9–2

CONTRARIAN INDUSTRY RATIOS 1970–1996

The price-to-value ratio of the cheapest stocks in the lowest 20% of industries is much lower than the price-to-value ratios of the cheapest stocks in the highest 20% of industries. Yet the returns of the cheapest 20% of stocks in each group are nearly identical.

	Lowest 20% of Industries		*Highest 20% of Industries*	
	Ratio	*Return*	*Ratio*	*Return*
Low P/E	6.5	19.1%	11.0	16.8%
Low P/CF	3.2	16.9%	6.5	16.5%
Low P/BV	0.7	18.4%	1.4	17.4%
Low P/D*	8.1%	15.6%	3.8%	17.1%

* THE P/D IS LISTED AS DIVIDEND YIELD.

goes. Earnings, instead of growing at 25%, grow at 20%. The difference is devastating to the stock. Perceptions of its prospects change and the market unmercifully punishes it. Now, even excellent growth is met with skepticism, and any failure to meet expectations continues the pummeling. The combination of impossibly high expectations and the competitive and organizational problems (endemic to high and extremely profitable growth) take their toll.

But moving back from the "why" to the "how," let's look at another reason this approach can help you. Buying the lowest valued stocks in each major industry opens a much larger investment universe than is available using an "absolute" contrarian strategy. Investing in the absolutely cheapest stocks, no matter which of the previous methods you pick, gives the investor only the bottom 20% or 40% of stocks in the marketplace from which to select. With a relative industry strategy, you get a crack at the entire market.[6]

The advantage of the relative contrarian strategy is that you have far more diversification by industry than you do in the original contrarian strategies. This diversification should protect you from the underperformance that occurs when the most out-of-favor stocks and industries in the market are taboo. Thus, if groups like communications or biotech are headed for the stars, you will not feel left out. You will also not be positioned only in the most disliked groups that may underperform for months or sometimes years.

Although the returns of the relative industry strategies are moderately below those of the absolute strategies, psychological pressure is often the determining factor that may recommend these new methods. It is difficult for individual investors, and even more so for professionals, to take unpopular positions for long periods, even if they are right in the end.

With the inane focus on quarterly performance, by some consultants and clients, a pro who lags for too long can easily get the ax. True, he or she may prove right, but all too frequently it is "dead right." For the individual, the psychological pressures to run for the hills are difficult or impossible to resist. After all, it is the psychological pressures that keep people from following contrarian strategies in the first place.

The Defensive Team: Part II

"Do I still get to have my cake and eat it too?" many investors might ask of the relative industry strategies. "We see they provide impressive returns over time, but how good are they in down markets?" Very good in-

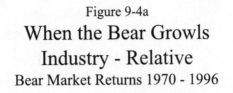

Figure 9-4a

When the Bear Growls
Industry - Relative
Bear Market Returns 1970 - 1996

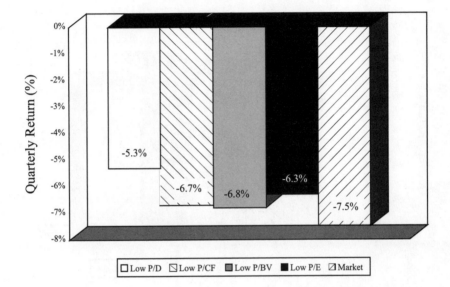

deed, as Figure 9–4a demonstrates. As with absolute contrarian strategies in chapter 7 (Figure 7–5), we measured the bear market returns for
all the down quarters in the 27-year time period. Once again, all four
strategies outperform the market handily in the 34 quarters when the
market declined. The price-to-dividend method again shines, declining
only –5.3% quarterly on average in down quarters against –7.5% for the
overall market. Similarly, Figure 9–4b shows all four relative industry
strategies outperform the market in the 74 quarters of our study when
stocks are heading up.

Next we'll turn to a number of issues important to shaping your investment approach.

Buy-and-Weed Strategies

In the preceding chapter we looked at the success of "buy-and-hold"
strategies. A twist on this approach is to buy a portfolio of contrarian
stocks and weed it periodically of stocks that move up to or above the

Figure 9-4b
When the Bull Roars
Industry - Relative
Bull Market Returns 1970 - 1996

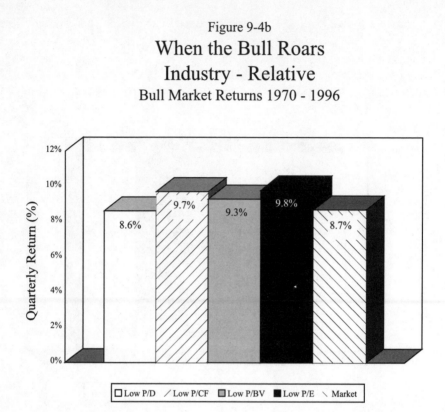

market ratios, or if they fail to perform as well as the market after a certain time. An overview of the studies indicated that returns normally diminished with long holding periods (ten years or more). Some methods (such as this) would thus raise overall return above the simple buy-and-hold strategy.

While this strategy introduces transaction costs, they should be quite small, since you should, on average, have only a few trades a year. The pruning process should also allow you to maintain a portfolio of contrarian stocks with above-average yields. In any case, whichever "mechanical" strategy you choose, you should have a good chance of outdoing the market while taking below-average risk and spending minimal time making selections.

Where Do I Get My Statistics?

You might ask how one determines quintiles. Brokerage firms, advisory services, and financial publications often advertise long lists of contrarian stocks (the Value Line Survey, for example, presents tables weekly of the hundred lowest P/Es, price-to-cash flow, price-to-book value, and highest yielding stocks of the 1,700 companies in its universe). Two other statistical data base providers, The American Association of Individual Investors (1–800–428–2244) and Investor's Alliance (1–800–804–5577), also offer disks of company information that allow screening, for a minimal fee.

To select contrarian stocks on your own, some simple rules should suffice. First, take a broad market index, like the S&P 500, for which the current P/E ratio, price-to-cash flow, price-to-book value, and dividend yield can easily be found from a variety of sources. The current P/E ratio of the S&P 500, in December 1997, is about 24.2, its price-to-cash flow 18.1, price-to-book value 5.4, and yield 1.6%.

Pick well-established companies. A rule of thumb might be to use a 20% discount or more from the S&P 500 for any of the first three measures and a yield of at least 1% above the market for the fourth. The deeper the discount from the S&P 500, the further into contrarian territory you go.

There is nothing magical about picking the bottom 20% by any one of the first three measures. It was simply a good cut-off point for a computer. As we found in virtually all of the contrarian studies, this group outperformed the market consistently.

A simple method should work fairly effectively if you do not have the actual quintiles for these strategies. How do you find the ratios themselves? *The Wall Street Journal*, *Barron's*, and the financial sections of most major daily newspapers will have the P/E ratio right next to the stock, calculated on latest 12-month reported earnings. It is a relatively easy matter to run down the column and find stocks at a 20% discount from the market multiple (or more or less, as you choose). Yield is also found daily in the financial section of any large newspaper. Once again, you can compare it with the average yield of the S&P 500, which is readily available from a number of sources. As indicated, price-to-cash flow and price-to-book value can be obtained at low cost from Value Line or a variety of other services.

Realistically, there are a number of approaches to contrarian strategies in addition to the eclectic approach that I favor personally. All are strongly documented statistically. While I don't believe contrarian investing need necessarily be the final answer to stock selection for everyone, it has consistently performed better in both good and bad markets. It is the only system I know of that effectively and systematically checks investor overreactions—by far the largest and most important source of investor error.

What Contrarian Strategies Won't Do for You

Whether you opt for the eclectic contrarian strategy, or you take the contrarian bit between your teeth and attack the market without any form of security analysis, keep in mind that the strategies are relative rather than absolute. This means that they won't help you decide when to get in or when to get out of stocks. Whether the market is high or low, you will receive no warning signals to sell in the first place or buy in the second.

What contrarian strategies should do is give you the best relative opportunities for your capital. Which means that in a rising market, your stocks ought to do better than the averages, and in a falling market they should decline less. As we have seen, the long-term returns of holding contrarian stocks through bull and bear markets are breathtaking; the longer the period, the more impressive the results. In chapter 13, we will provide some impressive evidence that owning stocks has been the best way to go, not only for the past decade but for the past 200 years.

Alternatives to Contrarian Strategies

MUTUAL FUNDS

Perhaps you wish to participate in the stock market, but do not want to make your own investment decisions. Or perhaps your capital is too limited to get a fully diversified contrarian portfolio.

With limited funds, the best approach would seem to be to purchase a mutual fund with a broad portfolio. There are a large number of sources to help you in the selection process including Lipper, Morningstar, The Value Line Mutual Fund Service, *Forbes,* and *Barron's.**
These will provide you with quarterly information on the fund's performance and its record over the number of years it has been in public hands. Select a fund that has a strategy you are in tune with, and that has outperformed the market for a significant period. This will narrow the bewildering number of funds out there to a handful. Also, make sure the manager who built the record is still running the fund. Table 9–3 gives you the returns of some of the better value mutual funds through bull and bear markets in the last five and ten years. The results are taken from the Morningstar Mutual Fund Survey.

For the investor who, having read about the difficulty of outperforming markets, decides an index fund is the best choice, that's easy too.

---

* *Forbes* ranks funds at least through two bear markets to get its bear-market rankings. The As are the top 5% relative to all stock funds, the Fs the bottom 5%.

Table 9–3

BEST PERFORMING VALUE FUNDS: 5- AND 10-YEAR RANKINGS

As of 12/31/97

Company	Asset Size ($Millions)	5-Yr. Return	10-Yr. Return
Davis NY Venture	4,462	22.0%	21.1%
Kemper-Dreman High Return A	3,170	22.0%	19.8%*
Fidelity Destiny II	3,693	22.4%	21.1%
Mutual Shares	7,755	20.0%	17.4%
Sequoia	3,468	23.0%	19.4%
Vanguard/Windsor II	23,545	20.7%	18.2%

*RETURN FOR KEMPER-DREMAN HIGH RETURN FUND SINCE INCEPTION, 3/18/88.

SOURCES OF DATA: LIPPER ANALYTICAL SERVICES

Vanguard, for example, provides a low-cost index fund that replicates the S&P 500 and another one that replicates the Russell 2000 (small cap—smaller market value companies).*

CLOSED-END INVESTMENT COMPANIES

A broad portfolio also can be acquired by purchasing a closed-end investment company. These companies, unlike mutual funds, do not continuously issue and redeem shares: their number of shares outstanding is fixed. Most of the larger closed-end funds listed on the New York Stock Exchange trade at a discount from the value of their assets. Table 9–4 indicates the average discount over the last five years.

The discounts, provided weekly in *The Wall Street Journal, Barron's,* and *The New York Times,* usually vary between 5% and 15%. If the discounts are larger than average, as they tend to be during a market decline, it is often a buying opportunity.[7]

Foreign and Country Funds: Myth and Reality

Until recently, foreign markets were the rage. Billions flowed into China, the Pacific Rim, and Latin America, while more conservative investors bet on the European and Japanese markets. Should you get into the act? Maybe, but you have to be careful.

---

* For information, contact The Vanguard Group at 1–800–860–8394 or at www.VANGUARD. COM.

Don't just jump in because the concept is exciting. Speculative activity in China, Hong Kong, and Mexico has cost investors billions of dollars in recent years. The idea that there are zillions of Chinese yearning to buy anything from an offshore company at fat profits is bunk. The people who buy this thesis remind me of the moonstruck English investors who lined up to purchase shares in the South Sea Company several centuries ago, convinced it owned mountains of gold and diamonds in the Indies.

Some of these markets certainly have potential, but if history is a guide, it takes years to develop large profits. When the realization dawned in the fall of 1997 that the payoff was further off than anticipated, and that a bumpy road lay ahead for a while, many of the Pacific Rim markets free-fell. Korea, Thailand, Malaysia, and many other formerly booming economies came within a hair's breadth of default debt and required well over $100 billion in bailouts by the International Monetary Fund and the banks of major industrial nations to save the day. As a result of this and similar crises, in mid-December of 1997 the Morgan Stanley index of emerging markets returned only 27% for the most recent five years, 198% in the most recent ten. This compared to 151% and 425% respectively for the S&P 500. That's right, in the past 10 years the "dull S&P" provided more than double the return of the emerging market countries, without the currency and other risks inherent in these markets. Some bonus for investing abroad!

Does this sound spoilsport? Maybe you remember the red-hot German closed-end funds that sold at large premiums to asset value on the prospects of the reunification of Germany and the collapse of commu-

Table 9–4
CLOSED-END INVESTMENT COMPANIES
As of 12/31/96

Company	Asset Size	Average Discount 5-years
Adams Express	1099.4	−9.92
Gabelli Equity	1041.1	−0.38
General American Investors	597.8	−9.58
Liberty All-Star Equity Fund	953.6	−1.08
Quest for Value Capital	890.9	−11.18
Royce Value Trust	440.9	−7.60
Salomon Brothers Fund	1588.4	−11.86
Tricontinental	2991.9	−13.70

SOURCE: PREPARED FROM MORNINGSTAR DATA.

nism. A number of the premiums on closed-end funds went to 50% or 100%. But German reunification proved much costlier than expected and the premiums evaporated. You could have lost half or more of your capital purchasing these closed-end funds at their peak. The same was true in the mid 1990s in the Mexican and other Latin American markets, as well as in other developing countries.

Lesson one, then, is that foreign investing is anything but a panacea. You have to apply the same contrarian principles you apply in U.S. markets. The 1997 debacle in the Pacific Rim markets is a classic example. Be extra careful to avoid the waves of speculation that often dominate in these areas. Even buying an index fund may not help much. In 1990 the Japanese market was in the stratosphere, trading at P/E multiples of 80 to 90 times earnings.

Sure, it's high by our standards, we heard from the experts on Japanese stocks at the time, but the value is there. Japanese markets, like Japanese snow, are different.* Nippon Telephone, for example, traded at a P/E of 160 and had a market value many times larger than AT&T, although AT&T was several times its size. This one market made up fully 60% of the value of all stocks outside the U.S. before it collapsed in the early 1990s.

Another important consideration is that when you buy foreign companies, you are taking an exchange rate risk that can greatly add to or detract from your total return. In the years that the markets abroad outpaced those in the U.S., the gains were often more a consequence of a weak dollar than of strong markets overseas. Thus, when the dollar dropped in recent years, a good part of the fabulous returns on foreign portfolios—trumpeted in many funds' advertising—were not from the markets themselves but were there because these stocks were simply worth more with a cheaper U.S. dollar. More recently, with the stronger dollar, the situation reversed. Behind much of the glamour of investing abroad, then, is simply speculation that foreign currencies will go up and the dollar down.

Remember, too, that foreign stocks looked strong in the early nineties because of the Japanese bubble. The fast-climbing Japanese market in tandem with the falling U.S. dollar made investing abroad appear to be a lay-up. When the Japanese market began to unravel in the early nineties, the foreign indexes fell apart.

Table 9–5 gives you the returns of global and foreign stock funds taken from Morningstar Mutual Funds. Glance at the third column,

---

* That Japanese snow was different was an argument Japanese ski manufacturers used against the import of foreign ski equipment for some time.

Table 9–5

TOTAL RETURNS OF INTERNATIONAL STOCK FUNDS
VERSUS THE S&P 500 AS OF 12/31/96

	3 years	5 years	10 years	Average P/E	Average Market Capitalization*
International Stock Funds	6.1%	10.1%	9.6%	25	4,500
Standard & Poor 500	19.7%	15.2%	15.3%	21	5,850

* IN $ MILLIONS.
SOURCE: PREPARED FROM MORNINGSTAR DATA.

which shows ten-year annualized returns. The average international fund does not approach the S&P 500, let alone the returns from contrarian strategies. Also, look at the average weighted P/E for foreign funds. It is 25, significantly higher than the P/Es we would buy following my strategies. Finally, look at the median market size these funds are buying. They are somewhat smaller than the stocks we would look at with contrarian strategies.

Over any reasonable period of time, then, investing abroad has not done any better—and oftentimes worse—than investing in the United States. Not only have the major domestic averages provided excellent returns overall, but you avoid the worries of currency fluctuations and also stay clear of thinly-traded speculative markets and geo-political considerations.

Remember too, all foreign countries are not equally safe. I feel more comfortable investing in Western Europe and Canada, or, if the P/Es come down, in Japan. I would not invest in South America or other regions with a record of debt defaults and restructurings. Our banks have taken a whipping in these countries, often losing 50 cents on the dollar on loans to their governments. The underwriters of foreign securities assure us that things are different now. Maybe, but who can say that a government that has defaulted on debt won't change the rules again?

Having talked about the dangers involved in investing abroad, I hasten to add that there are opportunities in foreign stocks. One of the best for individual investors is to buy foreign securities traded in the U.S. markets. This avoids the high costs of overseas brokerage, safekeeping charges, and converting small amounts of foreign exchange at high spreads. American Depository Receipts (ADRs) represent a stated number of shares of a foreign stock traded in the U.S. Many of the larger

ADRs are listed on the New York Stock Exchange and most have detailed financial information available in English.

The mechanics are simple because a large number of foreign stocks, funds, and other financial instruments are actively traded here. Foreign stocks can make good sense, because they sometimes trade at lower values, using contrarian indicators, than do domestic companies in the same industry. Unilever, for example, the giant Dutch-based consumer products company, is nearly the same size as Procter & Gamble. The company has a lower P/E and a higher yield than the American consumer products companies, although the growth rates are similar. Other foreign companies that present better value than their American counterparts can be found by looking through the Value Line Investment Survey or the S&P stock report sheets.

You might use these stocks, as I do, to find better values in a particular industry than are available domestically, or else to produce a diversified portfolio both by country and by industry. Such giants as Royal Dutch, Sony, Nestle N.V., and Philips are all traded here, most on the NYSE. Using ADRs, you can structure a well-diversified foreign portfolio. By coincidence, many of these large, well-established ADRs pass the contrarian criteria easily. But remember, the currency risk doesn't disappear. If the dollar spikes up against the currency the stock was issued in, the price will drop, and vice-versa.

There are a number of conservative ways, then, to approach markets abroad. The first is to buy an index fund, or a close substitute, that represents the weighted value of stocks outside the U.S. If I were to buy a foreign fund, this would be my preference, because currently there are no contrarian funds with acceptable records in these markets.[8]

The second is to buy large foreign companies that have ADRs trading here and that fit in with a contrarian strategy, as was described. The latter is something I have done often with the portfolios I manage, with good success.

A third alternative that sometimes proves quite lucrative is to buy closed-end funds that invest in major countries with good outlooks and political stability, when these funds are unpopular.

The first rule of investing abroad is identical to the first rule of investing at home: buy 'em when they're cheap, not when everybody is on the bandwagon and the media hype is in full swing. With hot initial public offerings (IPOs) and concept stocks at home, we know that after a euphoric price run-up there is an inevitable hangover.

If you buy a country fund, you should, of course, look for the same contrarian characteristics. Four examples of country funds that have been cheap in recent years:

- The Germany Fund traded at more than double its net asset value at the peak of "Europe 1992" enthusiasm in 1991. Since then, the stock has declined to a discount of 17% by late 1997.
- The Spain Fund, at the height of the investor euphoria in 1989, traded at almost triple its net asset value. In late 1997, it traded at a discount of nearly 14%.
- Scudder New Europe traded at a 20% discount in late 1997.
- Vanguard International Equity Index European is a no-load index fund. Its expense ratio of 30 basis points is only one-sixth that of most funds investing in Europe.*

One final word of warning on foreign closed-end funds: don't buy countries considered to have great prospects, which trade at a premium to their net asset value. The average closed-end fund normally trades at a 10% discount or more to the underlying asset value of its portfolio. Be wary of a premium; it probably won't last. When a country or sector fund gets "hot," as the Spain Fund did in 1989, enthusiastic folks pushed it to an enormous premium, as we saw, before it slid back to a discount. Investors caught in such a swing from premium to discount lost as much as 50% of their assets, after underwriting fees. This can occur with little or no movement in the underlying foreign stock market itself. This is another segment of the new-issues game that puts big bucks into the underwriters' pockets at the expense of the investor.

Next we'll turn to one of the toughest questions that must be addressed using contrarian—or for that matter any other—strategy. When should you sell?

When to Sell?

Regardless of the strategy you use, one of your most difficult decisions is when to sell. There are almost as many answers to the problem as there are investors, but even among professionals, few religiously follow their own sell rules. Psychological forces dislocate most sell decisions, often disastrously. I have seen many a money manager set stringent sell targets, and did so myself in my earlier years. But as the

---

* The expense ratio of a fund is the annual charges the fund takes, including management fees. This comes right out of the investors' pockets. These ratios average 1.20% for the industry and can run as high as 2% to 3% a year. The lower the expense ratio for a comparable fund the more favorable it is to the investor.

stock moved rapidly toward the pre-set price, more and more good news usually accompanied its rise.

If the stock was originally purchased at $20 with the sell target at $40, and it shot through $40, the manager would often bump the sell price higher. Forty would become $50, $50 would be stretched to $60. This frequently resulted in the manager taking "the round trip": riding a stock all the way up, only to ride it all the way down again.

Given what we know, it seems that the safest approach, once again, is to rely on mechanical guidelines, which filter out much of the emotional content of the decision. The general rule I use is this, which I'll call Rule 21:

RULE 21

Sell a stock when its P/E ratio (or other contrarian indicator) approaches that of the overall market, regardless of how favorable prospects may appear. Replace it with another contrarian stock.

For example, assume we are using the low P/E strategy and the market P/E is 22. If one of our stocks, (say PNC Bank), bought at a P/E of 10, went up to 22, we would sell it and replace it with another low P/E stock.*

The first guideline then is simple: Pick a sell point when you buy a stock. If it reaches that point, grit your teeth, brace yourself, and get rid of it. You probably will be unhappy because the issue often will go higher. But why be greedy? You've made a good gain, and that's what the game is all about. (The only exception is when you have an almost sure takeover situation.)

Picking a sell point, however, doesn't necessarily mean selling a stock just because it has gone up. If you are a low price-to-book value (P/BV) player, for example, you may find that even after a stock has risen sharply it still sells at a below-market P/BV because its book value has continued to go up. Often, stocks remain at low P/BVs for years, despite doubling or even tripling in price, because book value has also doubled or tripled, keeping the P/BV ratio low. The same is true for low price-to-earnings, price-to-cash flow, or high dividend yields.

Another question is how long should you hold a stock that has not worked out. Investors all too often fall in love with their holdings. I have

---

* Naturally, as prices change over time, the weightings of stocks in the portfolio will differ. When stocks are sold, the effort should be made to bring the weightings more into balance with one another.

seen portfolios loaded with dozens of companies that look good on paper but that have long been dogs in the market, resulting in poor returns.

Again, there are many partial answers to this problem, but I think 2½ to 3 years is an adequate waiting period. (For a cyclical stock with a drop in earnings, this might be stretched to three-and-a-half years.) If after that time the stock still disappoints, sell it. John Templeton, one of the masters of value investing, used a six-year time span. You be the judge, but stick to your time frame and don't be stubborn.

Another important rule is to sell a stock immediately if the long-term fundamentals deteriorate significantly. No matter how painstaking the research, something can go wrong, worsening a company's or an industry's outlook dramatically. I'm not talking about a poor quarter or a temporary surprise that a stock will snap back from, but major changes that weaken a company's prospects. Under these conditions, I have found that taking your lumps immediately and moving on usually results in the smallest loss.

To summarize: don't be stubborn, don't be greedy, and don't be afraid to take small losses. Above all, when you buy a stock, make a mental decision as to the level at which you will sell it—and stick to that decision. You may lose a few points at the top, but you'll make a lot more than you'll lose in the long run.

A further question may arise with sell strategies using the eclectic approach. Suppose you have a portfolio of 25 or 30 stocks and find a new one that ranks much higher by our indicators, while trading at a lower contrarian ratio than stocks you already own. A switch might then be made, but keep in mind the principle of a fixed number of stocks in the portfolio: each time one is purchased, another one should be sold. Because you are bringing in more judgment in switching, and therefore more opportunity for error, changes of this sort should be relatively rare in order to avoid the dangers of overtrading. Or, as horse players like to say, "Stay away from the switches."

A supplementary rule is, do not sell a stock that attains a high P/E multiple solely because of a decline in earnings, either through a large one-time charge or because of temporary business conditions. It is true that by using the contrarian approach you can acquire a number of clinkers that are nearing peak earnings and will incur income declines, whether because they are cyclical or for other reasons. However, we know the overall superior record of contrarian stocks, which contains numbers of such companies. Thus, if you have adequate diversification, both by the number of stocks and by industry, this should not be a major problem.

Also, the price drop will often be an overreaction to the anticipated decline in earnings. Take the case of Compaq, trading at $9 in early 1991. At the time it was trading at a P/E of 14—under that of the S&P 500. Earnings declined that year by almost 50%, and Compaq's multiple rose above the market's as the stock fell as low as 3⅛. By the latter part of 1994, however, the stock was over $15, and by late-1997 it had moved up to $79, rising far more than the spurting S&P over this time, while staying at a below-market P/E.

In this chapter, we have looked at the relative-industry contrarian strategy, as well as a number of additional ways to use the other strategies we have developed. We also examined a number of techniques for people with limited capital, and looked at the question of whether you should invest abroad. Next, let's turn to the heart of why contrarian strategies work with such consistency: the predictability of investor overreaction. Armed with this knowledge, we have a far better chance of not stampeding with the herd, whether in euphoria or panic, and have a real possibility of benefiting from the greatest opportunity of all—investing in crisis.

10

Knowing Your Market Odds

I N THIS section we have seen that investors make systematic errors in predicting which will be the "best" and "worst" stocks. We have also been looking at the strategies and techniques that will allow you to benefit from their mistakes. Now it's time to examine why investors, many of whom are highly knowledgeable about markets, go off the deep end time after time. Overreaction is the main reason people make repeated and predictable errors, the linchpin of contrarian strategies

However, investor overreaction is only one way that people repeatedly swing widely away from rational behavior. The psychological pressures we are discussing might also account for such anomalies as soothsayers' warnings resulting in the evacuation of London in the early sixteenth century, on the lighter side, and to fans rioting murderously at a soccer game, or to lynchings, on the darker.

We will see in chapter 16 that the most gentle peer pressure can lead us to bad decisions, even when the facts are straightforward and easy to distinguish. But when reality is complex and the situation is hard to read, "social reality"—the consensus of the group, no matter how far-fetched—can take a grip on the mind, and turn strong, rational, independent people into sheep. Or, to find a metaphor more appropriate to human beings, lone wolves join the pack and follow anyone who acts like an alpha male.

But the psychological findings on group peer behavior provide only a part of the answer. Investors, even professionals, fall prey to important logical fallacies and psychological failings. Some of the latter are relatively new; others have been known for decades. These psychological pressures impact our decisions under conditions of uncertainty in a very predictable manner, not only in the marketplace, but in virtually every aspect of our lives. The bottom line is that these powerful forces lead most people to make the same mistakes time and again. Understanding them is your best protection against stampeding with the crowd, and perhaps profiting from their mistakes instead. But as you read on you'll see it's much easier said than done.

Improving Your Market Odds

Despite what many economists and financial theorists assume, people are not good intuitive statisticians, particularly under difficult conditions. They do not calculate odds properly when making investment decisions, which causes consistent errors. First, we must learn why such mistakes occur so frequently. Once their nature is understood, we can develop a set of rules to help monitor our decisions and to provide a shield against serious mishap. We will then see how the contrarian strategies presented above are anchored upon these intuitive statistical limitations. We can then apply the same principles to other investment opportunities outside of financial markets, and be in a position to profit from crisis and panic in the marketplace itself.

In Simplification We Believe

Let's quickly review the limitations of man's information-processing capabilities, a sort of black hole that is constantly exerting great force on his decisions. We briefly looked at the problem in chapter 6. According to Nobel laureate Herbert Simon, people are swamped with information and react consciously to only a small part of it. Simon also stated that when overwhelmed with facts, we select a small part of them and usually reach a different conclusion from what the entire data set would suggest.

Researchers have found that people react to this avalanche of data by adopting shortcuts or rules of thumb rather than formally calculating the actual odds of a given outcome. Known to psychologists as *judgmental heuristics* in technical jargon, these shortcuts are learning and simplifying strategies we use for managing large amounts of information. Backed by the experience of a lifetime, most of these judgmental shortcuts work exceptionally well, and allow us to cope with data that would otherwise overwhelm us.

Driving a car down a superhighway, for example, you concentrate only on operating the vehicle, on other traffic, and on traffic signs, screening out thousands of other distracting and disruptive bits of information. The rule of thumb is to focus solely on what directly affects our driving, and the rule is obviously a good one.

We also use selective processes in dealing with probabilities: in many of our decisions and judgments, we tend to be intuitive statisticians. We apply mental shortcuts that work well most of the time. We think our odds of survival are better when driving at 55 miles an hour than at 90 miles an hour, although few of us have ever bothered to check the actual numbers. A professional basketball team is likely to beat an amateur one, if the "amateurs" are not "The Dream Team"; a discount computer store will probably sell personal computers more cheaply than Macy's or Bloomingdale's. And we might expect to get to a city 300 miles away faster by air than by ground (if it is not a United Express flight to a Colorado ski resort). There are dozens of examples that such procedures are valuable and immensely timesaving.

But being an intuitive statistician has limitations as well as blessings. The very simplifying processes that are normally efficient time-savers lead to systematic mistakes in investment decisions. They can make you believe the odds are dramatically different from what they actually are. As a result, they consistently shortchange the investor.

The distortions produced by the subjectively calculated probabilities are large, systematic, and difficult to eliminate, even after people have been made fully aware of them, as we'll see next.

It Ain't Necessarily So

Let us first look at one of the most common of the cognitive biases that Daniel Kahneman of Princeton and the late Amos Tversky of Stanford (whom we met earlier) call "representativeness." The two professors show it's a natural human tendency to draw analogies and see identical situations where none exist.

In the market, this means labeling two companies, or two market environments, as the same when the actual resemblance is superficial. Give people a little information and, *click!,* they pull out a picture they're familiar with, though it may only remotely represent the current situation.

An example: the aftermath of the 1987 crash. In five trading days the Dow fell 742 points, culminating with the 508 point decline on Black Monday, October 19. This wiped out almost $1 trillion of value. "Is this

1929?" asked the media in bold headlines. Many investors taking this heuristical shortcut cowered in cash. They were caught up in the false parallel between 1987 and 1929.

Why? At the time, the situations seemed eerily similar. We had not had a stock market crash for 58 years. Generations grew up believing that because a Depression followed the 1929 Crash it would always happen this way. A large part of Wall Street's experts, the media, and the investing public agreed.

Overlooked was that the two crashes had only the remotest similarity. In the first place, 1929 was a special case. The nation has had numerous panics and crashes in the nineteenth and early twentieth centuries without a depression. Crashes or no, the thriving American economy always bounced back in short order.

In recounting how often they occurred, Victor Niederhoffer, in his insightful book, *The Education of a Speculator,* notes that Henry Clews wrote after the panic of 1837 that "Prices dropped to zero." The same observer casually stated a few pages later, "The panic of 1857 was much more severe."[1] Clews doesn't say whether in the latter panic sellers actually had to pay buyers to cart away their stocks or bonds. In neither case was there a depression. So crash and depression were not synonymous.

More important, it was apparent even then that the economic and investment climate was entirely different. My *Forbes* column of May 2, 1988, noted some of the differences clearly visible at the time. The column stated that although market savants and publications were presenting charts showing the breathtaking similarity between the market post-crash in 1988 with that of 1929, there was far less to it than met the eye. Back then the market rallied smartly after the debacle before beginning a free-fall in the spring of 1930, and many experts believed history would repeat itself 58 years later.

The similarities were obvious. The major averages had moved up 20% from the Oct. 19, 1987, bottom and then skidded lower, again in a manner similar to early 1930. But as I warned readers: a chart, unlike a picture, is not always worth a thousand words; sometimes it is just downright misleading.

The economic and investment fundamentals of 1988 were worlds apart from those of 1930. At that time economic and financial conditions were beginning to blow apart, as the worst depression in the nation's history rapidly approached.

It was hard for even the most fervent gloom-and-doomer to argue that a parallel situation existed after the 1987 crash. The economy was rolling along at a rate above most estimates pre-crash and sharply above the recession levels projected in the weeks following the October 19 debacle.

Stock fundamentals were encouraging. The P/E of the S&P 500 was a little over 13 times earnings, down sharply from the 20 times earnings just prior to the 1987 crash, and below the long-term average of 15 to 16. The underlying fundamentals of the two periods were dramatically different. 1929 it wasn't. Investors who followed the representativeness bias missed an enormous buying opportunity: by July, 1997, the market quadrupled from that time.

The representativeness heuristic covers a number of common decision-making errors. Kahneman and Tversky defined this heuristic as a subjective judgment of the extent to which the event in question "is similar in essential properties to its parent population" or "reflects the salient features of the process by which it is generated."[2] People often judge probabilities "by the degree to which A is representative of B, that is, by the degree to which A resembles B."[3]

What are A and B? It depends. If you are estimating the probability that A came from B, A might be a person and B might be a group, say of doctors. The judgment you want to make in this case is the probability A is also a doctor. Or A might be an event and B might be a potential cause. Again you are judging the probability that A comes from B. A, for example, would be the similarity or representativeness in people's minds of the 1987 crash to B which, in this case, would be the 1929 crash and depression.

Because the definition of representativeness is abstract and a little hard to understand, let's look at some more concrete examples of how this heuristic works, and how it can lead to major mistakes in many situations.

First, it may give too much emphasis to the similarities between events (or samples), but not to the probability that they will occur. Again looking at the 1987 crash, it appeared similar to 1929 in its stunning decline, but this by itself did not mean that a Great Depression would follow. In fact, as we have seen, there have been many crashes, but only one Great Depression. Still, the dramatic event of the 1929 Crash followed by the Great Depression was an overpowering image. After the 1987 crash, people did not step back and try to logically assess what the probabilities were that the next event would occur in an identical manner. Rather, by using the representativeness heuristic, or mental shortcut, they assumed this would be the outcome.

Second, representativeness may reduce the importance of variables that are critical in determining the event's probability. Again using the crash as an illustration, the major differences between the situations in

1987 and 1929, outlined in the *Forbes* article, were downplayed, with the focus solely on the market's plunge.

This type of representativeness bias occurs time and again in the marketplace. During the Gulf Crisis in the last half of 1990, for example, the stock market fell dramatically on the fears of a worldwide shortage of oil. The seizing of the Kuwaiti oil fields by Iraq, and the subsequent embargo on Iraqi oil, triggered the bias for both investors and the media. The surface similarities to the past indicated an oil shortage, followed by a skyrocketing increase in price, culminating in runaway inflation, as was the case in 1981, or a severe recession as in 1973–1974. Markets plunged, as investors fearfully recalled the battered sales of large cars and other gas-guzzlers including yachts (whose prices dropped sharply) as well as other economic horrors.

The representativeness bias worked in an identical manner to the way it had after the 1987 crash. Yet 1990 was dramatically different from 1973 or 1981.

I warned about the dangers of false parallels in a column written at the time.[4] While it was impossible to predict the outcome of the Persian Gulf Crisis, the world was not facing a major protracted increase in oil prices.

Still, market pundits immediately compared this oil crisis with those of 1973/1974 and 1979/1980. Back in 1980, for example, oil experts stated that crude would reach $100 a barrel by the end of the decade, at the latest. Then, too, leading dailies ran front-page series for months on how higher oil prices would permanently damage the economy. Some of the statistics conjured up to back the predictions were terrifying. One showed that at the then-current price of oil, almost the entire capital of the Western world would flow into the coffers of OPEC (Organization of Petroleum Exporting Countries) members. Another demonstrated that Saudi Arabia would accumulate more capital in six or seven years than the value of all stocks on the NYSE.

What actually happened? By the late 1980s oil had dropped to as low as $12 a barrel. Fear sells newspapers and keeps people glued to the tube, but fear does not make money in the stock market.

But all of this was forgotten as the crisis developed in the late summer of 1990. In fact, the differences between the Gulf Crisis and the two previous oil crises were remarkable. In 1990 the world was facing an oil glut, not the shortages of the two earlier occasions. Oil prices, rather than tripling as they did in the seventies, were up only about 30% in the 1990 crisis. Too, this time around the OPEC members had not banded together to increase prices. Instead they had mostly condemned the Iraqi aggression and felt threatened by it. The OPEC cartel indicated it would make up the Iraq-Kuwait difference to keep prices from rising further. With the 50-year-plus supply the Saudis and some of the other producers had, and their pressing need for hard cash, economic considerations ranked up there with altruism. Finally, there was a unanimity among the major powers in response to the crisis that had not occurred in well over a century.

The analysis strongly indicated that oil prices were not destined to move higher for long, if at all. The panic that gripped many investors had created the finest buying opportunity of the decade.

You can see the representativeness bias resulted in a near identical investor reaction to the Gulf Crisis as it did to the 1987 crash. First, people put undue weight on the surface similarities between the potential oil crisis of 1990 and those of 1973/1974 and 1980. Secondly, investors again downplayed the critical differences between the two periods the article outlined, which were far more important than the casual resemblances. Again, the bias contributed to major investor errors in decision-making.

As I'm sure you have guessed, the representativeness heuristic can apply just as forcefully to a company or an industry as to the market as a whole. Here is one such an example:

In 1993 Dell Computer collapsed on Wall Street, losing 50% of its value in months. One day it had a market capitalization of $4.6 billion; six months later, it was just over $2.2 billion. Same company but worth less than half as much, and trading at only 4.6 times the previous year's earnings. What caused the drop? Earnings were weak, as the company took some major charges while repositioning its personal computer lines, and restructuring its marketing.

What probably happened was this: two other industry leaders, IBM and Digital Equipment Corporation (DEC), were weak, and investors lumped the three companies together. IBM was in temporary trouble, while DEC's was more serious. Dell was not. It was a very different kind of company with different products. Its repositioning was fabulously successful and it went on to become a major player in the personal computer (PC) industry. If you had bought it at its 1993 low, you would have increased your money more than 59-fold by late 1997. The representativeness bias worked the same way as in the two previous examples.

Kahneman and Tversky's findings, which have been repeatedly confirmed, are particularly important to our understanding of stock market errors and lead us to this rule of investing:

RULE 22

Look beyond obvious similarities between a current investment situation and one that appears equivalent in the past. Consider other important factors that may result in a markedly different outcome.

The Law of Small Numbers

The representativeness bias is responsible at least in part for a number of other major and oft-repeated errors. All mutual fund organizations work from the principle that investors flock to better-performing mutual funds—even though financial researchers have shown that the "hot" funds in one time period are often the poorest performers in another. The final verdict on the sizzling funds in the 1982/1983 market was disastrous. Ditto for the aggressive-growth funds of 1991 to 1997. Investors lost billions of dollars in these funds. Many, although far more risky, could not hold a candle to the long-term records of many conservative, blue-chip mutual funds.

Still, people are continually enticed by such "hot" performance, even if it lasts for brief periods. Because of this susceptibility, brokers or analysts who have had one or two stocks move up sharply, or technicians who call one turn correctly, are believed to have established a credible record and can readily find market followings.

Likewise, an advisory service that is right for a brief time can beat its drums loudly. One market-letter writer was featured prominently in the Sunday *New York Times* for being bearish in July of 1996, as the market dropped rapidly. He was right for three weeks but missed the enormous rally of the prior 18 months, as well as the subsequent rise for the balance of 1996, which kept him out of the market as it spiked 80%.

In fact, it doesn't matter if the advisor is wrong repeatedly, the name of the game is to get a dramatic prediction out there. A well-timed call can bring huge rewards to a popular newsletter writer. Eugene Lerner, a former finance professor who heads Disciplined Investment Advisors, a market-letter writer, speaking of what making a bearish call in a declining market can do, said, "If the market goes down for the next three years you'll be as rich as Croesus. . . . The next time around, everyone will listen to you."[5] With hundreds and hundreds of advisory letters out there someone has to be right. Again, it's just the odds.

Elaine Garzarelli gained near immortality when she purportedly "called" the 1987 crash. Although, as the market strategist for Shearson

Lehman, her forecast was never published in a research report, nor indeed communicated to its clients, she still received widespread recognition and publicity for this call, which was made in a short TV interview on CNBC.

Since this "brilliant call," her record, according to a fellow strategist, "has been somewhat mixed, like most of us."[6] Still, her remark on CNBC that the Dow could drop sharply from its then 5300 level rocked an already nervous market on July 23, 1996. What had been a 40-point gain for the Dow turned into a 40-point loss, a good deal of which was attributed to her comments. Only a few days earlier, Ms. Garzarelli had predicted the Dow would rise to 6400 from its then value of 5400. *Even so, people widely followed her because of "the great call in 1987."*

Stan Weinstein, editor of *The Professional Tape Reader*, an advisory letter headquartered in Hollywood, Florida, advertises week after week that the market is heading south. He naturally tells potential subscribers that following his advice will make them mega-bucks. Mr. Weinstein's track record leaves much to be desired. According to the *Hulbert Financial Digest*, his advice has significantly underperformed the market.[7]

The truth is, market-letter writers have been wrong in their judgments far more often than they would like to remember. However, advisors understand that the public considers short-term results meaningful when they are, more often than not, simply chance. Those in the public eye usually gain large numbers of new subscribers for being right by random luck.

Which brings us to another important probability error that falls under the broad rubric of representativeness. Amos Tversky and Daniel Kahneman call this one the "law of small numbers."[8] Examining journals in psychology and education, they found that researchers systematically overstated the importance of findings taken from small samples. The statistically valid "law of large numbers" states that large samples will usually be highly representative of the population from which they are drawn; for example, public opinion polls are fairly accurate because they draw on large and representative groups. The smaller the sample used, however (or the shorter the record), the more likely the findings are chance rather than meaningful.

Yet the Tversky and Kahneman study showed that typical psychological or educational experimenters gamble their research theories on samples so small that the results have a very high probability of being chance.[9] This is the same as gambling on the single good call of an investment advisor. The psychologists and educators are far too confident in the significance of results based on a few observations or a short period of time, even though they are trained in statistical techniques and are aware of the dangers.

Note how readily people overgeneralize the meaning of a small number of supporting facts. Limited statistical evidence seems to satisfy our intuition no matter how inadequate the depiction of reality. Sometimes the evidence we accept runs to the absurd. A good example of the major overemphasis on small numbers is the almost blind faith investors place in governmental economic releases on employment, industrial production, the consumer price index, the money supply, the leading economic indicators, et cetera.

These statistics frequently trigger major stock- and bond-market reactions, particularly if the news is bad. For example, investors are concerned about the possibility of rising prices. If the unemployment rate drops two-tenths of one percent in a month when it was expected to be unchanged, or if industrial production climbs slightly more than the experts expected, stock prices can fall, at times sharply.

Should this happen? No. Flash statistics, more times than not, are near worthless. Initial economic and Fed figures are revised significantly for weeks or months after their release, as new and "better" information flows in. Thus, an increase in the money supply can turn into a decrease, or a large drop in the leading indicators can change to a moderate increase. These revisions occur with such regularity you would think that investors, particularly pros, would treat them with the skepticism they deserve.

Alas, the real world refuses to follow the textbooks. Experience notwithstanding, investors treat as gospel all authoritative-sounding releases that they think pinpoint the development of important trends.

An example of how instant news threw investors into a tailspin occurred in July of 1996. Preliminary statistics indicated the economy was beginning to gain steam. The flash figures showed that GDP (gross domestic product) would rise at a 3% rate in the next several quarters, a rate higher than expected. Many people, convinced by these statistics that rising interest rates were imminent, bailed out of the stock market that month. To the end of that year, the GDP growth figures had been revised down significantly (unofficially, a minimum of a dozen times, and officially at least twice). The market rocketed ahead to new highs to August 1997, but a lot of investors had retreated to the sidelines on the preliminary bad news.

Just as irrational is the overreaction to every utterance by a Greenspan or other senior Fed or government official, no matter how offhanded. Like ancient priests examining chicken entrails to foretell events, many pros scrutinize every remark and act upon it immediately, even though they are not sure what it is they are acting on. Remember here the advice of a world champion chess player when asked how to avoid making a bad move. His answer: "Sit on your hands."

But professional investors don't sit on their hands; they dance on tiptoe, ready to flit after the least particle of information as if it were a strongly documented trend. The law of small numbers, in such cases, results in decisions sometimes bordering on the inane.

Tversky and Kahneman's findings, which have been repeatedly confirmed, are particularly important to our understanding of some stock market errors and lead to another rule that investors should follow:

RULE 23

Don't be influenced by the short-term record of a money manager, broker, analyst, or advisor, no matter how impressive; don't accept cursory economic or investment news without significant substantiation.

The law of averages indicates that many experts will have excellent records—usually playing popular trends—often for months and sometimes for several years, only to stumble disastrously later. If you buy the record just after a period of spectacular performance, chances are the letter writer or manager will not sustain it.

This is the sad lesson to be learned from the records of the market-letter writers above and from the turbo-charged, aggressive growth managers of mutual funds in the mid-eighties, many of whom forlornly traded their hot hands in for a bartender's apron or UPS uniforms after decimating their clients' portfolios. It is the same lesson that investors over the centuries have had to relearn with each new supposedly unbeatable market opportunity.

A Variation of the Previous Problem

A third flaw, in many ways parallel to the second, also indicates man's shortcomings as an intuitive statistician. In making decisions, we become overly immersed in the details of a particular situation and neglect the outcome of similar situations in our experience. These past outcomes are called *prior probabilities,* and logically should help to guide similar choices in the present.[10]

But they tend not to. This shows up clearly in an experiment made with a group of advanced psychology students.[11] The group was given a brief personality analysis of a graduate student, said to have been written by a psychologist who had conducted some tests several years earlier. The analysis was not only outdated but contained no indication of the subject's academic preference. Psychology students are taught that profiles of this sort can be enormously inaccurate. The study, which follows, was intended to provide them with nothing of practical value.

Here it is:

Tom W. is of high intelligence, although lacking in true creativity. He has a need for order and clarity and for neat and tidy systems in which every detail finds its appropriate place. His writing is dull and rather mechanical, occasionally enlivened by somewhat corny puns and flashes of imagination of the sci-fi type. He has a strong drive for competence. He seems to have little feeling and little sympathy for other people, and does not enjoy interacting with others. Self-centered, he nevertheless has a deep moral sense.

Tom W. is currently a graduate student. Please rank the following nine fields of graduate specialization in order of the likelihood that Tom W. is now a student in that field. Let rank one be the most probable choice:

    Business Administration
    Computer Sciences
    Engineering
    Humanities and Education
    Law
    Library Science
    Medicine
    Physical and Life Sciences
    Social Science and Social Work

Given the lack of substantive content, the graduate students should have ignored the analysis entirely, and made choices by the percentage of graduate students in each field—information that had been provided for them. It was assumed they would act upon the real data. At least, according to the laws of normative probability, this was what was expected of them. According to these laws, the more unreliable the available information in a specific situation (called the *case rate*—in this example the profile of Tom W.), the more one should rely on established percentages (called the *base rate*—in this instance the percentage of students enrolled in each field).

Did the group look at the base rate percentages? No. This experiment and others like it demonstrated that the students relied entirely upon the profile and decided that computer sciences and engineering were the two most probable fields for Tom W. to enter, even though each had relatively few people in them. In spite of their training to the contrary, the psychology students based their decisions on unreliable information, ignoring the more pertinent data. Nonetheless they were confident they were made on the facts.

A parallel example in the stock market is the emphasis people put on the outlook for each exciting initial public offering or concept stock (the case rate), even though the substantiating data is usually flimsy at best. Still, investors rarely examine the high probability of loss in such issues (the base rate). Instead, most buyers of hot IPOs in the 1980s and 1990s focused on the individual story and forgot that over 80% of these issues had dropped in price after the 1962 and 1968 market breaks. Here again, the prior probabilities, although essential, were ignored. Which brings us to another rule of decision-making:

RULE 24

Don't rely solely on the "case rate." Take into account the "base rate"—the prior probabilities of profit or loss.

The greater the complexity and uncertainty in the investment situation, the less emphasis you should place on your current appraisal, and the more you should look to the rate of success or failure of similar situations in the past for guidance.

Put another way, rather than attempting to obtain every fact and sliver of information about a difficult investment situation (much of which is contradictory, irrelevant, and difficult to evaluate correctly), you should, if possible, gauge the long-term record of success or failure of a particular course of action.[12]

The same rule could be applied to a broad number of investment situations. For example, if you like a concept stock, you might take a cross-section of favorites of other periods and see how they worked out; or if you decide to try your hand at market timing, examine how well the system you selected has worked over time.

In each instance, the information in the particular case being examined should, where possible, be supplemented by evidence of the long-term record of similar situations—the base rate—before making your decision.

Regression to the Mean

The three previous cognitive biases, stemming from representativeness, buttress one of the most important and consistent sources of investment error. As intuitive statisticians, we do not comprehend the principle of *regression to the mean.* Although the terminology sounds formidable, the concept is simple. This statistical phenomenon was noted over 100 years ago by Sir Francis Galton, a pioneer in eugenics, and is important to avoiding this major market error.

In studying the height of men, Galton found that the tallest men usually had shorter sons, while the shortest men usually had taller sons. Since many tall men come from families of average height, they are likely to have children shorter than they are, and vice versa. In both cases, the height of the children was less extreme than the height of the fathers.

The study of this phenomenon gave rise to the term *regression,* which has since been documented in many areas. The effects of regression are all around us. In our experience, most outstanding fathers have somewhat disappointing sons, brilliant wives have duller husbands, people who seem to be ill-adjusted often improve, and those considered extraordinarily fortunate eventually have a run of bad luck.

Regression to the mean, although alien to us intuitively, occurs frequently.[13] Take the reaction we have to a baseball player's batting average. Although a player may be hitting .300 for the season, his batting will be uneven. He will not get three hits in every ten times at bat. Sometimes he will bat .500 or more, well above his average (or mean), and other times he will be lucky to hit .125. Over 162 games, whether the batter hits .125 or .500 in any dozen or so games makes little difference to the average. But rather than realizing that the player's performance over a week or a month can deviate widely from his season's average, we tend to focus only on the immediate past record. The player is believed to be in a "hitting streak" or a "slump." Fans, sportscasters, and, unfortunately, the players themselves place too much emphasis on brief periods and forget the long-term average, to which the players will likely regress.

Regression occurs in many instances where it is not expected and yet is bound to happen. Israeli Air Force flight instructors were chagrined after they praised a student for a successful execution of a complex maneuver, because it was normally followed by a poorer one the next time. Conversely, when they criticized a bad maneuver, a better one usually followed. What they did not understand was that at the level of training of these student pilots, there was no more consistency in their maneuvers than in the daily batting figures of baseball players. Bad exercises would be followed by well-executed ones and vice versa. Their flying regressed to the mean. Correlating the maneuver quality to their remarks, the instructors erroneously concluded that criticism was helpful to learning and praise detrimental, a conclusion universally rejected by learning theory researchers.[14]

How does this work in the stock market? According to the classic work on stock returns of Ibbotson and Sinquefield, then at the University of Chicago,[15] stocks have returned 10.5% annually (price appreciation and dividends) over the last 70 years, against a return of about 5.6% for bonds. An earlier study by the Cowles Commission showed much the same return for stocks going back to the 1880s.

As Figure 10–1 shows, however, the return has been anything but consistent—not unlike the number of hits a .300 career hitter will get in individual games over a few weeks. There have been long periods when stocks have returned more than the 10.5% mean. Within each of these periods, there have been times when stocks performed sensationally, rising sometimes 50% or more in a year. At other times, they have seemed to free-fall. Stocks, then, although they have a consistent average, also have "streaks" and "slumps."

For investors, the long-term rate of return of common stocks, like the batting average of a ballplayer, is the important thing to remember. However, as intuitive statisticians, we find it very hard to do so. *Market history provides a continuous example of our adherence to the belief that deviations from the norm are, in fact, the new norm.*

The investor of 1927 and 1928 or 1996 and 1997 thought that returns of 30 to 40% were in order from that time on, although they diverged far from the mean. In 1932 and 1974, he believed huge losses were inevitable, although they, too, deviated sharply from the long-term mean. The investor of mid-1982, observing the insipid performance of the Dow Jones Industrial Average (which was lower at the time than in 1965) believed stocks were no longer a viable investment instrument.

Business Week ran a cover story, just before the Great Bull Market began in July 1982, entitled "The Death of Equities."[16] In 1987, after the Dow had nearly quadrupled its level of 1982, I attended a dinner of money managers just prior to the crash. The almost universal opinion at the table was that stocks would go much higher. The table was right—for another ten days.

The same scenarios have been enacted at every major market peak and trough. Studies of investment advisor buying and selling indicate that most experts are closely tied, if not pilloried, to the current market's movement. The prevalent belief is always that extreme returns—

Figure 10-1

Annual Stock Returns

1926 - 1996

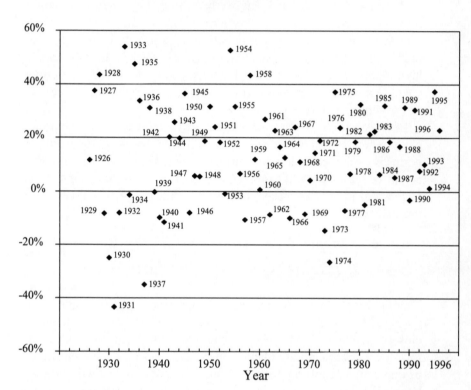

whether positive or negative—will persist. The far more likely probability is that they are the outliers on a chart plotting returns, and that succeeding patterns will regress towards the mean.

We can mask the relevance of these long-term returns by detailed
study of a specific trend and by intense involvement in it.[17] Even those
who are aware of these long-term standards cannot always see them
clearly because of preoccupation with short-term conditions. This leads
to a fourth protective rule:

RULE 25

**Don't be seduced by recent rates of return for individual stocks
or the market when they deviate sharply from past norms (the**

"case rate"). Long-term returns of stocks (the "base rate") are far more likely to be established again. If returns are particularly high or low, they are likely to be abnormal.

Returns that are extremely high or low should be treated as deviations from long-term norms. *The long-term return of the market might be viewed like the average height of men.* Just as it is unlikely that abnormally tall men will beget even taller men, it is unlikely that abnormally high returns will follow already high returns. In both cases, the principle of regression to the mean will most probably apply, and the next series of returns will be less extreme.

Because experts in the stock market are no more aware of the principle of regression than anyone else, each sharp price deviation from past norms is explained by a new, spurious theory. This, together with other cognitive biases we will examine, leaves the investor vulnerable to the fashions of the marketplace, however far removed prices may be from intrinsic worth.

If It Looks Good, It Must Taste Good

There is yet another powerful heuristic bias stemming from representativeness. This is the intuitive belief that inputs and outputs should be closely correlated. We believe, in other words, that consistent inputs allow greater predictability than inconsistent ones. Tests have shown, for example, that people are far more confident that a student will regularly have a B average if he has two B's rather than an A and a C, although the belief is not statistically valid.[18] Or if the description of a company is very favorable, "a very high profit is most representative of that description," and vice-versa.[19] This fallacy usually leads to consistent errors in the market.

The direct application of this finding is the manner in which investors equate a good stock with a rising price and a poor stock with a falling one. One of the most common questions analysts, money managers, or brokers are asked is, "If the stock is so good, why doesn't it go up?" or, "If contrarian strategies are so successful why aren't they working now?" The answer, of course, is that the value (the input) is often not recognized in the price (the output) for quite some time. Yet investors demand such immediate, though incorrect, feedback—and can make serious mistakes as a consequence.

Another interesting aspect of this phenomenon is that investors mistakenly tend to place high confidence in extreme inputs or outputs. As we have seen, Internet stocks in the mid-1990s were believed to have sensational prospects (the input), which was confirmed by prices that moved up astronomically—as much as 10- or even 20-fold (the output). The seemingly strong fundamentals went hand-in-hand with sharply rising prices for HMO stocks in the mid-1980s or for the computer leasing and medical technology stocks of 1968 and 1973. Extreme correlations look good and people are willing to accept them as reliable auguries, but as generations of investors have learned the hard way, they aren't.

The same thinking is applied to each crash and panic. Here the earnings estimates and outlooks (the inputs) erode as prices drop. Graham and Dodd, astute market clinicians that they were, saw the input–output relationship clearly. They wrote that "an inevitable rule of the market is that the prevalent theory of common stock valuations has developed in rather close conjunction with the change in the level of prices."[20] The consistency of this behavior leads us to our next contrarian rule:

RULE 26

Don't expect the strategy you adopt will prove a quick success in the market; give it a reasonable time to work out.

Demanding immediate success invariably leads to playing the fads or fashions currently performing well rather than investing on a solid basis. A course of investment, once charted, should be given time to work. Patience is a crucial but rare investment commodity. The problem is not as simple as it may appear; studies have shown that businessmen and other investors abhor uncertainty.[21] To most people in the marketplace, quick input-output matching is an expected condition of successful investing.

On Shark Attacks and Falling Airplane Parts

What is a more likely cause of death in the U.S.: being killed by a shark or by pieces falling from an airplane?[22] Most people will answer that shark attacks are more probable. Shark attacks receive far more publicity than deaths from falling plane parts, and they are certainly far more graphic to imagine, especially if you've seen *Jaws*. Yet dying from falling airplane parts is thirty times more likely than being killed by a shark attack.[23]

This is an example of *availability*, a heuristic which causes major investor errors. According to Tversky and Kahneman,[24] this is a mental rule of thumb by which people "assess the frequency of a class or the probability of an event by the ease with which instances or occurrences can be brought to mind."

As with most heuristics, or mental shortcuts, availability usually works quite well. By relying on availability to estimate the frequency or probability of an event, decision-makers are able to simplify what might otherwise be very difficult judgments.[25]

This judgmental shortcut is accurate most of the time because we normally recall events more easily that have occurred frequently. Unfortunately, our recall is influenced by other factors besides frequency, such as how recently the events have occurred, or how salient or emotionally charged they are.[26] People recall good or bad events out of proportion to their actual frequency. The chances of being mauled by a grizzly bear at a national park are only one or two per million visitors, and the death rate is lower. Casualties from shark attacks are probably an even smaller percentage of swimmers in coastal waters. But because of the emotionally charged nature of the dangers, we think such attacks happen much oftener than they really do.

It is the occurrence of disasters, rather than their probabilities of happening, that has an important impact on our buying of casualty insurance. The purchase of earthquake and airline insurance goes up sharply after a calamity, as does flood insurance.[27]

As a result, the availability rule of thumb breaks down, leading to systematic biases. The bottom line is that availability, like most heuristics, causes us to frequently misread probabilities, and get into investment difficulties as a result.

Recency, saliency, and emotionally charged events often dominate decision-making in the stock market. Statements by experts, crowd participation, and recent experience strongly incline the investor to follow the prevailing trend.

In the 1990s, small-capitalization growth stocks rocketed ahead of other equities. By early July 1996 this was almost the only game in town. The experience is repeated and salient to the investor, while the disastrous aftermath of the earlier speculation in aggressive growth issues in the sixties, seventies, and eighties has receded far back into memory.

The tendency of recent and salient events to move people away from the base-rate or long-term probabilities cannot be exaggerated. Time and again, we toss aside our long-term valuation guidelines because of the spectacular performance of seemingly sure winners. As psychologists have pointed out, this bias is tenacious.

A moment's reflection shows that this judgmental bias reinforces the others. Recent and salient events, whether positive or negative, strongly influence judgments of the future. People, it appears, become prisoners of such experience and view the future as an extension of the immediate past. The more memorable the circumstances, the more they are expected to persist, no matter how out-of-line with prior norms.

The defense here, as in Rule 26, is to keep your eye on the long-term. While there is certainly no assured way to put recent or memorable experiences into absolute perspective, it might be helpful during periods of extreme pessimism or optimism to wander back to your library. If the market is tanking, reread the financial periodicals from the last major break. If you can, pick up *The Wall Street Journal,* turn to the market section, and read the wailing and sighing of expert after expert in August and September of 1990, just before the market began one of its sharpest recoveries. Similarly, when we have another speculative market, it would not be a bad idea to check the *Journal* again and read the comments made during the 1979 to 1983 or 1991 to 1998 bubbles. While rereading the daily press is not an elixir, I think it will help.

Anchoring and Hindsight Biases

We might briefly look a two other systematic biases that are relevant to the investment scene and tend to fix investment errors firmly in place. They are also difficult to correct, since they reinforce the others. The first is known as *anchoring*,[28] another simplifying heuristic. In a complex situation, such as the marketplace, we will choose some natural starting point, such as a stock's current price, as a first cut at its value, and will make adjustments from there. The adjustments are typically insufficient. Thus, an investor in 1997 might have thought a price of $91 was too high for Cascade Communications, a leader in PC networking, and that $80 was more appropriate. But Cascade Communications was grossly overvalued at $91 and dropped to $22 before recovering modestly.

Again, the best defense against this bias appears to be in our earlier rule: *If the returns are particularly high or low, they are probably abnormal.*

The final bias is interesting. In looking back at past mistakes, researchers have found, people believe that each error could have been seen much more clearly, if only they hadn't been wearing dark or rose-colored glasses. The inevitability of what happened seems obvious in retrospect. *Hindsight bias* seriously impairs proper assessment of past errors and significantly limits what can be learned from experience.[29]

I remember lunching with a number of money managers in 1991. They were bullish on the market, which was moving up strongly at the time. One manager, looking at the upsurge of financial stocks from the depressed levels of 1990, asked rhetorically, "How could we not have bought the financial stocks then?" In 1988, he asked the same question about other ultracheap companies after the much more damaging 1987 crash. He'll likely ask it again after the next major surge.

This bias too is difficult to handle. That walk to the library may be as good a solution as any. I think you will see that the mistakes were far less obvious than they appear today.

Decisional Biases and Market Fashions

Chapter 16 will detail the seductiveness of current market fashions, how prudent investors could be swept away by the lure of huge profits in mania after mania through the centuries. Now, with some knowledge of decisional biases, we can understand why the tug of fashion has always been so persistent and so influential on both the market population and the expert opinion of the day.

Whatever the fashion, the experts could demonstrate that the performance of a given investment was statistically superior to other less-favored ones in the immediate past, and sometimes stayed that way for fairly long periods.

Tulip bulbs appreciated sharply for seven years until 1637. A Dutch expert in that year could easily show that for more than a decade tulips had returned considerably more than buildings, shops, or farms. The recent record was exciting, and rising prices seemed to justify more of the same.

The pattern continually repeats itself. A buyer of canal bonds in the 1830s or blue-chip stocks in 1929 could argue that though the instruments were dear, each had been a vastly superior holding in the recent past. Along with the 1929 Crash and the Depression came a decade-and-a-half passion for government bonds at near-zero interest rates.

Investing in good-grade common stocks again came into vogue in the 1950s and 1960s. By the end of the decade, the superior record of stocks through the postwar era had put investing in bonds in disrepute. *Institutional Investor*, a magazine exceptionally adept at catching the prevailing trends, presented a dinosaur on the cover of its February 1969 issue with the caption, "CAN THE BOND MARKET SURVIVE?" The article continued: "In the long run, the public market for straight debt might become obsolete."

The accumulation of stocks occurred just as their rates of return were beginning to decrease. Bonds immediately went on to provide better returns than stocks. Of course, as we know, it happened all over again. In 1982, the greatest bull market of the century for stocks began—naturally at the time institutional funds were stampeding out of equities. As always after a major miscalculation, perceptions shifted radically. Money managers once again tilted sharply towards stocks, with enormous flows of new moneys pouring into equities in the past decade and a half.

Behind the statistics on expert failure, we saw that the professionals tended to play the fashions of the day, whatever they were. One fund manager, at the height of the two-tier market in 1972/1973, noting the skyrocketing prices of large growth stocks at the time, said that their performance stood out "like a beacon in the night." Both the growth stocks and the concept stocks were clobbered shortly thereafter.

Although market history provides convincing testimony about the ephemeral nature of fashion, it has captivated generation after generation of investors. Each fashion has its supporting statistics, the law of small numbers. The fashions are salient and easy to recall and are, of course, confirmed by rising prices—the inputs and outputs again. These biases, all of which interact, make it natural to project the prevailing trend well into the future. The common error each time is that, although the trend may have lasted for months, even for years, it was not representative and was often far removed from the performance of equities or bonds over longer periods (regression to the mean). In hindsight, we can readily see the errors and wonder why, if they were so obvious, we did not see them earlier.

The heuristic biases, which are all interactive, seem to flourish particularly well in the stock market and to result in a high rate of investor error. We are too apt to look at insufficient information in order to confirm a course of action, we are too inclined to put great emphasis on recent or emotionally compelling events, and we expect our decisions to be met with quick market confirmation. The more we discuss a course of action and identify with it, the less we believe prior standards are valid. So each trend and fashion looks unique, is identified as such, and inevitably takes its toll. Knowledge that no fashion prevails for long is dismissed.

Shortcuts to Disaster

We find, then, that the information-processing shortcuts—heuristics—which are highly efficient and timesaving in day-to-day situations, work systematically against us in the marketplace.

Only in recent years has it been recognized that people simply don't follow probability theory under conditions of uncertainty. The implications of these cognitive biases are enormous, not only in economics, management, and investments, but in virtually every area of decision-making. The tendency to underestimate or ignore prior probabilities in making a decision is undoubtedly the most significant problem of intuitive prediction in fields as diverse as financial analysis, accounting, geography, engineering, and military intelligence.[30]

Cognitive biases, which affect each of us to a greater or lesser extent, are locked more firmly into place by the group pressures described earlier. When our own cognitive biases are reinforced by the powerful influence of experts and peer groups we respect, and who interpret information in the same way, the pressure to follow becomes compelling.

It's important then to have some protective rules against the tug of prevailing fashion. Let's briefly review the five rules we've looked at in this chapter:

RULE 22

Look beyond obvious similarities between a current investment situation and one that appears equivalent in the past. Consider other important factors that may result in a markedly different outcome.

RULE 23

Don't be influenced by the short-term record of a money manager, broker, analyst, or advisor, no matter how impressive; don't accept cursory economic or investment news without significant substantiation.

RULE 24

Don't rely solely on the "case rate." Take into account the "base rate"—the prior probabilities of profit or loss.

RULE 25

Don't be seduced by recent rates of return for individual stocks or the market when they deviate sharply from past norms (the "case rate"). Long-term returns of stocks (the "base rate") are far more likely to be established again. If returns are particularly high or low, they are likely to be abnormal.

RULE 26

Don't expect the strategy you adopt will prove a quick success in the market; give it a reasonable time to work out.

Frankly, the above rules are going to be a lot harder to follow than you think, because the cognitive biases are anything but phantoms. They can reveal a dozen reasons why you should abandon a course, naturally all expertly masking the real motives for doing so.

Other work in cognitive psychology indicates that even when people are warned of such biases they appear not to be able to adjust for their effects.[31] So it will take a good deal of concentration and effort on your part to avoid these pitfalls. However, the effort to understand their pull should prove rewarding and should help you avoid many a serious error.

Heuristic biases, interacting with other psychological forces, lead to consistent overreaction in markets. Let's next turn to how similar and predictable the psychology of overreaction is not only in the stock market but in other areas, from collecting art to investing in junk bonds.

11

Profiting from Investor Overreaction

OVERREACTION plays a part in virtually every aspect of human activity. When two North Vietnamese torpedo boats attacked a U.S. Navy destroyer, Congress gave President Johnson emergency powers that virtually abrogated their right to declare war. Historians now question whether the torpedo boats were remotely near the destroyer, or even at the scene. Yet, Congress's reaction was the major reason for the enormous escalation of the war.

Overreaction is almost a given in military thinking. After their ignominious defeat in the Franco-Prussian War of 1870, the French General Staff attributed the loss to lack of the dash and daring that had characterized French armies under Napoleon I. The marshals and generals overreacted by stressing elan above all else, even though there had been revolutionary changes in weaponry since Napoleon's time. For 44 years afterwards, French military maneuvers concentrated on fixed bayonet attacks in closely packed ranks, the tactic that had won the Emperor victory after victory.

But 1914 was not 1812. When World War I started, the cream of the French army was slaughtered by the rapid precision fire of the German machine guns and the enormous destructive power of their artillery. The overreaction to the Prussian defeat resulted in 250,000 French dead in the first six weeks of the war alone, about the total number of American soldiers killed in action in World War II.

The Pervasiveness of Investor Overreaction

Overreaction is one of the most predictable features of markets. In chapter 16 we will look at the amazing similarities between the overreactions in the IPO and aggressive-growth markets of 1977 to 1983 and 1991 to 1997. Investors in the market of the nineties bought almost the identical stocks, for the same exciting reasons, as the ones that were massacred a decade earlier. Only this time the excesses were more extreme, and the correction even more severe. On July 10, 1996, Nasdaq took a larger intra-day drop than the day of the crash in 1987. Such high fliers as America Online plummeted from $78 to $38 (where it still was priced at a modest 166 times earnings), and Presstek from $200 to $58 (still 212 times earnings). And that was for openers. The second wave beginning in the fall of 1997 began to take many of the major winners apart.

We noted in chapter 9 how people frenziedly flocked into emerging markets in the 1990s. Again no price was too high to get into the Hong Kong and other Pacific Rim markets, or into Russia, the former Eastern Bloc, or Latin American stocks. The stock indices of these countries soared. Billions of dollars pouring into illiquid markets again made increase in prices a self-fulfilling prophecy—for a while.

As we also saw in chapter 9, by late 1997 the emerging Asian markets dropped sharply, the South Korean market reaching a 10-year low. Such reactions are a way of life in markets, even for the bluest of the blue chips. They prevent investors from seeing opportunities when they almost stumble into them.

In August of 1982, investors and the media were extremely bearish on the stock market only weeks before the great bull market began that lifted the Dow Jones Industrial Average more than ninefold. Again the negative sentiment was enormously overplayed. By many standards stocks were at their lowest levels since the 1930s. But because prices were actually below where they were 12 years earlier, people could not see the vast potential in equities. This overreaction caused them to avoid the stock market like the plague, even though stocks were in the bargain basement.[1] The Dow, adjusted for inflation, was under 80, not far from the lows of the Great Depression, while book value, according to John Templeton (again adjusted for inflation), was at a greater discount to market price than at any point in the century. There was exceptional value out there.

Investor overreaction, this time on the negative outlook for stocks, resulted in the majority missing the greatest stock market opportunity in several generations.

At the same time, bonds were cheaper in real terms than at any time in 100 years. Another overreaction was also taking place concurrently with the blacklisting of stocks: the almost paranoid fear of long-term bonds, even though their value was unparalleled. Such reactions can often be captured while they are unfolding, if you are aware of some of your cognitive and other psychological limitations.

The reactions are almost almost always accompanied with headlines, ebullience, or fear. Interest rates, said West German Chancellor Helmut Schmidt in 1982, are "higher today than at any time since Christ walked the earth."[2] It was the opportunity of a lifetime for brave investors who could step up to the plate to buy something that had done badly for the past 30 years. Bond prices had not only discounted all the negatives that had already happened, but a carload of negatives that never would happen.

Almost everyone back then thought that bonds were a terrible long-term investment, good only for the occasional trading profit. But experience teaches us that when "everyone" comes to the same conclusion, that conclusion is just about always wrong.

Only months later investors took a dispassionate look at the available values in the bond market and prices went through the roof. People who recognized this major overreaction and acted on it made a bundle. Thirty-year, zero-coupon treasuries, for example, appreciated over 100% in about 6 months.

But a caveat is in order here. Seeing an overreaction and acting on one are two different things. If you can act on it you can make major money, but it's a heck of a lot harder than it looks. Too, there is the small matter of timing. You may be dead right on the overreaction, but way off on the timing. Take a call made on the Japanese market in 1987.[3]

The Japanese market seemed not just overpriced, said an observer, but was at the mania stage, ranking with tulip fever or 1928/1929 in its speculative frenzy. Why was he sure? Because the symptoms of all manias are remarkably similar. Just as remarkable, in every case the idiocies are generally overlooked until after each bubble bursts.

To tick off some of the major symptoms:

1. Absurdly high prices. The average P/E of the Nikkei 225 was 86 times estimated 1987 earnings. (The peak for the U.S. market in 1929 was 20 times.)

2. Experts on the Japanese investment scene wrote that the market was shooting skyward because of a shortage of stock. This argument was identical to the one used to explain why the market would continue

to rise for years to come by some of the most important players in the late twenties, according to J. Kenneth Galbraith's classic *The Great Crash—1929*.

3. It was more profitable to speculate than manufacture. An estimated 20% to 30% of Japanese corporate profits came from stock-market trading. The situation was similar to tulipmania, in which Dutch industry and commerce slowed down so that merchants could pick off far easier profits from tulip bulbs.

4. Japanese institutions were large holders of stocks and would never sell. Ha! So were the vast U.S. trusts of the late 1920s, until the market unraveled and everyone ran for his life.

5. "The Japanese market was unique," stated experts, and "this uniqueness will lead inevitably to higher prices." The identical statement has been made in every mania in financial history.

Well, the observer—who happened to be me—was almost right. The prediction of the Japanese market being overvalued was dead on. However, it was a mite premature—the statement was made on August 24, 1987, when the Nikkei 225 was at 25,760, and it rose to over 38,000 by 1990, some 50% higher, before it blew apart. And—oh yes—there was another slight problem with the forecast. It assumed a Japanese crash would come before a setback in the American market. We had a minor one that year that saw U.S. markets plummet 33% in mid-October.

There's a lesson to the story. Overreactions are very predictable using the valuation guidelines I've outlined, but actual corrections are impossible to forecast. Certainly all the telltale pennants were in place in the summer of 1987. Still, had an investor sold at that time, even though the market increased sharply, he or she could have rebought the same holdings 45% cheaper ten years later.

In the past few decades there have also been numerous overreactions in nonfinancial markets where investors rushed in only to have their net worth decimated. In the seventies, Chinese ceramics were increasing at a 23% annual rate, U.S. stamps at 23.5%, rare books at 21%, Art Deco at 19%, and old master paintings at 15.4%.

Faced with a stock market that was going nowhere, major economic uncertainty, and baffling inflation, people became more willing to speculate on the past, as represented by precious metals, jewelry, or artwork, rather than in the future of the American stock market.

This overreaction ended like all the others, of course, with collectibles and precious metals now worth a fraction of what they were at the time. Silver, then fetching as high as $49.50 a troy ounce, was $6.24 in late 1997, while gold was down from $875 an ounce to around $290. In the same period, the Dow Jones Industrial Average has risen from 850 to 7900.

A similar overreaction occurred in the art market in the 1980s. A prosperous economy and a good stock market sent art on a wild joyride. Many contemporary paintings (art created after the Second World War) went up as much as 20- and 30-fold, while the stately blue chips (Impressionist and Modern) of this market appreciated a more demure ten times. With the major increase in wealth in Japan, the Middle East, the U.S., and elsewhere, thousands of new investors turned to art. There was a shortage of good paintings relative to demand, said the experts. After all, you could never create another Impressionist painting. The "shortage of good stock" thesis, as we just saw, was one of the most widely held investor beliefs in the years prior to 1929.

The auction houses never had it better. Bidding wars took paintings up to many times expert appraisal values. The atmosphere became carnival at staid Sotheby's and Christie's, where dignified auctioneers with Oxford accents presided in tails. The thronged galleries applauded each sale that went over the appraisal price, which in itself had soared outside of the range of reality. In some auctions 70% of the paintings sold above the estimates. Van Gogh's *Portrait of Dr. Gachet* was auctioned off for $82,500,000, while Renoir's *Au Moulin de la Galette* went for $78,100,000.

But as always, overreaction corrects. By late 1990, a recession, a falling stock market, and serious financial problems in Japan, where buying had been exceptionally heavy, particularly for Impressionist works, killed art prices. Impressionists dropped 50%, while the Yuppie aficionados who bought contemporary paintings for six figures from the recent "hot contemporary artists" now saw their prized conversation pieces drop to virtually nothing.

How quickly the tide changes. By 1990 and 1991 the atmosphere in the auction houses was sheer gloom. Painting after painting "passed" (was not sold), even though the appraised prices had been reduced substantially. I was able to buy a good Picasso in 1991 for one-third of what it had sold for only two years earlier, during a forced liquidation by a Swedish bank. Although the overall art market stabilized by mid-1997, most prices are still well below their highs. The pattern, whether it is overenthusiasm or overpessimism, is ever recurring.

We have galloped briefly through some of the major overreactions of recent years. Dozens of others have similar radar plots. As a contrarian you might ask, "besides the contrarian strategies outlined, are there any other types of predictable overreactions that can make me a winner?" Fortunately, the answer is a definite yes.

Junk Bonds: A Money-Making Overreaction

The most consistent evidence supporting another workable overreaction strategy is buying high-yield bonds, as their proponents would call them—junk as they are known in the trade. Junk bonds are issues rated BB or lower by the credit agencies.

I can imagine some snickers, because the common perception is that these bonds are a passel of bankruptcy candidates steering toward the corporate scrap heap. But hang on. Studies stretching from 1900 to the 1980s show the performance of this group to be nothing short of remarkable.

The Hickman report, the grandfather of studies in this area, analyzed the returns on public and private corporate debt between 1900 and 1945.[4] The result: lower-grade bonds yielded 50% more on average than their higher-grade counterparts, after adjusting for defaults (the failure to make timely payment of interest or principal).

More interesting, perhaps, was the default rate—only 1.7% annually through a span that included the Great Depression. Too, defaults were not substantially larger in the lower- than the higher-quality ratings.

T. R. Atkinson, updating the Hickman study from 1945 to 1965, discovered that the default rate in that period was even lower, averaging only one in a thousand issues annually.[5] A later study extending the results to the end of 1981 found the annual default rate to be between 1.5 and 1.9 issues per thousand with a yield premium of 4% or more above higher-grade bonds. In other words, if you held a diversified portfolio of junk bonds, the added income was 20 times more than the average amount lost in a default. Not a bad risk/reward ratio in anyone's book.

Perhaps even more surprising was that default was not the nightmare everyone thought. Quite the contrary, the greatest gains were made on the bonds purchased at or near the date of default.

Although at first glance the findings are puzzling, they mesh perfectly with the reasons that contrarian stocks consistently outperform the market. Investors shun both high-income bonds and the out-of-favor stocks because their prospects seem less clear than for favored issues. To buy these risky critters they demand a large increase in return. After all, who wants a Dell Computer or a Woolworth bond when they can have the unquestioned safety of a Warner Communications or a Microsoft?

Even worse is a bond that defaults. "If it does," the consensus goes, "forget price—just sell." With large quantities suddenly dropping on the market and few buyers, prices become cheap, cheap. Benjamin Graham wrote about the pattern of institutions dumping such bonds more than 50 years ago, and he consistently made good money buying their mistakes. Not much has changed since then.

But if you are thinking of playing against knee-jerk thinking, you should be familiar with some of the background. The studies that junk bonds provided outstanding rate of return were carried out primarily before the 1980s. Lower rated credits could be more easily analyzed to assess their potential. Indeed Mike Milken in his earlier days made enormous money for his clients, and to a lesser extent for himself, carrying out precisely this analysis. In "artistic" terms I'd refer to this period as "early Milken."

Later, after the junk bond market grew exponentially and investors clamored for higher-yielding issues, Drexel Burnham and scores of other supposedly respectable firms filled the need with bonds that promised high yields, but with such poor credit quality, that large numbers stumbled or died near the starting gate. I would call the period, which ran through the last half of the 1980s, "late Milken." This crop of junk bonds had little in common with its earlier counterparts, and resulted in large losses for many buyers, as well as bringing down a number of major S&Ls who chased the impossibly high yields. Quality has improved since then, but you have to know what you're doing.

First, diversify widely to protect yourself from the odd bad egg that can creep into your portfolio. Fortunately, large numbers of such bonds exist. (According to Securities Data Company, $178.45 billion worth of junk bonds were issued during the five years ending 1996.)

Second, these bonds aren't for everyone. You have to understand the ins and outs of financial statement analysis, have detailed knowledge of the markets, and have nerves of cast iron. You should also own a dozen or more for adequate diversification.

An easier way for most investors to play this opportunity is to buy a junk bond mutual fund with a good 5- and 10-year record. Table 11–1 offers a number of such funds to consider.

If you can keep your own knees from jerking, you will find a very rewarding overreaction.

Table 11–1
JUNK BOND FUNDS
1987–1997

	10-year Return as of 11/30/97	Load	Phone Number
Fidelity Advisor High Yield	14.9%	3.5%	800-522-7297
Merrill Lynch Corp-High Income	12.4%	4.0%	800-637-3863
Federated High Income Bond	12.6%	4.5%	800-341-7400
AIM High Yield	12.4%	4.75%	800-347-1919
Seligman High Inc-Hi Yield Bond	12.5%	4.75%	800-221-7844
Oppenheimer Champion Income	13.0%	4.75%	800-525-7048
Kemper High Yield	11.6%	4.5%	800-621-1048
Putnam High Yield Advantage	11.6%	4.75%	800-225-1581

SOURCE: PREPARED FROM MORNINGSTAR DATA

Earnings Surprise: Another Profitable Overreaction

You can frequently harness the powerful effects of a disappointing earnings surprise by buying GARP (Growth at a Reasonable Price) companies after they have been blasted. A good company trading at an above average P/E will often break sharply on bad news. The trick is to evaluate the earnings surprise. Is it something that will alter the company permanently? Or is it simply analysts' overoptimism or some other unpredictable but short-term negative event? Surprise need not be earnings related. Temporary loss of market share, industry price-cutting, a slowing of sales, and a host of other factors can also result in highly valued companies plummeting.

Still, earnings surprises are the most common investor overreaction. For example, Intel dropped 20% in three days when reported earnings in its June 1995 quarter were up strongly, but still 4% below the analysts' consensus forecast. Earnings continued to grow briskly and the stock almost tripled by the summer of 1997.

Is this an isolated example? Not at all.

Hewlett-Packard announced in late September 1992 that its quarterly earnings would come in below analysts' estimates. The next day the stock dived 13 points, or 18%, on huge volume. The carnage was out of all proportion to the cause: on a shortfall of a few tens of millions of dollars, the stock lost $3.5 billion in market value. In today's market, disproportionate drops caused by earnings shortfalls are, if anything, becoming more and more frequent.

How should the smart investor react? Buy right after the plunge? Or wait till the dust clears? It's a tough call, but my advice would be to let the dust clear. Don't be a hero and charge into the initial panic. If you like a stock blown out by disappointing news, it pays to sit on the sidelines for a while. In all probability, you will get plenty of chances to buy it cheaper in the next 90 days.

The nature of the Street's research explains why the phenomenon occurs so consistently. Analysts react to surprises by slashing their quarterly estimates on the announcement of the disappointing news. Even so, the changes in their projections are usually not large enough for the next few quarters or the following year.

When there is a negative surprise, the poorer results, even for first-rate companies, are likely to continue for a while. It takes time to ride through an unanticipated rough stretch. As a result, the initial shock is often followed by later, if lesser shocks, which continue to pressure price.

So be patient. If a company you like comes out with an announcement that shakes the market's confidence, play the waiting game. It should pay off well over time. In the case of Hewlett-Packard, this is exactly what happened. The surprise was caused by a slowdown of sales in its European instrumentation businesses, not by its fast-growing computer peripheral lines. The stock bounced back from $14¾ at the time of the surprise to over $60 in December of 1997. Investors got a classic GARP double play with the P/E rising from about 16, under market at the time, to 21.6, on earnings that tripled.

If you know a company well, reacting to negative earnings surprises can make you a bundle.

The Investor Overreaction Hypothesis

Although the term "investor overreaction" is as old as markets, I put forth a statistically testable explanation of how it worked in *Contrarian Investment Strategy* in 1980. Based primarily on the psychological forces we examined earlier, the hypothesis states that investors overreact to events in a predictable fashion: they consistently overvalue the prospects of "best" investments and undervalue those of the "worst." They extrapolate positive or negative outlooks well into the future, pushing prices of favored stocks to excessive premiums and out-of-favor stocks to deep discounts. (Performance of "best" and "worst" stocks can be directly compared, of course, but "best" and "worst" investments can be things other than stocks, and "best" might be in a different market than "worst.")[6]

In 1981, for example, "best" investments included gold—at over $800 an ounce—and "worst" tax-exempt municipal bonds, yielding as high as 15%. Bonds soon rose sharply while gold plummeted. Premiums or discounts on favored or unfavored investments can be substantial and last a long time.

Specifically, the Investor Overreaction Hypothesis predicts that after earnings or other surprises, investments previously considered to be "best" underperform, while those considered to be "worst" significantly outperform, as both regress towards a more average valuation. The hypothesis also states that the maximum price swing is produced by negative surprises on "best" stocks and positive surprises on "worst." On the other hand, positive surprise on favored stocks and negative surprises on out-of-favor stocks—reinforcing events—corroborate the market's opinion of these stocks and have a lesser impact on price movements than event-triggers (see chapter 6).

Finally, the overreaction hypothesis holds that even without the occurrence of an event trigger, the "best" and "worst" investments regress towards the market average. Because the investor overreaction hypothesis is based on psychological principles, it is likely to apply in other markets and in fields outside of investments and economics where risk and uncertainty exist.

The Investor Overreaction Hypothesis makes these predictions:

1. "Best" stocks underperform the market, while "worst" stocks outperform, for long periods.

2. Positive surprises boost "worst" stocks significantly more than they do "best" stocks.

3. Negative surprises knock "best" stocks down much more than "worst" stocks.

4. There are two distinct categories of surprise: *event triggers* (positive surprises on "worst" stocks, and negative surprises on "best"), and *reinforcing events* (negative surprises on "worst" stocks and positive surprises on "best"). Event triggers result in much larger price movements than do reinforcing events.

5. The differences will be significant only in the extreme quintiles, with a minimal impact on the 60% of stocks in the middle.

The hypothesis states that overreaction occurs before the announcement of an earnings or other surprise. A correction of the previous overreaction occurs after the surprise. "Best" stocks move lower relative to the market, while "worst" stocks move higher, for a relatively long time following a surprise.

It may fall short of a ten commandants for contrarians, but remember, all five predictions of the investor overreaction hypothesis have been confirmed to a high level of statistical probability in the studies reviewed in chapter 6.

Is It a Horse?

Even though it looks like a horse, smells like a horse, and gallops like a horse, is it really a horse? In a word, though we have demonstrated the important qualities of contrarian strategies, can we really prove that investor psychology is the cause of these overreactions, rather than some other undetected factors? This is an important question, because if we can prove it, we can develop even more powerful strategies to take advantage of overreactions. So far as I know, this question has not been explored before.

The key is whether the fundamentals of favored stocks deteriorate, resulting in sharply lower prices, while those of out-of favor issues improve, markedly boosting their performance. If this is the case, then the price changes are merely a reflection of deteriorating fundamentals for "best" stocks, an argument which will no doubt be made by our efficient market friends. Stock prices, they will say, are doing no more than responding to new events, which is exactly what they are expected to do in an efficient market. Sorry, guys, but no.

A study I did in collaboration with Eric Lufkin pinpoints exactly how powerful the psychological effects of overreaction are. It shows how overpriced the "best" (and underpriced the "worst") stocks become before they correct, as well as how small the underlying changes in a stock's fundamentals actually are that cause such major price moves.[7]

To do this we used the Compustat 1500 from 1973 to 1996 and selected five of the most widely used fundamental measures to characterize how good or bad the outlook for a company was. These were return on equity (ROE), profit margin, growth in sales, growth in cash flow, and growth in earnings. The higher each of these measures is, the more promising a company appears to investors. We averaged each of these measurements for five-year periods.[8] These measurements, which we'll call *growth and profitability indicators,* demonstrate how rapidly a company is growing and how profitable this growth is.[9]

Next we determined how much the growth and profitability indicators changed for both the lowest and highest price-to-earnings, price-to-cash flow, price-to-book value, and price-to-dividend quintiles. This tells us if improvement in the underlying indicators is the real cause of outperformance for the out of-favor stocks and underperformance for the favorites.

Figure 11–1 and Table 11–2 show the results. Figure 11–1 measures the returns of the lowest 20%, and the highest 20% of price-to-book value stocks for the five years after the portfolios are set up (Period A, 0 to +5 years). We can see at a glance that low price-to-book value stocks do significantly better than high P/BVs. For the five-year holding periods between 1973 and 1996 they return 153%, some 64% more than the highest price-to-book value group, and 34% more than the market.[10]

The next question is whether the fundamentals of low price-to-book stocks have improved (and those of high price-to-book deteriorated) enough to be responsible for this impressive price reversal.

To answer this question, we take the five growth and profitability indicators and average them over the same five-year periods that we just

Figure 11–1

Back from the Future

How Stocks Perform Before and After They Move
Into the "Best" and "Worst" Groups
1973–1996

	Price Movement Before	Price Movement After
	–5 to 0 Years	0 to +5 Years
Low P/BV	56.2%	153.3%
High P/BV	363.5%	88.8%
Market	141.3%	119.1%

–5 years	0	+5 years

Measuring points of Best and Worst Groups

Year 0 ⟶ Point at which portfolios of best and worst stocks are assembled

Period A:

Years 0 to +5⟶ Performance from point 0 to 5 years later

Period B:

Years –5 to 0⟶ Backplaying performance for the 5 years before point 0

Table 11–2
GROWTH AND PROFITABILITY INDICATORS
1973–1996

		−10 to −5 Years	−5 to 0 Years	0 to +5 Years
Cash Flow Growth	Low P/BV	11.5%	9.9%	12.2%
	High P/BV	21.3%	26.1%	15.8%
	Market	14.3%	15.5%	12.2%
Sales Growth	Low P/BV	12.4%	10.4%	6.8%
	High P/BV	18.0%	21.0%	14.9%
	Market	13.8%	13.6%	10.1%
Earnings Growth	Low P/BV	9.3%	6.4%	11.6%
	High P/BV	18.6%	24.6%	12.1%
	Market	12.2%	14.2%	10.6%
Return on Equity	Low P/BV	10.5%	9.7%	8.1%
	High P/BV	15.3%	17.9%	17.4%
	Market	12.4%	13.0%	12.3%
Profit Margin	Low P/BV	9.8%	7.4%	5.3%
	High P/BV	12.2%	13.6%	12.8%
	Market	11.1%	10.2%	8.7%

An investor buys stocks based on growth and profitability indicators:

- **0:** Measuring point of best and worst groups (point at which portfolios are formed).
- **0 to +5 years (Period A):** The period during which the portfolio is held.
- **−5 to 0 Years (Period B):** Investors use this period 5 years before to 0, and 0 to +5 years, to determine pricing in Period A (0 to +5 years) in Figure 11–1.
- **−5 to −10 Years:** Investors use this period, as well as −5 to 0 years, to determine pricing in Period B (−5 years up to 0), in Figure 11–1.

measured performance (Period A, 0 to +5 years). Table 11–2 (column 3), gives these results.

We then look back at the growth and profitability indicators from the point we began our stock performance measurements (point 0). When evaluating stocks at this point, investors examine the record of each of the five important indicators for the previous five years (−5 to 0), to decide which stocks have the most favorable and least favorable prospects. This second set of growth and profitability indicators is shown in Table 11–2, column 2.

Finally, we compare the two sets of growth and profitability indicators in columns 2 and 3 of Table 11–2, to see whether the changes in these indicators are the chief cause of "best" and "worst" stock price movements or whether it is investor overreaction.

Are the higher returns for the low price-to-book value stocks the result of their fundamentals improving sharply, while those of high price-to-book value drop through the floor? *Not at all.*

As Table 11–2, column 3 shows: three of the five growth and profitability indicators for the low price-to-book value group do not improve but continue to decline in the five years that their stock prices surge. Two of these measures, profit margins and sales growth, actually deteriorate significantly. Sales growth, for example, dropped from 10.4% a year to 6.8%, as the lowest price-to-book value stocks shot out the lights. Only earnings-per-share growth improves: 6.4% to 11.6% annually over this five-year period.

The growth and profitability indicators of high price-to-book value stocks also deteriorate some (see Table 11–2, columns 2 and 3), but are still well above the market average in every case, and much higher than these indicators for the lowest price-to-book value group, except for earnings growth. Yet the high price-to-book value stock performance is abysmal. As columns two and three of the table show, the collapse in fundamentals of best stocks and a major improvement in those of worst stocks just doesn't happen. The cause of the dramatically better returns of this contrarian group lies elsewhere. The only conclusion left is that investors do indeed overreact predictably and continually to the prospects of "best" and "worst" stocks.

As we have seen, even mild disappointments in "best" stocks will drive them lower, while positive news has almost no effect. For the lowest price-to-book value quintile the results are precisely the opposite. Investors have overreacted to their poorer prospects so strikingly that even when their fundamentals continue to get worse over this five-year period, the stocks, like a corked bottle, still pop out of the water. Nothing else to this time shows investor overreaction so clearly.[11]

Other research also confirms that investor psychology is the cause of the overreactions. In the study discussed in chapter 6, showing the effects of surprise, we found that even five years after we measured an earnings surprise, "best" stocks still had much higher P/E, P/BV, and P/CF ratios than "worst" stocks.[12] For example, though high P/E stocks experiencing negative surprises decline more than 44%, relative to the market, their average P/E at the end of five years is 17, well above the 13 for the market. Conversely, though the lowest P/E group with positive surprises provide a 35% above-market return after the five years of our study, the average P/E multiple for the lowest group is 10, still well below the market's at the end of this time.

What this shows is that the prior overvaluation of the "best" and undervaluation of the "worst" groups was so large that even after these major price re-evaluations, they still trade at premiums and discounts respectively to the market. That investors still price "best" stocks at a premium to the averages after five years indicates they are believed to continue to have above-market prospects, albeit not as good as they were thought to be earlier. The price decline can only be attributed to the overpricing of "best" stocks originally. In the case of "worst" stocks, the situation is reversed. Investors price them at a discount to the market, indicating their outlooks continue to be thought below average.

That the P/E multiples of "worst" stocks are still below-market after outperforming for five years (and "best" stocks are above-market after the underperformance) indicates major overpricing of "best" stocks and underpricing of "worst" occurs prior to the surprise. "Best" companies are still believed to have better prospects than the market, and so trade at higher P/E multiples five years later, but the multiples have come down significantly, indicating the prospects are not nearly as exciting as was believed originally.

Although the outlooks for "worst" companies are evaluated more favorably, they are still considered to be poorer than those of the average stock. The measurements for low price/earnings, price-to-book value, price-to-cash flow, and high yield are similar.[13]

An independent verification of overreaction comes from a study done by Fuller, Huberts, and Levinson.[14] These researchers showed that the lowest P/E group experiences the smallest earnings growth for periods in excess of five years. Similarly, "best" companies show the highest rate of earnings growth for five years. Analysts apparently do predict which companies will have above- and below-normal growth over time.[15] This finding is important because it demonstrates that, although the fundamentals don't change dramatically in either the case of "best" or "worst" stocks, investors continually overprice favorites and discount unpopular issues.

What we see then is that it is not changes in the underlying outlooks that appear to be the primary cause of the major price re-evaluations of "best" and "worst" stocks; rather it is the overreaction to the exciting or lackluster prospects of companies that often results in best stocks being priced far too dearly, and worst stocks much too cheaply.

The Dark Side of the Moon

Some readers and certainly many academics will ask when the overreaction begins. The academic literature seems uncertain on this point, but appears to say overreaction occurs during the time the contrarian stocks bounce back. Nothing is further from the truth. Contrarian stocks recover from their previously depressed prices in that period, while high-priced issues decline. The overreaction, as I use the term, takes place earlier, during the period when the favorite stocks are becoming overpriced, as they move up to the highest price-to-book value (or highest price/earnings, price-to-cash flow or price-to-dividend quintiles) and when unfavored stocks are being knocked down to the bargain basement group.[16]

What happens to the prices of favored stocks before they have reached their highest price-to-book value, or price/earnings, price-to-cash flow, or price-to-dividend ratios, and to out-of-favor issues before they hit the bottoms of these groupings? If overreaction is the powerful force I believe it is, we should expect two things to occur. Favorite stocks should outperform the market as they move up to the priciest quintile, and the unloved and unwanted stocks should underperform, as they drop towards the lowest quintile. If the investor overreaction hypothesis is correct, then, we should have two distinct and opposite overreactions taking place concurrently, and continuing for a number of years. Favored stocks should become increasingly overpriced, and out-of-favor issues should get increasingly less expensive. Does it really happen this way?

To find out we took the same period measured in Table 11–2, 1973–1996, and the same stocks from the Compustat 1500. However, instead of measuring the returns of best and worst price-to-book value groups for the next five years (Period A, column 2, Figure 11–1), we now asked the computer to do a backplay of the same portfolios, this time calculating the returns for the stocks in the highest and lowest price-to-book value quintiles for the prior five years (Period B, years –5 to 0). The performance is shown in Figure 11–1, column 1.[17] We call this study the "Dark Side of the Moon," because no one had examined how stocks behave as they are moving towards their highest or lowest price-to-book levels.

The only way we can construct the portfolios in Figure 11–1, column 1, is by initially sorting the Compustat 1500 into highest, lowest, and middle groups by price-to-book value (or other contrarian indicators) at point 0. If we didn't know the lowest and highest price-to-book value portfolios to start with, we could not backplay their results without the aid of an expert in the occult, or at least a first-rate astrologer.

Measuring returns in the past allows us to find out how the "worst" price-to-book value portfolios acted as they fell out of favor, and the "best" stocks performed as they became increasingly hotter issues. If we are right, we should find that favorites provided excellent returns over this period (–5 to 0 years), while the contrarian stocks performed badly. Figure 11–1 indicates this is precisely what happened.[18]

As Figure 11–1 column 1 demonstrates, the results are rather remarkable. The highest price-to-book value stocks do 6.5 times as well as the lowest in the five years they moved towards their highest valuations and the worst issues moved towards the lowest. This is about 7½ times the outperformance that the lowest 20% of price-to-book value stocks originally showed over the highest, in the five years after they reached the bottom P/BV group (Period A, 0 to +5 years).

The highest price-to-book value stocks also outperformed the market by an astounding 157% in the five-year period before they reached the highest P/BV quintile. Again, this is almost 5.5 times the outperformance that the lowest price-to-book value group showed against the market in Period A.

These are stunning returns, but unfortunately, as we have seen, we can only get them by picking a group of stocks, like the Compustat database, dividing them into lowest, middle, and highest price-to-book value groupings, and then looking back five years from this point to see how they made out. If you know that astrologer, you can make big bucks this way. But if he or she is that good, they probably can make more in the market or at the track themselves.

Back to reality. In the five years after they are in the highest price-to-book value quintile we saw that the top group underperformed the market by 34%, after advancing 157% more than the market in the previous 5 years—so they are still far ahead of the market over the full 10 years. This indicates the initial five-year overvaluation was so large that a further correction can take place, which is in fact what happens as we saw in some of the longer buy-and-hold contrarian studies (see chapter 8, Table 8–1).

Similarly, in the five years after they reach their lowest valuations as a group, the lowest price-to-book value stocks increase 29% more than the market. This is only a fraction of the 151% they plummeted relative to the market in the previous five years, again indicating the initial overreaction may not have been completely corrected. This turns out to be the case in the buy and hold contrarian studies we viewed in chapters 8 and 9.

Finally, look again at Table 11–2, this time at columns 1 and 2. You'll see that the average of the growth and profitability indicators in column 1 for the five years before we measured the returns of the highest price-to-book value group retroactively (years –10 to –5) is very high. Investors at the beginning of the five-year period we just backplayed (year –5) could look back at the excellent characteristics of the best stocks, which is almost certainly the reason they bid prices so high in this period (years –5 to 0).

Moreover, the good times just kept rolling along. Table 11–2, column 2, shows that the growth and profitability measures for the favorites kept improving in this period from those in column 1. Earnings growth, for example, accelerated from a well-above-market 18.6% annually (column 1) to 24.6% (column 2), while sales growth increased from 18% annually to 21%. Looking back five years, the best stocks not only had excellent growth and profitability indicators in years –5 to –10, but were reinforced by progressively better growth and profit indicators in the period in which they were shooting out the lights (years –5 to 0).

The lowest group is almost a mirror image. Growth and profitability ratios, already lackluster for the five-year period before the retroactive returns were measured (years –10 to –5, column 1, Table 11–2) continued to deteriorate. Investors, already seeing mediocre results, watch them get progressively worse during the five years these stocks are falling to their lowest valuations (years –5 to 0, column 2, Table 11–2). The negative opinion of this group at the beginning of this period continues to be reinforced, and results in the substantial underperformance we see.

People almost certainly place too much emphasis on the growth and profitability indicators shown in Table 11–2, thereby carrying the prices of stocks which appear to have "best" and "worst" prospects to extremes.

It is the size of the overreactions that leads to the superior returns of worst stocks and inferior returns of best stocks after they reach the highest and lowest price-to-book value quintiles. This prior overreaction is the basis for the success of contrarian strategies.

Because the compelling psychological forces do not change, overreaction works just as surely with the investor today as it has in all markets of the past.

Other Voices

In the past decade, investor overreaction has become a hot topic not only among Wall Streeters but within financial academia. As chance would have it, two academic researchers, Werner DeBondt and Richard Thaler, discovered a similar hypothesis six years after I had published the thesis in *Contrarian Investment Strategy.* Their statistical findings, which show that stocks underperforming in one period often outperform the market in the next period, provide further backing for the Investor Overreaction Hypothesis.[19]

DeBondt and Thaler do ask a good question, "What is an appropriate reaction?" They answer it by stating that extreme price movements in one direction should be followed by subsequent price movement in the opposite direction. They add that the more extreme the price movement is in one direction the greater the subsequent adjustment will be. Their answer is supported by our findings (Figure 11–1 and Table 11–2).

Regression to the Mean Revisited

When you think about it, the old proverb that no tree grows to the sky certainly makes sense in the marketplace. We might refer again to the principle of regression to the mean. In a dynamic environment there will be periods of excellent growth and profitability, which create the seeds of greater competition and lower growth some time in the future. On the other hand, for companies and industries undergoing difficulties, their lowered expansion, reduction of overhead, and belt tightening often bear the fruit of above-average growth once again.

In *Security Analysis,* Graham succinctly summed up the problems of analyzing corporate fortunes:

> The truth of our corporate venture is quite otherwise [than investors think]. Extremely few companies have been able to show a high rate of uninterrupted growth for long periods of time. Remarkably few also of the large companies suffer ultimate extinction. For most, this history is one of vicissitudes, of ups and downs, with changes in their relative standing.[20]

Let's transform this into a more compact contrarian rule:

RULE 27

The push toward an average rate of return is a fundamental principle of competitive markets.

Yet it is one that investors never seem to learn. It is also the reason that the superior performance of contrarian stocks and the inferior returns of the most pricey stocks are so consistent.

The highly favored stocks and the contrarian cases represent extremes. The probability is high that future returns will be more in line with more average companies. But most investors do not see it this way. Instead, they tend to view the current trend as the norm, no matter how extreme it is within a probability distribution. The consistent overreaction to current trends opens up a great opportunity for the investor—putting you ahead of the crowd, so to speak. Which brings us to an important rule:

RULE 28

It is far safer to project a continuation of the psychological reactions of investors than it is to project the visibility of the companies themselves.

From the prior performance of contrarian stocks we have seen this approach work with remarkable reliability for over 60 years. It is true, of course, that there are excellent companies that will continue to chalk up above-average growth for years or decades to come, and there are especially talented investors who will find them at reasonable prices. But for most of us, whether individual or expert, the odds of winning at this game are pretty slim.

As I hope it is now apparent, contrarian strategies are powered by investor overreaction. Whether one is buying cheap stocks or junk bonds, the psychological forces are the same. Though it is not yet possible to quantify strategies to markets such as art or real estate, overreaction occurs in them in an identical manner. Investor overreaction is one of the most powerful tools for making money in markets. Let's next look at an outstanding opportunity that overreaction presents—panic in a company, an industry or in the market itself.

PART IV

INVESTING IN THE 21ST CENTURY

12

Crisis Investing

IN 1956, a young American Congressman wrote *Profiles in Courage,* a book that dealt with how ten important Americans successfully handled crises. It was a best seller, and catapulted John F. Kennedy into the public eye. People have always been fascinated by how an individual or group soberly faces a crisis and surmounts it, or even turns it to advantage. Crisis, indeed, can clothe a man in glory. In the darkest days of 1940, with France already prostrate under the Nazi heel, and with Britain's survival being calculated in weeks, Winston Churchill stood before the House of Commons and uttered the immortal words, "We shall never surrender." In the 1960s, Martin Luther King marched past glowering mobs and police armed with cattle prods, believing that only through peaceful confrontation and crisis would civil rights be won.

On the other hand, crisis can clothe us in ignominy. Crisis has always victimized investors—and the walking wounded are everywhere. Some even seem to carry their scars as a badge of courage, as if surviving terrible losses was at least some compensation. However, it doesn't have to be that way. Crisis also opens the door to large profits. But you had better don your general's hat and flak jacket. To make this killing you have to charge "into the valley of death" while overreaction is roaring and thundering all around you.

First: Know Your Enemy

A market crisis presents an outstanding opportunity to profit, because it lets loose overreaction at its wildest. In a crisis or panic, the normal guidelines of value disappear. People no longer examine what a stock is worth; instead they are fixated by prices cascading ever lower. The falling prices are reinforced by expert and peer opinion that things must get worse.

Further, the event triggering the crisis is always considered to be something entirely new: nothing in our experience shows us how to cope with the current catastrophe. "Sell, sell, sell," the savants chorus. "No matter how low prices have fallen, they are destined to go lower yet."

It is through this rout of panicky investors—who as they rush past you shout how awful conditions are up ahead—that you must resolutely advance. However, as this section will show, you will certainly not go in unarmed. If you can shield yourself with the psychological armor provided in the previous chapters, you have an opportunity to make major gains. (Okay, if you have a swagger stick to smack against your jodhpurs, it couldn't hurt.)

To see that it is possible to keep your cool, and benefit from the enormous overreaction a crisis brings, let's return to an old battlefield. We'll look at the Gulf Crisis, at its worst in the fall of 1990. The Dow Jones Industrial Average had been knocked down over 15% in the midst of the most severe panic in bank and financial stocks since the Great Depression.

Here's the rule to remember as we re-create the heady crisis that got the nineties off with a bang.

RULE 29

Political and financial crises lead investors to sell stocks. This is precisely the wrong reaction. Buy during a panic, don't sell.

My *Forbes* column on October 22, 1990, describes the environment at the time.

With the world seemingly on the brink of war, should you buy now, sell or stay on the sidelines? Although thousands of Wall Street reports have been devoted to every major crisis through the years, no coherent strategy has ever been developed to cope with these recurring but frightening confrontations. The advice given by experts over time has almost always been a knee-jerk recommendation to sell.

After examining the 11 major crises of the postwar period, I found that this has been exactly the wrong thing to do, in every single case. Analyzing the subsequent market action also makes it clear that there is

Table 12–1

APPRECIATING CRISIS

Performance of the Dow Jones Industrial Average through 11 major postwar crises.

		Appreciation	
	Market low after crisis	*1 year later*	*2 years later*
Berlin Blockade	7/19/48	–3.3%	13.2%
Korean War	7/13/50	28.8%	39.3%
1962 stock market break	6/26/62	32.3%	55.1%
Cuban missile crisis	10/23/62	33.8%	57.3%
Kennedy assassination	11/22/63	25.0%	33.0%
Gulf of Tonkin	8/6/64	7.2%	3.1%
1969/70 stock market break	5/26/70	43.6%	53.9%
1973/74 stock market break	12/6/74	42.2%	66.5%
1979/80 oil crisis	3/27/80	27.9%	5.9%
1987 crash	10/19/87	22.9%	54.3%
1990 Persian Gulf War	8/23/90	23.6%	31.3%
Average appreciation		25.8%	37.5%

a definite way to react to a crisis and a very high probability that you can profit, regardless of whether the roots of the crisis are financial, monetary or political.

Table 12–1 shows the eleven major crises since World War II, ranging from the Berlin blockade in 1948 (when we stood eyeball-to-eyeball with the Soviets on the brink of war) to the crash of 1987 (the worst of the twentieth century). Of the 11, 6 were political; the other 5 were brought on by economic, investment or financial factors.

The figure measures the Dow Jones Industrial Average at the bottom of each crisis, when experts predicted prices could only tumble lower, along with the subsequent performance one and two years later. A glance at the record tells it all. The consistency of results is remarkable. An investor would have made good money one year later in 10 of the 11 crises, and would have lost in only one, and then a mere 3.3%. The average gain one year later would have been 25.8% with the gains ranging as high as 43.6% after the 1969 to 1970 break and 42.2% after the 1973 to 1974 bear market.

Holding stocks for two years after a crisis resulted in spectacular returns. A buyer would have made money in all 11 crises, with an average two-year gain of almost 38%, and appreciation ranging up to 66.5% after the market decline of 1973/1974. Granted, no one buys at the bottom, but even if an investor were 10% or 15% off the mark, he or she would still have made big bucks buying into the crisis. . . . Although gut-wrenching, holding—and even buying—in a panic is a winning strategy.

Symptoms of a Crisis

How do we know when a crisis has arrived? The symptoms are anything but hard to find, and usually are downright unavoidable. They appear on prime time news or in banner headlines, whether it was the Iraqi invasion of Kuwait in 1990, the stock market crash of 1987, or the bear market of 1973/1974. In each case, the crisis is the major news of the day. Legions of experts are interviewed, most making dour forecasts of structural damage to the nation. A common theme is "things will never be the same again."

Because the nation, if not the world, is focused on the crisis, the media is in its glory. I remember that after the 1987 crash I received scores of phone calls from reporters because of my prior work on panics and crashes. During the course of one call, it became apparent the reporter had little understanding of the stock market. I asked him (diplomatically, I hope) if he had covered the investment scene for long. "No," he replied, "I normally cover obits, but my editor yanked me off them; he said this was more important."

A crisis sells newspapers, builds ratings, and peddles advertising. CNN devoted most of its resources to the Gulf Crisis and the Gulf War for months. Before the shooting started, CNN's creative programmers produced feature after feature about the ramifications of a Gulf War. The military situation became a gigantic, worldwide, pregame Superbowl show, lasting months. Chart after chart showed the weapons of the two teams—I mean, armies: attack fighters, bombers, infantry and armored divisions, missiles, artillery, poison gas, ad infinitum. So that you would not turn away from your screen, the forces of the opposing teams looked equally matched. Many people, myself included, were swept up by the news, so much so that we watched virtually the same dispatches over and over.

In point of fact, many experts and quite a number of lay people knew it was not going to be even close, as subsequent events bore out. True, the Iraqi military had a large number of armored divisions, equipped with the most sophisticated Soviet tanks. However, it had shown itself all but incompetent to handle them during the eight-year Iraq-Iran war that had ended only a few years earlier. The best effort by an Iraqi Patton was to move several regiments about twenty miles in one major battle. It had never been able to maneuver even one armored division with much success. To rapidly strike out and coordinate the attack of half a dozen divisions would have required divine intervention. There was even less to say about their vaunted air force.

The point is that in crisis, most people do not make objective evaluations. The enormous disparity in quality and effectiveness of allied weaponry and men was, to my knowledge, never discussed. Rather, the media focused overwhelmingly on the devastating problems the U.S. faced. The result was that in the third quarter of 1990, the market had its fourth worst drop of the postwar period.

A confluence of factors fed the stock market crisis. One of the most important, as noted in chapter 10, was the fear of a major new energy crisis that would cripple American industry, leave millions shivering in cold homes, and create long lines at the gas pumps, patiently waiting hours for a gallon or two of "black gold."

Perception and reality were poles apart. As was obvious even at the time, the energy panic had no basis in fact. The fear of a world shortage of oil did not stand up to even the most cursory examination.

But an important rule to learn in crisis investing is that, true or false, the perceptions driving stock prices take on a life of their own.

This leads to the second rule of crisis investing, which, simple as it is, most investors overlook.

RULE 30

In a crisis, carefully analyze the reasons put forward to support lower stock prices—more often than not they will disintegrate under scrutiny.

But crises are usually multifaceted, which often leads to multifaceted market opportunities. The mania in commercial real estate in the 1980s* led to the worst drop in prices in the postwar period.

Real estate markets tumbled 50%, and even 75% in some areas, with no security behind many of the projects. The banks, S&Ls, and insurance companies were heavily involved. A full-fledged panic in financial stocks began during the Gulf Crisis, in August of 1990. Banks, S&Ls, insurance companies, and other financial stocks, already down sharply because of real estate problems, went into a free fall. Fears were now voiced about the viability of the banking system itself, and doubts were expressed as to whether it could withstand the shock of trillion-dollar losses in real estate. From the beginning of the year to the end of Sep-

---

* We will examine this bubble in more detail in chapter 16.

tember of 1990, money center and regional banks dropped 50%.[1] Some financial stocks fell as much as 80% from their previous highs.

Essentials for Crisis Investing

When you're in a crisis, how do you know that this time is not the exception, that this is not the rerun of 1929? Sure the charts show how well you would have done in each crisis in the past, but charts are cold comfort when you're watching the tsunami approach. To answer the question and give you a set of systematic rules, let's take the 1990 financial crisis as our case study.

Bank stocks were ultracheap, trading at about 50% of their market values of 9 months earlier. Many banks were priced at 60% or less of book value. At these prices they more than discounted their potential real estate losses, even applying the tighter accounting standards on delinquent loans that the bank examiners had recently put into effect, which often required significantly larger loss reserves.

"Well and good," you might say, "but a number of these banks did belly up. How can you tell which banks to buy and which to pass on?"

You can't. But a number of criteria I used should help you increase your odds substantially. First, we were careful to buy banks that were financially sound. We researched the hundred largest regional banks to see which had recently taken loss reserves that seemed to adequately cover their bad real estate loans.[2]

Second, after writing off these large debts, I required them to have more than adequate capital to meet any further unanticipated or undiscovered losses.

Third, we paid careful attention to financial ratios. The banks we bought had to have enough capital to be well over the regulators' minimum requirements. Since the name of the game was to buy banks that had a very strong chance of survival, financial ratios were critical to our analysis. Not surprisingly, a large number of banks met our standards— again indicating how much investors had overreacted to the crisis.

Take PNC, a large bank holding company headquartered in Pittsburgh. The bank increased its loan loss reserves by $761 million in 1990, after boosting them by an abnormally large $332 million the year before. At the time, management indicated it believed it had reserved fully against its potential real estate losses, marking the portfolio down to the value it thought it would receive in the then depressed market. Even after taking major write-offs for real estate in 1990, PNC still had a core capital ratio of 5.7%, well above the regulators' requirements. Its book value after the large write-off was $13.40 a share. The stock traded down to under $6.00. At this level its market price was only 44% of a conservative valuation of book value. By comparison, the price-to-book value of the S&P 500 was about 2.5 times. PNC was thus priced at a mere 16% of the book value of the market. Unless management was misrepresenting the situation or had no accounting controls, the bank appeared dirt cheap.

But there's more. PNC never cut its dividend, which had been raised in the crisis to $1.06 a share from $1.00 the year before. During the panic in the fall of 1990, it yielded a lip-smacking 14%. The yield was a major inducement to buy the stock, but even more important than the dividend itself, you may recall from chapter 8, was the implicit vote of confidence by management and the board of directors in the bank's future. If they were less sure the situation was under control, a dividend cut or else omitting it entirely would have been far more appropriate. This would have forestalled punishing personal lawsuits if things went awry. Too, the regulatory authorities, which at this point were ultraconservative in their examination of possible bad loans, would not have tolerated a high dividend, or indeed any dividend, if the bank didn't appear to be financially sound.

To end the episode, PNC's earnings recovered sharply in 1991 and 1992, and by early 1993 the stock had almost sextupled, reaching $35 a share. Not a bad bounce considering the 14% yield in the interim. Dividends continued to increase and by year-end 1997 were 47% above the 1990 rate.

There were numerous banks that met the same criteria. Another example, First Chicago, should provide additional flavor of the times. The bank, which traded at $28 in the fall of 1989, was rocked by the financial crisis and fell as low as $8 a share as investors' fears about its large real estate holdings made them question its continued viability.[3] The facts were similar to those of PNC. The bank took large loss reserves, primarily for bad real estate debts, in 1989, 1990, and 1991, with the highest being a charge of $516 million in 1990. Still, the company's capital remained well above the regulators' requirements. Near the bottom, First Chicago traded at only 40% of book value, once again a fraction of the S&P 500.

The board of directors, as in the case of PNC, maintained the dividend, resulting in a stock yield of over 14% near the low. Here again was a severe overreaction. By late 1997 the stock had moved up to $80, tenfolding from its 1990 low.

One of the most important characteristics of a crisis—at least to the contrarian investor—is the abundance of opportunities. Sometimes excellent stocks collapse when there is nothing wrong with them. Take the case of Federal Home Loan Mortgage Corporation, referred to on the Street as "Freddy Mac." (This company and the Federal National Mortgage Association—"Fannie Mae"—are the country's two largest originators of mortgage securities on housing.) To 1990, Freddy Mac had a record of earnings growth that would make many a CEO of an emerging growth company envious. For the previous 15 years its income increased at a better than 20% clip. Earnings continued to move ahead in 1990, but the stock dropped off the charts with the other financial stocks during the panic. Then, in the fourth quarter of 1990, the company reported it would take a one-time charge on a small part of its multifamily mortgages.

Horror of horrors, a negative earnings surprise in an industry where the password was panic. When the smoke cleared, the stock had dropped from $8½ a share in late 1989 to under $2¾, or almost 70%. At its low it was trading at a P/E of about 4.5 times earnings and yielding 5%, even though earnings after the write-off would still be 5% higher in 1990 than in the previous year. Careful analysis indicated that there was nothing wrong with the company, and that the growth rate of the past was likely to continue.

Management statements corroborated this analysis. We bought the stock, and growth did continue at an above-average rate. Earnings increased 33% in 1991 and more than doubled by 1994. Dividends also rose over 100% in the same period. The stock moved up to $11 by early 1994, on its way to $42 in late 1997, or more than 15 times its price at the 1990 low.

Hedging Your Bets

As these examples illustrate, crisis brings enormous opportunity, but there is always the fear that something can go wrong. Any one of the banks, even though they appeared sharply undervalued by our value criteria, could have made a mistake on its loss reserves, thus putting it into greater financial difficulty than was apparent. In fact, this happened in one or two cases, which was a remarkably low percentage of the thousands of the banks that were publicly traded.

Still, if you're conservative, you want to guard against this risk. The best way is to have adequate diversification. As a money manager, I did this by buying a fairly large number of banks, with none accounting for more than 2% of our overall holdings (although we had over 25% of our equity portfolios in this industry, and over 35% for the Kemper-Dreman High Return Fund). We expected to lose one and possibly two banks as a result of management underestimating real estate losses. Even given this loss ratio we believed we would do significantly better than the market.

As it turned out, thanks to the financial screens outlined above, we did not own a single bank that went under. Our returns in this area were exceptional. From the fourth quarter of 1990 to the end of 1997 the banking index outpaced a rapidly rising market, increasing 578% vs. 231% for the S&P 500.

In looking back, it may look like a cakewalk (due to hindsight bias), but at the time it was anything but easy. In my case, I had reasonably good background, I knew about overreaction, cognitive errors, group decision errors, and theoretically should have been battle-hardened by the similar crises I went through in the previous three decades. So when the financial crisis of 1990 exploded it should have been a layup.

Nothing could be further from the truth. True, I moved in with relish snapping up bargain after bargain. Trouble was, this was not the bottom, as it almost never is. Some of the temporary reverses were stunning.

First Fidelity Bank, which we bought after it dropped from $45 to $17, and met all the criteria outlined above, was under $13 two weeks later. That's right, the stock dropped another 25% in ten trading days. The thought crossed my mind that three more weeks of this and it could be valueless.* Other bank and financial stocks we bought behaved the same way. In spite of my background, the nagging question of whether this time it was different still went through my mind. None of us can escape the anxiety and doubt that permeates a crisis.

Panic

In a market crisis, panic occurs frequently. Enrico Quarantelli writes in *The Nature and Conditions of Panic* that the most important condition for the emergence and continuation of panic is a feeling of entrapment with an impending threat.[4] Whether the person is independent or part of a group, the feeling of being trapped predominates.

---

* As it turned out, $17 for First Fidelty Bank wasn't so bad after all. It was taken over by First Union at $65 in late 1995 and, adjusted for the takeover by First Union, was $134 at the end of 1997.

Psychological experiments have duplicated conditions of near panic. In one experiment, corks were placed in a bottle attached to strings. The neck of the bottle was so narrow that only one cork could be passed through at a time. The subjects were told the bottle would be filled with water and they would have to get their cork out before this occurred or they would receive an electric shock. As the bottle filled with water slowly, there was adequate time to do this if each subject went in order. This, of course, did not happen. A wild melee ensued, similar to panic in a theater fire, and very few got their corks out in time.

Quarantelli, although discussing physical panic, accurately describes conditions observed in the securities market. People see the threat as immediate and believe that their survival depends on taking instant action. In a panic there is a total collapse of the constraints to flee. In the overwhelming desire to save oneself, self-control is overcome by fear and actions become highly self-centered.

In a financial crunch, for example, when a new consensus occurs there is a sense of entrapment in these stocks, a realization of the danger, and a desire to run. Even with the knowledge that their actions could trigger a stampede (because their selling would dwarf normal buying), large numbers of professionals rush for the exit at the same time, only to be trampled by the crowd.

The psychological barriers against following contrarian strategies in times of crisis are high. Panic doesn't just affect sellers, it often keeps even experienced buyers away. But it is surmountable. I related the missed-bottom incident to a seminar I was conducting on "The Psychology of Markets" at the Harvard Medical School Conference in 1995 to show how powerful psychological forces could be even on supposedly well-trained experts.

A psychologist in the audience then made what I thought was an excellent suggestion. She pointed out that people are being taught to cope with trauma in other areas, and suggested similar training for investors. Individuals, psychologists believe, can be trained to cope with panic by analyzing the fears leading up to it, thereby reducing their potency and allowing the person to deal with them. This is done in fields where crisis can be deadly if not handled properly.

This kind of training starts by exposing the student to all aspects of the potential trauma-producing situation. The subject is taught to understand that in panic his perceptions are distorted by fear, and that he should tick off the points covered by the training to see how many of them apply to the current event. Flight simulators, which allow airline and combat pilots to apply their skills and experience in unexpected

crisis-producing situations, are one example of such training. Because trauma is both repetitive and costly in the marketplace, the introduction of training of this sort, at least on an experimental basis, would seem beneficial.

Value Lifelines in a Crisis

In the last sections we examined how oversold the financial stocks became in that crisis. While not of the same magnitude, we saw in chapter 10 how cheap the pharmaceutical stocks became as investors lost confidence in their futures in 1993/1994. The common denominator in all crises is a sharp drop in prices fostered by a serious investor overreaction, whether on a major scale as occurred with financial stocks, or on a somewhat reduced level as was the case with pharmaceuticals. It is precisely this large drop, often in the order of 50% or more, that allows you to set up the lifeline I spoke of in the previous section. You can apply a systematic set of value lifelines to an investor overreaction and measure how far prices have deviated from their normal levels.

Table 12–2a shows the normal P/E, price-to-book value, and dividend relationships for bank stocks one year before the crisis, at its crisis low point, and one year after the crisis. Look at the price-to-book ratio. It falls from 1.6 to .9 at the bottom of the crisis. In effect you have a fire sale with the price of the merchandise chopped to about half the level it was at only a year or two before. Note too that the price-to-book ratio increased dramatically over the next year, from 0.9 to 1.6. The higher price-to-book ratio indicates the stocks have almost doubled from their 1990 lows.*

Another good indicator is dividend yield. In Table 12–2a you can see how sharply it has risen at the bottom of the crisis from its more normal level one year earlier. Yields more than doubled from the year before the crisis to its height, moving up from 4.1% in the second quarter of 1989 to an astonishing 8.8% at the height in the third quarter of 1990. They then fall back to 3.9% one year later. Though the dividend rates on bank stocks have shown an impressive rate of increase during this period, prices have risen even more rapidly, more than doubling for the industry as a whole—not a bad reason for a substantially reduced dividend yield.

---

* By late 1997 banks were being acquired at prices as high as 4—and in the case of Barnett Banks, 5—times book value.

Table 12–2a

PRECRISIS, CRISIS, AND POSTCRISIS FUNDAMENTALS—BANKS STOCKS

Bank Stocks	*Precrisis* *1 year before*	*Crisis* *September 30, 1990*	*Postcrisis* *1 year after*
Price to Earnings	9.4	6.3	12.6
Price to Book	1.6	0.9	1.6
Dividend Yield	4.1%	8.8%	3.9%

The major lifeline in a crisis is that fundamental values increase dramatically in your favor because of rapidly falling stock prices. Whereas before the panic you got a dividend yield of 4.1% on the average bank, you now get 8.8%. Where the banks in the S&P 500 previously traded at 1.6 times book value, they now trade at half of this ratio—and this after deducting large write-offs for bad loans.*

Now look at Figure 12–1, which shows the price performance of bank stocks in the S&P 500 (25 banks) compared to the performance of the S&P itself. As the chart makes obvious, investing in a crisis pays off handsomely. What perhaps is not so obvious is that banks continued to outperform the S&P 500 for years after the crisis ended, including a 195% spurt from 1995 to the end of 1997. Why is this so?

Part of the reason is that banks have been a low P/E industry for years. The crisis just made them that much cheaper. Even when their multiples were restored to more normal levels, they still traded at a substantial discount to the S&P 500 by almost all of the contrarian indicators. The banking crisis allowed the value shopper to buy bargain merchandise at a fraction of the going rate.

Look now at Table 12–2b, which shows the investment fundamentals before, during, and after the crisis in pharmaceutical stocks from the first quarter of 1993 to early 1995. Once again note the substantial drop in the contrarian indicators, P/E, price to book, and yield, at the bottom of the crisis. The indicators are much higher than for banks, because pharmaceuticals are normally a high multiple industry. Nevertheless the patterns are the same.

Price-to-book value, for example, falls from 10.0 before the crisis to 5.5, while yield expands from 2.0% before to 3.7% at the height of the crisis. Finally P/E drops from 26.0 before to 16.5 at the peak of the overreaction, even though many drug companies took substantial one-time

---

* Price/earnings is not a good indicator in this case, because many of the bank stocks are reporting only marginal earnings or losses, making this ratio unrealistic.

Figure 12-1
Crisis Price Performance
S&P 500, Banks, and Drug Stocks

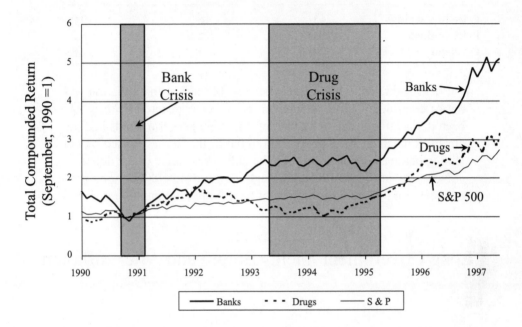

write-offs at this time, increasing the P/E ratios at the bottom.* Also note how price-to-book value and price-to-earnings rose and yield dropped one year later, indicating the dramatic bounce-back in prices. This is shown in Figure 12–1, which demonstrates how handily the pharmaceuticals whipped the rapidly rising S&P 500 from the bottom of the crisis.

Finally, let's examine from a value standpoint the opportunity available in the bond crisis of 1982, discussed briefly in the last chapter. In this case the most important value yardstick is yield after inflation for a nontaxable account, or yield after taxes and inflation for a taxable account. At the height of the panic on long bonds, 30-year Treasuries were yielding over 15%. This yield could be guaranteed by buying zero-coupon bonds (securities that pay no interest but instead are sold at discounts large enough to include the interest rate over the life of the bond.)[5] Municipal bonds yielded as high as 15%. Municipal bonds, of course, are exempt from Federal income taxes.

---

* For some peculiar reason—possibly that Hillary C. was looking disapprovingly at their large profits.

Table 12–2b

PRECRISIS, CRISIS, AND POSTCRISIS FUNDAMENTALS—PHARMACEUTICAL STOCKS

Pharmaceuticals	*Precrisis* *1 year before*	*Crisis* *September 30, 1990*	*Postcrisis* *1 year after*
Price to Earnings	26.0	16.5	19.0
Price to Book	10.0	5.5	6.2
Dividend Yield	2.0%	3.7%	2.8%

Prices had risen to these levels because of the fear that inflation was out of control. Inflation, accompanied by sky-high interest rates, had been devastating to the bond market. Many longer-term bonds had declined as much as 50%, in addition to the further losses caused by declining purchasing power through the falling real value of the dollar.

Now look at Figure 12–2. Although the yields in 1982 on long government bonds were their highest of the century, the inflation rate was

Figure 12-2

Long Government Yields Before and After Inflation

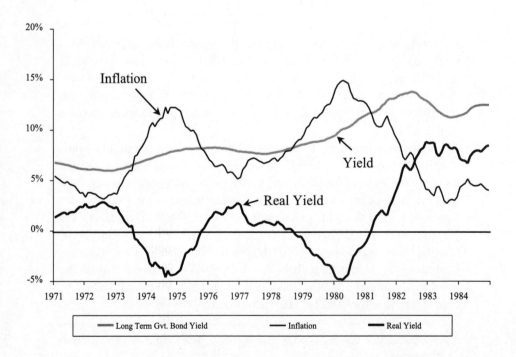

down significantly from its 1980 peak. Normally the yield on government bonds after deducting inflation is 1½% to 2%. In early 1982 this "real yield" stood at over 5%,[6] and, with inflation declining, reached 6% within a few months. So once again the price/value ratios provided investors with double the margin of safety or more in crisis than under more normal circumstances. Shortly thereafter, as noted in the previous chapter, bonds had one of the sharpest rallies of the century, with 30-year zero-coupon governments more than doubling in months.

The bottom line to the investor is that crisis investing pays off, whether it is for the stock market as a whole, a single industry, the bond market, or other markets. It is the ultimate way of playing investor overreaction. *If you get the combination of a panicky market and an industry or sector panic, such as occurred with financial stocks, the potential rewards are that much larger.*

Two key rules for investing in crisis were presented on pages 262 and 265. Here's a third.

RULE 31

(A) **Diversify extensively. No matter how cheap a group of stocks looks, you never know for sure that you aren't getting a clinker.**

(B) **Use the value lifelines as explained. In a crisis, these criteria get dramatically better as prices plummet, markedly improving your chances of a big score.**

What Are the Risks of Crisis Investing?

What unique risk factors should you look at if you decide to invest in a crisis? Measuring risk—as value managers, including myself, use the phrase—involves several factors, all of which become substantially more important in crisis.

1. The first is a company's financial strength, its ability to sail through tough times unscathed. If I buy a group with enormous financial muscle, like the pharmaceuticals, I have very little chance of losing my capital because of financial problems. That's why I devote a lot of attention to balance sheets and other measures of financial strength, including debt to capital structure. Look no further than the LBO (leveraged buyout) excesses of the 1980s to see the merits of this one.

2. The second measure of risk is adequate diversification (which we have already touched on). Not only by industry but by company and by sector. No matter how cheap a company or industry appears, things can still go wrong. That's why in the bank crisis we only took small positions in any single bank, even though the good regional banks traded at giveaway prices. The industry was dirt cheap and there were enough strong banks whose prices had been clobbered to build a diversified portfolio without taking much risk on any single one. Similarly, we didn't put all our chips into the banking industry, or even the financial sector, although it appeared to be a screaming buy. Had we done so we would have chalked up a much larger score. However, the risk of keeping all the eggs in one basket was just too high.

3. The third measure of risk involves price, certainly a lesser consideration in a crisis, but nevertheless still there. Even if a company is a tower of financial strength, that doesn't mean I haven't paid too much for its stock. This is particularly true in a panic. As we have seen, in a crisis you can demand even lower price-to-value ratios than in more normal times. What's more you will get them! So don't be overanxious as stocks free-fall. What looks dirt cheap can often drop another 20% or 30%. Remember my experience with First Fidelity Bank.

These value measures of risk can not only be used to avoid losing money in normal markets but are essential armor if you want to enter the world of crisis investing. In a world of panic, with perceptions of danger greatly magnified, you must have a number of benchmarks to keep your perspective.

Panic brings out the worst fears about a company or an industry. Often, as in the case of the bank stocks during the financial crisis of 1990, the focus is on whether the company or industry in question can survive. This is where financial strength is critical. By looking at the balance sheet and other financial statements, you or your financial consultant can get a good idea of whether the company has the staying power to ride through a crisis relatively unscathed.

The measurements I gave you—on low price/earnings, price-to-cash-flow, price-to-book value, yield—can be supplemented by a number of important financial ratios outlined in chapter 3. Combining these yardsticks provides a clearer perspective of the financial risk you are taking, and thus whether you should buy the stock in a crisis.

Last, but certainly not the least important, the psychological aspect of the risk situation must be held at bay. Although, to this time, it has not been examined in the marketplace, it is normally most pervasive in periods of uncertainty and crisis. As I'm sure will come as no surprise to you, risk is anything but a one-dimensional measure.

The Psychology of Risk

Paul Slovic, a distinguished cognitive researcher we met earlier, has devoted much time to studying the psychological factors that shape judgments of risk. Research on the psychological perception of risk shows that people tend to respond to hazards they perceive. As chapter 10 indicated, psychological studies of flood insurance sales demonstrate that they are heavily influenced by recent experience. Thus, local businessmen will buy more insurance after a flood, when the experience is poignant, than they did, on the same floodplain, before the natural disaster. Similarly, travelers buy more insurance after an airplane crash.

In a panic, investor perceptions similarly can vary on the most clearcut of investment criteria. Balance sheets, statements of profit and loss, financial ratios—all of which usually seem almost fixed in concrete—can look dramatically different to investors in anxiety-producing conditions. Questions arise in a period of great angst, sometimes valid, but more frequently frightened reactions about the worth of inventories, plants, product lines, and a host of other company variables.

If a PC manufacturer in a period of crisis writes down the value of some outdated inventory, questions are likely to surface not only about the value of the company's inventory but about the entire industry. Balance sheets which have appeared to bristle with strength are now questioned and perhaps challenged, with an accompanying drop in stock prices.

Trustworthiness, which has been studied by social psychologists within the domain of interpersonal perception, also has a bearing here.[7] Credibility has been shown to be hard to acquire (many reinforcing instances are needed to attain it) and easy to lose. As Paul Slovic summed it up, "When it comes to winning trust the playing field is not level. It is tilted towards distrust. . . ."[8]

Again, looking at risk, our perceptions can run wild on the most feeble of evidence. Companies with cast-iron balance sheets or product lines can be severely jarred by a minor industry player reporting the need for an upward revision of its reserves or a cash squeeze. First Chicago NBD, for example, lost over a billion dollars in market value when it reported a slight increase in its reserves for bad credit card debt in the second quarter of 1996. Credit cards, considered enormous money makers, were suddenly viewed with suspicion. How bad were these losses likely to be, could they result in a crisis possibly on par with real estate at the beginning of the decade?

Nervousness continued for several months, although the bank said at the time the increase in the reserve was likely to be a one-time charge, which it was. But coming as it did, when investors were apprehensive about the outlook for financial stocks, the perception of the risk exposure from a minor problem increased dramatically. Psychology then can change perceptions even on matters that normally appear black or white.

In the last few pages, we examined the question of what risks you take investing in a crisis environment. We saw that even the most stable risk measures can, like a trick mirror, reflect a different image to investors under varying psychological conditions. While there is not a simple formula for measuring the risk you might be facing, a combination of the price/value ratios I've recommended will put you well ahead of the conventional wisdom of the day.

Remember, too, there are many dimensions to risk. It is not volatility alone, the most widely used measure of risk. Volatility cannot take into account crisis, and has other major limitations. The stocks that perform the worst in some down markets may be precisely the ones you want to buy, as my examples made clear.

Next, a more basic question: how to structure your portfolio to maximize your returns over time while attempting to minimize your exposure. We'll look at the returns over many decades of stocks, T-bills, long bonds, and other investments for a compelling (and nonintuitive) answer.

13

An Investment for All Seasons

WHO hasn't heard this old saw? If the Algonquian Indians had invested the $24 they received from the Dutch in 1626 in payment for Manhattan Island at 6%, they would have $55 billion today? Or marveled at the sagacity of collectors who in the 1870s paid what seems almost pocket change today—a thousand or two—for Impressionist paintings, now worth $3 million or $4 million? Awesome, or so it seems until you look at the returns of stocks over long periods.

What *is* astonishing is that returns on equities surpass just about any other investment. And you don't need the penetrating eye of the collector who can spot the genius of a Degas or a Monet and weed out the hundreds of popular and pricey artists of the day destined for obscurity.

This chapter will demonstrate just how well equities have performed over time. I'm not speaking of discovering a Microsoft in the 1980s or an IBM a few decades earlier. I'm talking of the returns the stock averages have provided over the years. This is before the sizable extra returns that contrarian strategies add. Equally important to the investor, as I will make clear, is the crucial but little-known fact that stocks are not a risky investment, if you hold them for a number of years. In fact, they are one of the safest investments for putting away money for your retirement or your children's education.

Finally, we will see that stocks also keep their value better than almost any other investment through hyperinflation and most other crises. We will also look into using this little appreciated but well-documented information to build a portfolio for your individual needs.

Stock Returns Over Time

When I wrote *Contrarian Investment Strategy* in 1980, stocks were more out of favor than they had been in 15 years. As we saw in chapter 11, collectibles, diamonds, precious metals, and bonds burnt up the track in the previous eight years, while stocks lagged badly. If you had asked investors back then for the last place they wanted to put new money for their retirement, most would have said common stocks.

If these investors had had this chapter in front of them at the time, I think many of them would have changed their decisions instantaneously. Figure 13–1, from Jeremy J. Siegel's first-rate book, *Stocks for the Long Run,* provides the rates of return from 1802 to 1996 for stocks, bonds, Treasury bills, gold, and the dollar after adjusting for inflation.[1] As the chart indicates, the best way to make your money grow over a long period of time is to invest in the stocks of good companies.

The figures are staggering. A dollar invested in stocks over the life of the study became $512,232 (including reinvested dividends)—and this after inflation. Before inflation, it became $6,770,887. Bonds and Trea-

Figure 13–1

Stocks Have It

Total Return Indexes 1802–1996 (inflation adjusted)

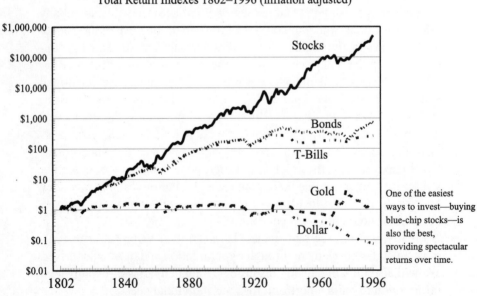

One of the easiest ways to invest—buying blue-chip stocks—is also the best, providing spectacular returns over time.

Source: Jeremy J. Siegel, *Stocks for the Long Run* (McGraw-Hill, 1994), reproduced with permission of the McGraw-Hill Companies.

sury bills (all interest is reinvested) are not even in the same league. A dollar invested in bonds in 1802 increased to 721 dollars at the end of 1996, after inflation, while one invested in T-bills increased to 262 dollars. Gold, one of the hottest investments in the late 1970s, barely keeps up with inflation; a dollar here only rose by 12 cents in 195 years. And look at the dollar itself. By 1996 the poor greenback had lost 92% of the purchasing power it had in 1802.

Let's put stock returns under the microscope. Sure the returns are enormous, but don't the historians say that most of the increase came in the late nineteenth century, with the great railroad boom and the rapid industrialization of the country; or even earlier when stocks of canal companies were the rapidly expanding blue chips of the day? They do, but most historians aren't statisticians. The question is whether the returns are heavily weighted in one or two periods. Table 13–1, again based on Siegel's numbers (and the Dreman Foundation's after 1945), demonstrates that they are not.

Table 13–1

ANNUAL RETURNS TO STOCKS, LONG-TERM GOVERNMENT BONDS, T-BILLS AND GOLD: ADJUSTED FOR INFLATION

1802–1996

	Stocks	*Bonds*	*Bills*	*Nominal Yield*	*Gold*	*Inflation*
Periods						
1802–1996	7.0%	3.4%	2.9%	4.3%	.06%	1.3%
1871–1996	6.9	2.7	1.7	3.7	.01	2.0
Major Subperiods						
1802–1870	7.0	4.8	5.1	5.2	.18	.11
1871–1925	6.6	3.7	3.2	3.8	−.82	.60
1926–1996	7.2	1.9	.59	3.7	.63	3.1
Postwar Periods						
1946–1996	7.5	.86	.42	4.8	−.13	4.4
1946–1962	9.9	−1.4	−1.3	1.7	−3.0	3.1
1963–1979	1.4	−2.6	−.05	5.5	10.9	5.6
1980–1996	11.5	6.8	2.7	7.2	−7.4	4.4

• All returns are averages for the period, expressed as percentages.
• "Nominal Yield" is the mean annual T-Bill return before inflation.
• "Inflation" is the average increase in the Consumer Price Index.
• Data: All data 1802–1945, Gold data 1802–1995: Jeremy Siegel.
     All other data 1946–1996: Dreman Foundation.

The table shows the return of stocks, along with Treasury bills, long government bonds, and gold, adjusted for inflation over time.*

The collectors of Monets or Degas in the 1870s, although they made a killing, made only a fraction of the amount on an inflation-adjusted basis. In fact, I went back to the 1870s and calculated these returns, which came to 6% annually, only 73% of the amount they would have made investing in stocks over the same period.† The returns we should focus on are the inflation-adjusted ones, because they represent the increase in purchasing power from an investment over time.

From 1802 to 1996 our long-lived investor increased his capital by 7% annually, after adjusting for inflation, but before taxes. Now glance at the three major subperiods of the study: 1802–1870, 1871–1925, and 1926–1996. The rate of return in all these periods is remarkably similar, 7%, 6.6%, and 7.2%. Those born more recently than 1802 might say, "This is ancient history. How have stocks done since World War II?"

The postwar return, at 7.5% after inflation, is actually a little better than the 6.8% annually over the previous 143 years. Breaking down the postwar returns further, the real returns (column 1) are positive for stocks in all three postwar periods. Even in the 1963–1979 period, the worst period for stocks in the past 50 years, you still would have increased your real purchasing power by about 1½% a year, while almost tripling it in nominal dollars.

What about the investor who bought stocks at the top of the market in 1929, and then watched in horror as they lost 90% of their value by 1932? Surely this is the exception to the rule. Nope. It took time—15 years—but the investor buying stocks near the market high in August of 1929 came out slightly ahead after inflation. She had retained her entire purchasing power in the worst period for stocks in American history.

"But," someone might say, "buying bonds or T-bills at the same time would have put cautious investors miles ahead, particularly with the deflation of the early thirties." Again no. Had an investor purchased bonds at the top of the 1929 market, he would have lost a staggering 86% of his capital in real terms in the same 30-year period, while buying T-bills would have cost him over 92%. Sharp market drops in 1921, 1973/1974, 1987, and 1990 all had similar outcomes. Rather than getting killed, equity investors who didn't panic were big winners over time.

---

* Nominal returns are much higher for these investments because they are not adjusted for inflation, thus exaggerating the results in terms of real purchasing power.

† The nominal return is used in both cases.

Over nearly two centuries, stocks have returned 7.0% after inflation. Put another way, this means you double your real capital in stocks every 10 years and 6 months. After 21 years your real capital increases four-fold, after 42 years—not an impossible time for people in their twenties or even early thirties—it increases 16 times.

Look again at the table, but this time at the returns of bonds and T-bills after inflation over the same periods. Long government bonds (column 2) and T-bills (column 3) significantly underperformed stocks over 195 years. T-bills returned 2.9% and long bonds returned 3.4%, compared to 7% for equities. Stocks provided almost two-and-a-half times as much annually as T-bills and double the amount of bonds. That is one heck of a lot of outperformance. For gold bugs the news is even worse. Over this time, stocks returned 117 times as much as gold on average each year.

But this is only for openers. Glance at the three major subperiods of the study. The disparity between stocks and the other investments becomes larger with the passage of time. In the 1802 to 1870 period stocks outperformed T-bills by 1.9%, or 37% annually. Stocks returned 106% more than T-bills in the 1871 to 1925 period, and 12 times as much annually from 1926 to 1996. Bond returns, though marginally better than T-bills, were also dwarfed by stocks.

Gold was a nonevent throughout. Holding money in gold, the ultimate investment of the prophets of doom, is simply a joke with rising prices. In the postwar period gold actually decreased capital by a fraction of a percentage point annually. Some ultimate investment!

Stocks outperformed T-bills 73% of the time for all five-year periods between 1802 and 1996, 81% for ten-year periods, 95% and 97% respectively for 20- and 30-year periods. The results after the war are better yet. For any five-year period stocks outdistanced T-bills 82% of the time, and for any 20-year or 30-year period 100% of the time. The comparisons with long bonds are nearly identical.

What do all these rather remarkable numbers tell us? Clearly that stocks are a far better long-term investment than bonds or Treasury bills. I'm not the first to make this statement, however.

In 1924 Edgar Lawrence Smith, a New York investment banker, wrote a book rejecting the conventional wisdom that high-grade bonds were a superior long-term investment to stocks.[2] Smith's data went from the Civil War to the 1920s. His book, *Common Stocks as Long Term Investments,* although highly praised at the time, was in retrospect viewed as one of the contributors to the 1929 crash. Smith was lambasted for decades in books reviewing this debacle. Smith turned out to be somewhat of a prophet, though. He had also written that even if an investor bought stocks at the top, there was only a 6% chance that he or she would have to wait 6 to 15 years to break even. There is no record that Smith anticipated circumstances nearly as extreme as the Crash and the Great Depression, yet, as was indicated, it took an investor only 15 years to recover the money invested at the 1929 peak.

John Jacob Raskob, a director of General Motors and a major market figure of the era, also wore horns after the 1929 crash. Raskob, in an oft-quoted article in *The Ladies Home Journal,* stated that an investor putting $15 a month into blue-chip stocks could accumulate $80,000 over the next 20 years. Raskob's timing was admittedly not quite perfect—the article appeared only a few days before the Dow hit its then all-time high on September 3, 1929. Too, his estimates, based on the enormous rates of return of the 1920s bull market, were a touch optimistic—24% a year, or over three times the rate of return of the previous 50 years. As a result, he too was ridiculed by historians as an example of the inane advice experts provided at the time. Wildly optimistic projections and terrible timing not withstanding, anyone following Raskob's advice would have more capital than a person putting money into T-bills at the same time—only four years later. Further, the investor's stock portfolio, while not reaching $80,000 in 20 years, would still be a respectable $60,000 in 30 years.[3]

Although inflation and taxes in the 1920s still had a minimal impact on the returns of T-bills or bonds, the superiority of investing in stocks was already recognized. Another leading advocate of stocks at the time was Irving Fisher of Yale, the outstanding American economist of his day. Unfortunately, his reputation was tarred by an 11-word sentence he made days before the 1929 Crash: "Stocks are now at what looks like a permanently high plateau."

All the same, Fisher foresaw the superior returns of equities clearly in the mid-twenties:

> It seems then that the stock market overrates the safety of "safe" securities and pays too much for them, that it underrates the riskiness of risky securities and pays too little for them . . . and finally that it mistakes the steadiness of money income from a bond for a steadiness of real income which it does not possess. In steadiness of real income or purchasing power, a list of diversified common stocks surpasses bonds.[4]

These prophetic sentiments were echoed by John Maynard Keynes and other leading economists and financial figures of the time.

Though the evidence was accumulating, the 1929 Crash and ensuing market collapse resulted in the perception that stocks were a risky investment, while bonds were a safe haven, persisting for several more decades. As strong as the superior performance of stocks over T-bills and bonds was in 1802 to 1945, it was only a part of the picture. The inflationary story that crippled the returns of T-bills and bonds only began after World War II. It is here we must look to find what the truly risky investments are.

The Investment Revolution

To 1945 inflation was a nonfactor in markets. The 1940 dollar, for example, still had 88 cents of the purchasing power of the 1802 greenback. But since 1945 inflation has moved up relentlessly. The dollar today, as Figure 13-1 demonstrated, has only 8% of the purchasing power it had in 1802. From 1946 to 1996, prices rose 4.4% annually, or over 15 times as fast as the rate for the previous 143 years. Inflation has precipitated a revolution in investment markets that has irrevocably changed the investments that will preserve and enhance your capital, as well as those that will destroy it.

Since 1945, inflation and taxes—the twin horses of the apocalypse—have made a disaster of the prudent method of savings we learned from our parents and grandparents. Figure 13-2 shows the inflation-adjusted returns on Treasury bills, Government bonds, and stocks before and after taxes since World War II. If an investor put $100,000 into T-bills in 1946, after inflation it would have increased to $124,000, a gain of only $\frac{4}{10}$ of 1% annually. At this rate, it would take 150 years to double your capital. Bonds did only slightly better: $100,000 in 1946 became $155,000 by the end of 1996, or a gain of under 1% annually. Unfortunately, millions of Americans holding bonds, T-bills, money-market funds, and other fixed-income investments have been trampled by inflation, the first of the deadly horsemen. It's almost as though the Feds hired Jesse James to separate you from your savings.

By comparison, investing $100,000 in stocks hit the jackpot. It became $4,035,000, thirty-three times as much as T-bills and 26 times as much as bonds in the same time. *Although stocks have done better than bonds since at least the early 1800s, they have dominated markets in the postwar period.* After adjusting for inflation, stocks returned 7.5% annually in this period, 18 times more than T-bills and nine times as much as bonds.

But bad as the results for bonds and T-bills are, they only get worse when the second horseman of the apocalypse rides through. If you pay income taxes on your investments, the disparity between stocks and

Figure 13-2

THE FEDS HIRE JESSE JAMES

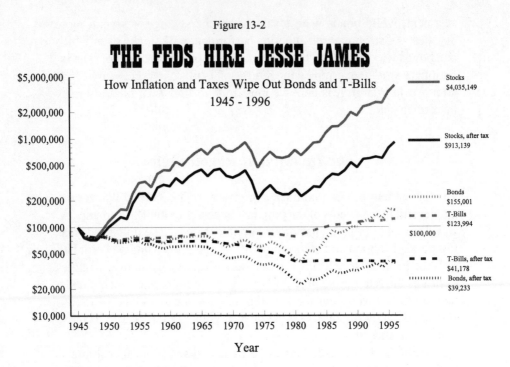

How Inflation and Taxes Wipe Out Bonds and T-Bills
1945 - 1996

Stocks
$4,035,149

Stocks, after tax
$913,139

Bonds
$155,001

T-Bills
$123,994

$100,000

T-Bills, after tax
$41,178

Bonds, after tax
$39,233

Year

All figures are inflation-adjusted.

bonds increases dramatically. As the chart also shows, the after-tax and inflation-adjusted return of T-bills and government bonds, for an investor in a higher tax bracket, has been negative since 1946. An individual in a 50% bracket who put money into T-bills or government bonds after World War II,* and kept reinvesting in these instruments to 1996, lost the major part of his or her capital. Investing $100,000 in T-bills, after adjusting for inflation and taxes, left only $41,200, while in bonds it dwindled to $39,200. By comparison, if an investor had put $100,000 into blue-chip stocks, he would have $913,000 after inflation and taxes, or nine times his original investment.

---

* The tax bracket went as high as 75% to 90% for a part of the postwar period.

Fighting the Last War

To get a better historical perspective on how radically changed the investment world became after 1945, look again at Table 13–1. Over the entire 200-year period, prices increased at only 1.3% annually. But glance at the major subperiods. In the first two, inflation was almost nonexistent, rising only .1% and .6%. Yet if you look back at the stock returns for these periods, you'll see that stocks still did better than bonds, with returns almost 50% higher annually in the first major subperiod (1802–1870), and getting progressively larger in the next two subperiods. In the last major subperiod (1926–1996) stocks returned 3½ times as much as bonds annually, and nine times as much after the War.*

Columns 2 and 3 of Table 13–1, and Figure 13–2, also provide some historical background on how devastating inflation has been to bonds and T-bills. Although the real return for bonds after inflation was 3.4% annually over the 1802 to 1996 period, it dropped to under 1% for the 50 years ending 1996. That's right, the historic return of bonds was cut by almost 75% after the War! For T-bills, as column 3 demonstrates, it was even worse. Their long-term inflation-adjusted return plummeted by 87% after 1945. At best, bonds and T-bills merely preserve your purchasing power after inflation. Holding stocks would have increased your real capital 40 times in the 50 years after the war. It would have taken you 140 years in a T-bill or money market fund to even double your money in constant dollars.

Is inflation going to stop? I doubt it. It has been brought down to a more moderate 3.6% rate in the 1982 to 1996 period, but this is still higher than the 3% Arthur Burns, chairman of the Federal Reserve, considered intolerable in the sixties. Burns warned repeatedly that such high rates would mean the end of Western Civilization as we know it.

Although chairman after chairman of the Fed has tried to stomp out inflation, price rises are pernicious. Prices have risen in 49 of the 51 years since the war. The last year prices went down was in 1954 and the decrease was under 1%.

While this chapter is not a tract on the causes of inflation, but rather its effects on various types of investments, it is still obvious that the postwar period is different from any period in the past. E. H. Phelps and Sheila V. Hopkins published a 700-year study of consumer price indices in England—food, fuel, clothing etc.—beginning about 1250.[5] Through 1933, inflation and deflation took place with remarkable regularity. Af-

---

* In 1940 the greenback still had 86% of its 1802 purchasing power.

ter remaining on a plateau for 300 years, prices exploded in the century following 1550, fueled by the plundered gold and silver of the Inca and Aztec empires, rising to about three times the level of the previous three centuries. This was the classic type of inflation economists understand so well—too much money chasing too few goods. The primitive production capacity of the time could not keep up with the vast increase in money supply, and wild inflation resulted, first in Spain and shortly thereafter in England. Prices then remained stationary for almost 300 years and were actually higher in 1650 than they were in 1932.

So, with the exception of odd and quickly corrected price surges (at least when looked at over the long historical time span), the world enjoyed relative price stability. For example, prices rose 75% between 1350 and 1370, but by 1380 they were lower than they had been in 1350. Similar surges and corrections accompanied most major wars. In Victorian England, prices were so stable that government bonds returned only 2.5%.

Over this entire time there have been only two periods of sustained inflation (the one beginning in the sixteenth century and lasting 100 years, and the one starting after World War II). The current inflationary period is by far the worse of the two. By the end of 1974, prices had risen over 480% in 28 years, and by the end of 1996, 780%. Prices were now 100 times as high as in 1250, and 34 times as high as in 1550.

As we know, the price rise in the postwar period is the only one that has shown no sign of a reversal. While other periods, even the 1500s, show deflationary dips, the current inflation has moved continuously higher with virtually no respite.

What do we make of this? It seems obvious the Keynsian revolution, a part of which is the belief that governments could run surpluses in good times and deficits in bad to improve the economy, has been one of the primary causes. This country and most others in the Western world seem to have gotten Keynes half right. They fully understand the principle of deficits (which seem to be increasing progressively in size over time), but run them in expansions as well as recessions. They have never learned the concept of surpluses in boom periods, despite the pledges of even the most tight-fisted presidential and congressional candidates when they are running for office.

Deficits are unquestionably inflationary, in spite of the government's efforts to shrink them away by higher inflation. The loss of most of their investment by a generation of Americans, who scratched out their meager savings in the Great Depression and then patriotically put them into Government War bonds at 2½% or 3%, is an example of the enormous decrease in purchasing power because of inflation, and, oh yes, just as big a debt reduction in real terms for the Government.

But there are other well-recognized causes of inflation. Entitlement programs and social welfare, set up in the 1930s under the New Deal and expanded many times on all governmental levels since the war, make it very hard to reduce budget deficits. So does the ever-increasing national debt, now 25% of the GDP (gross domestic product). While we are seeing the first major attempts to reduce some entitlement programs, it appears at the time of this writing that it will be a long, uphill battle. Conscientious efforts have been made to reduce the deficit, and indeed the first balanced budget since the sixties was projected in January 1998. Still, some costly new event that costs billions of dollars inevitably comes along to hinder the process. The S&L bailout, the Gulf War, Bosnia, Iraq, Somalia, Haiti, numerous natural disasters are all examples of this type of unbudgeted phenomenon. In sum, it is hard to get control of spending for a myriad of reasons, only a few of which are listed here. That means a balanced budget, or more unrealistically, a budget surplus over time, is going to be more difficult to maintain than many believe.

After World War II another crucial new socioeconomic variable was introduced into the inflation picture in the United States—a variable that has been important ever since. In traditional microeconomic theory, labor is treated as a commodity, and its cost, like those of all other commodities, might rise or fall according to changing market conditions. In 1946 Congress passed the Full Employment Act, making labor something different. In the parlance of some economists, labor is an administered market—or a market in which the flexibility of price movement is restrained.[6]

In the labor market from the end of the war to the early eighties, wages were expected to be renegotiated upward regardless of prosperity or recession. And to the early eighties, at least, to move up faster than the rate of inflation. Wages, then, were a major contributor to rising prices at that time.

Through the rest of the eighties to the present, however, higher unemployment and a free trade policy resulted in wage rates showing a significant slowdown, as many jobs—and at times entire industries—were exported abroad. These factors led to a drop in the percentage of American workers who were union members, reducing further the power to increase wages.

Even so, inflation has risen steadily at over 3%. Much of the increase came from the service part of the economy, now projected to be over

60% of GDP, and continuing to grow rapidly. The service segment has been estimated to have increased its pricing in high single-digit or low double-digit figures in recent years, accounting for a significant share of the continuing inflation.

Since 1980, two major contributors to price increases in the previous two decades—oil and commodities—have actually been declining, and in inflation-adjusted dollars are well below their peak levels of 15 years ago. Although there is still a reasonable supply of oil, the dynamics of oil pricing could change rapidly for political or economic reasons. The Saudi Arabian Royal Family, for example, is under increasing pressure from the country's Islamic fundamentalists.

The Royal Family is clinging to power in the face of an increasing undercurrent favoring Islamic fundamentalist change. If such a change does occur, it is quite conceivable—with Saudi Arabia being by far the largest oil exporter in the Middle East—that the resulting shocks could send oil prices soaring again, and inflation with it. A price increase could also come from other totally unpredictable events that could limit production or rejuvenate the OPEC Cartel.

Finally, commodity prices, after lows in the early 1990s, could again head higher, as could wage rates. Thus three major causes of inflation in the 1970s and early 1980s, which have been dormant as prices continued to rise in recent years, all appear to have the potential of rekindling. If this does take place, we could be faced with inflation at higher rates than the 3.5% of the past 10 years.

The bottom line is that inflation rates are likely to stay at current levels or increase in the years ahead. Which indicates the outlook for bonds, T-bills, and other debt continues to be mediocre.

Enter the Second Horseman

Table 13–1 showed how the disparity between the rates of return of stocks and government debt spiked sharply with the much higher rates of inflation endemic to the postwar period. Table 13–2 is identical to Table 13–1 in format, but returns for stocks, bonds, and T-bills are calculated using a 50% income tax rate.[7]

Over the entire 1802 to 1996 period stocks provided a 5.9% annual return after both inflation and taxes, almost triple the return of T-bills and more than 2½ times the return of long government bonds. Again glance at the three major subperiods. As you can see, the disparity in returns grows larger as the years pass. As is evident with rising inflation and taxes, both bond and T-bill returns, positive in the preceding two

Table 13–2

ANNUAL RETURNS TO STOCKS, LONG-TERM GOVERNMENT BONDS, T-BILLS AND
GOLD: ADJUSTED FOR INFLATION AND TAXES
1802–1996

	Stocks	Bonds	Bills	Nominal Yield	Gold	Inflation
Periods						
1802–1996	5.9%	2.3%	2.1%	3.5%	.06%	1.3%
1871–1996	5.2	.97	.54	2.6	.01	2.0
Major Subperiods						
1802–1870	7.0	4.8	5.1	5.2	.18	.11
1871–1925	6.6	3.2	2.7	3.3	−.82	.60
1926–1996	4.2	−.71	−1.1	2.0	.63	3.1
Postwar Periods						
1946–1996	3.8	−1.8	−1.8	2.6	−.13	4.4
1946–1962	5.7	−2.8	−2.1	.85	−3.0	3.1
1963–1979	−2.3	−4.4	−2.7	2.8	10.9	5.6
1980–1996	8.3	1.9	−.34	4.0	−7.4	4.4

• All returns are averages for the period, expressed as percentages.
• "Nominal Yield" is the mean annual T-Bill return before inflation.
• "Inflation" is the average increase in the Consumer Price Index.
• Data: All data 1802–1945, Gold data 1802–1995: Jeremy Siegel.
               All other data 1946–1996: Dreman Foundation.
• Tax rates: Income: 50% 1914–1987; 35% 1988–1996.
               Capital Gains: 25% 1914–1996.

major subperiods, turn negative in the 1926 to 1996 period, while stocks—despite two enormous crashes in 1929 and 1987—still provide a 4.2% annual return.

The postwar period really lights up the scoreboard. As Table 13–2 demonstrates, T-bill returns were negative for the 50 years following 1945 after inflation and taxes, while bond returns were in the red for the first 34 years. Stocks outperformed bonds and T-bills in every single subperiod between 1945 and 1996. Even in the 1963 to 1979 period, when stocks had a negative annual return of –2.3% after inflation and taxes, it was still better than the –4.4% of bonds or –2.7% of T-bills. Gold, for the sharp-eyed reader, did better during this time, providing an average return of 10.9% annually, but for the whole 1945 to 1996 period it was in the red, –0.13% a year.

The outperformance of stocks, which was significant in the 1802 to 1870 period, when inflation was a nonevent and income taxes were almost nonexistent,* increased substantially in the 1871 to 1925 period when inflation was low and income taxes were only beginning to come into effect. The bottom line is that from 1945 on, with both higher inflation and income taxes, it was simply no contest. Stocks dramatically enhanced your purchasing power; bonds and T-bills drained it.

A New Investment Era

Stocks outperformed bonds, as Edgar Lawrence Smith, Irving Fisher, and John Maynard Keynes noted as far back as the twenties. However, what comes out in bold face is that inflation and taxes changed the game entirely after the war. Before 1945 stocks had an excellent chance of outperforming T-bills and bonds; now the bet is overwhelming. Just as important, the time required for stocks to outperform fixed-income securities has decreased significantly.

Because the twin horsemen of the apocalypse—inflation and taxes—target debt securities, the probabilities of stocks outperforming bonds and T-bills become much higher for shorter holding periods after 1945 than in the previous 145 years. In one year, the odds of stocks outperforming T-bills (after inflation but before taxes) rise from 60% in the pre-1945 world to 67% after 1945; in a two-year period from 61% to 78%; in 15 years they move from 88% to 92%; and in 20 years they increase from 92% to 100%.

The argument becomes stronger the longer an investor can keep his or her funds in stocks. What is clear is that if you are putting savings away for more than a few years, the major portion should be invested in high-quality stocks. But isn't this more risky? We'll look at this question carefully in the next chapter. The answers might surprise you.

Investing in Doomsday

It doesn't happen often, but it happens: the economy of a country disintegrates violently. Sometimes it's hyperinflation, sometimes by a crushing military defeat and occupation. How do stocks and bonds cope in these radical situations? In the past 80 years there unfortunately have been enough such occurrences to draw a pretty good picture.

---

* A 5% federal tax on income over $1,000 was imposed during the Civil War and continued until 1872. The information about how many people bothered to pay Uncle Sam back then is not available.

Let's start with the case of the investor who decided to invest a large amount of money in 1913. The world had been at relative peace for almost a hundred years, with minimum inflation. Being conservative, the investor chose only bonds and, to be fully secure, he picked only government securities. To be extra sure, he went one step further and diversified by buying the obligations of the six strongest powers on Earth.

If he had put them in a safety deposit box inaccessible to him for 10 years, he would have come back to find the bonds of Russia, Austria-Hungary, and Germany valueless, and those of England and France having only a small fraction of their former value because of inflation. Only the bonds of the United States would still possess the greater part of their purchasing power. His assets would have been decimated; yet at the time he made them, the safety of his investments was unquestionably superb. Debt securities failed miserably in this period of major political change and rampant inflation.

Or consider the Weimar Republic in Germany after the First World War (1919 to 1933). As we all know, this was a classic case of hyperinflation. It took billions of Deutschmarks to buy a loaf of bread. One story is told of a man who loaded a wheelbarrow with Deutschmarks to go to the grocery store. When he came out the wheelbarrow, not the money, was missing. German bonds, once the most gilt-edged securities in Europe, went to nothing. But the German stock market behaved differently. Stocks dropped sharply in the first year of hyperinflation and then began to recover. By 1929, they had entirely regained their purchasing power despite the hyperinflation.

The unconditional surrenders of the Germans and Japanese that ended World War II, followed by the Allied occupations, resulted in a crash of the stocks and bonds of these economies. German stocks plummeted to about a tenth of their former prices, while its bonds became wallpaper. But by the late 1950s the German stock market had regained its previous highs in real purchasing power, and by the early 1980s matched the spectacular increase of the American market since 1925.

The case of Japan was almost identical. By 1945 the Japanese stock market in real terms had dropped well over 90% from its high in the early 1940s. By the late 1980s it had risen about 6,700% from its lows. Japanese bonds, however, adjusted for inflation, fell almost 90% by the end of the war. Fifty years later they still only had 25% of the purchasing power of the early 1940s, despite the country's miraculous recovery and prosperity. Inflation again.

Brazil, Argentina, and other Latin American countries, as well, have had high inflation for decades. At the beginning of each bout of hyperinflation the stock markets turned down for a period, but then rallied to more than offset the ravages of runaway prices.

Why do stocks do so well in these extreme conditions, while the capital of bond holders is dissipated? Land, plants, machinery, equipment, and inventories adjust to their replacement cost in real terms. A company in Germany might have had a value of 1,000,000 Deutschmarks before the hyperinflation, and might have moved to 10 billion afterwards. The real value of the company had not changed.

But, an astute reader might ask, if rising prices adjust only to the value of assets in real terms, why aren't gold and precious metals far higher too? The answer is that the productive assets of a company are capable of producing a stream of increasing earnings. A pharmaceutical company trades at many times the worth of its physical assets. The market recognizes this and adjusts the price in the inflated currency to approximate its real worth. Gold and other precious metals only keep up with inflation; they have no growth potential.

The holder of bonds, T-bills, or other fixed income investments has no such protection. Anyone who buys a bond or a T-bill or an annuity is guaranteed the payment of a fixed amount of dollars, marks, or yen. If inflation effectively takes capital away—tough. From what we've seen in this chapter these investments look precarious at best.* But remember, this new investment world, where inflation constantly erodes the value of bonds, T-bills, and other fixed income savings, is only a little over 50 years old. The conventional wisdom of many hundreds of years is that inflation is a nonevent. We might have been amused by the 2½% interest the English received on their government bonds in the eighteenth and nineteenth centuries. But 2½ percent was a reasonable rate of return in a period of price stability that lasted for centuries.

Too, the conventional wisdom of our time focuses to a large extent on dollar value, not real value. Even today, knowing the terrible toll inflation has taken, the vast majority of fiduciaries, from bank trust departments to money managers, recommend a significant portion of the portfolio be in bonds and T-bills or other short-term investments. A portfolio that is 65% or more in equities and 35% or less in fixed income is considered reasonably aggressive. Fifty to 55% equity and 45 to 50% fixed income is far more the norm. If I were to recommend to the trustees of a pension fund, whose retirement funds our firm manages, that they put 90% into stocks (knowing they will not need the money for

---

* The new Treasury Bonds first issued in early 1997, which adjust both principal and interest for inflation, change this for tax-free accounts. However from the initial yields at least, it appears the return will still be well below those of stocks over time.

decades) I would be considered imprudent and irresponsible. I would have violated the basic tenet of conventional modern investing, keeping a significant portion of the funds in "safe investments," namely bonds, T-bills or their equivalents. And if the market dropped sharply, I might be successfully sued, even if I made the case presented in this chapter.

To Sum Up

We have seen that stocks are a far better investment than most other financial alternatives, particularly T-bills and bonds and other debt instruments you might own. The postwar period has entirely changed the investment environment. Returns on stocks adjusted for inflation or for inflation and taxes are higher relative to bonds and T-bills than at any time in the past.

Clearly, the conventional wisdom that fixed-income investments are safe is unsound. If you are saving to buy a house or a car or have another use for funds within a few years, then T-bills, money market funds, or short-term bonds are certainly reasonable. In a short period stocks are simply too unpredictable to depend on. However, once you push the window beyond four or five years, you should keep the large proportion of your assets in stocks or another investment, such as real estate, where there is a long-term record of outperforming both inflation and taxes. Be careful though. Real estate and other investments require a much higher level of expertise than do stocks. If you do not have it, I'd suggest you stay with the excellent record of blue-chip equities.

Not only do stocks sharply outperform bonds and T-bills over time, they also have remarkable recuperative power from major disasters, whether from a market crash or from economic disintegration.

The lesson then is to buy blue-chip stocks with funds you can salt away for some time. Forget bonds and T-bills as investments over the long term. No, this advice is not the conventional wisdom of the day. It certainly wasn't the wisdom of some of the seers of value investing of markets past. Graham and Dodd with "their margin of safety" come to mind in particular. But we must remember that they were writing in a period of little inflation, and in the early thirties, deflation. Astute observers that they were, I'm convinced they would have been among the first to understand the new realities of today's investment world and would offer similar advice.

I am sure you'll hear that this approach is "too aggressive," but inflation is the reality of our times. It is a reality that is difficult for many to perceive, because it goes against the advice of generations of intelligent and conservative investment advisors and fiduciaries as to what was prudent.

Indeed, it goes against the principle we were taught from childhood—that the safest way to save was putting our money in the bank.

Contrarian strategies fit in well with this new advice. As we saw, we can get a higher-than-market return by using any of the four primary methods that I discussed, low P/Es, low price-to-cash flow, low price-to-book value, or buying the lowest-priced stocks in an industry. Contrarian strategies work best over time, which ties in well with the plans of a long-term investor. Such strategies should be able to enhance inflation-adjusted returns by 1% to 2% annually over a period of years.

Next let's look at how risk affects your portfolio. Does the current universally employed risk measure—short term volatility—capture the inflationary aspects of a postwar economy? As the following chapter will show, we can develop more practical ways of identifying risk, and thus be able to protect ourselves from the major investment risks of our times—which will soon mean a brand new century.

14

What Is Risk?

O<small>F ALL</small> the evils the investor must face, the devil of risk is perhaps the most treacherous. At this point it's time to step back and ask a basic question: are the risk measures you use effective? Or could they actually impede good investment decisions?

We saw in the last chapter how a new form of risk sprang full born at the investor after the Second World War: the risk of loss of purchasing power though inflation and taxes. This risk is far more severe than financial risk, because it is universal. Its effects continuously erode the value of fixed-income securities, whether gilt-edged Treasury-bills and government bonds, or high-yielding junk bonds.

Cutting through the myths to a realistic assessment of the actual risks you face today will lead to dramatically different conclusions about the kinds and amounts of investments you should own.

It Seemed So Simple

What then is risk? To the academics who built the efficient market hypothesis (EMH) and modern portfolio theory (MPT) the answer is obvious. Risk is an A–B–C commodity. According to this theory, investors are risk-averse: they are willing to take more risk for higher payoffs and will accept lower returns if they take less risk. A simple but elegant theory.

How does one measure risk? That too is simple. As we saw in chapter 3, it was defined by Markowitz, Sharpe, et al., as volatility: the greater the volatility of a stock or portfolio, whether measured by standard deviation or beta, the greater the risk. A mutual fund of common stock that fluctuates more than the market is considered to be more risky and has a higher beta. One that fluctuates less is less risky and has a lower beta.[1] How did these professors know that investors measured risk strictly by the volatility of the stock? They didn't, nor did they do any research to find out, other than the original studies of the correlation between volatility and return, with results which were mixed at best. The academics simply declared it as fact. Importantly, this definition of risk was easy to use to build complex market models, and that's what the professors wanted to do.

Economists find this view of risk compelling, if not obsessional, because it is the way the rational man *should* behave according to economic theory. If investors are risk-averse in markets, and the academics can show this to be so by their definition, then the economist has proof of a central concept—or pet crotchet—of economic theory. Voilà! Man is a rational decision-maker. If investors will take greater risk only if they receive higher returns—Eureka! A six lane highway opens between investment markets and microeconomic theory. By this highway, investment markets deliver to economic theory the ultimate payload: proof positive of rational behavior in markets. Right or wrong, the idea is too seductive for economists to pass up.

But the critical question is still there, why this measure of risk rather than the analysis of a company's financial strength, earnings power, outstanding debt, or dozens of other measures that Graham and Dodd or corporate management use? Sure, this one is alluring to economic types, but what else has it got going for it?

You don't have to look all that closely to see large holes in this definition begin to appear. Investors may not like volatility in down markets, but they certainly don't object to their stocks outperforming the averages on the upside. What about the psychological and financial risk that we looked at in crisis investing, or the risk of loss of capital through inflation in chapter 13? Finally, the headlong charge into aggressive stocks, which are highly volatile and return little, certainly contradicts the definition. From the beginning, then, this definition of risk seemed unrealistic.

Whether unrealistic or not, an entire generation has been trained to believe risk is volatility. Perhaps you read the various guides on how to select mutual funds by their volatility. Possibly you accept these measures without question. Most people do. But in truth they are faulty.

In the first place it has been known for decades that there is no correlation between risk, as the academics define it, and return. Higher volatility does not give better results, nor lower volatility worse.

J. Michael Murphy in an important but little-read article in the *Journal of Portfolio Management* in the fall of 1977 reviewed the research on risk.[2] Some of the conclusions were startling, at least for EMH and MPT believers. Murphy cited four studies that indicated that "realized returns tend to be higher than expected for low-risk securities, and lower than expected for high-risk securities . . . or that the [risk-reward] relationship was far weaker than expected."[3] Murphy continued: "Other important studies have concluded that there is not necessarily any *stable* long-term relationship between risk and return;[4] that there often may be virtually no relationship between return achieved and risk taken;[5] and that high volatility unit trusts were not compensated by greater returns"[6] [italics original].[7]

Another paper by Haugen & Heins (1975) analyzing risk concluded with the statement: "The results of our empirical effort do not support the conventional hypothesis that risk—systematic or otherwise—generates a special reward."[8] Remember this research was done in the mid to late seventies, just as MPT and the concept of risk-adjusted returns were starting the investment revolution, and over a decade before Nobel Prizes were awarded to its advocates.

The lack of correlation between risk and return was not the only problem troubling academic researchers. More basic was the failure of volatility measures to remain constant over time, which is central to both the efficient market hypothesis and modern portfolio theory. Although beta is the most widely used of all volatility measures, a beta that can accurately predict future volatility has eluded researchers since the beginning. The original betas constructed by Sharpe, Lintner, and Mossin were shown to have no predictive power, that is, the volatility in one period had little or no correlation with that in the next. A stock could pass from violent fluctuation to lamb-like docility.

Since the cornerstone of MPT and an implicit assumption of EMH is that all investors are risk-averse, in the same manner, the absence of a demonstrable beta was a serious problem for the researchers from the beginning. If investors are risk-averse, beta or other risk-volatility measures must have predictive power. That they have not, that there is no correlation between past and future betas was a major anomaly, a "black hole" in the theory. Without a tenable theory of risk, the efficient market hypothesis was an endangered species.

Barr Rosenberg, a well-respected researcher, developed a widely used multifactor beta, which included a large number of other inputs besides volatility to measure the risk of specific securities. These multifactor betas were often called "Barr's Bionic Betas." Unfortunately, they were as hapless as their predecessors. Other betas were experimented with, all with the same result. Future betas of both individual stocks and portfolios were not predictable from their past volatility.

The evidence for the most part was kept on the back burner until Eugene Fama put out his own paper on risk and return in 1992. Fama had previously published a paper in 1973 (coauthored with James MacBeth) that indicated higher beta led to higher returns.[9] It was one of the instrumental pieces in building MPT. This time collaborating with Kenneth French, also of the University of Chicago, the researchers examined 9,500 stocks from 1963 to 1990.[10] Their conclusion was that a stock's risk, measured by beta, was not a reliable predictor of performance.

Fama and French found that stocks with low betas performed roughly as well as stocks with high betas. Fama stated that "beta as the sole variable in explaining returns on stocks . . . is dead."[11] Write this on the tombstone: "What we are saying is that over the last 50 years, knowing the volatility of an equity doesn't tell you much about the stock's return."[12] Yes, make it a large stone, maybe even a mausoleum.

An article in *Fortune* concluded: "Beta, say the boys from Chicago, is bogus."[13] The *Chicago Tribune* summed it up well: "Some of its best-known adherents have now become detractors."[14]

If not beta, then what? If risk cannot be measured by volatility, how should it be determined? According to French, "What investors really get paid for is holding dogs."[15] Their study, as we saw in chapter 7, indicated that stocks with the lowest price-to-book ratios and lowest P/Es provide the highest returns over time, as do smaller capitalization companies. Stock returns are more positively related to these measurements than to beta or other similar risk criteria.[16]

Fama added: "One risk factor isn't going to do it." Investors must look beyond beta to a multifactor calculation of risk, which includes some value measurements and other criteria.[17]

Buried with this canon of modern finance is modern portfolio theory, as well as a good part of EMH. Fama's new findings rejected much of the academic work of the past, including his own. He said at beta's graveside, "we always knew the world was more complicated."[18] He may have known it, however he did not state it for more than two decades.

Fama's statement that "beta is dead" was the shot at risk heard round the world. As one finance professor put it in discussing the Fama and French findings:

[M]odern finance today resembles a Meso-American religion, one in which the high priest not only sacrifices the followers—but even the church itself. The field has been so indoctrinated and dogmatized that only those who promoted the leading model from the start are allowed to destroy it.[19]

The academics also devised measures to adjust risk by dividing performance by volatility. I might return 15% a year and my competitor 30%, but if her portfolio were much more volatile than mine, I would have the better risk-adjusted returns.

It turns out it could all come from the Wizard of Oz. But why is that a surprise? Beta gives the appearance of being a highly sophisticated mathematical formula, but is constructed while looking into a rearview mirror. It takes inputs that seemed to correlate with volatility in the past, then states they will work again in the future. This is not good science. Because some variables moved in step with volatility for a number of years, does not mean that they initiated it. Most often, such correlations are sheer coincidence.

I wrote almost two decades ago that betas, built as they were on spurious correlations with past inputs, were unlikely to work in the future. This is precisely what has happened.

This is not just ivory tower stuff, as we've seen. Beta and other forms of risk measurement decide how hundreds of billions of dollars are invested by pension funds and other institutional investors. High betas are no-nos while the money manager who delivers satisfactory returns with a low-beta portfolio is lionized.[20]

A billion-dollar industry, selling beta and similar measurements, has grown and prospered. The academic definition of risk is almost universally used by legions of mutual fund advisers and pension fund consultants. They advise clients on the mutual funds to buy, or the money managers to hire or fire, by the volatility of their investment returns.

Take Morningstar, for example; the largest service monitoring mutual funds. Although it is an excellent and easily readable source that I refer to often, its concept of risk is problematical. Morningstar's "five stars," its top ranking, widely followed and much sought after, is anchored on dubious assumptions of how you should measure risk.* The returns of a mutual fund are calculated every month against the interest earned on a 90-day T-bill or other "riskless investment." If a fund falls behind this benchmark—or worse yet has the misfortune of underperforming the market for relatively short periods—it is branded as "risky." In fairness

---

* Approximately 90% of all new mutual fund sales in 1997 had Morningstar 4 or 5 star rankings, testifying to the enormous influence of this publication.

to Morningstar, it cautioned its readers not to treat its rankings as gospel. Other ranking systems have not taken this step.

Which leads us back to the dollars you shell out for risk ratings today. While I respect Morningstar as a storehouse of mutual fund information, I believe its rankings, and others like them, built as they are on some variation of volatility, are dangerous to you. They can steer you away from some of the finest value funds, just as you should be looking at them, and guide you to pricey ones with weak finances because they are temporarily shooting out the lights in a sizzling sector.

This is exactly what happened with aggressive growth funds that owned stocks priced in the stratosphere from 1995 through July of 1997. Many billions poured into these funds, which invested in a limited portfolio of small-cap growth stocks. Until they plummeted. Not a few had high ratings from the various consultants and ranking systems that measured risk in terms of volatility.

Yet, looking through the rearview mirror is exactly what almost all of these risk measurement services do. Investors have been hurt when low risk ratings were awarded to money market funds, such as Piper Jaffrey's, that then fell apart. The ranking systems had no way of picking up the fact that the funds, by using derivatives, were as dangerous an investment as the most speculative stock fund.

The point is that when you are told what is risky and what is not, read the fine print of the ranking agency very carefully. If it's based on beta or volatility measurements such as I've described, stay well clear of the advice. This brings us to an important rule.

RULE 32

Volatility is not risk. Avoid investment advice based on volatility.

The simplistic risk measurements commonly used today can get you into trouble, or cause you to miss opportunities. Sometimes even the bluest of blue chips tumble sharply and become very volatile for a while (as the banks and the pharmaceuticals have done in this decade). This volatility is not something to shy away from, it's the gift of opportunity. For the value buyer, the more a stock is driven down by panic selling, the better. People warned away from this volatility lost enormous potential profits.

The rearview mirror approach also cannot detect either of the two key risk measures that we looked at in chapter 12, which allow you to avoid stocks that are overpriced or those that are weak financially. More than a few high rankings have gone into the tank as a result. Many more, particularly of the emerging growth or aggressive growth variety, are on their way.

Other Risk Measurements

We have seen that volatility, and its crowning achievement beta, do not work, although beta is still the risk measurement most widely followed by consultants and mutual fund advisors. The question then is what else is out there? Actually, there are some good looking new models that measure risk. One of the popular tickets today is called semivariance.

Semivariance measures the performance of your portfolio only in a down market or in down quarters, to see how it holds up relative to the market. The theory behind it states that investors are happy enough to beat the market when it is rising, but want to see their portfolios fall less than the averages when the bear growls. You'd be surprised at the acrimony of the academic debate about whether to accept this sensible-seeming measurement instead of volatility. Some researchers consider outperformance (or volatility) of the market on the upside equally distasteful to investors as their portfolios dropping more than the market on the way down. The theorists may know some hidden secrets we don't, but I've yet to meet an investor who, watching his portfolio move briskly ahead of the market, considered it more risky.

You might recall we used semivariance in all our contrarian tests of down markets. Regardless of which value benchmark we tried, each contrarian portfolio passed the semivariance test by outperforming the market in down quarters.

However, although I think semivariance is a better measure than volatility, I am not happy with it as the basic definition of risk, because it still states that investors assume risk is price volatility alone. Price fluctuations are only one of the risk factors that investors face.

As we have seen, there are risks endemic to both the investment and business worlds that cannot be put into a neat little statistical package that measures volatility and returns—nor can the impact of inflation on your investment results in the future. Let's turn to what I believe is a better approach to assessing risk.

The Riskless Investments

During most of American financial history, preservation of capital, rather than appreciation, was the most important criterion of investment management. In 1830, Justice Samuel Putnam of the Massachusetts Supreme Court rendered the decision that was to serve as the critical guideline for management of money for over 130 years. He said in part:

> All that can be required of a trustee to invest is that he conduct himself faithfully and exercise a source of discretion. He is to observe how men of prudence and intelligence manage their own affairs, not in regard to speculation but in regard to the permanent disposition of their funds, considering the probable income as well as the probable safety of the capital to be invested.

Thus was born the famous "prudent man rule" defining the responsibilities of a trustee handling funds for others. It was the cornerstone of American fiduciary practice until well into the 1970s, and is still an important guideline for the courts today.

Before 1945, as we have seen, with a few brief exceptions, inflation was not a serious problem in this country. The prudent man might be expected to stay primarily in bonds and Treasury bills with small amounts of income-yielding common stocks and revenue-producing real estate. A dollar's a dollar, this line of thinking ran. The bank or insurance company, and most other fiduciaries, were considered to have fulfilled their obligations to their clients by keeping the principal intact in dollar terms, not in terms of purchasing power.

But as we know, there has been a radical change in the real value of the dollar since the Second World War. Today's dollar has only a sliver of the purchasing power it had in 1802. People's perceptions and the law often lag behind changing conditions by decades. Thus the preservation of capital in dollars, rather than in purchasing power, is still viewed as the fiduciary's major responsibility. The focus on the dollar itself, not on what it can buy, is the backbone of the bond market, bank accounts, life insurance policies, and scores of other financial products. If taken to court, most fiduciaries would probably still win today if they had preserved their clients' dollars, no matter how much the purchasing power had shrunk.

Investors forget, or still have not learned, how destructive inflation and taxes are to their fixed income investments. The magic of compound interest makes it appear so easy—and riskless—particularly if you buy U.S. government securities, supposedly the safest investment around.

Toward a Realistic Definition of Risk

We have seen that risk, as the academics defined it, was eventually rejected by efficient market types themselves. Higher volatility did not provide the promised higher returns, nor lower volatility lower results. This leads us back to square one. We can now construct a more sensible theory of risk measurement, one that takes into account the pitfalls you face today.

As noted in the last chapter, an all-encompassing strain of risk permanently entered the investment environment for the first time after World War II. The virulent new risk is called inflation. Nothing is safe from this virus, although its major victims are savings accounts, T-bills, bonds, and other types of fixed-income investments. For these investments, there is no antidote. While a relatively small number of companies may flounder financially or go under in any normal period, credit risk is far less dangerous than inflation risk.* And government bonds or T-bills eliminate credit risk entirely. Not so for inflationary risk. Inflationary pressures after the Second World War have radically and completely altered the return distributions of stocks, bonds and T-bills.

Are Stocks More Risky?

The wisdom of the ages has always been that bonds are less risky than stocks over time. Bondholders of a company, after all, had far less financial risk than the shareholders. If a company ran into financial problems it could cut its dividend to shareholders, but it had to maintain interest payments and repay the bond principal when it was due. Otherwise, the company was in default and the creditors got everything the company owned before the shareholders got a penny.

A large company like a railroad would have many classes of debt securities. These range from first mortgage, to second mortgage, to debentures. The holders of the first mortgage securities were entitled to every dollar they were owed before the second mortgage holders got anything, and so on. Preferred shares were a hybrid that paid more than bonds, but stood behind all debt holders in the schedule of repayment in case of financial difficulty.

Graham and Dodd devoted a large part of their book to how to analyze the bonds and debentures of companies, as did many other serious

---

* With the exception of some calamitous event such as the Great Depression.

students of security analysis of the period. Writing in the thirties, the major risk investors had to face was financial. The risk of inflation was an insignificant concern at that time.

The rapid inflation of the postwar period has turned all risk calculations topsy-turvy. While stocks have always had higher returns than T-bills or bonds over time, as we saw in the last chapter, the disparity between the three classes of financial investment widened enormously after 1945. Since the Second World War, moreover, cumulative stock returns, adjusted for inflation, have moved exponentially higher than T-bills or bonds for periods of 15 years or more. Inflation destroys the returns of T-bills, government bonds, and all other debt securities. Yet few investors put this enormous outperformance of stocks over debt securities into their risk calculations.

Table 14–1 shows the inflation-adjusted returns of stocks, bonds, and T-bills for periods of 1 to 30 years in the postwar period. As the table indicates, the longer the holding period the greater the differences. The first row in column 1 demonstrates that stocks provided a 7.5% annual return on average over the entire period after inflation. At the end of 5 years, capital you've invested in stocks increased 44%, more than doubling after 10 years, and almost nine-folding after 30. With government bonds and T-bills the rate of increase moves up at a snail's pace. After 10 years, bonds (column 2) expand your initial capital by only 9%, after 30 years by only 29%. The rate of increase for T-bills is lower yet (column 3). After a decade, adjusted for inflation, your capital would have increased 4%, after two decades by 9%.

Table 14–1
COMPOUNDED RETURNS AFTER INFLATION
1946–1996

Holding Portfolio for . . .	*Returns*			*Percent of times stocks beat*	
	Stocks	*Bonds*	*T-bills*	*Bonds*	*T-bills*
1 year	7.5%	0.9%	0.4%	65%	67%
2 years	15.6%	1.7%	0.9%	73%	78%
3 years	24.3%	2.6%	1.3%	78%	90%
4 years	33.6%	3.5%	1.7%	82%	84%
5 years	43.7%	4.4%	2.1%	84%	82%
10 years	106.5%	9.0%	4.3%	94%	86%
15 years	196.7%	13.8%	6.5%	100%	94%
20 years	326.3%	18.8%	8.8%	100%	100%
25 years	512.6%	24.0%	11.1%	100%	100%
30 years	780.3%	29.4%	13.5%	100%	100%

"This is well and good," you might say, "but stocks fluctuate. What are the odds that stocks will outperform bonds or T-bills over various periods of time?" Good question. It is one thing to see that stocks outperform over the long term, but as Keynes once remarked, "In the long term we're all dead." How do they do then for somewhat shorter periods?

Column 4 shows the percent of times stocks beat bonds for periods varying from one to 30 years, and column 5 provides the same information for T-bills. As you can see, it's a slam dunk for stocks after four years. Holding stocks, you have an 82% chance of doing better than bonds after inflation, and an 84% shot of outperforming T-bills after 48 months, moving up progressively to a 100% chance of outperforming bonds, and a 94% chance of beating T-bills in 15 years. Beyond 15 years the odds favoring stocks surge to 100%. For longer periods, stocks are clearly the least risky of these three categories of investments.

Let's look at how stocks and bonds have performed over other periods in the past. Table 14–2 shows the probabilities of stocks outperforming bonds and T-bills after inflation over different intervals between 1802 and 1945. Three periods are analyzed, 1802 to 1870, 1871 to 1945, and 1946 to 1996. In each period the probabilities of stocks outperforming bonds and bonds beating T-bills is measured from 1 to 30 years. The table indicates the probabilities of stocks outperforming bonds or T-bills increase with time. More importantly, the odds are higher for any period from 1 to 20 years in the post World War II period than in the previous 145 years.

For 5 years the odds of stocks beating T-bills and Treasury bonds rise from about 70% in the two earlier periods to 82% after World War II. In the 1945 to 1996 period stocks had a 100% chance of outperforming T-bills for all 20-year periods, but by that time they clearly outperform even without the increasing inflation of the postwar period. Stocks had an 87% chance of beating T-bills after 20 years over the 1802 to 1870 period, which increased to 99% for the 1871 to 1945 time span.

Do you sense something wrong here? T-bills, the "risk-free" investment of modern portfolio theory, are providing far worse returns over time than the "risky" ones—common stocks. But wait—there is more.

Enter again the "second horseman" for bonds and T-bills—taxes. After taxes, the returns on fixed-income securities drop dramatically. For all their allure, buying long-term governments is about as safe and profitable as having been heavily margined in stocks just before October 19, 1987. We saw in chapter 13 that if an investor in a 50% tax bracket put $100,000 into long Treasury bonds after World War II, he would have only $39,200 of his purchasing power left in 1996. That's right, inflation and taxes had eaten up over 60% of the investment.

Table 14–2

FREQUENCY OF STOCKS OUTPERFORMING BONDS & T-BILLS, BONDS OUTPERFORMING T-BILLS, INFLATION-ADJUSTED 1802–1996

Holding Portfolio for . . .		Stocks Beat Bonds	Stocks Beat T-bills	Bonds Beat T-bills
1 year	1802–1870	63.8%	59.4%	44.9%
	1871–1945	57.3%	61.3%	58.7%
	1946–1996	64.7%	66.7%	43.1%
2 years	1802–1870	63.8%	59.4%	42.0%
	1871–1945	60.0%	62.7%	65.3%
	1946–1996	72.6%	78.4%	51.0%
5 years	1802–1870	65.2%	69.6%	40.6%
	1871–1945	65.3%	69.3%	69.3%
	1946–1996	84.3%	82.4%	51.0%
10 years	1802–1870	78.3%	75.4%	40.6%
	1871–1945	80.0%	85.3%	76.0%
	1946–1996	94.1%	86.3%	43.1%
20 years	1802–1870	87.0%	87.0%	30.4%
	1871–1945	92.0%	98.7%	74.7%
	1946–1996	100.0%	100.0%	53.0%
30 years	1802–1870	98.6%	92.8%	17.4%
	1871–1945	97.3%	100.0%	76.0%
	1946–1996	100.0%	100.0%	58.8%

DATA: 1802–1945, JEREMY SIEGEL; 1946–1996: DREMAN FOUNDATION.

The results were equally bad for T-bills. Lower tax brackets don't help the T-bill or Treasury bond buyer that much.* Finally, had the investor put $100,000 into blue-chip stocks, the "risky" investment with the same 50% tax rate after inflation, the portfolio would have appreciated to $913,000 over the 50-year period. The capital invested in equities would be worth 23 times as much than if placed in T-bills or bonds.

Table 14-3 is identical in format to Table 14–1, but shows the returns after both inflation and taxes for stocks, bonds, and T-bills for periods of 1 to 30 years through the postwar period. Stocks compound at almost

---

* See endnote #7, chapter 13, for a description of how taxes were calculated.

Table 14–3

COMPOUNDED RETURNS AFTER INFLATION AND TAXES

1946–1996

Holding Portfolio for . . .	Returns			Percent of times stocks beat	
	Stocks	*Bonds*	*T-bills*	*Bonds*	*T-bills*
1 year	4.4%	−1.8%	−1.7%	67%	67%
2 years	9.1%	−3.6%	−3.4%	76%	80%
3 years	13.9%	−5.4%	−5.1%	84%	86%
4 years	18.9%	−7.1%	−6.7%	86%	86%
5 years	24.2%	−8.8%	−8.3%	88%	82%
10 years	54.3%	−16.8%	−16.0%	90%	86%
15 years	91.7%	−24.1%	−23.0%	100%	92%
20 years	138.1%	−30.7%	−29.4%	100%	100%
25 years	195.7%	−36.8%	−35.3%	100%	100%
30 years	267.3%	−42.3%	−40.7%	100%	100%

5% annually adjusted for inflation and taxes. In 10 years the investor has increased her capital by over 54%; in 20 it is up 138%.

With bonds or T-bills it's a dirge. The longer you hold them the louder the organ plays. After 10 years, both will cost you over 16% of your capital; after 20 years, 30%, and so it goes. The last two columns again demonstrate the probabilities of stocks outperforming bonds and T-bills from periods of 1 to 30 years. After 4 years there is better than an 85% chance that stocks will outperform bonds and T-bills, and the odds build up significantly with time. By 15 years the odds are 100% that you'll do better in stocks than government bonds and 92% that you'll do better than T-bills. Investing in government securities, then, considered by most to be almost "riskless," is a classic loser's game.

Common stocks, as Tables 14–1 and 14–3 indicate, though a more volatile asset in any short period of time, provide much higher returns than T-bills and bonds over longer periods.

Is There Something Wrong with This Picture?

As Appendix A indicates, the starting point of modern portfolio theory is the return an investor receives on a riskless asset, normally a Treasury bill. The investor then selects a portfolio made up of risk-free and more risky assets, naturally measured by their volatility, to get the optimum mix for himself. *Trouble is, the "risk-free asset" of academic theory is one of the riskiest assets out there over time.*

It's apparent that this assumption of academic investment theory is far removed from reality. The rational investor should be concerned with the probability of maintaining and enhancing his savings, adjusted for inflation, for retirement, or other future needs. The time horizon of the large majority of investors is not months, quarters, or a year or two. It is many years away, because the need for funds to meet costs such as retirement, college tuitions, or similar goals is usually far off in the future. After all, that is why the government set up tax-deferred pension funds, IRAs, and similar programs to build savings, which tens of millions of investors participate in. The investment objective for most people is to maximize savings as safely as possible for the time when they will need to draw on them.

The major risk is not the short-term stock price volatility that many thousands of academic articles have been written about. Rather it is the possibility of not reaching your long-term investment goal through the growth of your funds in real terms. *To measure monthly or quarterly volatility and call it risk—for investors who have time horizons 5, 10, 15, or even 30 years away—is a completely inappropriate definition.* The volatility measurements provide only an illusion of safety. It's almost like saying that if I walk far out on a beach in Maine when the tide is very low, I am not at future risk. This is probably correct for an hour or two, but it is certainly a short-sighted view of my situation, especially as high tide starts rolling in.

A Better Way of Measuring Risk

Stocks may blow away T-bills and bonds over time, but as we saw, the focus of most investors, fiduciaries, and courts is still on financial risk. The far more potent and universal risk of inflation and taxes is a secondary consideration at best. Academic risk theory also accepts the conventional wisdom by making the T-bill the risk-free investment. The financial academics, like most market participants, also have not incorporated into their equations the largest postwar risk factor, the decrease in purchasing power through inflation.

Adjusting for inflation, supposedly risky assets like stocks become far safer. The probability that the investor holding stocks will double her capital every 10 years after inflation, quadruple every 20, combined with 100% odds that she will outperform T-bills or government bonds in 20 years, can hardly be called risky.* Conversely, the supposedly

* Through the postwar period.

"risk-free" assets actually display a large and increasing element of risk over time. For these reasons, we need a new definition of risk that incorporates the effects of inflation for investors in the postwar period along with the other types of risk inherent to these investments.

What then is a better way of measuring your investment risk? While there can be many definitions even in the business and investment worlds, a good starting point is the preservation and enhancement of your purchasing power in real terms. The goal of investing is to protect and increase your portfolio in inflation-adjusted, and (where appropriate) tax-adjusted dollars over time.

A realistic definition of risk recognizes the potential loss of capital through inflation and taxes, and would include at least the following two factors:

1. The probability that the investment you chose will preserve your capital over the time you intend to invest your funds.

2. The probability the investments you select will outperform alternative investments for this period.

These measures of risk tell us the probabilities that we will both maintain our purchasing power and do better than alternative investments for the period we chose.* Unlike the academic volatility measures, these risk measures look to the appropriate time period in the future—5, 10, 15, 20, or 30 years—when the funds will be required. Market risk may be severe in a period of months or even for a few years, but as we saw, it diminishes rapidly over longer periods.

Tables 14–1, 14–2, and 14–3 tell us how stocks stack up against bonds and T-bills after inflation and taxes, and the probability that stocks will outperform them in any period of time. As is apparent, blue chip stocks are by far the best of the three financial investments over time. The careful reader might ask another question here. "O.K., I know the odds of stocks beating bonds and T-bills are increasingly high over time, but stocks have very good periods followed by years of lackluster results. What are my chances of capturing returns above those provided by bonds or T-bills?"

The answer is provided in Tables 14–4 and 14–5. Table 14–4 shows the probability of getting stock returns as low as 25% of the average return for stocks in the postwar period (column 2) to as high as 150 percent of the average return (column 8) after inflation. The probability of return is shown for periods of 1 to 30 years.

---

* For the taxable investor, also considering the impact of taxes.

Table 14–4

PROBABILITY OF STOCKS MEETING VARIOUS LEVELS OF RETURN
1.0 = Starting investment, inflation-adjusted
1946–1996

	25% of Market Return		50% of Market Return		100% of Market Return		150% of Market Return			
	(1)	*(2)*	*(3)*	*(4)*	*(5)*	*(6)*	*(7)*	*(8)*	*(9)*	*(10)*
	Average		*Average*		*Average*		*Average*		*Average*	*Average*
	Stock		*Stock*		*Stock*		*Stock*		*Bond*	*T-bill*
Holding	*Port-*		*Port-*		*Port-*		*Port-*		*Port-*	*Port-*
Portfolio	*folio*	*Prob-*	*folio*	*Prob-*	*folio*	*Prob-*	*folio*	*Prob-*	*folio*	*folio*
for	*Value*	*ability**	*Value*	*ability**	*Value*	*ability**	*Value*	*ability**	*Value*	*Value*
1 year	1.02	(67%)	1.04	(61%)	1.08	(53%)	1.11	(47%)	1.01	1.00
5 years	1.11	(82%)	1.22	(71%)	1.44	(55%)	1.66	(39%)	1.04	1.02
10 years	1.27	(78%)	1.53	(76%)	2.06	(57%)	2.60	(39%)	1.09	1.04
15 years	1.49	(78%)	1.98	(71%)	2.97	(65%)	3.95	(45%)	1.14	1.07
20 years	1.82	(82%)	2.63	(67%)	4.26	(61%)	5.89	(41%)	1.19	1.09
25 years	2.28	(94%)	3.56	(67%)	6.13	(51%)	8.69	(41%)	1.24	1.11
30 years	2.95	(100%)	4.90	(67%)	8.80	(45%)	12.70	(37%)	1.29	1.13

* The probability that a portfolio will be above the value shown.

Column 1 is the total portfolio value, or *wealth relative,* in academic jargon, for every period from 1 to 30 years, if you only earned 25% of the average return for stocks for each period. Column 2 indicates what your probabilities are of earning more than 25%. The probabilities, with minor exceptions, of earning more than 25% increase with time. Thus, holding the portfolio with a starting value of 1, you have a 67% probability or better (column 2) of it returning at least 2% (1.02, column 1) at the end of one year. The 2% is 25% of the average annual return of stocks over the past 50 years after inflation. After 10 years it has a 78% probability of increasing more than 27% (1.27, column 1); after 25 years a 94% probability of returning 128% more than your initial investment (2.28, column 1). So the 25% of the market return represents "a worst case for stocks," one that should not persist over time.

Next, glance over at the portfolio values of bonds and T-bills. *You can see that even if you take a worst case of receiving only 25% of the stock market's average return, you still do better in stocks than in either bonds or T-bills for any period.* By 2 years your portfolio is noticeably ahead, and in 25 years it does about twice as well. Remember again this is almost a doomsday scenario; the chance of making only 25% of the normal market return is only 6 in 100 when you invest for as long as 25 years. You have a 94% (column 2) chance of doing better. But worst case or no, you still do better in equities than in T-bills or bonds.

As you increase the number of years you hold stocks versus debt securities, the comparisons only get better. If you received only 50% of the market return for 10 years your portfolio would be worth 40% more than in bonds and 47% more than in T-bills. What's more there is a 76% chance (column 4) that you would do better than that. If you receive the market return over time, as we saw before, you score big. After 15 years (column 5), you would almost triple the returns from bonds or T-bills. Moreover you have a 64% chance of reaching or surpassing this figure (column 6). After 25 years, your net worth is over 5 times what it would be in debt instruments, and so on.

Not that you need to strike it rich with the types of returns we have just seen, but there is also a reasonable chance you could outperform the market over time. If you did so, as column 7 indicates, the returns bury those in bonds and T-bills. In this happy situation the investor almost quadruples the return of debt instruments in 15 years, and about quintuples them in 20 years.

There you have it. Once again stocks provide higher rewards over time than bonds or T-bills even under poor circumstances, and shoot out the lights under better conditions. The decision of where to place money should not be that difficult.

Table 14–5 is identical in format to Table 14–4, but also includes income taxes.* Once again a portfolio of stocks, after taxes and inflation, does better than bonds or T-bills whether you get 25% of the average return on stocks or 150% for any period they are held. Taking the lowest return on stocks—25% of the market average—for 5 years, the portfolio increases by 6% (1.06, column 1), whereas portfolios of bonds and T-bills lose 9% and 8% respectively (.91 column 9 and .92 column 10). Moreover, as the frequency distribution shows, you have a 67% chance of being at or above this return (column 2). Again, as the time periods increase, stocks substantially outperform bonds and T-bills under all the scenarios.

I have tried to answer in two separate ways the question of how much risk there is in holding stocks instead of bonds and T-bills. First, we asked how often stocks would outperform T-bills or government bonds after inflation for periods varying from 1 to 30 years in the postwar period in Table 14–1, and after inflation and taxes in Table 14–3. We saw that stocks won in a breeze in both cases; the longer the time period the

---

* A 50% bracket is used for comparative purposes; however, lowering it to 40%–45%, which will be the effective rate on short-term gains including state income taxes in a number of large states (23%–26% on long-term gains), will not affect the results significantly.

Table 14–5

PROBABILITY OF STOCKS MEETING VARIOUS LEVELS OF RETURN
1.0 = Starting investment, inflation- and tax-adjusted
1946–1996

	25% of Market Return		50% of Market Return		100% of Market Return		150% of Market Return			
	(1)	*(2)*	*(3)*	*(4)*	*(5)*	*(6)*	*(7)*	*(8)*	*(9)*	*(10)*
	Average		*Average*		*Average*		*Average*		*Average*	*Average*
	Stock		*Stock*		*Stock*		*Stock*		*Bond*	*T-bill*
Holding	*Port-*		*Port-*		*Port-*		*Port-*		*Port-*	*Port-*
Portfolio	*folio*	*Prob-*	*folio*	*Prob-*	*folio*	*Prob-*	*folio*	*Prob-*	*folio*	*folio*
for	*Value*	*ability**	*Value*	*ability**	*Value*	*ability**	*Value*	*ability**	*Value*	*Value*
1 year	1.01	(59%)	1.02	(57%)	1.04	(55%)	1.07	(53%)	.98	.98
5 years	1.06	(67%)	1.12	(65%)	1.24	(51%)	1.36	(45%)	.91	.92
10 years	1.14	(76%)	1.27	(71%)	1.54	(61%)	1.81	(45%)	.83	.84
15 years	1.23	(71%)	1.46	(69%)	1.92	(63%)	2.37	(47%)	.76	.77
20 years	1.35	(69%)	1.69	(63%)	2.38	(61%)	3.07	(45%)	.69	.71
25 years	1.49	(73%)	1.98	(61%)	2.96	(49%)	3.94	(43%)	.63	.65
30 years	1.67	(82%)	2.34	(63%)	3.67	(43%)	5.01	(41%)	.58	.59

* The probability that a portfolio will be above the value shown.

more they outperformed. The risk of T-bills or bonds providing inferior returns to stocks is large and increasing after 3 to 5 years.

Second, we examined the risk that stock returns would drop off sharply from their long-term norms in Table 14–4 and Table 14–5. Once again, we saw even if this happened (if, for example, stocks provided only 25% of their normal return over time) they still outperformed the debt instruments by a significant margin after as little as 5 to 10 years.

Let's now go back to the two measures that we said should be incorporated into a good definition of risk:

1. The probability that the investment you chose will preserve your capital over the time you intend to invest your funds.

2. The probability the investments you select will outperform alternative investments for this period.

The conclusion is obvious—stocks meet both of these criteria. Using this analysis of risk in the postwar period, stocks are the least risky investments over time. If you are in your thirties, for example, and have a goal of retiring at 65, you should buy blue-chip stocks because you have a 100% chance of both preserving and enhancing your capital, as well as outperforming bonds and T-bills. The probabilities are also high that you will outperform debt securities manyfold. Though not as high, the odds are still overwhelming for 15 years and reasonably good at 4 or 5 years. From a risk perspective, bonds and T-bills give you increasingly short odds after only a few years. They are not the investments you want to build your future upon.

What we see then is the development of a new approach to risk analysis, which tries to more realistically appraise the risk of holding various types of investments over the time the investor intends to invest his or her funds. The analysis allows you to not only determine the odds that your returns will outperform or underperform other types of investments, but also the probabilities to determine by how much. This risk measurement framework could also be adapted to valuing real estate, precious metals, or other investments, if you can find records of their performance over longer periods. If you chose to measure how you would do in Old Masters, other art, or collectibles relative to equities, as an example, there is an index dating back to the 1960s from Sotheby, which *Barron's* reports each week.

While this approach to risk can certainly be fine-tuned, it allows you to more accurately assess your exposures in the postwar investment world, one very different from any investment environment of the past.

We examined one last category of risk in the previous chapter: how financial investments react when an economic system breaks down through hyperinflation, such as has occurred in Latin America for decades; or in Germany in the early twenties; or when an economy is destroyed, as in Germany and Japan after World War II. Fortunately this kind of risk is not a consideration for domestic investments, but it can certainly affect your investments abroad. As we saw, the findings also strongly support the risk strategies we have developed in this chapter.

Now let's turn to market pitfalls. Have you heard these?

- Small caps should make you major money over time.
- Nasdaq, which billed itself as the stock market for the next 100 years, is a place you should keep most of your money.
- You can always trust the numbers, anybody's numbers, as long as they're given to you in writing.

15

Small Stocks, Nasdaq, and Other Market Pitfalls

A POWERFUL idea can move mountains. With the publication of *Malleus Maleficarum—The Witches' Hammer,* in 1487, the idea swept through Europe that Christianity was thickly beset with the minions of Satan. It was the duty of the faithful to root them out and destroy them, before they destroyed the world. The ensuing panic lasted 200 years and saw tens of thousands tortured, strangled, burned alive.

The belief was so dominant that any allegation of witchly powers was accepted without hesitation. Their bodies were said to be made of "light air" that could pass through the densest substance with ease. They multiplied quickly, and their ranks were swelled by demons and the souls of the wicked. Johannes Weir, a physician of Cleves, and an authority on witchcraft, asserted in the 1560s that there were exactly 7,405,926 demons of the air, divided neatly into 72 battalions, each led by a prince or a captain.

The air was filled with them, and the careless could inhale thousands in a single yawn. They would then merrily wreak havoc on the inner anatomy, causing intense pain. In great multitudes they created tornadoes and whirlwinds on land, violent storms at sea, and delighted in destroying both nature and the works of man. (It's surprising the producers of B-grade horror flicks searching for new material don't make more use of the idea.)

Wizards and witches met weekly for their Friday night "Sabbath" with Satan. Attendance was compulsory; failure to show up resulted in the miscreants being lashed by demons with rods made of serpents or scorpions.

King James I of England fretted openly about what to do with this infestation of evil that threatened to take over all the kingdoms of Europe. Crisis inevitably breeds opportunity, and this was no exception. Witch hunting became a lucrative profession. The leaders in the field had their own state-of-the-art detection devices. One was the knowledge that only a witch or a sorcerer could float on water when their hands and feet were bound and their bodies wrapped in a sheet or blanket. Hundreds of thousands of people were put to this test. If they floated they were burned at the stake; if they drowned, they were innocent. Also accepted as indisputable proof of witchcraft was that no witch could recite the Lord's Prayer or scriptures from the Bible correctly. If someone on trial for witchcraft mispronounced or missed a word in front of a massed group of hostile accusers, which under this pressure was a strong possibility, her fate was sealed.

Widely accepted beliefs often appear silly, sometimes horrifying in hindsight. Unfortunately they occur just as often today. We will examine several in this chapter. First take the popular and costly myth that small stocks have a long record of outperforming their larger-sized siblings. At first glance, the logic is simple and compelling: small companies, often in rapidly expanding industries, are cheaper and are growing much faster than larger ones. That makes their stocks a better bet than old-fashioned, lumbering giants of industry.

Statistics brought forth in the early eighties supposedly supported this contention. So popular has the notion become that hundreds of billions of dollars have been invested by millions of investors in pint-size companies. Again, as in the case of witches and sorcerers, the belief was unfounded. With barely a ripple or a trace, investors' money sank beneath the waves. It is important for you to be aware of the pitfalls in this area.

The Small Company Blues

The beginnings were highly principled. Two young Ph.D. candidates at the University of Chicago, Rolf Banz and Marc Reinganum, were engaged in the lofty cause of defending the efficient market hypothesis in the late 1970s when it was initially challenged by the findings of the low P/E strategy. The two wrote their Ph.D. theses on the validity of the small-cap effect. Some of the leading figures of efficient markets, including Eugene Fama, Roger Ibbotson, and Myron Scholes, sat on their dissertation committees.

Here's where the myth got its first academic blessing. Rolf Banz "proved" that small stocks outperformed large companies over time. Mark Reinganum concluded that there was no low P/E effect; rather it was a small-cap effect. Without the small stock effect, low P/E stocks did not beat the market.

Banz studied the performance of companies listed on the New York Stock Exchange between 1926 and 1979. He placed stocks in five equal groups by market value for five-year periods over the length of the study. For the entire 54 years the average rate of return on small companies was 11.6%, compared to 8.8% for large stocks.

The results were published in the *Journal of Financial Economics* in March 1981, but the preliminary findings were given to *Fortune* almost a year earlier, at the time a strong believer in efficient markets. It then did a feature on the work.[1]

As *Fortune* summed it up,

> [T]he small-stock phenomenon has indirectly refuted the most serious challenge yet to the efficient-market theory. A number of researchers have demonstrated that portfolios of stocks with low price-earnings ratios have regularly outperformed the market averages. *That finding, trumpeted by David Dreman in his book* Contrarian Investment Strategy, *is wholly inconsistent with an efficient market. It turns out, however, that low P/E stocks appear to offer superior returns only because small stocks have lower P/Es, on average, than large ones.* [Emphasis mine.]

Why did smaller companies do better? Banz didn't know. "There is no theoretical foundation for such an effect," he said. "We do not even know whether the factor is size itself or whether size is just a proxy for one or more true but unknown factors correlated with size."[2] Although admittedly unsure of what these findings signified, Drs. Banz and Reinganum used them to dismiss the low P/E strategy. To quote Banz again in *Pensions and Investment Age,* a periodical widely read by pension fund and money managers: "We still do not know why the [size] effect exists . . . however, no other thesis, such as . . . Dreman's Contrarian Investment Strategy, explain[s] the effect."[3]

My curiosity more than a little whetted by the *Fortune* article and Banz's statements about the failure of low P/E, I undertook my own research on the subject. What did Banz actually discover? My findings indicated that some of his work looked right at first glance. But look out! The reasons are far different from what Professor Banz and the efficient market researchers might think, and once again illustrate the danger of using statistics blindly.

The Banz findings did not pertain to small caps at all, since he used as a sample all the companies on the New York Stock Exchange (NYSE). Back in the late 1920s when his study began, and through the next several decades, even more than today, the NYSE was America's blue-chip market. Only the largest and most widely held companies were admitted through its portals. The bottom 20% of NYSE stocks are much larger than what are normally considered small companies. The Curb, later the American Stock Exchange, was where the larger of the second tier of companies traded, and after that came the over-the-counter and the various regional markets. Banz, or certainly his blue-ribbon thesis committee, should have known that a representative group of smaller companies did not trade on the Big Board. At best it was a study of how the bottom 20% of larger companies performed. Error number one then was serious in itself—Banz's study simply did not measure the performance of small stocks.

But this was only the beginning of a rather remarkable string. He showed that small companies had sparkling returns near the bottom of the Great Depression. That's right, they moved up over 100% in the 1931 to 1935 period, whipping their largest brethren easily. How was this possible, you might ask, when we know this was a time that small companies had the greatest financial difficulties and highest bankruptcy rates in American history? Figure 15–1, taken from the *Fortune* article discussing the Banz study, shows this supposed result as well as portraying an investor happily riding the pole of the giant payoff of small stocks in the 1941 to 1945 period, dollars floating all around him.

Banz, a financial statistician (as are virtually all of the current generation of investment Ph.D.s), apparently had little idea of what was in his sample, which resulted in a second major error. Banz's computer sort automatically placed numbers of troubled companies on the NYSE in his smallest group in the 1931 to 1935 period. Near the bottom of the Great Depression, some were in or approaching Chapter 11, which resulted in a drastic shrinkage of their market values, dumping them into the smallest capitalization group. Banz was often measuring larger companies that had been whittled down to small companies in this extremely troubled time—not small companies that were growing into major concerns by rapidly improving market share and profitability as he and many others conjectured. A fair number subsequently recovered, accompanied by dramatic increases in price.

Many capitalizations had shrunk drastically in the 1930s—the average company value for the smallest stock group on the NYSE at the beginning of 1931, for example, was a piddling $640,000—that's correct, I didn't leave out any zeros.

Some of the reasons for survival were not a little strange. For example, the Electric Boat Company, which became a part of General Dynamics, sailed through this period with giant gains, because it won an $8 million settlement in the World Court from the German government.

Figure 15–1

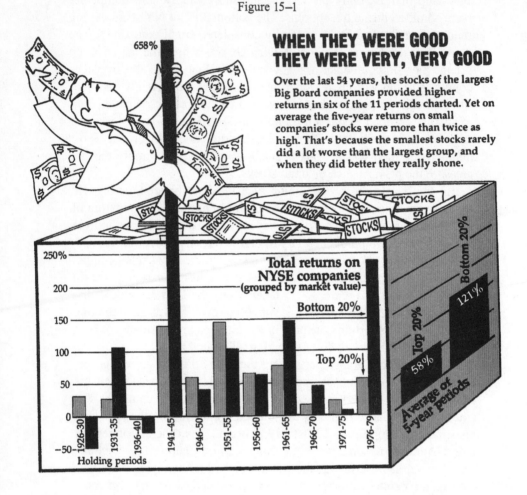

WHEN THEY WERE GOOD THEY WERE VERY, VERY GOOD

Over the last 54 years, the stocks of the largest Big Board companies provided higher returns in six of the 11 periods charted. Yet on average the five-year returns on small companies' stocks were more than twice as high. That's because the smallest stocks rarely did a lot worse than the largest group, and when they did better they really shone.

Copyright: *Fortune,* June 30, 1980; reprinted by permission. Chart by Parios Studio.

The reason: the Imperial German Navy had "borrowed" a number of its submarine patents without permission in 1911 and 1912, before the start of World War I. Without this windfall, the company would have gone down for the third time.

The second and more damaging error also stemmed from contemporary financial researchers' near obsession with statistical tests, applied all too often with little understanding of the underlying data or market mechanisms. Banz and his thesis advisors completely overlooked how illiquid the market was in the 1930 to 1945 period. At the beginning of

1931 some companies were in receivership, although they were still listed on the Exchange. Many traded at a fraction of a dollar, a number going as low as ¼ or ¹⁄₁₆. The average price of the bottom 20% of stocks on the New York Stock Exchange was only $3.34 a share over the 1931 to 1935 period.

By 1935, 30% of these companies were delisted. It took only four survivors (Atlas Tack, Spiegel May Stern, Evans Products, and United Dyewood) to improve the average performance of each remaining stock in the cheapie group by 43%.

And here is the hitch: these were companies that just couldn't be bought! The markets were so thin that a number of these stocks traded only a few hundred shares a week, if that. Moreover, the spread was enormous for the pint-sized stocks, averaging 45% between what the buyer was willing to pay and the seller was willing to offer the stocks at. (These are the spreads for the lowest 20% of stocks on the last day of each of the 20 quarters in the 1931 to 1935 period, taken from *The New York Times*.)

That's right, if you wanted to buy a stock at market and had to pay the offering price, your cost went up 45%. How much stock could you buy if you decided to grit your teeth and pay 45% more? Very little. An investor could buy only a few hundred shares, if that, for the majority of these issues. The average volume for the 139 stocks of the smallest-sized group on the NYSE was 240 shares a day through the five-year period. (This number is inflated because a few issues traded several thousand shares.)

The median volume was 100 shares at the beginning of 1931. Moreover the market continued to be almost illiquid through the entire 1931 to 1935 period. A startling 58% of these stocks did not trade on any given day.[4]

Not only did the researchers believe one could easily trade these stocks, they took a price between the bid and the offer price and did not consider that with the gigantic spread and low volume, the price was completely theoretical. The Banz study simply assumed the stock could be bought or sold in the middle of the spread,* thus paying absolutely no commissions and other transaction costs.

---

* If the stock did not trade, the CRSP database (Center for Research in Security Prices, University of Chicago), which Banz and many others have used for small cap studies, substitutes the midpoint of the bid/ask spread for an actual price. However, CRSP does not list the bids and asks themselves for any stocks before 1962. We obtained them by combing through newspaper listings published at the time.

With the average price of a share in the small-cap group at about $3⅜, using the 45% spread in the 1931 to 1935 period, the bid would be about $2.625 and the asking price $4.00. The buyer, according to Banz, could blithely waltz in and buy any amount of stock in the middle (3⅜), and not pay any commission to boot, which on small stocks could be as high as 3% of the price. The lucky buyer in 1941 could do the same thing. This assumption is key to a large part of academic financial research, which assumes markets are efficient and therefore transaction costs are a non-factor.* In addition to commissions, Banz also ignores that even tiny amounts of buying, possibly only 100 shares, could drive the stock price up sharply, which is why these prices often skyrocketed.

Just how far-fetched some of this analysis is can be seen from the following calculations. If someone were willing to pursue such a strategy, and buy every share of the small-cap group traded on average on any day during the 1931 to 1935 period, the theoretical cost would only be $111,422.† But if you tried to do so, the trading volume would be doubled, which would drive prices much higher than the $111,422 figure. This only considers shares that traded; remember that 58% of the pint-sized group did not trade at all on any given day during this five-year period. Remember too that the spread on the stocks that didn't trade was enormous. If an investor wanted to buy $1 million worth of these sure-fire winners, or if a savvy mutual fund wanted to put $100 million into this group, the prices would be driven up tenfold, maybe more, making the cost of this strategy inane.

Two clear-cut examples of how thin these markets were come from the second quarter of 1933 and the third quarter of 1932. Examining the second quarter of 1933 first, the supposedly midget companies returned an astonishing 319%, against 91% for their large-sized brethren. Small wonder the investor in the *Fortune* chart is jubilant.

But as Thomas Carlyle noted in the 1830s, "statistics are the greatest liars of them all." The small-cap statistics would not likely change Carlyle's opinion. In the second quarter of 1933 the market price was $1.35 for the average stock in the group and the average market value was only $263,000 for each company. These shares traded an average of 94 shares a day at the beginning of this period.

---

* This is not the only time that this conclusion has resulted in severely flawed ideas. The 1987 crash is the classic example. See my *Forbes* articles written before and after the crash—"Doomsday Machine," 3/23/87; "Thanks, Professor," 11/16/87; and "The Nominees Are . . . ," 3/21/88.

† Taking the average trading volume of 240 shares of the 139 companies in the bottom 20% resulted in this figure.

If you bought every stock that traded in the group, the total cost would have been a pittance: $17,470. Many readers' IRAs or other retirement funds I'm sure exceed this figure—even in constant dollars. But it gets worse. You could only buy 27% of the stocks traded; 73% of these stocks simply did not trade.

What was the average spread between the bid and offer of the 73% of these the stocks that didn't trade? It was an amazing 117%. If you wanted to buy 100 shares, you would have had to pay double the market price. That alone would wipe out 50% of the advantage of small over large cap stocks in their finest hour. With markets this thin, one shudders to think what 100,000 shares would push the price to.

The third quarter of 1932, when midget companies rose 160.7%, vs. 90.5% for the large caps, is a nearly identical example. The average market price for the bottom 20% was $1.09, the average volume was 32 shares, and 83% of the group did not trade. The total trading volume for the bottom 20% was $4,817 a day.

The 1941 to 1945 period, the best in the sample, shows again how little liquidity existed for pint-sized companies, even for those trading on the NYSE. The companies were minuscule, with the average size of the bottom 20% at $1.9 million. The average trading volume was very low, only 482 shares a day when this group of "big winners" was selected at the beginning of 1941.* The spread between the bid and the offer price was still large at 17%. Although the price was higher than in 1931, it would have only cost an investor about $335,000 to do all the trading on the NYSE in this group on a given day. Add the fact that more than 37% of the group did not trade on any trading day, and you can see that even a marginal increase in demand for these stocks would have driven prices through the roof, which is exactly what happened.

Without the two periods where pint-sized companies sparkled in the Banz study, 1931 to 1935 and 1941 to 1945, small stocks actually did no better than the market, with a far greater risk of going under. The new professors did not consider any of these factors.

But was the liquidity problem solely one affecting small-cap stocks or did it also apply to their larger brethren? The answer is that liquidity was lower for all stocks throughout this period, but it had a disproportionate effect on the smaller companies. For the large stocks the spread in 1931 to 1935 was 4.6%. (The median spread for large caps was 1.3% in 1931

---

* Taken again from the closing prices from *The New York Times* and *The Wall Street Journal* at the end of each quarter in the period. No bid/ask information for this period is available from any computer database that I am aware of, and not from CRSP.

to 1935, while small caps' was 20%.) The average large-cap volume was 4,842 shares, or 20 times that of the pint-sized group. In 1941 the spread was only 1.6%, and the volume was about six times that of the small group. Fewer of the larger companies did not trade on any single day, 13.2% vs. 58.1% of the small-cap group in the 1931 to 1935 period, and 11.0% versus 37.3% in the 1941 to 1945 period. Liquidity in bigger companies was a fraction of what it is today, but you could buy or sell them, which meant you could carry out a real, rather than a hypothetical, strategy.

A final problem that Banz and his blue-ribbon academic committee missed is connected to the others and magnifies the liquidity problem enormously. Numbers of the smaller-sized companies in the 1931 to 1945 period were in serious operating difficulties, particularly if they were once larger, financially sound firms. That was what originally won them their spurs to trade on the Big Board. An improvement in outlook would likely trigger a manifold price increase in one of the most illiquid securities markets in the nation's history. When the U.S. entered World War II, many firms which had barely stayed alive began to prosper.

The war was an enormous one-time boost to small cap companies, many of which had accumulated major losses in the past. Improving business and prior losses meant they paid little or no income taxes, rebuilding often drained financial resources. The larger companies, on the other hand, often profitable through the thirties, paid excess profit taxes up to 100%. The war was a splendid one-time boost to troubled small cap companies, a boost that the solid blue chips didn't get.

The 1930 to 1945 period happened once, and only once in American economic history, brought about by the worst crash and depression on record, followed by the nation's largest recovery. Add to this some of the most extreme illiquidity in market history. The key point is that it was extraordinary conditions, not rapidly growing small-sized firms, that accounted for the rocketlike returns.

In short this was a strategy that could not have been used by any but a handful of investors buying a few hundred shares here and there. Yet the Banz study is used to justify billions of dollars and millions of investors rushing in to buy small-sized companies. It's almost like locating a bridge on a map that does not detail its size or composition, and concluding the bridge is a steel span on a superhighway when it is in fact constructed of rope.

When I showed their results were problematical a year later, and the low P/E effect was very much alive, there was nary a word from the academic researchers. I've written five additional articles on small-cap research to the present time. The criticisms discussed above have never been challenged.

An Attack on Contrarian Strategies

Marc Reinganum's findings supported Banz's. Reinganum concluded from his work that the only low P/E effect is in small stocks.[5] In his work, Reinganum divided his P/Es into deciles. His lowest decile has a P/E ratio of slightly over 1, compared to 6.5 for his next lowest decile. A P/E of 1, of course, indicates serious trouble. Healthy companies—large or small—do not trade at one times earnings. (This in effect means the investor receives a 100% after tax payback on his investment each year on the stock.)

Most of the stocks in his low-P/E sample were very small. Twenty-two percent had market values of $13 million (which are inordinately small capitalizations in recent years), and fully 65% had market values under $68 million. By comparison, only 2.4% of companies in the largest capitalization decile traded at P/Es of 1.

What do Reinganum's results really show? Like Banz, he was actually measuring something very different from what he thought. In his case Reinganum is demonstrating a small, troubled company effect, not a low P/E effect. What these findings indicate is that investors react sharply to the financial difficulties of smaller companies. The fear of bankruptcy or severe operating problems drastically shrinks their prices. This reaction is even more severe than for larger companies. Small companies that recover bounce back sensationally; those that don't are delisted. This also seems supported by the fact that small companies normally trade at higher, not lower, P/Es than larger concerns. Again, the then-novice professor seems to have had little understanding of what lay under the statistics.

But what about other studies reputed to show the superior performance of small-cap stocks? Roger Ibbotson, a distinguished academic researcher, who is best known for his studies in collaboration with Rex Sinquefield on long-term returns on stocks and bonds, computed the value-weighted returns* on what was termed the second tier: all stocks other than the large companies in the S&P 500 from 1958 through

---

* A value-weighted index assigns a weighting to each stock in the index proportional to the market value of its stock.

1979.[6] Over this 22-year period the group's total return was 967% versus 504% for the S&P 500. Other researchers came up with similar effects.[7]

These findings too are problematic. By weighting companies by their market values, Ibbotson assigns small companies to a relatively minor part of the sample, although there may be several thousand of them. Second, the liquidity problems endemic to the Banz study are also imbedded in this one. Adjusting for transaction costs of small companies takes a big bite out of their returns. Compounding the difficulty is that there are large numbers of big companies that are not in the S&P 500. These stocks were put into the small company sample. Many of the large banks, insurance companies, and a good number of other bigger concerns traded on Nasdaq or its predecessor during this time. Weighting the companies by market size means the performance of 50 companies with a market value of $40 million, or 20 companies with a market value of $100 million, count for no more in performance than one company with a market value of $2 billion.

So what the study almost certainly calculated was the performance of medium and some larger-sized companies. In a word, the "small company effect" the researchers believed they were measuring was drowned out!

Another issue that questions the credibility of these results can be termed "survivorship bias." Many of the small companies measured ran into problems and dropped off the face of the earth. In the less rigorous databases prior to the 1980s, hundreds disappeared. Their businesses faded, and their stocks went off the screens unnoticed.* Of the scores of PC companies underwritten in the hot new issues market of the early eighties, very few are around today. The same was the case with the computer leasing companies of the late sixties and undoubtedly will be true of the Internet group shortly. The over-the-counter market, which at times traded over 5,000 companies, did not keep statistics on nonsurvivors. Also ignored is the high likelihood of price declines as failing companies near Chapter 11.

You should note two other points, if you own or are thinking of buying small-cap stocks. First, confirming evidence that small stocks do not do well over time comes from the Loughran and Ritter and Forbes studies of IPOs, which we will look more closely at in the next chapter. Loughran and Ritter examined 4,753 IPOs between 1970 and 1990.[8] They found the average return of these companies over five year periods was 3%, versus 11.3% for the S&P 500. No big bucks from small cap-

---

* Most likely traded, if at all, in "the pink sheets," where there are normally only one or two market-makers and spreads are enormous.

stocks here. This sample is much closer to what Banz or Ibbotson believe is small cap than those that were examined in their own studies.

The last point to be aware of is that small companies are expensive. Sure, everybody likes the idea, held forth by Banz and his colleagues, that thousands of these bargain basement values lie around waiting to be plucked up by the percipient investor. But once again we have a case of an exciting theory, in the words of Thomas Huxley, "killed off by nasty, ugly little facts." The average P/E of the Russell 2000* over the last 20 years has been above that of the S&P 500 consistently with only one or two exceptions since the index's inception in 1979. Dividend yield has also been significantly lower than that of large stocks, while price-to-book value has been higher than that of large caps about half the time. So once again small companies have not been in the bargain basement as a group—with one important exception that we'll look at shortly.

Right or wrong, the academic thinking swept through the investment world like a brush fire. Billions of dollars and probably millions of investors, either directly or indirectly through their retirement plans, have purchased small-cap stocks. What we have seen is that the Banz research, the major study demonstrating superior performance, is so seriously flawed that adjusting for only some of the errors wipes out most, if not all of its claims. There are also major questions about the Ibbotson study. But to me the most telling point is what happened when the professors took their pet theory out of the laboratory and put it into practice.

We Have a Tie-in to Mecca

What advocates of small-cap stocks may have lacked in research, they made up in chutzpah. Take Rex Sinquefield, who coauthored with Ibbotson. He became one of the founding partners in Dimensional Fund Advisors, a firm formed in late 1980 to take advantage of the small-cap effect. On the board or serving as advisors were ten high-powered University of Chicago professors or alumni, including Roger Ibbotson, Eugene Fama, Merton Miller, Myron Scholes, and Rolf Banz.[9] Sinquefield, when asked what he thought of active portfolio management, sneered, "crap."[10] Sinquefield was hyping his new small-cap product at the time, whose hype naturally included the spectacular performance I questioned above.

---

* The most commonly used index to measure small-cap performance.

Whether the figures were correct or incorrect, they were highly marketable. And Sinquefield was certainly an academic who could market. Here, as quoted in *Forbes* in a 1981 article, is part of the spiel. " 'Take the S&P 500 for 1930 through 1980; the return is 9½% a year. But for the bottom 20% in terms of market value, it's 14.6%' " The article continued, "Put another way: $1 million in S&P's 500 would have grown to $93 million, but to $924 million in the small companies. Better than that you can hardly do."

For further effect Sinquefield adds, " 'It's not a fluke. Our computer tells us it happens but none of us knows why.' " Sinquefield resoundingly concludes, " 'We're plugged into the academic world, where all the real good research is taking place. We have a kind of tie-in to Mecca.' "[11]

The *Forbes* article went on to report the reaction of some of the critics, including me. "*Forbes* columnist David Dreman's rebuff of Northwestern Professor Rolf Banz's favorable study of small company performance was like a slap in the face with a wet fish. Dreman says basically that the University of Chicago study was based on faulty data, which skewed the results. Dreman said of the Banz study, in effect, garbage in, garbage out."

Still, give credit where credit is due. The marketing of the product, and the founding of a major investment firm, Dimensional Fund Advisors (DFA), on it could make a case study at the Harvard Business School, even if the academic work was faulty and has proved costly to investors who followed it. By the end of 1996, Dimensional Fund Advisors had $11 billion under management, a good part from the small-cap product.

The professors associated with DFA went along with their Wall Street marketing cronies, happily wallowing in dollars. Ironically, it is this group, some of whom were among the original crusaders to save the public from the clutches of Wall Street ignorance, who refuse to answer reasonable criticisms of the performance of peanut stocks.

But, you might ask, were the small stock findings really as badly flawed as I've indicated? After all, as Sinquefield stated, they had a tie-in to Mecca as his firm was plugged into the finest academic research available. How well, then, did the Dimensional Advisor small-cap fund perform? Poorly, by any yardstick.

For the 5 years ending October 1990, the S&P 500 increased 77.6% in value, while the DFA Small Company Fund (called the 9–10 fund, which closely approximates the real small-cap universe) rose only 1.15%.[12] These figures come from an article by Marc Reinganum, which argues that over time there are predictable reversals. Large cap may beat small stocks in one 5-year period, and predictably will typically get beaten the next time around. Good sleight-of-hand! Alas, the "predictable reversal" Reinganum promised never came. From its inception in 1981 to the end of December 1997 the DFA 9–10 Fund trailed the S&P 500 by 54%. Some of the academics involved with the fund were disturbed by its performance. One said, "This has never happened before, we're stunned."

DFA continues to market the small-cap funds on the basis of the same problematical returns, reporting that small stocks earned 45% annually at the bottom of the Depression. Any novice in the math of compounding rates of returns knows that if you start with these enormous results as a base, whether they're correct or not, the S&P 500 is likely never to catch up. It appears, then, that Sinquefield's direct line to Mecca is out of order, and has been for the last 72 years.

Should You Give Up on Small Stocks?

Dr. Reinganum, as we saw, attempted to dismiss the low P/E findings as a small-cap effect. Nothing could be further from the truth, as Table 15–1 indicates. The study, from 1970 to 1996, is an update of one I published in *Forbes* on July 23, 1990. It shows two important investment findings. First it demonstrates that there is a low P/E effect regardless of the size of the company. Secondly it shows a definite small-cap effect, which results in superior returns to smaller companies—but this effect

Table 15–1
SMALL CAP OR SMALL LOW P/E?
1970–1996

When the Compustat tapes were divided into five groups by market size, and also sorted into five P/E groups, the annual returns (in the five columns below) of the lowest P/E were significantly better, regardless of the size of the company.

Market Capitalization*	Low P/E	2	3	4	High P/E	Market
$100–500 Million	18.6%	18.0%	15.7%	14.6%	12.5%	16.0%
$500 M–$1B	18.8	17.7	14.1	11.0	10.4	14.6
$1–2 Billion	15.9	15.1	13.7	12.4	10.3	13.7
$2–5 Billion	15.3	14.1	11.6	11.8	10.2	12.8
>$5 Billion	14.2	13.7	11.1	11.2	8.7	11.9

*MARKET CAPITALIZATION ON JANUARY 1, 1995.

is contributed entirely by small, low P/E stocks. Let's look at these results more closely.

The study was again done in collaboration with Dr. Eric Lufkin of the Dreman Foundation. To build our database, we took all the companies on the Compustat tapes with market value greater than $100 million[13] and divided them by both P/E and market size. The lowest 20% of stocks—as ranked by price-to-earnings ratios—are in column one, progressing to the highest 20% in column five. Looking across the table, the lowest 20% of stocks by market value ($100 million to $500 million) are in the top row, the largest 20% (larger than $5 billion) in the bottom row.

The lowest P/E group outperformed the highest group for companies in all five market-size categories. The low P/E effect exists for stocks with market values of $1 to $2 billion, as surely as at $100 to $500 million. The difference in returns is formidable. Had you invested $10,000 in the lowest P/Es of the lowest market-size group back in 1970, it would have been worth $1,003,000 in 1996—more than 4 times as much as the $240,000 for the highest P/E group.

The results are even more lopsided for companies in the second-lowest market cap range (row two). The lowest 20% of P/Es here provided an 18.8% annual return, versus 10.4% for the highest P/E group.

Moving to the largest stocks (stocks with a market value greater than $5 billion) in row five, the lowest P/E group provided a 14.2% return versus 11.9% for the group average and 8.7% for the highest P/E stocks. *What's more, these low P/E behemoths with supposedly sluggish futures outperform every category of high P/E stocks including even the smallest-cap group ($100 to $500 million) handily.*

The table also demonstrates that the low P/E strategy is even more effective as company size is reduced. Returns rise as market size decreases, but again we have to be very careful when we get down to "midget" companies. The superior returns, low P/E or not, are likely to be offset to some extent by higher transaction costs. In addition, there is the greater risk that the companies down here will not survive.

The study provides some backing for an investment strategy in medium-sized and smaller stocks almost identical to the one I recommend for large low P/E issues. With the smaller issues you must be prepared to buy them and hold them or the turnover costs will eat you up. This means you have to be very sure the stock is an extra-good value.

Here are five pointers that should be helpful in following the contrarian approach for smaller and medium-sized companies. As you can see they are little different from the rules given for their big brothers, but the penalties for breaking them could be even more severe for your portfolio.

Small-Cap Contrarian Rules

RULE 33

Small-cap investing: Buy companies that are strong financially (normally no more than 60% debt in the capital structure for a manufacturing firm).

RULE 34

Small-cap investing: Buy companies with increasing and well-protected dividends that also provide an above-market yield.

RULE 35

Small-cap investing: Pick companies with above-average earnings growth rates.

RULE 36

Small-cap investing: Diversify widely, particularly in small companies, because these issues have far less liquidity. A good portfolio should contain about twice as many stocks as an equivalent large-cap one.

RULE 37

Small-cap investing: Be patient. Nothing works every year, but when smaller caps click, returns are often tremendous.

What we see clearly is that the small-cap and low P/E effects are separate. Buying small companies *does* give you higher returns, but *only* if you select low P/E stocks.[14] The low P/E effect continues to be strong regardless of the size of the company. Even buying the largest group, the return on the lowest P/E quintile is significantly above the highest P/E set. Sanjoy Basu, in a 1983 paper, obtained similar results, showing that the low P/E effect occurs for companies of any size, and further, also demonstrated problems with Reinganum's methodology.[15]

Do these results hold for other contrarian strategies? Yes. We found very similar performance by using small-cap price-to-cash flow, small-cap price-to-book value, and, to a lesser extent, small-cap price-to-dividends. The price-to-book results are shown in Table 15–2. Buying

Table 15–2

SMALL CAP OR SMALL LOW PRICE-TO-BOOK?
1970–1996

When the Compustat tapes were divided into five groups by market size, and also sorted into five P/BV groups, the annual returns (in the five columns below) of the lowest P/BV were significantly better, regardless of the size of the company.

*Market Capitalization**	*Low P/BV*	*2*	*3*	*4*	*High P/BV*	*Market*
$100–500 Million	18.1%	17.1%	15.1%	14.0%	8.8%	14.8%
$500 M–$1B	18.2	15.9	14.0	11.9	8.7	14.0
$1–2 Billion	15.2	15.5	12.1	13.1	10.7	13.5
$2–5 Billion	16.2	13.9	11.4	11.7	9.7	12.9
> $5 Billion	15.0	12.5	12.6	9.9	10.0	12.2

*MARKET CAPITALIZATION ON JANUARY 1, 1995.

medium or small-cap stocks using one of the contrarian strategies not only provides higher returns over the highest P/E group, but magnifies them, because they outperform their larger co-peers. Once again, though, remember the caveat about the lack of liquidity and the transaction costs in the peanut-sized stocks.

Why do contrarian small-cap stocks do better? Although I cannot give you a definitive answer at this time, I think there are at least two reasons. First, these stocks are not glamorous, but are darn good businesses, such as the local bank or a small company in an unexciting but expanding industry. The stocks, like their big-cap siblings, get knocked down too far when they are unpopular and then recover just like their larger kin. Too, they are often overlooked by all but local or regional investors, and can thus plod along at cheap prices for years. Often a larger company sees they make a good fit, and they can also be bought on the cheap. A merger is consummated well above the previous trading range.

Naturally there have to be other caveats. I talked about survivorship bias in small cap stocks. Doesn't this also hold for small contrarian stocks? Not as much, but let's explore the question a little further. Usually the sizzlers are more thinly financed. Large numbers of IPOs swarm into the marketplace to meet the heavy demand for the concept of the day.

Analyzing Ritter's results, for example, indicates many IPOs were simply startups, usually high on expectation and low or nonexistent on actual revenues and earnings.[16] His 1991 study also showed that value industries had been in business for much longer than the concept industries. The average age of the value IPO was 12 years, compared to several for the glamour segment. (The study excluded penny stock offerings, and stocks not traded in major markets, as well as several other classifications which, if included, would probably have made the comparisons for the glamour sector even worse.).

What this boils down to is, yes, there is very likely a survivorship bias, but one that understates the returns of small-cap contrarian stocks and overstates those of high-priced small companies. Why? Because, as noted, contrarian companies are normally in unexciting but profitable industries that have the financial strength to endure. Failures are more likely to be in exciting new sectors where growth is rapid, but competition is intense and financing is flimsy. Innovation and technology advance rapidly, wiping out the temporary advantage of thousands of such companies.

The latter are the ones that likely dropped out of the less sophisticated databases a couple of decades back. While the jury is out until we get further proof, my assumption is that the returns of high flyers in the small-cap sample are overstated because of this problem. If a more comprehensive index could be constructed that included the thousands of IPOs brought forward in the last few decades, and not just the small-cap survivors, I believe the statistics favoring the small-cap contrarian strategies would be even stronger. I have stated for years that the small-cap effect is almost entirely a contrarian effect for this reason. Do I have any takers on this bet? Professors Banz, Reinganum—are you there?

Beware of Nasdaq and Small Stock Trading Costs

Before you rush out to buy small-cap contrarian stocks, remember they have the same narrow markets endemic to all small stocks. It will cost big to make a trade. Transaction costs are not only the costs of commissions for switching from one stock to another, which, while they can be high, would still leave you with a big part of the pie.

The more important spoiler is the spread: the difference between the price you can buy a stock for and what you can sell it for, which we examined in detail earlier. Even today, while having a relatively minor impact on larger companies, the spreads for pint-sized companies can be enormous—30% to 40%, sometimes more. It has been estimated that the average buy-sell or bid-ask spread of the Russell 2000 (the 2,000 smallest stocks among the top 3,000 traded) is 2.75%, against less than one half of 1% for the S&P 500. Remember, there are thousands of companies smaller than those indexed in the Russell 2000. Normally, the smaller the company the higher the spread. As we've also seen, the spread is often so high that it can completely nullify the theoretical advantage you get from buying small companies in the first place.

Here are some examples of how spreads affect prices in the real world.

First, as a general rule:

RULE 38

Small-company trading (e.g. Nasdaq): Don't trade thin issues with large spreads unless you are almost certain you have a big winner.

If the spread on a thinly traded stock is $2.50 to $3.50, for example, and remains constant when you go to sell, the issue will have to rise 40% before you can break even. With peanut-sized stocks this is precisely the type of spread you can be looking at. Anyone paying 30% or 40% every time he trades his portfolio is hardly likely to end up with the 925 times the amount invested (over 50 years) that some academics crowed about earlier. With charges like these, he (or his estate) would be lucky to come out with his skin.

Nasdaq, where most small companies trade, is a tough market not only for the average investor but for professionals as well. Its commercials on national TV a few years back asked, "Where do you go to find the next Microsoft?" The answer boomed: "Nasdaq, the stock market for the next 100 years." Nasdaq sells glamour and the opportunity to hit it big. Of course, the commercial doesn't remind you that for every Microsoft among midget issues, there are dozens and dozens of busts.

Behind the smooth pitch is a market consisting of about 500 computer-linked, over-the-counter dealers, including the majority of the country's largest brokerage firms, that trade in unlisted stocks.[17] The name of the game, until the Securities and Exchange Commission (SEC) recently stepped in, was to keep the spreads as wide as possible. An array of academic and regulatory studies have concluded that Nasdaq dealers have kept their spreads unnecessarily wide for years, skimming huge profits on securities trades at the expense of the investor. Researchers estimate that investors lose a cool $2 billion a year between the price at which dealers will buy stocks and the price at which they will sell.

According to Arthur Levitt, the head of the SEC and former chairman of the American Stock Exchange, "We found a singular lack of competition on Nasdaq. Where there are few incentives for dealers to compete on price, and few opportunities for investors to do so, the open and fair markets that we rely on are neither open nor fair."[18]

Although Nasdaq dealers justify the spread by stating they take the risk of owning the stock, many keep low inventories. In fact some stocks can have markets of only 100 by 100, or 500 by 500. This means that if you come to the dealer, 100 or 500 shares is all he has to trade at the price he posts. The lower the trading volume, the smaller the position the dealer is required to take and the higher the spread, particularly for low-priced, small-company stocks. In effect, the risk factor is often not large for the dealers, particularly when they have a spread of 20% or more, but it's great sleight of hand. Too, many of the dealers will back away from their bids or offers, even though they are often only for nominal amounts of stock. On October 19, 1995, for example, Morgan Stanley, one of the brokerage house giants, walked away from buying 500 shares of Intuit, Inc., at $49.25, which was its bid (the price Morgan Stanley was required to buy at to make a market). It continued to post $49.25 as the price it would pay for the stock for at least another 12 minutes.[19]

"Backing away" by the dealers results in investors paying higher prices when they buy, and receiving lower ones when they sell. Veteran traders say backing away occurs because there is little risk of penalty by the N.A.S.D. (National Association of Securities Dealers). To compound the problem, most traders are not interested in making a market but are primarily trading for their own accounts in the stocks in which they are market makers, according to Robert M. Gintel, of the Gintel Group of Mutual Funds. The dealers post quotes because Nasdaq rules require them to do so. But, said Gintel, "Out of twenty market makers for a stock, maybe two are interested in trading at any given time." The rest, he said, "will scurry like rabbits to get out of the way" of unsolicited trades, swiftly changing their quotes if an unwanted order comes in on which they cannot make an instant profit. Having traded myself in Nasdaq markets since its beginnings, I have seen this happen many times.

But, unfortunately, there's more. The staggering spreads are only the tip of the iceberg on thinly traded stocks. The purchase or sale can move the stock an additional 10% or more. When you come in to buy more than a minimal amount, the price goes up, even if the spread itself is already large. The dealer's bid naturally drops when there is a more-than-nominal order to sell and rises when there is a more-than-marginal amount to buy.

Let me give you an illustration. Several years back a friend of mine tried to buy 30,000 shares of a stock called Western Transmedia, then listed on Nasdaq's bulletin board. The bulletin board is a section of Nasdaq that trades 7,000 tiny companies with minimal liquidity and enormous spreads. The stock had close to seven million shares outstanding, and traded at $3½ bid, $4½ offered, or a modest spread of 30%. When my friend attempted to buy these shares, the stock moved up rapidly to 6½ bid, 7½ offered. Either the dealers had no inventory, or got wind of the size of the order, or both. There were no news announcements from the company or analysts' reports during this period. The cost to buy had risen a whopping 67%. Wisely, my friend canceled his buy order, whereupon the stock fell back to its original spread of 3½ to 4½ in weeks. Anyone see a slice more of that extra, small-company return disappearing here?

In late 1997, feeling the hot breath of Big Brother behind it, Nasdaq cracked down on its bulletin board by proposing stricter standards to the SEC. Though the Nasdaq name and its electronic trading system make it appear to be a regulated stock market, the bulletin board had almost no rules and no listing requirements. Said Barry R. Goldsmith, Nasdaq's chief enforcement officer, "It had the look and feel of a highly regulated market, and that was enabling people to perpetrate frauds."[20] In order to be listed, the only requirement was one broker who could act as a market maker. Not only were the spreads out of sight, but it was a hotbed of stock-market fraud because of serious manipulation by a number of unscrupulous brokerage firms. The crackdown came after the SEC investigations and F.B.I. sting in October 1996 of shady brokerage houses trading in smaller company stocks, which has resulted in the recent indictment of 55 promoters, brokers and small-company officers for fraud, with the probability of more coming. Talk about closing the barn door . . .

In bad markets or panic, as in the case of the crash of 1987, you don't have to worry about spreads—or for that matter fraud. The dealers simply vanish or don't answer their phones, as a number of major commissions investigating the crash brought out. This is classic price-gouging. There are few places where it is tolerated more than in trading small stocks.

Nasdaq was long considered a "club," ruled by a powerful trading committee made up of the executives of 18 large brokerage firms that traded heavily in Nasdaq stocks.[21] The spreads allegedly have been vigorously "policed" by the club. Thus market-makers narrowing their spreads have been chastised by senior members of the club for raising their buying price above those of other members or lowering their selling prices. If the market-maker has been really naughty he is, as in any old-line club, black-balled. No one will trade with the miscreant, effectively putting the firm out of the market. If they do this in a number of his major stocks, he's out of business. Artificially high spreads enforced by intimidation of rival dealers have been a way of life, some critics of Nasdaq contended, during its more than 25 years of existence.

Apparently it's not only contention. In June of 1997, one of the largest Nasdaq firms, Herzog, Heine & Gedult, settled a class-action suit brought on by a Department of Justice investigation, that will pay back investors $30.8 million.[22] The firm makes a market in 5,000 over-the-counter stocks. The suit charged that 35 brokerage firms colluded to keep trading spreads high on securities traded on Nasdaq between May 1989 and May 1994. The settlement amounted to 25% of the firm's capital. Two other large Nasdaq traders settled suits for multimillion-dollar sums earlier. At year-end 1997, two dozen Nasdaq dealers, including many of the nation's largest brokerage houses, were close to settling a $900 million class-action suit for these practices.

In the late summer and early fall of 1996, the SEC, after some years of study, came to an agreement with a reluctant Nasdaq on a number of trading reforms. The agency found that Nasdaq had failed to enforce compliance with the Exchange Act, "without justification or excuse." The most important reform was to try and limit the power of the club by forcing a number of trading changes, such as requiring a dealer to post an investor's bid or ask on the system if it is between the spread. The system began on an experimental basis for a limited number of stocks in early 1997. Nasdaq also agreed to spend $100 million in the next five years to enhance its system of market surveillance, which according to many critics was virtually nonexistent to then.

Naturally the club was not happy at the prospects of a curtailment of profits. At the time of the agreement some knowledgeable sources estimated profits would be slashed by one-third. Said Benjamin F. Edwards, the chairman of A. G. Edwards, a major regional broker, commonly regarded as old-line in protecting clients' interests, "I think the SEC has been blind to the economic facts of life."[23]

What does this all mean to you? It is still too early to state with any assurance how much protection you have gained. Some of the most rigorous proposals to curb the spreads were not adopted by the SEC. While the jury is still out, to me it seems that many of the costly old practices will continue with only minimal restraints. This means that it is still up to you as an investor to protect yourself against excessive spreads.

How? To begin with, don't be mesmerized by low commission rates. The commission may be only a small part of the cost of buying or selling a stock.

Let me explain. For a stock trading on Nasdaq, the commission may be under a penny a share at the cheapest discount firms. However, the broker is usually paid an additional fee of several cents per share to direct the business to a particular over-the-counter house. That's right, the broker can get as much as double the fee that it charges in commission to you for directing the business.

Why is the Nasdaq house willing to pay for the right to exercise your order? You guessed it, to earn the spread. If the spread is, say, $8 to $8½, the Nasdaq dealer will make 50 cents per share on the deal, and can easily afford to pay for your broker to direct the order to him. A discount broker, who charges very low commissions, or any other for that matter, would be sorely tempted to send your order to a dealer who will take a fat spread. What you gain on the commission you may lose many times on the spread. So don't rush to brokers who offer you a penny a share commission on Nasdaq trades.

True, the same thing often happens on the Amex and even the NYSE to folks who put in a market order to save a few pennies on commissions. But because Nasdaq does trade by far the largest number of small companies, the excesses are much greater in this market. Since market orders on any but the most liquid stocks can cost 25 cents or more in the bid-ask spread, transaction costs can again be many times the commission savings. For the few extra dollars it costs to put in a limit order, you can save many times that on the spread.

I can't say it too often: Watch those spreads. There is no free lunch, especially on Wall Street. If you are getting super low commissions, it's highly unlikely you are also receiving the same attention to execution. This then brings us to a rule:

RULE 39

When making a trade in small, illiquid stocks, consider not only commissions, but also the bid/ask spread to see how large your total cost will be.

It often pays to deal with a market-maker directly (many of the large national brokerage houses are market-makers on hundreds of over-the-counter stocks). You will probably get as good or a better execution this way, without paying any commission. (You don't pay commission if the dealer buys or sells to you in a principal transaction.) Finally, use a limit order—give the broker a fixed price to buy or sell at—and change it when necessary.

Table 15–3
SMALL CAP VALUE FUNDS
As of 11/28/97

	5-year return	*3-year return*	*Phone Number*
Franklin Balance Investment	20.7%	24.0%	800–342–5236
Longleaf Partners Small Cap	20.6%	25.7%	800–445–9469
Kemper Small Cap Value	18.7%	30.0%	800–621–1048
MAS Institutional Small Cap Value	27.4%	30.3%	800–354–8185
T. Rowe Price Small Cap Value	20.8%	26.8%	800–638–5660
Vanguard Index Small Cap Stock	18.0%	24.3%	800–662–7447

SOURCE: PREPARED FROM LISTINGS IN *THE WALL STREET JOURNAL.*

In summary, there can certainly be a performance advantage for you in buying pint-sized contrarian stocks. But this advantage can easily be negated by the spread. In fact if you trade frequently, you can very easily come out behind, even though you have been right on every pick. Paying 10%, 20%, or more every time you buy or sell takes a big chunk out of your capital. As we saw, the academic studies that noted the huge returns from small-sized companies never considered this issue.

Should you abandon the small-cap market entirely? No, but if you go into it, avoid companies where the dealers have large trading spreads. Remember, most are trading for their own accounts, a virtually automatic conflict of interest. Second, and this also applies to larger stocks that are illiquid—use limit orders. A third good choice for the investor who wants to capture the higher returns theoretically available in small-sized stocks is to buy a small-cap value mutual fund. Table 15–3 lists several that I would consider.

Next we'll turn to market indices, another example of an investor pitfall where seeing is not believing.

The Index Trap

Most professional investors and increasingly large numbers of individuals compare how they do against an index. While this is a good benchmark most of the time, there are problems that you should be aware of. Take the granddaddy and most widely followed index of them all, the Dow Jones Industrial Average.

Far from being an accurate proxy for the stock market as a whole, the Dow index—and most other indexes—are just lists of bellwether stocks selected by a committee. The Dow Jones is made up of 30 stocks using a pricing method established over a century ago. Trouble is, the stocks in the average have been changed over the years, based on the decisions of a small group working within the Dow Jones organization. Little is known about how these people pick stocks for the average, yet their choices can significantly change the level of this index.

On March 14, 1939, one particular stock was dropped from the index. Why? It was "just another dull office equipment supplier." The name of the company was IBM. AT&T was substituted. You know the rest. With stock dividends, splits, and rights offerings, IBM moved up 635.2 times over the next four decades before the keepers of the gate saw fit to restore it to the index in June of 1979. Its replacement, AT&T, moved up 6 times in the same period.

Had IBM been kept throughout, the Dow would have been around 9,000 in 1997 (nearer to 15,000 if the appreciation were not adjusted downward after each stock split, according to the formula, to equally weight the average).

You see, in a sense, the Dow keepers are just stock pickers—and just as fallible. When the time came to restore IBM, something had to be dropped. It was Chrysler, then barely breathing. Kicked out of the index, Chrysler staged a sensational comeback. Since then, Chrysler has appreciated 1324% to IBM's 82%, or 16 times as much. Chalk up a bunch more points, had IBM not been added back. Never underestimate the ability of a committee to arrive at the wrong decision.

Okay, how about the S&P 500? Similar pattern. In the late sixties, for example, the REITs (real estate investment trusts) were put in very near their all time highs, only to be dropped in 1974 at a fraction of those prices near their lows. Gambling stocks were added in 1979 and oil service companies in 1981—both near their market peaks—which they never regained. And so it goes.

The makeup of many indexes, then, simply reflects the conventional stock-picker wisdom of a given time. Investors believe stock market indexes mirror markets completely insulated from popular fashions. Not true. Because stock selection or deletion is an art, the index is not a mirror but more like a painting that differs, sometimes dramatically, from the reality it attempts to portray. This subjective element in stock indexes is something most people, including experts, are unaware of. In the end, ironically, index investors get exactly what they attempted to avoid—human error.

Since there are many indexes, some are performing much better than others at any given time. Small stock indexes were popular well after the small cap markets turned south in mid-1983. Over ten years to the early 1980s, the Value Line Index (which is a long-standing record of 1,700 equally weighted stocks) did sensationally, but only because it recovered from the sharp drop in the prior ten.

You should be extra careful of specialty indexes put out by investment houses or other parties that have a vested interest in demonstrating excellent performance for a particular group of stocks. One of the leading technology houses, for example, puts out an index of high-tech stocks that outperformed the market manyfold since its inception in the early 1970s. The brokerage house uses a rather unique index-selection formula. When stocks it originally held in the index don't perform well, it drops them retroactively, sometimes ten years after the fact, and substitutes the major high-tech winners of the day instead. Naturally it puts them into the index at the prices they were trading at on the dates they were retroactively selected, which results in instant performance. The excellent record of its index indicates the firm obviously knows its stuff, and helps the company to bring in substantial business. I wrote a *Forbes* column on November 3, 1986, on this somewhat out-of-the-ordinary stock selection process. We checked as of mid-1997, and found that the practices had changed little.

In the end then you are not getting an index based on the performance of growth stocks of the seventies, eighties, or nineties, but one that is built using the luxury of hindsight. If we could bottle this formula, we'd all be rich.

The moral is clear. Steer away from these sweeping generalizations based on flimsy evidence, wherever they occur. This is particularly true of indexes that can be self-serving to the people who construct them. Which brings us, you will not be surprised to learn, to another widespread performance deception.

Tailor-Made Performance Records

I don't want to make you totally paranoid about indexes and performance records, but I don't think it would be completely honest to hold back on two categories of bogus performance that can do you in.

The first is *supercharged results*. These can come out of a mutual fund, and are unlikely to be maintained. The point is so important that I think it ought to be made into a contrarian rule:

RULE 40

Avoid the small, fast-track mutual funds. The track often ends at the bottom of a cliff.

Forbes's "1984 Annual Mutual Fund Survey" (Aug. 27) summed it up well: "A tiny fund scorches the track, brings in big money and sends late investors into the tank." Nothing has changed since that time; in fact it's become worse. By late 1997, the sizzling fast-track funds of the nineties were falling behind, with some of the former outstanding performers down 20% to 25% for the year alone.

The better the performance in a market where fast-track stocks are shooting out the lights, the more advertising the mutual fund sponsor pours into the fund (often a virtual new entry with a short but spectacular record), and the more publicity is generated in the press. Inevitably, most investors get in near the top—just in time to get blasted away. Buying fast-track funds is like paying full price for last year's fashion just before the new lines are shown.

Here are some ways to avoid this shuffle. The first is not to buy a fund of $50 million if its returns have been made by some fast-track method. The record at $50 million usually doesn't continue as the fund grows into hundreds of millions or billions. That's true especially if a good part of the increase has come from spectacular gains at the beginning, when the small fund had only a minute part of present assets under management.

Second, go beyond the record itself and find out how it was achieved. If you are uncomfortable with what makes the fund tick, stay away—it's likely to explode. This is also true of a widely known practice currently being investigated by the SEC, of one or two funds in a fund family receiving most of the group's allotment of hot IPOs. That's done in order to "spike" their performance. Again these are usually smaller funds in trendy industries that can attract big bucks if the record is sizzling. Allocating major portions of hot IPOs to them gives them instant performance. Nobody much looks at how the fund did it. The answer once more is close scrutiny of any small fund you buy.

Finally let's glance briefly at the record of the investment advisor. A good friend of mine, the late Ted Halligan, spent most of his career placing money managers with clients. "I never met a manager who didn't say he was in the top percentile in performance," Halligan once told me wryly.

So how do you separate the claims from the truth? Getting accurate numbers of a manager's performance over a long period is more difficult than you might think. Even sophisticated investors, who depend on consultants to do their digging, often get bad numbers. A former retail broker, who once lived near me, wiped out his original clientele in the early eighties playing hot, "junior oil" stocks, just before they went into the tank. With his commission gauge rapidly moving toward empty, he started his own money management firm. He hyped it as "conservative value" and entirely fabricated an outstanding eight-year record.

Did anyone, including a number of consultants, question his numbers? Heck no. The fantasy performance built him a nice business.

Or take a recent group of small-cap stock-pickers who started their business after several years as marketers for another firm. None had the experience they claimed. These fellows launched their firm with a mouthwatering record, little of which was theirs. What they did was to "simply borrow" the excellent performance record of the firm they had previously worked for. Even several large consultants didn't bother to check, until made aware of the problem by anxious clients. Their performance was a disaster.

It's not only the out-and-out frauds that can suck you in. As my friend Halligan also observed, everyone has a winning streak. At some point the canny manager can get coverage from naive reporters who fail to note that the performance owed its sizzle to a handful of risky stocks— while over three to five years the results were near the bottom of the barrel.

Checking the performance numbers of money managers is harder work than for mutual funds, where the figures better be good or it's "go directly to jail." The SEC has issued detailed rules for how a manager must calculate performance, and most firms with assets of $1.5 billion to $2 billion or more are audited regularly. Still, the unscrupulous manager can, in effect, keep "two sets of books." One for marketing and the other, the real performance numbers, for SEC audits. (This was the technique of the former junior oil manager I discussed earlier.)

Short of outright lying, investment managers can do other cute things with their figures. One prestigious "white-shoe" firm sent a letter to many of our clients a few years ago claiming their style easily beat our firm's low P/E investing record and backed the claim with an impressive chart.

Curious, I read the footnotes and found that the record was not one investment style but a blend of carefully chosen methods, ranging from foreign to momentum to growth, with the portfolio heavily weighted in the style that had the best performance in a given year. Call it "hindsight investing."

The final numbers game is played by some prominent national consultants. They offer their clients multimanager investment packages for value, growth, momentum, and various other performance styles. The managers they show you naturally knock the socks off their peers. What the consultants don't tell you is that they prepackage the managers with the best records at a given time—again, selection by hindsight.

The moral: Don't just take somebody's word for it. Ask for audited ten-year numbers for each of their managers. Find out whether they are the same team used three to five years back. If you hear a gulp, it's time to move on. A few hours spent researching records and asking for the performance of representative portfolios can save you big bucks.

In this chapter, we looked at the facts and myths of investing in small-sized companies, the Nasdaq follies, as well as a number of other ways even astute investors can get blindsided. In the next we will ask how much the opinions and beliefs of groups of investors we respect can influence our investment decisions—invariably for the worst.

PART V

PSYCHOLOGY AND MARKETS

16

The Zany World of Rationality

Do you remember New Math? Or perhaps you were subjected to it in elementary school. As a popular shorthand term, New Math stood for the revised mathematics curriculum introduced in the 1970s as a reform effort. Supposedly the new program would enable students to understand the meaning behind basic mathematics, rather than just manipulate numbers by rote. That was the theory.

What parents found was that, first, they could no longer help their children with their homework in arithmetic. They just didn't understand it. Secondly, their children weren't learning to add or subtract. They could draw set diagrams, but 2 + 2 wasn't on the teaching agenda. Needless to say, parents shouldered their scythes and pitchforks and headed for the Board of Education, for they held the strange belief that their kids would need to be able to do simple, practical arithmetic.

Now comes the interesting part. The new reforms weren't abandoned, but were stirred in with the old practices. Students get a little bit of both. Substitute the efficient market hypothesis for New Math, and you have a pretty good idea of what happened on Wall Street. As we have seen, EMH was a product of academia, but, like the New Math, something went wrong when it left the classroom. None of its prophecies were fulfilled, and its basic teachings were disputed by an increasingly impressive body of evidence.

Despite the steady rain of contradictory evidence, the high priests continued to dismiss, minimize, or trivialize it. All the same, the findings not only questioned the essence of the theory, but also threw down the gauntlet to a major tenet of economics: is man really the rational, almost omniscient creature that he must be in order for the EMH faith to stand? This chapter and the next will delve into that question. The answer will explain why the investment methods I recommend work so reliably over time.

Chapter 10 demonstrated the remarkable power of cognitive biases to lead individual investors away from the rational behavior assumed by the theorists and to seduce them into major market errors. Errors so systematic that people aware of them can use the strategies outlined to exploit them with high odds of success.

But there's more. The cognitive biases do not act on individual investors as if each were in a separate cocoon. Heuristic biases have the strength they have demonstrated because humans interact in almost everything they do. Few of us escape the opinions of others. The investment inputs that affect us to a greater or lesser extent also affect the experts we respect, as well as tens of thousands of market participants. In the marketplace then, these biases not only lead investors into errors on their own, but the opinions of others serve to reinforce these mistakes and justify the course we take, no matter how foolhardy it is. As this chapter will demonstrate, there is strong evidence that the power of the group or the crowd, when interacting with the cognitive errors we all fall victim to individually in markets, like dousing flames with kerosene, serve to substantially extend and magnify the blaze.

Observers have watched the absurd behavior of people in market manias or bubbles for hundreds of years. The "Madness of Crowds," "group folly," or "the herd mentality" have been described in innumerable chronicles. In fact, the market has been an arena where groups or crowds have shown some of the least rational behavior on record, as we'll see next. But it is only in the second half of the twentieth century that these behavioral phenomena have been looked at scientifically and psychologists have begun to categorize and analyze them.

Let's begin our study of "rational behavior in markets" by examining the antics of millions of people who first discovered the promise of stocks in the mid-nineties.

The Former Comrades Meet the Market

Naturally, I would hardly expect you to believe that solid, well-educated American investors could fall prey to such ludicrous behavior. Rather let's turn to the tragicomic events surrounding MMM, the largest investment company in Russia, for an example of how reasonable people go off the deep end when pursuing instant wealth. By 1994, free enterprise and its natural by-product, the urge to get rich quick, had hit Russia with a vengeance. Millions of people from "babushkas" to yuppies were chasing quick fortunes. Though scores of slick con artists conspired to clip the newest capitalists, no one was better at it than Sergei Mavrodi, the head of MMM. Mavrodi was a promoter par excellence even by the tough standards of western hype. Spending millions on TV and newspaper advertising, MMM became as well recognized in Russia as Coca-Cola in this country.

Lyonya Golubakov, a fictional MMM shareholder, was as much an icon in Russia as the Marlboro Man is here. Plain-talking, vodka-swilling Golubakov, the protagonist of a major series of television commercials, had found the key to wealth. The polished commercials portrayed him getting rich and fulfilling the Russian dream as MMM would have it. Rolling in rubles from his investment in MMM, Golubakov goes off to San Francisco for a World Cup Soccer game, while his brother can only weep and beat his breast at his lack of foresight in not purchasing the stock. With slick advertising, Golubakov becomes the Russian Horatio Alger.[1]

MMM advertised that it could make its shareholders modestly rich—promising a 3,000% return annually. It portrayed itself as the vehicle to gain dazzling wealth, creature comforts, and luxurious living.[2] Russian investors swallowed the bait. At its height, MMM had an estimated five to ten million shareholders—more than GM, Microsoft, and Exxon combined.*

What was MMM really? A gigantic pyramid scheme—no more. New stock was sold at the market price, which soared in the first part of 1994. MMM could well afford to redeem the few shares coming in, because thousands of buyers lined up to buy at increasingly higher prices.[3]

What did the company do? When polled, virtually none of the shareholders knew. It had no earnings, revealed no investments, and explained no financial strategy. What investors did know was that its stock skyrocketed and people made fortunes. From February, when the shares were first issued, to July 23, 1994, it was the goose that laid the golden egg. In American dollars, the price rose from $1 to $65. In five months, MMM almost doubled the rise in the Dow Jones in the past 70 years!

Like all good dreams, it had to end. In mid-1994, the Russian Government began to investigate MMM. Finding no business of any sort behind the company, it issued warnings to the Russian public. In two days the stock crashed from $60 to 46 cents. As is always the case with bubbles, the aftermath was harsh.

---

* According to Value Line, General Motors has approximately 860,000 shareholders, Exxon has 606,579, and Microsoft has roughly 35,650, for a total of 1,500,000; far less than MMM's reported ownership.

Ten thousand Russians mobbed the streets in front of MMM's offices and the colonnaded headquarters of Moscow's Commodity Exchange, smashing windows, pushing, shoving, sleeping in the streets and on sidewalks, and offering bribes of thousands of dollars to cut to the head of the line, as they desperately tried to redeem their shares.[4] Some stared blankly into space wondering what had become of their savings, others called for hunger strikes, and several threatened to immolate themselves. The firm then announced it was nearly bankrupt and shares would be redeemed at $\frac{1}{100}$ of their previous value.

Ex-comrade Mavrodi did not lose his cool. He blamed the entire crash on government meddling, stating none of this would have happened had they let "free enterprise take its course." He promised that "in two or three months the price will return to its previous level of ten thousand rubles." As an added kicker, he offered to immediately redeem the shares of the most needy at $50. "We, unlike the state, have never deceived you, and never will," he announced. He also stated that the fund was on the verge of a super breakthrough in which the shares would be sold in the U.S., Germany, and other countries. A large number of shareholders believed him in spite of their enormous losses. Queues formed to buy MMM shares in August—mere weeks after the crash—even after the government had exposed MMM as a gigantic pyramid scheme.

A good promoter has nine lives. After being carted off to jail for tax evasion shortly after the collapse, Mavrodi came up with another audacious scheme. Russian law gives a member of parliament immunity from prosecution for all but the most serious crimes. Mavrodi ran for parliament in a district with large numbers of MMM owners. He never set foot in the district, relying instead on the same media blitz that drew millions of Russians to MMM. He urged people to vote for him so he could save the firm, portraying himself as the little man pitted against the bureaucratic state. For those who didn't have the misfortune of owning shares, he guaranteed to make the district a "little Switzerland," promising $10 million of his own money for the project. Not surprisingly, he won.[5]

At his victory party, safe from prosecution, he could fess up. He told 3,000 supporters at the celebration that the resurrection of MMM would be put off indefinitely, and walked out, naturally with his large fortune intact. People exploded in anger, ripping up worthless shares as they finally realized there was no hope.

The MMM scam shows how easy it is for people to fling their life savings on a wild-eyed scheme they know nothing about. Sure, we might think, there are a few madmen out there who will bet their fortunes on a throw of the dice. But, which of us won't say, *I* know better than that.

I'm no fool, *I'm* no compulsive gambler. Still, millions bought these odds with MMM, all doing the same remarkably foolish thing.

What makes vast numbers squander their savings on such a harebrained promotion? Strange as it appears, can we dismiss these poor folks thronging the streets, desperately buying and selling worthless paper, as simply naive investors in a totally undeveloped market?

Let's look at this question next.

You Can Never Go Wrong in Real Estate

The rational man, like the Loch Ness monster, is sighted often but photographed rarely. Everybody claims to invest rationally, but point a camera at them when speculative opportunities arise, and something fogs the film. The developed photo fails to show any sign of that rational being beloved by economic theorists. What usually can be made out instead is a blurred image of a frenzied crowd.

In the 1980s, the behavior of well-trained professionals in American, Western European, and Japanese real estate, considered to be among the world's most sophisticated markets, underscores this point.

In *The Graduate,* a guest at Dustin Hoffman's graduation party takes him aside and whispers one word to him—plastics. That's where fortunes would be made in the 1960s. In the 1980s it was to be commercial real estate. The beginnings, as they often are, were sound enough. The remarkable boom in real estate was triggered by its impeccable performance in the past. Real estate had a solid record of appreciation since the war, and, like stocks, was an excellent shield against inflation. Because it had only gone higher in the past 40 years, it was inevitable, the smart money believed (and all money thinks it is smart), that it would continue to soar.

Big bucks flowed into commercial real estate. Banks, after losing heavily on third world loans, eagerly poured money into real estate. With prices ratcheting up, savings and loans, insurance companies, and other financial institutions increased their commitments, while the nation's gargantuan pension funds entered this market, many for the first time.

Real estate syndicators could sell their merchandise at 110% of its assessed value, which was stretched liberally. This meant the developer was given all the costs of land and construction, plus his overhead and profit—often before a cubic yard of earth was moved. In the past, conservative institutions (usually banks) would only offer developers interim financing, well secured by other collateral, and for a fraction of the overall development cost. The rules had most definitely changed. Buyers were so excited by real estate (usually the loans were accompanied by equity participations) that they often forgot even the most rudimentary valuation standards.

The equity investor found a multitude of other advantages, including tax write-offs and leverage. Say, for example, that I bought a property with an 80% mortgage. Suppose further that the property doubled after five years—conservative in the eighties. I would have sixfolded, not doubled my money, since I had put up only 20% of the price. Because interest, depreciation, and other expenses were tax deductible, I could write them off against other income, thus minimizing their impact. Not a bad deal.

When commercial real estate appreciated at a 15% clip through the early eighties, everyone wanted on the bandwagon. Pension consultants urged their major clients to jump in. A large number of the decisions were based on modern portfolio theory. After all, here was a place where they could make 15% or higher returns. Much more than the stock market. Better yet, it added diversification and lowered beta, which, according to their efficient market training, made the returns greater still.[6] Large pension funds placed major money in questionable ventures, many near the top.

Consultants often urged their clients to invest with managers who had hot hands. Here we see a bit of the bizarre. Unlike the stock market, which appraises the value of a stock on every trade, the real estate manager was allowed to appraise his own properties. He simply assigned a value to the client's property at year's end. That he took 20% of the increase in appraisal price, which could run up to 30% or 40% of the property's value, or that scads of new money swarmed to him because of the fabulous returns—created with the stroke of a pen—didn't seem to impugn his impartiality. Not unlike declaring four aces and raking in the pot without a showdown. As a money manager, I'm a little envious. Here is a market that a deserving manager should find only in paradise.

Does this sound zany? Of course it does. Nonetheless, it was done by many of the largest corporate pension funds, on the advice of some of the most blue-chip consultants in the country. Once again, a crowd mesmerized by the image of limitless wealth threw caution to the winds and headed for the cliff.

In Japan, although property prices had increased ten times in a few years, the major banks loaned money at approximately 100% of a proposed project's value. After all, believed investors in the late 1980s, Japanese real estate, like Japanese stocks, could never go down. It was little different in the West. Commercial space for rent expanded enormously. The U.S. Government reported in early 1996 that retail space, for example, had doubled since 1988.

The influx of money fueled construction. Developers would build and purchasers buy almost anything. Partnerships popped up like mushrooms. Like the Florida Land Bubble of the mid-twenties, which sold swampland, often under water, almost any project could be sold. Almost anything, that is. When promoters peddled projects that even their normally frenzied buyers wouldn't touch, there was always a brokerage house in the wings with clients clamoring to buy into the partnership. These deals *really* smelled. Fortunately for the clients, the large markups and poor quality of some of them forced the SEC to step in. The brokerage houses ultimately ate billions of dollars in losses.

"Just how did the commercial real estate mother lode of the last decade turn into the fool's gold of the 1990s?" asked a financial publication.[7] Demand for commercial real estate, partially created by expanding international trade, banking, and brokerage operations in the seventies and early eighties, accelerated property appreciation.

Ironically, as loan officers scrambled to acquire property, the same banks and insurance companies were sharply reducing their space requirements. From 1980 to mid-1992, the office vacancy rate in Manhattan jumped from 2.9% to 17%, in London from 2% to 20%, and in Toronto from 1.8% to over 13%. The 1987 stock market crash launched a worldwide retrenchment in financial services. Though the stock market subsequently tripled from its previous high, jobs had declined 10% from their peak.

The end was devastating, not only for the newly rich developers with their recently acquired Gulf Streams, yachts, or trophy wives, but for hundreds of thousands who had their savings in this sector. The marvelous leverage that enriched investors on the way up, bankrupted them on the way down. A 50% drop, with 20% equity and 80% borrowed funds, resulted in a 250% loss. If the investor had guaranteed payment—good-bye. Even some of the shrewdest international developers went under; the Reichman Brothers of Canada lost billions on the Canary Wharf Project in London. "The Donald" filed Chapter 11 on the Trump Taj Mahal Casino to avoid personal bankruptcy proceedings. As one periodical put it, "Not many people realize how stunningly big the commercial real estate debacle is."[8] The savings and loan industry was devastated. The Government had to form the Resolution Trust to acquire the assets of insolvent S&Ls, which it then sold at 50% or less of the price on the books. By mid-1992, an estimated one trillion dollars was lost in the U.S. alone—more than the cost of the 1987 crash.[9] Worldwide, it may have been many times this figure.

The people who were buying commercial real estate were not rubes. They were loan officers and other razor-sharp professionals worldwide, many of whom had devoted their entire careers to evaluating properties. These experts made bad loans that nearly wiped out the U.S. savings and loan industry, pushed the banking and insurance industries to the brink, and launched the worst panic on the stocks of financial companies since the Great Depression. Internationally, the damage was comparable.

Once again, image had leveled investors the world over.

The Madness of Crowds

In the last two sections, we witnessed the bizarre behavior of large groups of normally sane people in a financial mania. Speculative fever or mania characterizes various periods in various countries where the prevailing investor belief pushes the price of stocks or commodities or land far above traditional standards of value. The prices stay up for weeks, for months, sometimes for years, which reinforces investor confidence and sends prices higher still.

To those caught up in the situation, it can be a heady experience. The everyday rules of the game are discarded. Profits equal to years of hard work are made in days; dreams of a lifetime are realized in months. The climb in prices becomes the obsessive topic of conversation, and dramatic stories circulate, usually embellished with each telling, of the fortunes made by individuals who got in early. In every case, the experts are sucked in, condoning the price rises and predicting higher levels. Those still on the sidelines seem to be wasting a golden opportunity, and more and more people are drawn into the boiling cauldron. It is like discovering a lottery where odds have veered suddenly and dramatically in the player's favor. When investors see that the wildest gambles are rewarded with success, the voices of reason and moderation are drowned in the roar. The great bubble of hope, unreason, confidence, and greed floats upward. Of course, all bubbles, real or figurative, come to the same end.

These observations are anything but new. In 1852, Charles Mackay wrote his classic *Extraordinary Popular Delusions and the Madness of Crowds*. Mackay described the strange behavior of people swept away by popular ideas. To the uninvolved, these ideas appear bizarre, as they do to most of the participants afterwards. The work details a number of delusions, ranging from the evacuation of London in 1524, because of the prediction of its fortune tellers that the Thames, that most docile of rivers, would suddenly rise from its banks and sweep away the city, to the preoccupation of science in the Middle Ages with alchemy, to graphic descriptions of bizarre financial bubbles. Crowd behavior in the marketplace was every bit as strange to Mackay as any other mania he documented.

The book has been widely read on Wall Street since the turn of the century. Mackay foreshadowed by 150 years the study of the intricate and varying psychology of the marketplace. Bernard Baruch, an outstanding investor of the earlier part of the century, wrote the preface for the reissue of Mackay's book, and was fond of giving copies to young people coming into the industry to help them understand the powerful psychological forces often unleashed in markets.

Mackay was expert at capturing the mood of the crowd. He relates how speculators, driven to frenzy by the rise in price of the South Sea Company shares in 1720, searched London for the next big winner, just as investors look for the next Intel or Microsoft today. Ideas that were far-fetched, if not in la-la land, attracted scores of buyers. Companies were sold to extract oil from radishes, make gold out of sea water, and even to bring up hellfire—presumably an early form of central heating.

At its height, the South Sea Company had a market value of 500 million pounds, roughly five times the cash in all of Europe. In retrospect, the enormous valuation placed on the company seems absurd, yet the crowd believed it was only the beginning. The end came, as it came to MMM 275 years later. In days the wealth of thousands was swept away.

As Mackay observes:

> We find that whole communities suddenly fix their minds upon one subject, and go mad in its pursuit; that millions of people become simultaneously impressed with one delusion and run after it. . . . Sober nations have all at once become desperate gamblers, and risked almost their existence upon the turn of a piece of paper. . . . Men, it has been well said, think in herds . . . they go mad in herds, while they only recover their senses slowly and one by one.[10]

Some Common Features of Manias

We have now considered a number of manias, two recent, the other hundreds of years earlier. All had nearly identical characteristics. Dozens of others, from tulipmania in the Holland of the 1630s to the Mississippi Bubble in the France of 1720 to the Florida Land Bubble in the late 1920s, had nearly identical characteristics.

First, prices were taken far in excess of real value. Real estate was wildly overvalued in the 1980s, and MMM had no substance at all. Second, the crowd bought the concept by the hundreds of thousands in the case of real estate in the 1980s and by the millions in the Russian case. Third, reality (or rationality) excused itself almost completely. Prices rose an astounding amount: 6,500% for MMM, within months. Is it madness to buy a stock that traded at $1,000 a few months back for $20,000 today, when the underlying value has not changed in the least? The answer has always been yes. Still, people have done so repeatedly in the past and will do so again.

How can so many people be part of such a colossal folly? For further perspective let's turn to another early student of crowd psychology.

The Characteristics of a Crowd

Another early observer of the strange behavior of crowds was a Frenchman named Gustave Le Bon, who in 1895 wrote *The Crowd*. Like Charles Mackay's work, it is a classic. Le Bon's work contains some remarkable insights into the behavior of crowds, many of which apply to the lemming-like actions of investors.

One of the most striking features of the crowd to Le Bon was its difficulty in separating the imagined from the real.

> A crowd thinks in images, and the image itself calls up a series of other images, having no logical connection with the first . . . A crowd scarcely distinguishes between the subjective and the objective. It accepts as real the images invoked in its mind, though they most often have only a very distant relation with the observed facts. . . . Crowds being only capable of thinking in images are only to be impressed by images.[11]

At times, as Le Bon saw, the image evokes cruel behavior; the belief in "one true faith" sent millions to their deaths over the centuries, and the "isms" of this century have taken tens of millions of lives. At other times, the image can inspire heroism, as with the crowd that stood against the Chinese tanks in Tiananmen Square, or the Russians who lined up almost weaponless to protect the parliament building against the well-armed KGB attack in 1991. With the benefit of hindsight, the image may become droll, as when London was abandoned to the Thames. But to capture the crowd, the image must always be simple. Le Bon believed the individual regresses in a crowd and "descends several rungs in the ladder of civilization. Isolated, he may be a cultivated individual; in a crowd he is a barbarian. He possesses the spontaneity, the violence, the ferocity, and also the enthusiasm and heroism of primitive beings."[12]

Le Bon, like Mackay, was an insightful student of crowd actions. Since neither had the benefit of the psychological studies of group and crowd behavior of the twentieth century, both were less than sympathetic observers. Yet their descriptions of crowd behavior are remarkably applicable to what occurs in financial markets today. All the elements are present: numbers of people, intense excitement, and that essential, simple, beguiling image—instant wealth. Each image carries the crowd into the realm of fantasy, and sometimes beyond the boundaries of sanity.

As Le Bon foresaw, the image is not only simple and enticing, but seemingly infallible. And, as he predicted, people lose their individuality. Crowd contagion sweeps intellectuals, artists, nobles, and businessmen in every period as easily as it does the average investor.

The World of Social Reality

The vision of desperate investors scurrying about in a collapsing market trying to save themselves from their own foolhardiness may be amusing, but are there lessons for today's market?

History shows that group madness is not necessarily short-lived. The fear of the flooding of the Thames lasted many months; the real estate bubble was in full bloom for four or five years; the burning of witches went on for centuries. In each of these cases, the image created its own reality, reshaping the perceptions, actions, and attitudes of the crowd. How were such strange realities brought into being, and why should supposedly rational people succumb to them?

Social psychologists tell us that our beliefs, values, and attitudes lie along a continuum. At one extreme are those based on indisputable physical evidence. If I throw a crystal vase against a wall, it will shatter; or if I walk only in shorts into a blizzard, I'll probably freeze. Such outcomes, termed physical reality, are obvious and do not require other people's confirmation. At the other end of the continuum are beliefs and attitudes that, though important to us, lack firm support. Available facts are sparse and hard to evaluate. In this category are such questions as the existence of a Creator, whether there is a "best" political system, or, of primary interest here, what a stock is really worth.

Psychologists have demonstrated that the vaguer and more complex a situation, the more we rely on other people, both for clarification and as touchstones for our own views. This helps us reduce our uncertainty toward our own beliefs. French investors, for example, attempting to assimilate contradictory facts to put a value on Mississippi shares, undoubtedly sought the opinions of other intelligent investors. When people use the opinions of others as yardsticks to determine the correctness of their own views, they are using what psychologists call social comparison processes.

We do this frequently, rarely giving it a second thought. I was once in an Oriental restaurant in New York, where the restrooms were marked with hieroglyphics. I was stymied, until another man strolled confidently through one of the doors.

Similarly, a speaker may gauge the worth of his talk from the audience's reaction. After one of his speeches, Lincoln, judging from what he thought was a disappointing response from the crowd, turned to a friend and said, "That plow won't scour." The speech was the Gettysburg Address.[13]

The greater the anxiety and the more indeterminate the situation, the more readily we rely on the behavior of others, treating the information we receive as no less real than if we had directly observed it from physical reality. We forget its personal and tentative nature.

The term *social reality* refers to how a group of people perceives reality. As Leon Festinger, who first proposed the theory, described it: "When the dependence upon physical reality is low, the dependence on social reality is correspondingly high. An opinion, attitude, or belief is 'correct, valid, and proper' to the extent that it is anchored in the group of people with similar beliefs, opinions, and attitudes."[14] The ensuing social reality can then be a strange amalgam of objective criteria and crowd fancy. Facts, such as are available, can be twisted to conform to prevailing opinions.

This brings us back to the odd aberrations of people in crowds. In each instance, those involved found the information vague, complex, and anxiety producing. Few standards existed to help them. The real estate developers may have been right; after all, they had an almost flawless record for 45 years. During the roaring bull markets of the 1920s and late 1990's, one could see the substantial gains made by those who bought early; top Wall Streeters, shrewd businessmen, and some of the country's wealthiest people were buying stocks and making fortunes, while the experts hopped from foot to foot shouting that it was a "New Era—it's only the beginning."

People then, as now, hesitated, were anxious, and looked to individuals they respected to compare opinions. Great numbers were drawn by the need to examine their own views with those of the group; the larger

its nucleus, the greater the attraction of its beliefs to those who had initially resisted them.

The record outside of the laboratory is not much different. Because there are so few objective guidelines, social reality has always had a merry time in the fashion world, for men and women alike. At the turn of the century, the dictate was for women's hemlines to drag along the ground; in other periods, they were well above the knee. In the late nineteenth century, to be au courant demanded an exceptionally narrow waist (seventeen or eighteen inches), and many a poor woman had her floating ribs removed to fit herself to the fashion image. After Twiggy, the skeletal English model of the 1960s, the fashion world had demand for hundreds of Twiggy look-alikes. Whether the increase in anorexia is partially due to this trend would make an interesting study.

Fashions and fads are no different today. Take meditation. Although its benefits have been recognized for thousands of years, the need to communicate with oneself has become almost contagious in recent years. Friends of mine now go away—with spouses—for a week or more to meditate. No sailing, skiing, tennis, or hiking, no way—you've got to get to know your spiritual self better. I've had friends leave the unspiritual isolation of a beautiful Rocky Mountain home or the Maine coastline to find spiritual bliss. Where do you go to meditate? To the splendid isolation of a Canyon Ranch, a La Quinta, or a Greenbriar, of course. Here, you can find solitude within a group at a mere $1,000 a day—and that often includes five-star spa food as well. Maybe this isn't a fad, but only a recession will show if spirituality can be attained alone and on the cheap.

Does the same hold true of fashions in the marketplace? Uncertainty, anxiety, lack of objective reality, and violent shifts in the image of the group drives crowd behavior here, too. Each picture of "reality" was established and maintained by consensus of the group. In every mania, the group was swept by an image of spectacular wealth, which changed its behavior. The new social reality was fabricated of the dreams, hopes, and greed of thousands of investors. Many, watching a particular bubble, have seen this clearly. Yet, most could still believe that things really would be different this time. Almost identical scenarios have been played out over the centuries, whatever the "image" of instant wealth.

The Reinforcement of Group Opinion

Social reality offers an interesting explanation of why crowd behavior can often go off the charts. Research in social psychology demonstrates how easily people are drawn together under conditions of uncertainty and even mild anxiety.

An excellent demonstration was devised by psychologist Muzafer Sherif.[15] Sherif took advantage of the little-known auto-kinetic light phenomenon. A stationary pinpoint of light beamed in a darkened room for a few seconds actually appears to move. Sherif asked his subjects to calculate the extent of the perceived movement as carefully as possible. With no reference points upon which to anchor judgment in the blackened room, individuals gave answers ranging from a few inches to eighty feet—the latter subject believing he was in a gymnasium rather than a small room.

After 100 trial sets, Sherif charted the median guess of each subject. Figure 16–1 shows that it ranged from 1 to over 8 inches (as the line on the extreme left of both charts indicates). However when subjects were brought together, the judgments converged. Figure 16–1 panel a indicates the amount of convergence in each succeeding 100 tests with two people present; Figure 16–1 panel b with three. In the latter case, from individual medians varying from under an inch to almost 8 inches, the group's convergence by the third 100-set test moved to slightly over 2 inches.

Sherif added another variable by including a confederate. If the subject estimated the light moved 20 inches, the confederate might estimate

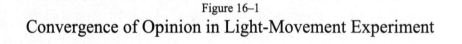

Figure 16–1

Convergence of Opinion in Light-Movement Experiment

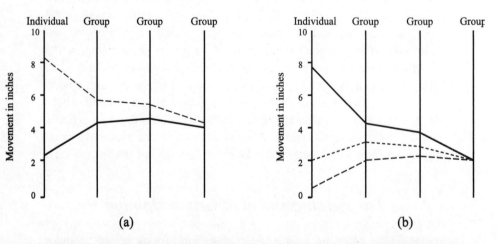

two. His influence was enormous. By the end of the trials, most subject's estimates came very close to those of the confederate's, which remained stable throughout. Without pressure of any sort, a naive subject's judgment could be shifted as much as 80%!

Writing of these experiments, psychologist William Samuels noted:

> The majority of subjects in such studies indicate little awareness that their perceptions have been manipulated by the estimates of others, for they maintain that they had previously made their own estimates before the others spoke. The influence process then may be a rather subtle phenomenon. Partners who are well liked, who have high status, who are reputed to be competent on the judgmental task, or who merely exude self-confidence when announcing their estimates are all especially effective in influencing a subject's personal norm of movements.[16]

Because denizens of the stock market eat uncertainty for breakfast, opinions frequently move toward a consensus, and as in the auto-kinetic light experiment, usually toward the most authoritative sounding or outspoken points of view available—those of the experts. Then throw in anxiety, another powerful force leading toward consensus. The stock market is uncertain and difficult during the best of times, and in its worst moments can induce first-rate terror. People find it natural under such circumstances to take comfort and security in the opinions of savvy, smart money. Small wonder that the consensus of the many looks like refuge, rather than a trap.

Earlier, we saw just how elusive the anchor of objective reality—and concepts of value based on it—actually are. It is not surprising, then, that when reality returned, speculators dashed frantically down the streets of Moscow a few years back, or down Exchange Alley, where "South Sea" shares were traded, two and a half centuries earlier.

How Not to Get Rich

Some readers will quite naturally ask if the strange behaviors viewed in this chapter aren't just anomalies. "True," they might say, "Mackay and Le Bon, although insightful on the behavior of crowds, were, after all, nothing more than keen observers. While Leon Festinger's Theory of Social Reality and other research on group behavior are interesting, is there any evidence that they really work?" In fact, this has always been the economist's chief dispute with the psychologist. "Your hypothesis is interesting, but how widely does it apply?" In short, "Where's the beef?" Let's look at this question through the perspective of investor reaction to initial public offerings (IPOs).

Unfortunately, more knowledgeable investors or no, the perfectly rational person is also not likely to be found in the American IPO markets. These markets too have had periods of euphoria, followed by panics and crashes.

Since the 1960s alone, no fewer than four major IPO bubbles have puffed up and popped, each reaching levels of crowd madness comparable to any in the past. Perhaps this area of what they would surely have regarded as "crowd folly" would have attracted Mackay and Le Bon the most. Mackay would have been fascinated by how the crowd, reinforced by expert thinking, could time and again be stampeded into paying ridiculous prices for companies of little value, only to watch the subsequent panic and freefall. Le Bon would be intrigued by the power of the image that seized expert and average investor alike, and resulted in the same disastrous mistakes only a few years apart.

Each new issue has some cutting edge product or service absolutely guaranteed to coin money. In the IPO market of the early eighties, one of the captivating images was that of new pharmaceutical and other products that would come from genetic engineering. On October 14, 1980, Genentech, then a four-year-old biotechnology company, went public. In an unprecedented 20-minute trading spree, its stock soared from $35 to $89 a share, setting a record for the fastest per-share increase in Wall Street history. Five months later, Cetus, the oldest biotech concern, set another all-time IPO record by raising $107 million. People invested more than $3 billion in genetic engineering research during this period. Investor enthusiasm still continues 17 years later, even though product pickings and market gains have been meager to date. Laboratory breakthroughs do not easily translate into salable products.[17]

But if you're on a roll, who cares what's real and what's puff? People wear blinders against the enormous risks IPOs represent. The Value Line New Issue Survey analyzed a group of proposed IPOs and found that many were start-ups, perhaps 95% dream and 5% product. The survey also found that quite a few had only one or two full-time employees (some had none). The majority attempted to go public with absolutely no earnings at 20 to 100 times their book value prior to the offering. Curiously, most people who bought these issues could pass a Breathalyzer.

Did these folks even care what price they paid for a piece of the action? Apparently not. Recent work done by Robert Shiller,[18] a respected behavioral economist at Yale, shows that if an investor wanted to buy a hundred shares of a company (say at $10), it didn't matter to him if the company had one million shares to sell or, having split, had five million shares. The investor would still pay $10 a share for his hundred shares, even though he now received only a fifth of the presplit profits. It was immaterial to these speculators, Shiller found, because they were convinced the price would go higher. Is this irrational? Of course it is. It borders on the pathological. No sane person would pay five times the price a house was valued at a few minutes earlier. But people look at IPOs differently. Again, they are heavily influenced, if not drugged, by the powerful impact of investor psychology.

The results have been disastrous to investors. In 1994, Professor J. Ritter and Tim Loughran completed the most comprehensive study of new issues made to date. The study followed the returns of 4,753 IPOs traded on the New York Stock Exchange, the AMEX, and Nasdaq between 1970 and 1990.[19] The average return for IPOs was 3% annually compared to 11.3% for the S&P 500. Put another way, investing $10,000 in the S&P 500 over these 20 years would have returned 751%, vs. 81% for the IPOs. The far safer stocks of the S&P did almost ten times as well.

But this wasn't the worst of it. The median return for these almost 5,000 initial public offerings was down 39%. That's right. If you couldn't get that handful of red-hot IPOs that doubled or even tripled on the first trade—and nobody but the largest money managers, mutual funds, or other major investors could—then you'd lose a good chunk of your original investment. You have less chance of making money in the new issue market—and millions of investors play this game —than by betting a single number in roulette.

An earlier study by Professor Ritter showed how trendy new issues were.[20] For example, most new issues go public near the top of an IPO market, when the demand is the greatest and the value of the merchandise is at its lowest. Fully 61% of IPOs went public in 1983, the absolute peak of the 1977 to 1983 mania. How many went public in the first five years when the quality was at its best? Try 6%. The study also showed that the hottest concept industries at the time subsequently performed horribly. After the energy crisis in the late 1970s and early 1980s, superheated oil and gas stocks returned a horrific − 43.9%, vs. 34.7% for the benchmark of established energy companies.

Other studies support the authors' results. H. Nejat Seyhun[21] reported that the market beat a sample of 2,298 IPOs for 6 years, while Mario Levis[22] showed that a group of British IPOs underperformed the U.K. averages for 3 years. Further research indicated that IPO fundamentals fell after the offerings, indicating a deteriorating business picture precisely when investors were most excited by the stock.[23]

Did any IPOs outperform? Yes, value stocks were the anomalies, consistently beating the market according to the earlier Ritter study.

Loughran and Ritter conclude: "Our evidence is consistent with a market where firms take advantage of transitory windows of opportunity by issuing equity when, on average, they are substantially overvalued."[24] The authors might have added that the evidence does not prove that the market is efficient but that stock hucksters certainly are.

Forbes, in a December 1985 cover story, entitled "Why New Issues Are Lousy Investments," came out with similar results.[25] The magazine traced the performance of 2,800 new IPOs between January 1, 1975, and June 30, 1984. After eliminating the penny stocks (whose records are normally far worse) as did Loughran and Ritter, the study measured 1,922 IPOs. The IPOs raised $27.5 billion, of which $2 billion went to the investment bankers. *Forbes* calculated the average appreciation over the period was 3% annually, vs. 14.8% for the S&P 500. The 3% a year is roughly in line with the Loughran-Ritter study.

The *Forbes* study also found that only 4 of 10 stocks went up at all in the 10 years measured. Among the new issues, 1 in 25 ended in bankruptcy, another 1 in 8 was down 95% or more, and almost 50% were down at least 50% versus the averages. According to the *Forbes* study, technology was, not surprisingly, one of the hottest areas. Four big IPO underwriting houses specializing in this area came to be known as the "four horsemen" in 1982/1983, near the last IPO market peak. These houses dished out a multitude of new issues in biotechnology, personal computer companies, software, disk drive companies, and the like. At the time, the issues were so hot that only the largest and best paying clients (in commission dollars for other business) could hope to get even a small fraction of what they wanted. How did these issues, underwritten by the very best of the technology houses, do? The batting average wouldn't make it in Class C baseball.

Alex Brown, one of the most respected technology underwriters, had only 26 of its 82 issues outperform the S&P 500 over the ten-year life of the study. Hambrecht & Quist, another widely respected technology house, showed that 25 of 94 outperformed. L&F Rothschild, Underberg, Towbin had 21 of 88; Robertson, Coleman & Stephens had only 11 out of 45. Remember these issues were sizzlers at the time. Most people could not buy them at the offering prices, but had to pay substantial premiums, making the results far worse. Although a large part of the *Forbes* sample consisted of technology IPOs, less than 20% of the top 100 performers came from this sector. *Forbes* concluded, "Technology, the most glamorous field of all, proved to be a trap for investors."

It did not require a crystal ball to see the end of the mania of the eighties coming. When it came the results were devastating. Technology stocks were decimated, and one of the four horsemen went out of business, while the others pared back their operations drastically—for a time. Biotechnology stocks suffered the same fate. The P/E multiples on new IPOs were chopped in half between mid-1983 and mid-1985, declining from 31.8 to 16.5.[26] The 1983 to 1985 IPO plunge was the worst on record. It occurred even as the largest bull market of the century made sweeping gains, loosening even further the barrier between quality equities and pure speculation.

Here We Go Again

I thought things would cool off for a while after the devastating drop following the 1983 bubble. I was wrong. No matter how much we study the subject, we are shocked anew at the power of "the image" in markets. Even Mackay and Le Bon would have gasped to see how quickly the crowd, after absorbing gut-wrenching setbacks, came back to follow near-identical images.

At this writing, as described above, we are in the largest IPO frenzy on record—one that dwarfs 1983's in size and lunacy. In 1983, $12.5 billion was underwritten in new issues, 70% or 80% of which was lost over the next several years. By 1993, the public poured $34.2 billion into new issues, almost triple the dollar amount they had gambled in 1983, the previous peak year. By 1996, the figure had reached $48.8 billion, dwarfing any IPO mania in the past.[27] Stephen Woodsum, a managing partner of Summit Partners, a Boston-based venture capital firm, marveled, "I don't think we have ever seen a sustained period in which the IPO market was this good."[28] Marvel he might. From 1990 to the end of 1995, the S&P new issue index was up 538% against a rise of 84% for the S&P 500. The gains were again in the realm of fantasy.

Were investors buying new and different concepts this time around? Heck no, the focus was on almost the identical stocks purchased in the last market. Technology, be it computer or medical, satellite or space stocks, was hotter than ever, as were biotech and fast-food stocks. HMOs and health-care companies also got a big play, as did dozens of other exciting ideas.

Billions have been made in IPOs having the least whiff of Internet. Speculators salivated over the Internet much as the French did over the Mississippi Territory, or Eve over the apple. Netscape, a developer of a Web browser, went public in August 1995 at $28 and shot up to $175, where it was priced at a mere 375 times earnings. UUNet, an Internet access provider, went public in May 1995 at $14 and closed the first day at $26. Spyglass was issued at $17 on June 27, 1995, and almost reached $100.

Then there was Yahoo, 1996's hottest new Internet stock. It went public on April 12 at $13 and opened at $24½, running rapidly up to $43, a gain of 231%. Turnover topped 17 million shares, or more than 6 times the 2.6 million shares originally issued. The company, which was founded by a pair of Stanford University students, sported a market value of over a billion dollars the day it was sold to the public. The stock traded at 77 times optimistic forecasts of 1997 revenues. All this on the dream of connecting every American home and—judging from its price—a few extraterrestrials. It's bad taste to even ask about earnings—the company operated at a loss.

IPOs in many other sectors did just as well. Amati Communications, a data-networking company, saw its price rocket 1,651% on lightning-like earnings growth in the 12 months to June 1996. L.L. Knickerbocker, a pint-sized company in home shopping, appreciated 14-fold. Diana Corporation, another recent IPO operating in the "related areas"—at least to hungry buyers—of food and telecommunications, increased 12 times over the same period. Accustaff, a temporary help provider, shot up ninefold over the same 12 months, to a market value of almost $2 billion.

In all, by late June 1996, 682 concept stocks had doubled over the previous 12 months, according to Baseline Data Service, with the overall market up less than 28%.[29] Thirty-five had gained 500% or more, while 114 had quadrupled. The hockey-stick charts were alarming to a number of veteran market observers, who said that even in the go-go years of the 1960s and 1980s, there was never such widespread speculative froth for small- to medium-sized growth companies.

Michael DiCarlo, who managed the hot John Hancock Special Equities Fund (up 72% in the 12 months ending May 31, 1995), was a pro who wasn't worried. He maintained that even a stock that has tripled or quadrupled isn't necessarily overvalued. "If you buy growth at a discount, then a stock can triple in value and it still makes sense to own it," he contended. Mr. DiCarlo, like thousands of others, was betting his clients' money, if not his career, that he could accurately project earnings years into the future. As was demonstrated in chapter 5, the odds are against him.

However, the odds definitely favored the sellers of the hot IPOs, resulting in some minor modifications in their life styles. At 5:59 A.M., on August 2, 1995, according to *USA Today*, Reed Hastings had $8,000 in his bank account and lived in an unheated cottage near San Francisco. At 6:01 A.M., as founder of Pure Software, he was a multimillionaire.[30] Hundreds of his employees have made fortunes or near fortunes in stock options. Secretaries and other lower- and middle-level employees were given stock options worth years of salary.

And the underwriters we met previously, with their not exactly earth-shaking records, were back with bells on. Three of the four horsemen, Hambrecht and Quist, Alex Brown & Sons, and Robertson Stephens, had banner years in 1996. Scores of other investment houses made big bucks selling IPO dreams to enthusiastic buyers.

As Table 16–1 shows, many Internet stocks more than doubled in a few months. What were the facts behind the craze? The theme that dominated an Internet investment conference in mid-1996 was that, popular as it is, nobody knows its ultimate promise, nor, therefore, the prospects for Internet stocks. The potential of the Internet for electronic commerce—ultimately its greatest value—is a gigantic imponderable. Too, none of the companies noted above has a shot at becoming a financial blockbuster unless Internet access becomes much easier, and unless many more people, including the less affluent, embrace it.

In the words of Donna Hoffman, business professor at Vanderbilt University, who is exploring business opportunities on the Internet, "Significant barriers to commercialization, especially on the World Wide Web, preclude the predictable and smooth development of commercial opportunities on this 'hot' new medium."[31]

Table 16–1

STAR WARS IV

Rational Behavior Strikes Back in the IPO Market

Issuer	Business	Issue Date	Offer Price	High	Closing Price 12/31/97	Percent change from high
Netscape	Internet Navigation	8/9/95	28	87	24	− 72%
Spyglass	Internet Technology	6/27/95	17	61	5	− 92%
E-Trade	On-Line Brokerage	8/16/96	10.50	48	23	− 52%
Diamond Multi	Multimedia Technology	4/13/96	17	43	9	− 79%
US Satellites	Satellite Broadcasting	2/1/96	27	39	8	− 79%
Xylan Corp	Networking Products	3/12/96	26	76	15	− 80%
CompuServe	On-Line Service	4/19/96	30	36	12	− 67%
Intuit	Accounting Software	3/12/93	20	89	41	− 54%

SOURCE: PREPARED FROM FACTSET DATA.

Some pundits believe Netscape's net browser software is a dubious source of revenue. Said one in late 1995, "They've gotten 75% of the market by giving their product away. I'd have hoped for 100%."[32] But priced at a cheap 375 times earnings, wasn't it worth the shot? Internet service providers, such as America OnLine, Netcom, UUNet, and other similar sizzlers, dispense dial-up services, which, according to one analyst, are about as close as you can come to a commodity business.

So there you have it: little or no earnings and a big question mark. Many companies will never break even, and those marginally in the black need enormous capital expenditures to support expanding customer bases. All the same, the overwhelming crowd enthusiasm and enormous price run-ups made investors believe the Internet was the greatest discovery since electricity, or maybe even the wheel. The final sign of a market where social reality diverges widely from the underlying facts is the opinions of experts condoning the speculation.

A cover story in *Business Week* picks up the enthusiasm well:

The IPO market is fueling the innovations that are transforming the U.S. economy into the world's productivity powerhouse. The driving force behind the technological revolution changing the way we live and work is the maverick, the risk-taker—in other words, the entrepreneur. And backing the entrepreneur is the most sophisticated capital market in the world. Says Netscape's [Jim] Clark, "IPOs supply the fuel that makes these dreams go. Without it, you die. . . ."[33]

But are the prices paid for these state-of-the-art tech companies justifiable? For perspective, look back to 1969. Technology had just put men on the moon, while a new way of storing, retrieving, and accessing vast amounts of data was revolutionizing record-keeping. In the hot new-issue market of the period, no price was too high for Telex or Memorex, makers of computer tape drives and magnetic tapes. They also led the field in the new and advanced technology of disk drives. Nobody, certainly not stodgy IBM, could catch them. The market for disk drives and other storage devices seemed unlimited.[34]

The market bid up the price of Telex from $44 in August of 1969 to $142 the following February, and Memorex's stock from $80 to $174 in the same period. It didn't work quite that way, however. IBM survived, and along with numerous others, competed effectively. Price of storage devices fell. Eventually, Memorex and Telex merged, later the combined company filed for Chapter 11.[35] Investors lost everything. Now consider that the price rises of these companies in the go-go market of the late sixties, long considered the classic example of IPO speculation, are a fraction of the gains of the Internet stocks and other IPO winners in the present bubble.

Devastating Changes in Perception

Many of us believe a collapse is inevitable. The only question is when. However, even without an IPO crash, the leading new issues have dropped significantly as investors reassess their initially optimistic outlook. Professor Ritter, in mid-March of 1997, measured the performance of the 21 hottest new IPOs for the previous four years. The list included Boston Chicken, Yahoo, Netscape, Shiva, and Tivoli Systems. To make this elite group, the stocks had to run up at least 100% from their initial offering price by the end of the first day of trading (the point at which most investors could initially buy the stocks). How did the princes of the IPO market do from here on? Poorly. This elite group fell 60% from their highs by late December 1997.

Table 16–1 also shows how fast investor perceptions can change; some of the red-hot Internet concepts were down 50–90% or more from their highs by the end of 1997. Why were so many Internet stocks abandoned in the midst of a heated bull market? "Investors have become more realistic about how long it will take for many of the Internet companies to show any profit," according to Richard Shaffer, a principal of Technologic Partners, a New York-based technology research firm.[36]

The money managers and investors who bought those issues either forgot or did not know what had happened in past bubbles. This time was surely different.

Not Very Different

Psychology and the Stock Market, Contrarian Investment Strategy, and *The New Contrarian Investment Strategy* all discussed the characteristics of manias. What surprises me is how quickly the list has grown. Since 1977, when *Psychology and the Stock Market* was published, three new IPO bubbles have floated by.* This almost doubles the number of domestic bubbles in this century. The new manias have taken

---

* The IPO manias of 1976 to 1983 and 1989 to 1997, the gambling stock mania of 1979 to 1983, and in addition, the worldwide real estate craze of the second half of the eighties.

place in much more sophisticated markets, with more knowledgeable investors who, because of more stringent SEC regulations, are much better informed than any group in the past. Yet the characteristics of crowd behavior Mackay describes and Le Bon analyzed, though they go back centuries, closely resemble the U.S. markets of the past three decades. It is also remarkable how predictable and repetitive these crowd actions in markets are.[37]

Market history directly contradicts our academic friends who theorized that investors were always rational, completely unemotional creatures. Investors continually overestimate the outlook for some investments and underestimate the prospects of others. Often the euphoria or pessimism goes to extremes. Here we come to an important rule that we will observe time and again.

RULE 41

A given in markets is that perceptions change rapidly.

When they do, the values of favorite investments can wither quickly to a fraction of their previous prices, while unfavored investments are suddenly reevaluated sharply higher.

There is a common denominator among the South Sea Bubble, the IPOs, and stocks on the telecommunications superhighway. People driven by powerful cognitive and group psychological forces are far too optimistic or too pessimistic about the outlook for a stock, an industry, or the market. It doesn't matter whether we are looking at Florida swampland in the mid 1920s, the boom then bust in the real estate or the art markets in the eighties and early nineties, or IPOs in 1997.

The following table looks at manias in different eras. They range from tulipmania (when rare tulip bulbs sold for more than today's top-of-the-line Mercedes), through the English South Sea and French Mississippi bubbles of the early eighteenth century, to the manias of the past 75 years. As you can see, prices swing enormously when investor expectation changes from ebullient to pessimistic. The fate of American investors pursuing hot IPOs and concept stocks in the sixties, seventies, eighties, and nineties was not much different from that of the frenzied Dutch, English, and French crowds centuries earlier.

Four general principles seem to emerge from a study of financial speculations. First, an irresistible image of instant wealth is presented, forming a crowd around it.

Second, a social reality is created. Opinions converge and become "facts." Experts become cheerleaders approving events and exhorting

Table 16–2
MARKET BUBBLES THROUGH THE AGES

	High Price	*Low Price*	*Price Decline from High (in Percent)*
Holland, 1637			
Semper Augustus (tulip bulb)	5,500[a]	50[a]	99%
England, 1720			
South Sea Company	1,050[b]	129[b]	88%
France, 1720			
Mississippi Company	18,000[c]	200[c]	99%
IPO Bubble, 1961–62			
AMF	66⅜	10	84%
Brunswick	74⅞	13⅛	82%
Lionel	37⅞	4½	88%
Transitron	42⅜	6¼	85%
IPO Bubble, 1966–70			
Leasco Data Processing	57	7	88%
Litton Industries	104	15	86%
National Student Marketing	143	3½	98%
University Computing	186	13	93%
IPO's, 1979–90			
Ask Corp	130⅝	1/32	100%
Cullinet Software	33⅜	4⅛	88%
Floating Point Systems	46	7/16	99%
IPO's, 1989–97[d]			
Boston Chicken	41½	6 7/16	84%
Secure Computing	64½	11 13/16	82%
Objective Systems	56½	8⅜	85%
Shiva	87¼	8 9/16	90%

[a] FLORINS; [b] POUNDS STERLING; [c] LIVRES; [d] "LOW PRICE" = CLOSING PRICE ON DEC. 31,1997.

the crowd onward. Overconfidence dominates, standards and experience of many years are forgotten.

Third, the image in the Le Bon magic lantern suddenly changes, and anxiety replaces overconfidence. The distended bubble breaks and panic ensues.

Fourth, we do not, as investors, learn from our mistakes—things really do seem different each time, although they are really pretty much the same.

As we have seen, even though the investors of the 1980s and 1990s were armed with exacting fundamental tools, these did not save them from going as wild as the English and French of centuries earlier.

What I hope the chapter demonstrates, then, is that the cognitive biases we examined in chapter 10 often can be reinforced by expert, crowd, or group opinion in the marketplace. The result is the irrational investor behavior we have just reviewed.

I am sure you can see the striking dichotomy between the rationality assumed by the EMH advocates and what we saw of cognitive biases and crowd behavior. We have yet to capture even a snapshot of the EMHers' rational man. Instead, we have frame after frame of frenzied investors, in Bourse after Alley after Street, paying ridiculous prices for companies with little but sizzle, and ultimately, little hope of survival, let alone staggering profits. Something is amiss. Are the academic researchers and the market historians looking at behavior on the same planet?

The final chapter provides the answer to this question.

17

Beyond Efficient Markets

THERE is a much quoted line from George Santayana you have likely heard. "Those who cannot remember the past are condemned to repeat it."[1] (Although the world of finance seems chock full of good examples, Mr. Santayana was a philosopher, not an economist.) However, rarely, if ever, noted is what immediately precedes this famous one liner: "Progress, far from consisting in change, depends on retentiveness." Which suggests, to cast it in more specific terms, that your financial progress cannot be secured by embracing the fashion of the moment, whether it is a new stockbroker, a "hot" mutual fund, or the latest wrinkle in market theory. It is in remembering what works—and perhaps more important, what doesn't work—that guidance can be found and a strategy adopted that will serve you well over the long haul.

Much of this book has been a testament to such principles. Based on the historical record, we have examined the results of some of the traditional and current approaches to investing and found them wanting. In particular, we reviewed the development and ascendancy of a powerful new theory of markets, the efficient market hypothesis. Fittingly likened to a new religion, EMH has in the last three decades gained thousands upon thousands of converts, both in the academic institutions and among market professionals. Today, as we know, it affects every aspect of Wall Street thinking.

The theory brought order and structure where there had been chaos and bewilderment. Little opposed the swift conversion. There was nothing better, nothing that could more rationally ravel out the workings of financial markets. More and more investors, taught that fundamental and technical analysis were mere relics of a pagan cult, came to scorn all the "old" ideas.

It has been quite a change as Santayana would dub it, but progress? In a word, no. For as we approached the issue from many possible points of analysis, again we found that the theory could not produce the results EMH claimed were logically, if not mathematically, a foregone conclusion. To start off this chapter, we will take a close look at where EMH and its close ally MPT (modern portfolio theory) stand now. What lies ahead will be startling to some, highly provocative to others. For after an almost unopposed sweep through the marketplace of ideas, and despite fending off every criticism of genuine merit or substance, EMH and MPT both *continue to fail dramatically.*

Even more significantly, these theoretical pillars have failed by the measure of what they held forth as their strength. The statistical methods, for which several leading researchers were awarded Nobel prizes in economics, turned out to be valueless in the marketplace. Yet, even with the scientific underpinnings demolished, the faithful believe and still cling to EMH dogma. For that is what I believe it has become. Ironically, the original apostles of the faith prevailed because of their insistence that it was empirical evidence that mattered, not the dogmas of another day and age of investing.

As we count down the days to 2000, several loud horns outside the walls of this modern investment Jericho seem appropriate. If I can leave you with some counterblasts firmly etched in your mind, it may just wind up saving you a bundle.

There are serious problems with EMH beyond what we found in chapters 3 and 14. Dogma, whether in inappropriate statistics or astrology, will not save you in the marketplace. Everyone is going to want to find a better way, sooner or later. Naturally, the "sooner" will be the investors who are most likely to profit and prosper.

A recapitulation of EMH and MPT is warranted for two reasons. First, it's important to understand how much your investment portfolio depends on this theory. Second, it is necessary to see why these methods fail the reader, in order to be fully comfortable with the new contrarian strategies. There are no labels to warn you away from the EMH–MPT trap—lacking knowledge, you can easily be snared. A flawed theory is not market neutral; it can be destructive to the capital of the average and the sophisticated reader alike.

Understanding is essential to the contrarian approach, particularly during a market crisis, when the investment world seems to be collapsing. People who know what they are doing—and why—are usually the ones who seize the opportunities bobbing in the chaos. In crisis the "black box" investor usually throws away the box and runs.

The failure of these methods also has wide-ranging implications for both investment and economic theory as we enter a new century.

MPT Assumptions Revisited

As we discovered, MPT and EMH are supposedly based on rigorous assumptions, but many of them are highly unrealistic, if not downright foolish. We see in Appendix A a sampling of the gap between the MPT assumptions and reality, and in chapter 14, a similar gap for risk.

But let us ask the hidden question: do we *need* realistic assumptions? Or is EMH, like Riemannian geometry, a system beginning in fantasy and ending in reality? William Sharpe and many others admit that their assumptions may appear unrealistic, but argue they need not be absolutely accurate—this is a virtual impossibility. They point out that "the final test of a model is not how reasonable the assumptions behind it appear to be, but whether the model actually works." They add that this point has been expressed with great clarity and persuasiveness by Milton Friedman: "The relevant question to ask about the assumptions of a theory is not whether they are descriptively realistic, for they never are, but whether they are sufficiently good approximations for the purpose in hand. And the question can be answered only by seeing whether the theory works, which means whether it yields sufficiently accurate predictions."[2]

This brings us to the critical test of both EMH and MPT. Do they yield "sufficiently accurate predictions"? Or have their adherents thrown themselves to their own lions?

Problems, So Many Problems

EMH and MPT are based on the idea that men and women are rational creatures who are risk-averse by definition. People will only take greater risk if they can receive higher returns, and they will take the minimum risk at any level of return. So goes the theory.

Prior to these theories the existence of rationality could not be proved or disproved in any other area of economics. With the evolution of the social sciences and particularly the various branches of psychology, the assumption of rationality has come under heavy fire. Thus there has been an interminable debate between economists and other behavioral scientists about whether man is or is not rational, and an exhaustive number of books and articles written on the subject.

Efficient markets are the natural extension of the last 200 years of economic theory. Here at last was a place to take a stand, a stand that would once and for all establish that people behaved in the rational manner economists have assumed for centuries. Demonstrating that people actually behaved this way in financial markets would be almost akin to discovering the Holy Grail of economics.

It is not surprising then that the original "evidence" by Fama, Blume, Jensen, Scholes, et al., that markets were efficient was enthusiastically greeted by economists, perhaps nowhere more so than at the University of Chicago, one of the renowned bastions of laissez-faire. Equally logical was that Chicago became the intellectual heart of this dynamic new research.

Market economists threw down the gauntlet. So deep was their conviction that these theories would usher in the golden age of markets, if not economics, that they were convinced the statistics would bear them out.

As one academic noted: "You can see why the idea [of perfectly knowledgeable investors in the stock market] is intriguing. Where else can the economist find the ideal of the perfect market? Here is a place to take a stand if there is such a place."[3]

Chapter 14 showed that MPT, the model built to create and test strategies based on efficient markets (anchored on the direct relationship between a stock's volatility and its expected return) had gone down in flames. Investors do not measure risk in the way the theorists expected. The rigorous risk measurements they assumed investors undertook were so complex and required such mathematical ability as to be almost ludicrous.

Still such a risk measure is essential to the concept of efficient markets. Risk, as the researchers defined it, is the core of MPT thinking. Fama and French, for example, state that "If stocks are priced rationally, systematic differences in average returns are due to differences in risk. Thus with rational pricing, size [of company] and book to market must proxy for sensitivity to common risk factors in returns."[4] Fama thus regards the superior performance of contrarian strategies as compensation for investors' taking on additional risk. (However, said risk remains undiscovered, even by sophisticated academics . . . even by Fama himself.)

One wonders why Professor Fama or other investigators just don't go out and ask one or two typical investors who supposedly use these complex risk calculations, exactly how they figure them out. But no, markets are efficient because investors are risk averse, and they are risk averse because markets are efficient. This is the hole that the proud efficient market researchers have dug for themselves.

How strong is the evidence that supports EMH? From what we've seen, this revolutionary theory seems to have been built on the flimsiest of foundations—unkind critics might say a house of cards. The core of the hypothesis—the theory of the rational measurement of risk—was simply an untested assumption of financial academics, which was necessary to bind investment theory to economics. Yet for EMH to be correct it was essential that investors did measure risk in this way. The academics willed it to be true—and continue to do so today.

As noted, many EMH researchers are *still* looking for the market equivalent of the Holy Grail—proof that investors are risk-averse as they have defined it. Though it almost boggles the mind that some of the world's finest economists have trapped themselves in such a logically indefensible position, it follows directly from the economic research models followed in the postwar period.

The Crisis of Modern Economics

The most important reason researchers erred so badly on risk measurement is the manner in which EMH and most other economic investigators conduct their research. Since the Second World War the social sciences have attempted to become as rigorous as the physical sciences. No discipline has put more effort into this goal than economics. Starting about fifty years ago, economists held out high hopes that through mathematics they could make the dismal science as predictable as Einstein's theory of relativity or Kepler's laws of planetary motion. Nobel laureate Paul Samuelson, then a young professor of economics at MIT, was the first to integrate the techniques of differential equations, which had met with such success in physics, into a structured approach which could be used to study virtually any economic problem.

The key assumption was rationality: for a firm it meant maximizing profits, for an individual maximizing his or her economic desires. Rational behavior is the bedrock of Samuelson's work. This dubious platform allowed the economist to merrily build the most complex mathematical models. Economics could now be converted into a precise physical science.

The great majority of economic research gravitated in this direction, despite the warnings of some of the important economic thinkers of the past. John Maynard Keynes, for example, was trained as a mathematician but refused to build his classic theory on unrealistic assumptions. Like his teacher, the great Victorian economist Alfred Marshall, Keynes believed economics was a branch of logic, not a pseudo-natural science.

Marshall himself wrote that most economic phenomena do not lend themselves to mathematical equations, and warned against the danger of falling into the trap of overemphasizing the economic elements that could be most easily quantified.

The Samuelson revolution, however, with its emphasis on complex quantification parroting the physical sciences, came to totally dominate economics in the postwar period. Mathematics, which pre-Samuelson was a valuable but subordinate aid to reality-based assumptions, now rules economics. Good ideas are often ignored by economists simply because they are not written down in pages of highly complex statistical formulas, or don't employ equations using most of the letters of the Greek alphabet. The vast amount of research published in the academic journals contains minuscule additions to economic thinking, but is dressed in sophisticated mathematical models. Bad ideas planted in deep math tend to endure, even when the assumptions are questionable and evidence strongly contradicts the conclusions.

Economic ideas and principles once understood by educated readers are now unfathomable to all but the most highly trained mathematical researchers. This would be well and good if economics had achieved the predictability of a physical science.

But without realistic assumptions the dismal science has been broken down rather than rejuvenated by mathematics. As John Cassidy points out in an excellent article in *The New Yorker,* complex new mathematical theories such as those of Robert Lucas, a Nobel Prize winner from the University of Chicago, while causing a generation of novice economists to build ever more complex models, are discredited in the end, with no agreement on what should replace them.

Lucas's work concluded that the Federal Reserve should not actively guide the economy, but only increase the money supply at a constant rate.[5] The research came under sharp theoretical attack, again because at the core of Lucas's complex mathematical formulas were untenable simple assumptions such as supply always equals demand in all markets. (If this were true we could not have unemployment—the supply of workers would never exceed the demand for them.) Once the supply-demand assumption is dropped, few of Lucas's conclusions hold up. Commenting on the impracticality of Lucas's work, Joseph Stiglitz, then chairman of the President's Council of Economic Advisers, said, "You can't begin with the assumption of full employment when the President is worried about jobs—not only this President, but any President."[6]

Economics, traditionally one of the most important of the social sciences, has suffered a self-inflicted decline. Not all are unaware of this. In 1996 the Nobel Prize for economics was awarded to two men,

William Vickrey, an emeritus professor at Columbia (for a research paper in 1961) and James Mirless, a professor at Cambridge. Although the popular press extolled Vickrey's contribution as breaking fresh intellectual ground in fields as diverse as tax policy and government bond auctions, the professor denied the hyperbole. He said, "[it's] one of my digressions into abstract economics. . . . At best it's of minor significance in terms of human welfare."[7] When interviewed, he talked instead about other unrelated work he had done, which he considered far more important.

The failure of the complex statistical models to provide much insight into current economic problems has resulted in a cutback in hiring of economists by Wall Street and major corporations. Lawrence Myers, who before becoming a governor of the Federal Reserve, ran one of the nation's most successful economic forecasting firms, St. Louis-based Macroeconomic Advisers, said, "In our firm we always thanked Robert Lucas for giving us a virtual monopoly. Because of Lucas and others, for two decades no graduate students were trained who were capable of competing with us by building econometric models that had a hope of explaining short-term output and price dynamics. We educated a lot of macroeconomists who were trained to do only two things—teach macroeconomics to graduate students and publish in the journals. . . . [These economists] don't care what happens out there. [They] don't try to build models which are consistent with the real world."[8]

Complicated statistical analysis is no different in the investment arena, nor should it be, since it's another branch of economics. Simple assumptions are usually necessary as a platform for abstruse statistical methods. More complex assumptions, though far more descriptive of the real world, do not allow the development of the statistical analysis the researchers desire, or the academic journals will publish.

The assumption of total rationality is the mother lode of complex statistical analysis. It eliminates the need for any other psychological assumptions, which, though likely to provide better guidelines to investor behavior in the real world, would vastly complicate the analysis, and probably send it in directions completely away from the researchers' paradigm.

Given the simple assumption of rationality, researchers in the best tradition of the Samuelson Revolution can merrily take off to examine how the totally rational investor will approach markets. They can then use the most complex differential equations or other statistical methodology to discover new results. Whether these assumptions have the remotest connection to reality is irrelevant. Who cares?

Correlations Unlimited

The lack of realistic assumptions leads directly to the next level of error for EMH. Correlations are the lifeblood of the theory. Using complex statistical analysis, researchers often find correlations, which they take as proof of the existence of an important causal relationship. In the world as it is, unfortunately, correlations are frequently pure chance. The derivation of beta, as we saw in chapter 14, is an example of correlation fishing. The researchers simply went back and looked at volatility that seemed to correlate with stock returns in the past, and assumed it was as immutable as Newton's law of gravity—it would work the same way in the future.

One of the important premises laid down in the physical sciences centuries ago was that correlation does not prove causation. Writers on sci-

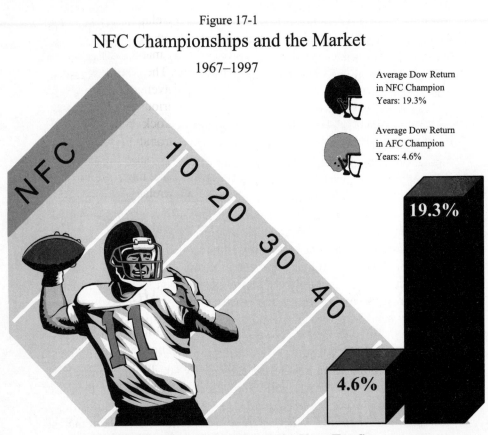

Figure 17-1

NFC Championships and the Market

1967–1997

Average Dow Return
in NFC Champion
Years: 19.3%

Average Dow Return
in AFC Champion
Years: 4.6%

NFC 19 Years, AFC 12 Years (31-Year Total)

entific method warn that findings that appear to support a hypothesis often are pure chance. The correlation may seem convincing, as does the EMH finding that professionals do not outperform the market. But this is not evidence of a cause-and-effect relationship; it does not *prove* the hypothesis that rational investors keep prices in line with real value.

Some Wall Streeters have long been aware of this problem. Two slightly ridiculous examples taken from the investment world will show what I mean. Several decades back, the late Ralph A. Rotnem of Smith Barney noticed a correlation between the height of women's hemlines and the level of the Dow Jones Industrial Average. In the 1920s hemlines rose and stock prices followed; both fell sharply in the early 1930s. In the first years of the 1960s, both hemlines and stocks worked higher. With hot pants the market surged ahead in the early 1970s. Hemlines obviously dictate the course of the Dow Jones Industrial Average. The hypothesis seemed repeatedly vindicated, but I doubt anyone would back this line of reasoning.

Another classic example of such a chance correlation is the NFL-stock market relationship. When a team from the original NFL has won the Super Bowl over its 31-year history, the market has gone up sharply the next year a large percentage of the time. The average is 19.3% over the 19 years they've won. This is double the average rate of return of stocks over time. When the AFC has been victorious, the market has gone up only 4.6%, less than half of the average stock return. The correlation is so strong that the T-test, a test of the probability of it being chance, is less than 1 in 25. But no serious investor believes the Super Bowl victory was the cause of the rising market. Like the hemline indicator, beta, and hundreds of similar academic correlations, it is sheer chance.

But false correlations were but one of the critical challenges to the theory.

The Vanishing Support for EMH

What about efficient markets themselves? Chapter 3 looked at how the theory was constructed and at some of the evidence presented in its support. Because of its impact on contemporary investors' decision-making, it is worthwhile to examine how "efficiency" stands up under scrutiny.

According to Fama,[9] if the necessary conditions for market efficiency are present—i.e. information is readily available to enough investors, and transaction costs are reasonable—there is no evidence of consistently superior or inferior returns to market participants.

Two lines of statistical research have developed purporting to show the efficiency of markets. The first is a group of studies that indicate money managers do not outperform markets, one of the two facets of the semi-strong form of EMH. The second is that markets quickly adjust to new information because of the rapid (and presumably correct) interpretation of events by investors. This tenet assumes that thousands of analysts, money managers, and other sophisticated investors search out and analyze all available information, constantly keeping prices in line with value.[10]

First let's examine the EMH premise that investors cannot consistently make money by using public information to find superior investments. Since it is difficult to assess how investors analyze information to determine undervalued stocks, tests of this premise focus on whether groups of investors have earned superior returns. Because the information is readily available, the group that most frequently serves as guinea pigs is the managers of mutual funds. The research, some of which we have examined, showed that mutual funds do not outperform the major averages, whether risk-adjusted or not (although the risk-adjusted studies are now certainly open to question), which supports the efficient market hypothesis. But wait.

An even more demanding challenge lay directly ahead. For the hypothesis to be invalid, not all investors, but only a reasonable number, are required to beat the market over time. The statistics of the original mutual fund researchers in the sixties and early seventies failed to turn up such above-average performance by any investors, the essential evidence required to make the EMH case.

On closer examination, the efficient market victory vanished. Studies we reviewed in chapter 14 demonstrated that the standard risk-adjustment tools the researchers used were too imprecise to detect even major fund outperformance of the averages. One showed, for example, that using Jensen's technique (one of the important mutual fund investigators) only one manager of the 115 measured demonstrated superior performance at a 95% confidence level (the lowest statistical level normally acceptable).[11]

Even to be flagged on the screen, the manager had to outperform the market by 5.83% annually for 14 years. When we remember a top manager might beat the market by 1½ or 2% a year over this length of time, the returns required by Jensen to pick up managers outperforming the averages were impossibly high. Only a manager in the league of a Buffett or Templeton might make the grade. One fund outperformed the market by 2.2% a year for 20 years, but according to Jensen's calculations, this superb performance was not statistically significant.[12]

In another study using standard risk adjustment techniques, the researchers showed it was not possible at a 95% confidence level to say a portfolio up more than 90% over ten years was better managed than another portfolio down 3%. It was also noted that "given a reasonable level of annual outperformance and variability (volatility), it takes about 70 years of quarterly data to achieve statistical significance at the 95% confidence level."[13]

One researcher, in an understatement, noted that the problem lay in weak statistical tools. Corroborating these findings, Lawrence Summers, later Deputy Secretary of the Treasury in the Clinton Administration, estimated that it would take 50,000 years' worth of data to disprove the theory to the satisfaction of the stalwarts. Indeed the EMH tools were so weak that it proved impossible to delineate even outstanding performance, which by sheer coincidence was the one thing that would invalidate the hypothesis.[14]

In spite of this and other evidence, the conclusions of Jensen's mutual fund study are still used to support the main premise of efficient markets. "There is very little evidence," wrote Jensen at the time, "that any individual fund was able to do significantly better than that which we expected from mere random chance."[15]

Even though risk measurements used by academic researchers were shown by Fama and others to be valueless, mutual fund performance has not been recalculated by EMH defenders to exclude their now refuted definitions of risk. We have just seen how these measurements resulted in outstanding performance not being detected. The records of most managers who consistently outperformed the market were wiped out by statistical gobbledygook.

The ghosts of beta and other academic risk measurements still walk the night, defending EMH and weeding out any above-average performance not permitted by the theory. This is not the only instance of such tactics being employed by the true believers, as we shall see.

Revenants and errors notwithstanding, superior performance could not be completely eliminated by the believers. We'll look at some of the ghost-busters next.

Those Dreadful Anomalies

The major challenge to the semi-strong form of EMH was whether groups of investors or investment strategies could beat the market. According to the hypothesis, none could do so with regularity.[16] The theorists, as we saw in the last section, focussed primarily on mutual funds, and, although the risk adjustment techniques are questionable, the evidence did show that funds as a group did little better or worse than the market over time.

However, this was not the final hurdle because, as noted, not all funds have to do better or worse consistently. In fact EMH makes a stronger statement: that *no group of investors or any investment strategy can do better than the market over time.* That's where the trouble starts.

There are methods, supported by a large body of evidence, that consistently do better than the market, as do some mutual funds and money managers. The $63 billion Magellan Fund, for example, with over a million shareholders, and under three separate money managers, has outperformed the market for well over a decade. So did John Templeton and John Neff, the latter running billions of dollars for the Windsor Fund for over two decades. How are these outstanding records possible using only public information? Is it sheer chance, as EMH adherents are forced to claim? If it is, we must look at how many other institutional investors have outperformed, using statistics that can actually detect superior performance, not filter it out inadvertently as Jensen's methods did. Whether large numbers of professional investors outperform or underperform the market is not settled, as the efficient marketeers would like to think; it's wide open. The emphatic statement by these academics that the research available corroborates its central tenet, that professionals perform in line with the market, is impossible to accept without further evidence.

However, while the jury may still be out on the last point, it has come in with a unanimous decision on another. The verdict is solidly against EMH. The tenet that managers do not outperform or underperform a market benchmark has a corollary: there is no method or system that can consistently provide higher returns over time. This may be the Waterloo of the hypothesis.

As we saw in chapters 6 to 9, a considerable body of literature demonstrates that contrarian strategies have produced significantly better returns than the market over many decades. The explanation for this explicitly contradicts the central tenet of EMH—that people behave with almost omniscient rationality in markets. As students of scientific method would anticipate, findings that threatened the existing beliefs were not met with garlands and victory parades by the new conquistadors.

Too, the Value Line ranking system has irked efficient market theorists for 30 years by demonstrating that an investor following its number one or number two rankings (its highest ranking classifications) would have outperformed the market handily. The Value Line System was tested by Fischer Black, one of the deans of EMH, who found that the odds of it being pure chance were infinitesimal.[17] This anomaly was also bothersome to the theory and resulted in a number of articles: some suggested risk-adjustment, others trading costs, others gleefully noting recent performance had slipped—unfortunately, it picked up again. The superior performance stood!

The tenet that no group of investors and no strategies should consistently underperform in an efficient market is another rock EMH founders on. Below-market performance has been turned in for decades by people who buy favorite stocks, as we saw in detail when we examined contrarian strategies. Another significant underperformance, as we have seen, is the research that shows that IPOs have been dogs in the marketplace for 20 years.[18] So overperformance and underperformance, for long periods, neither of which the semi-strong form of EMH states is possible, show us both sides of the anomaly coin.

The anomalies show no sign of going away after two decades of challenge; rather, they have been gaining increasing strength in the last few years, as dozens of articles examine contrarian effects. The most important anomaly—strategies that beat the averages over extended periods—has been documented by Eugene Fama himself. His own data contradict his contention that efficient markets have held up well, since by definition, no method can beat the market over time.

This large body of contradictory research defies the believers in efficient markets to dismiss or explain. Thus goes the first major canon of efficient markets. The glaring anomaly holes this major tenet of EMH below the waterline.

The Jury Is Out Again

The second major canon of EMH is the hypothesis that all new information is analyzed and almost immediately and accurately reflected into stock prices, thus preventing investors from beating the market. That the market reacts to some events quickly has been demonstrated by a number of researchers, as we saw in chapter 3. Stock splits do not result in higher prices, they state, indicating that this information is already reflected in their prices. The market reacts quickly to the announcement of mergers and acquisitions, they claim. They offer other, similar studies that seemingly back the semistrong form of EMH. Do these studies provide the convincing evidence the adherents claim?

The landmark study to show prices adjust to new information quickly was done by four leading researchers of the then-new faith—Eugene Fama, Lawrence Fisher, Michael Jensen, and Richard Roll. They examined all stock splits on the New York Stock Exchange from 1926 through 1960.[19] The results the investigators arrived at, using extremely sophisticated statistical techniques for the time, appear in Figure 17–2. The chart is adjusted to illustrate the returns for stock splits relative to the market on a monthly basis for the 29 months prior to the split and the 30 months following it.* (The distribution date of the new stock from the split is month 0 on the horizontal axis, and the 29 months preceding it are marked from –29 to 0. After the split, prices are followed in an identical manner to month 30.)

The above-average returns are measured on the vertical axis, on a cumulative basis, starting at month –29. The more steeply the dotted line rises, the higher the return relative to the market in the month. Figure 17–2 indicates that for the 29 months prior to the split, returns are high relative to the market compared to their historical relationship. After the splits, the returns are in line with their long-term relationships, and do not outperform the market. The authors conclude that their work provides strong support for the hypothesis that the market is efficient.

This study has been cited hundreds of times in academic papers and has been taught to tens of thousands of graduate students as one of the major research works upholding market efficiency. All the same, the findings may not support the researchers' conclusions but might present evidence that directly contradicts their claim that markets are efficient.

The researchers did not measure the right period in which news of a split would affect stock prices. The information enters the market at the time of the announcement (between months –4 and 0 on the chart), most often 2 to 4 months before the split is distributed. As noted, according to the semi-strong form of EMH, the news of stock splits is factored into prices almost immediately. By the time of the distribution of the split (point 0), the news was up to 4 months old, and the informational content was already fully reflected in the stock prices. The announcement date is the proper measuring point, as it is for earnings surprises, dividend increases or decreases, or other announcements that can have a major impact on stock prices.

---

* Strictly speaking, the chart shows "cumulative average residuals," which is statistical jargon saying that many effects—in this case the market return, the company's historical return, risk, etc.—have been taken into account. For our purposes, "cumulative above-market return" will suffice.

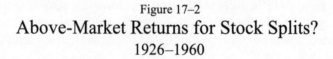

Figure 17–2
Above-Market Returns for Stock Splits?
1926–1960

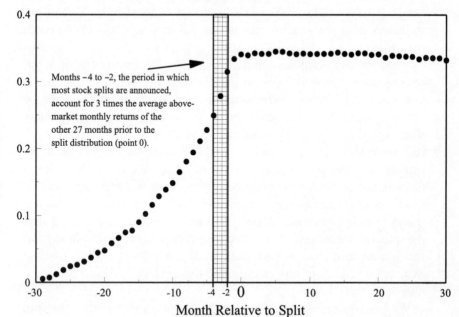

Month Relative to Split

Source: "The Adjustment of Stock Prices to New Information," *International Economic Review*,
February 1969, p.13. (Modified to show months -4 to -2.)

Instead, the academics used the month in which the stock split was actually distributed (Figure 17–2, month 0) as the starting point. Measuring of stock returns up to 4 months after the announcement date is almost meaningless.

From examining the chart it is obvious that the steepest run-up occurs during the time of the announcements of splits. In fact, the average extra monthly return for the four months in which the splits are announced is almost double the above-market returns in the previous 25 months. Fully 27% of the above-average return for the 29 months prior to the split distribution takes place in the 4 months in which the stock splits were announced. Moreover, 19% of this return occurred in the third and fourth months prior to the stock distribution. The returns during this time—which, as noted, is normally the period in which most stock splits are announced—are 3.3 times the above-market monthly return for the other 27 months before the splits were distributed.

This raises a difficult problem for the researchers. Given that by far the sharpest rise for the 29 months before the split distribution comes in this period, (months −4 to −2 in Figure 17–2), they must claim that all the price run-up took place before the split announcements in this period, or that the adjustment to the new higher prices came almost immediately after the announcements, so that investors could not benefit from them.

What the chart appears to show, assuming the majority of split announcements occurred 2 to 4 months prior to the stock distribution, is that stocks may indeed have provided above-average returns after the announcement date. The spike in prices in this period—again, more than triple the average high residual return of the previous 26 months—just seems too large to indicate otherwise. The adjustment to new information, then, appears not to have been immediate but to have taken place for some time, possibly weeks after the split's announcement. If this is the case their argument is invalid. The most logical conclusion is that the stocks continued to rise as a group for an extensive period after the split announcement. If true, the researchers' findings would support inefficiency, not efficiency in markets. However, the jury must be out until a clear-cut study supporting either this analysis or the authors' conclusion is carried out.

Why did the researchers not start their measurements when the split was announced, since they explain several times in the paper that this is the date that the new information enters the market? The answer was that the announcement date simply was not in their database.* Perhaps this was fortunate. If it were possible to place the split at the correct point, as the above analysis indicates, the conclusion might have been different.

The researchers don't stop there. They attempt to show an investor cannot benefit from the rapidly rising prices during the period of the split announcements. Not knowing the date of the announcements for the overall sample, or being able to measure from this point, makes this conjecture. Finally, in examining the returns after the split is distributed, the investigators say that since investors get no extra returns from this time on (point 0 on the chart) it's strong evidence that markets are efficient.

The statistics in the study seem to be interpreted differently for the varying time periods. For the original run-up from month −29 to months

---

* Except for a sample of only 52 of 904 splits, or under 6%, which the authors say supports their case.

−4 to −0, the higher prices are accepted as evidence that positive information pushes prices higher. For the 4 months during the stock split announcements themselves, when prices are rising fastest, the analysis concludes investors cannot profit from the information. After the split is distributed, they state the market correctly interprets the information. The conclusion reached, naturally, is that markets are efficient.

The major criticism of this study is that the researchers built a sweeping conclusion, by measuring the wrong date, that the split information would not affect the stock prices. As a result, the study does not "prove" that stock splits have no effect on stock prices—in fact the chart indicates that they very well might have, although, as noted, until the proper measuring point is used the jury is out on this question. What is more important is how the study has been used as strong support of efficient markets given the questions that have just been raised.

Finally, even if the researchers had measured from the right time periods and they could show that stock splits had no effect on prices—which the evidence seems to dispute—there is another serious problem with the study and others similar to it that attempt to demonstrate market efficiency by examining a simple event. We will examine this question shortly.

This study is considered by many as the best known supporting EMH. Without it and others that also have significant problems, the second pillar of EMH—that investors process information quickly and correctly—collapses.

More of the Same

Let's look at other studies that claim the market adjusts quickly to new information. The first was performed by Ball and Brown in 1968.[20] The two investigators examined the normal rates of return from 1946 to 1966 for 261 firms. They divided the stocks into two groups, those whose earnings in a given year increased relative to the market, and those whose earnings decreased. The performance was measured after each year end. They found that stocks whose earnings increased outperformed the market, while those that decreased underperformed the market. The researchers concluded the stock prices had already anticipated most of the news of earnings announcements.

The theorists overlooked one simple fact, well known to practitioners. Companies normally report quarterly (or, rarely, semiannually), not annually. The SEC has for many years required public companies to report this information within 90 days. Furthermore, even back then, analysts provided research reports on how companies were faring, supplemented often by press releases from company spokesmen. The researchers state that investors correctly judged the prospects of companies and thus determined the movement of their stock prices, when most times they actually had the information in hand to do so. To conclude the market is efficient from this rather obvious finding is stretching the point.

Another supposedly awesome bit of evidence to support the hypothesis was a study by Myron Scholes in 1972.[21] Scholes analyzed the effect of secondary offerings of stock and concluded that, on average, a stock declined 1% or 2% when such an offering is made. The largest declines resulted from the sale of stock by corporations or corporate officers. He also stated that the full price effects of a secondary are reflected in six days. Scholes concluded that since the SEC does not require the identification of the seller until six days after the offering, the market anticipates the informational content of the secondary, and is therefore efficient. Here again is a sweeping conclusion based on nominal price movements over a short period of time.

Secondary offerings normally bring stock prices down temporarily; this is almost a platitude. What is important is whether the stocks are brought down appropriately. How do they perform relative to the market 3, 6, or 12 months later? Too, many brokers disclose beforehand who the sellers are. To state the market anticipates this information, because the SEC does not require it, is a chancy conclusion. Often this information is provided anyway.

Several other studies examined how quickly markets integrate new information into stock prices. The first considers how companies react to the announcement of merger and tender offers. Fama, in his 1991 review of efficient markets, states,

> [I]n mergers and tender offers, the average increase in stock prices of target firms in the three days around the announcement is more than 15%. Since the average daily return on stocks is only .04% (10% per year divided by 250 trading days), different ways of measuring expected returns have little effect on the inference that target shares have large abnormal returns in the days around merger and tender announcements.[22]

EMH theorists, including Professor Fama, undoubtedly the most respected one of the day, make a major mistake in assuming that because stocks do respond to new information that they are also responding correctly. The event studies provide no evidence that this is the case. *They simply show that a merger or an acquisition moves prices.* To use a chess analogy, it's like concluding that if I move a chess piece after a move by Gary Kasparov or "Deep Blue" (take your pick), the fact that I pushed the piece puts me on their level of play. Nonsensical yes, but also the essence of the "proofs" of the theory.

The correct measurement would be not how firms respond in the three days around the initial merger or acquisition announcement, but how they respond relative to the price offered and the possibility of a higher offer (as was often the case through much of the 1980s, particularly with a hostile tender offer). The 15% that stocks appreciate around the date of the initial announcement of an offer is only a fraction of the approximately 30% or larger increase that shareholders receive when the offer is consummated. Even allowing for the occasional offer that is dropped, the first tender price appears far too low. The market again seems to be incorrect in its initial pricing of tender offers and mergers.

No evidence is provided that the initial reaction to the news is the correct reaction, as prices move up far too frequently from the trading levels following the announcements. This premise spawned a generation of risk arbitrageurs, who have made enormous returns on their capital.

Other Evidence Against Efficiency

While evidence of efficiency is quite a bit rarer than the theorists might admit, the evidence that markets do not adjust quickly to new information keeps mounting. Additionally Michaely, Thaler (one of the pioneers of behavioral finance), and Womack studied the subject in 1994.[23] The three researchers measured how stocks behaved after a dividend cut or increase during the 1964 to 1988 period. In the year after the announcement of a dividend cut, the average stock underperformed the market by 11%, and by 15.3% for the three-year period. In the year following a dividend increase it outperformed by 7.5%, and by 24.8% for the three years afterwards.[24] This study indicates again that markets do not adjust to new information quickly.

A number of other studies have shown that the market is slow to digest new information. Several researchers have found that when a company reports an earnings surprise (that is, a figure above or below the consensus of analysts' forecasts), prices move up when the surprises are positive, or down when they are negative, for the next three quarters.[25] Abarbanell and Bernard, as noted in chapter 6, have shown that analysts don't adjust their earnings estimates quickly after past mistakes.[26] The "buy and hold" contrarian strategies presented in chapters 8 and 9[27] demonstrated that "best" and "worst" stocks continued to outperform and underperform the market respectively for periods up to nine years.

These findings then appear to shoot another arrow through EMH.

Finally, Robert Shiller, a leading behavioral economist, argues that if markets were efficient, then looking back at history, stock market prices at a given time should be related to prices that we can say are "rational."[28] To find out if this is true, he looked back at prices that would be considered rational in light of dividends subsequently paid. The study covers the 1871 to 1979 period.

Shiller found the rational index he created after the fact follows a smooth and stable path, whereas the actual market index veers sharply above or below it for extended periods, displaying substantial volatility in doing so.

Shiller concludes: "[S]tock price volatility over the past century appear[s] to be far too high . . . to be attributed to new information about future real dividends."[29] In other words, markets over this long term did not respond accurately to information, but rather moved far higher or lower than was warranted by it.

A Leap of Faith

Even if the studies purporting that markets are efficient were not problematical, there is a much more serious question about them that was initially raised in chapter 4. The scientific findings were far too modest to justify the researchers' all-encompassing and revolutionary conclusions. What proof did the researchers have that the markets respond not only immediately but correctly to new information? None. They accepted market reaction to uncomplicated information as proof positive, not simply of reaction, but of the correct price reaction to the event. The investigators never attempted to test investors' ability to interpret far more complicated information, such as we've viewed throughout the text.

The pattern is common not only to EMH studies, but to most areas of mathematical economics. The researchers are very rigorous in their statistical analysis, but extremely liberal, if not specious, in their interpretation of broader issues. We saw this in their presentation of the studies that attempted to prove markets are efficient. The work looked at obvious examples that news affects markets. These findings, which one could call "slivers of efficiency," lead the researchers by quantum leaps to much broader conclusions. If markets can be impacted by news of mergers or secondary offerings, the reasoning goes, they must be equally capable of gathering and interpreting complex data about companies and industries, economic, monetary, and financial conditions, and the market itself.[30]

One must marvel at the boldness of these scholars, to build an all-encompassing theory on such flimsy evidence. It is an enormous leap of faith from these simple findings to the conclusion that the market correctly interprets all information, no matter how complex, almost instantaneously.

This is like saying that if my then six-year-old daughter could count to 100 without difficulty, she should also be able to comprehend the theory of relativity. While I'm sure that, if asked, she would have readily given me an answer to this, as she did to anything else, somehow I think it would miss the mark.

The Problem of Interpreting Information

The obvious next question is, how good are investors' interpretive capabilities? Even if the EMH studies are correct, do they prove markets are efficient?

The interpretation of information, as we have seen, is anything but easy. It is influenced by the psychological mood of the time, the response of market experts, the complexity of the data, and a host of other inputs. Examining the effects of a stock split is far simpler than deciding the proper level for bank shares in the midst of the 1990 financial crisis.

Let us examine the seemingly simple statement that enough buyers and sellers are aware of the meaning of all public information to keep prices in line with value. This statement subsumes two complex premises. If either can be shown to be inaccurate, the hypothesis can be dismissed on yet another count.

The first premise assumes investors not only have complete knowledge but can correctly interpret all information, past and present.

The second premise assumes that the sophisticated investors in the marketplace are rational in the classic economic sense of excluding all behavioral influences but one, the maximization of gain or the minimization of loss. Given new information, then, decision-making is as routine, automatic, and mechanical as the changing of a traffic light.

We have seen how difficult interpretation of information actually is. Perhaps this is why analysts so often project current trends to arrive at earnings forecasts or investors bet heavily on trendy stocks.

Although there is often a consensus by many sophisticated investors on the course of the market or the value of individual stocks, the difficulty of interpretation alone can push them far off the mark.

That investors obtain and correctly interpret not hundreds, but thousands, perhaps millions, of recondite facts is bedrock to the theory. This immensely complex undertaking, never subjected to testing, must be seriously questioned.

Summing It All Up

Unfortunately when put to the test, the tenets of EMH ring like a string of stunning military defeats. None of the risk measurements that the academics credit to rational investors have stood the test of time. The two key predictions of the theory, that investors cannot consistently beat the market and that markets respond to new information quickly or accurately, have both been discredited.

Finally, there is the major problem with the EMH assumption that investors can interpret vast amounts of data. Findings in cognitive psychology and other psychological disciplines demonstrate that this assumption is not accurate. To carry the chess analogy one step further, although millions play chess, there is only a score of Grand Masters, and only one Gary Kasparov (or to date one "Deep Blue"). If people are not equally adept at interpreting the complex world of the chessboard, can they be any better at interpreting the more complex and significantly more emotional world of markets? The simple EMH tests discussed previously showed that markets respond to new information; they did not demonstrate they responded correctly.

Towers Built in Sand

The history of science teaches us that, given capable, intelligent people, large errors normally do not occur in the development of a case, but rather in the assumptions upon which the work is based. Powerful statistical techniques without realistic assumptions take on a life of their own. As bad currency drives out good, three decades of bad constructs in finance and economics have driven out good science, leaving few useful contributions for the enormous effort expended.

To be fair, the concept of efficient markets has come under attack even by financial academics. Edward Saunders, using the work of Karl Popper, one of the important theorists on scientific method in the last half of the twentieth century, criticizes the scientific approach of EMH.[31] Popper stated in a famous analogy that to prove the theory that all swans are white, the researchers should not concentrate their efforts searching for more white swans. On the contrary they should search for black swans, because finding even one would destroy the theory.[32] EMH researchers have not followed Popper's teachings. Not only have they continued to search for white swans, but they have put together an unrelenting campaign to extinguish black swans—the anomalies that cannot exist if EMH is correct.

Thomas Kuhn in his classic work, *The Structure of Scientific Revolutions*,[33] takes a tolerant approach to the issue. It is essential, Kuhn writes, for scientists to have a paradigm from which to work. A paradigm, as you may recall from chapter 1, is the current body of theory the scientific community in a field accepts and works within.

Like an accepted judicial decision, says Kuhn, the paradigm is the body of knowledge that is used as a frame of reference from which to conduct new work. "Paradigms gain their status because they are more successful than their competitors in solving a few problems that the group of practitioners has come to recognize as acute."[34] Thus, efficient markets in the early years provided the explanation of prices fluctuating randomly, which showed why technicians could not consistently outperform markets. It provided a body of studies that appeared to indicate the market reflected new information almost instantaneously, thereby making it impossible for investors to act on it to outperform the averages.

Kuhn notes that "normal science does not aim at novelties of fact or theory and, when successful, finds none."[35] As the paradigm becomes widely accepted, its tools and methods become more deeply rooted in the solution of problems. The accepted tools for broadening the efficient market paradigm were beta and MPT.

The goal of normal science is not to question the reigning paradigm, but to explain the world as viewed through it. Anomalies that contradict the basic tenets of the paradigm are a serious challenge to it. A paradigm must be able to explain the anomalies or it will eventually be abandoned for a new one that does provide explanations that the first one cannot.

Thus scientists would naturally defend their paradigm. They prefer to believe that all swans are white and do not search for black ones. If they find black swans—the anomalies to EMH are such an example—they try to explain them within the theory. A change in a paradigm is a nerve-racking and difficult period with much acrimony.*

---

* Change undermines their basic approach. EMH and other such economic axioms allow people to proceed in the manner they know best. They are, after all, trained far more thoroughly in statistical method than in behavioral psychology.

Its adherents have a vested interest in upholding the validity of the old paradigm, because all their knowledge and experience is tied up in it. Rejecting their paradigm is often equivalent in a literal sense to rejecting their religion. Kuhn writes that many older scientists will never give up the current paradigm, others accept parts of it and try and integrate the old with the new. Usually, it takes a new generation of researchers to completely accept a new paradigm.

Kuhn also brings up a critical point. Scientists will never abandon a paradigm, no matter how harsh the criticism, unless they have a more compelling one to take its place, one that will solve most of the problems the old one could not. It is not surprising then, that even with the major challenges put to EMH, the hypothesis has not been abandoned. Even when the central tenets of the theory have been destroyed empirically, it lives on; as with Hydra, when one head is chopped off, two new ones grow in its place. Thus, when beta was destroyed, the deans of efficient markets stated there was another measure of risk out there waiting to be discovered; or when some value methods were shown to outperform the market, they claimed they were more risky. EMH is following the precise course of scientific discovery that Kuhn predicted.

Kuhn notes that new research is not only rejected, but its adherents have at times been punished. Thus, Bruno, a Renaissance poet and philosopher, was burned at the stake and Galileo was imprisoned. The fact that EMH researchers seem intolerant of work that opposes their theory is certainly predicted by the history of scientific discovery. Perhaps not surprisingly, there is no forum for dissenting thought, as the academic journals normally do not publish work they consider at odds with their paradigm, including that of knowledgeable Wall Streeters and psychologists.

Too, EMH adherents are not above attacking research that disagrees with the beliefs. In the early eighties for example, both *Barron's* and *Forbes* ran feature stories questioning the efficacy of EMH. The result was an onslaught of critical letters from hundreds of academics that lasted for months. The most common theme was, how could the magazines dare to challenge the work of the distinguished researchers?

Another disagreeable characteristic of changes in paradigms, demonstrated again with EMH, is the researchers' noticeable silence when they meet a challenge to their work that they cannot answer, as with the small cap theory and, for a long time, with beta and contrarian strategies.

Finally, as I noted in chapter 7, some of the researchers are not above taking credit for anomalies first found by nonacademic researchers— sometimes a decade or more before them. Perhaps even worse, the academic journals are, in effect, "in the pockets" of the major EMH researchers. They are not above publishing this work as being "newly discovered" by members of their group.

This then is the dark side of EMH. But, put it in context; it is not very different from the protest and rancor when any established body of knowledge is threatened by inexplicable facts.

If I have been somewhat harsh on EMH, it is because I cannot accept the manner in which its case has been built. Although I do not believe the hypothesis, I certainly respect the arduous experimental efforts made by the many researchers in this area. They have brought the winds of change to Wall Street, long overdue. Investors who are really interested in how the market works must genuinely appreciate these university researchers. Much of the research was necessarily tedious, dull, and time consuming, but it was essential in building the foundation of a new investment structure.

Without the thorough measurement of technical and fundamental performance records, Wall Street would have continued in the old, unsuccessful—often disastrous—ways, with no impetus toward change.

The New Paradigm

We have come a long way in the last 400 pages, from examining and rejecting conventional mores to finding a new and well-documented investment paradigm. This paradigm has its roots firmly imbedded in the psychology of the marketplace. As we now know, all the anomalies have one common denominator—investor psychology.

Psychology is both the reason for the consistently superior performance of the methods the financial academics cannot explain, as well as the consistently poorer results of those approaches that fail. Yet, psychology is not only misunderstood, but ruled out at source by most of the current generation of financial scholars.

The study of investor behavior in markets is still in an embryonic stage. Although we can statistically trace pattern after pattern of investor behavior, we know little of the dynamics of the complex interactions of cognitive, group, and other psychological forces that underlie them. Psychology offers the marketplace the opportunity to gain a much clearer understanding of what causes predictable behavior. The marketplace in turn offers the various branches of psychology a major laboratory to pinpoint patterns of behavior unlikely to be as statistically documented in such depth anywhere else.

Even if you agree with what I have written, it won't be an easy row to hoe. Psychological forces and conventional wisdom will continually tug us away from the investment decisions that have the highest chances of succeeding and towards the mediocre. Given the right circumstances, we'll convince ourselves we're seeing green, when we are actually sitting in one of the red rooms of our casino, betting away a big chunk of our savings.

Still, you have a good chance of doing well, if you can keep in mind the principles that drive contrarian strategies, and stay clear of the behavioral pitfalls that have taken their toll on so many generations of investors. When I wrote my first book, *Psychology and the Stock Market*, more than two decades ago, I was convinced that once readers saw clearly how effective a low P/E strategy was, and the reasons it worked, everyone would be on this bandwagon in a flash. The bandwagon is still empty 20 years later, although there are scores of self-professed contrarians around.

Contrarianism is more a catch-all term to describe counter-opinion to any aspect of markets, rather than the disciplined investment strategies outlined in this book. Thus Robertson Stephens has a contrarian fund that it advertises extensively in *The Wall Street Journal.* Its "contrarian strategies" are light-years away from those described in this book. There are also contrarian technicians, market timers, and from what I've read, astrologers.

No, the amazing thing is that even though many contrarian strategies are well known on the Street, they are not nearly as widely followed as I would have expected after more than two decades, in spite of the fact that the evidence supporting them has grown almost exponentially. Knowing the power of psychology on investment decisions back in 1977, I still badly underestimated its ability to inhibit winning strategies.

This is not bad news. For it means you have the same opportunities to use a contrarian approach that the investor of several decades ago did. If anything, the investment odds have shifted even more in your favor because of the numerous new contrarian strategies that we have demonstrated. Investing can be a probability game with the odds on your side. Going back to the image in chapter 1 of the green and red rooms in the casino, I think a careful reader should now be able to walk into the green rooms where the players are few but the winnings are big, and avoid the thronged red ones where most of the crowd is losing.

Do your homework, think for yourself, and prosper.

APPENDIX A

Modern Portfolio Theory

 T HE EFFICIENT market hypothesis (EMH) leads naturally to modern portfolio theory (MPT), a supposedly scientific way of explaining market behavior, quantifying risk, and outperforming the averages. This work, or parts of it, is still widely used to make investment decisions by many professional investors.

The father of modern portfolio theory is Dr. Harry Markowitz, a Nobel laureate. Markowitz framed the outline of MPT in his Ph.D. thesis in 1952. According to Markowitz, rational investors should be risk-averse. This means they should not be willing to take higher risk without receiving larger returns. Risk was defined by Markowitz, as by all subsequent efficient market researchers, in terms of short-term market fluctuations. The greater the volatility of the security or portfolio, the greater the risk. Whether this truly, or even approximately, defines risk is examined in this book.

Starting from this premise, however, Markowitz pointed out that holding different types of securities, or securities of different companies, would not significantly reduce the price movement of a portfolio.* Effective diversification requires securities that do not fluctuate in the same direction at the same time.

For each security, says Markowitz, it is necessary to establish expected return, volatility, and a covariance of return against every other

---

* If the direction and magnitude of the securities fluctuations were similar, the statistical term is that the stocks have a high degree of covariance. If they are dissimilar, they have a low degree of covariance.

security.* With this information, he showed how quadratic programming could calculate a set of optimal portfolios, which he called "efficient portfolios." An efficient portfolio would produce the highest level of return for a given level of risk. Any portfolio that produced the same return, but at a higher level of risk, would be considered inefficient. Similarly, a portfolio that produced a lower return for the same level of risk would also be considered inefficient.

The Markowitz model relies on a good understanding of statistics and an enormous number of calculations. Markowitz himself pointed this out, stating, "an analysis of 100 securities requires 100 expected returns, 100 variances and almost 5,000 covariances." Remember, well over 5,000 companies trade on the major U.S. exchanges and Nasdaq alone. In short, if investors were willing to follow this method, they would be overwhelmed by its computation.

Markowitz was a pioneer, rather than the founder of a working theory. Other academic researchers looked for ways to simplify his complex risk-reward equations.

THE CAPITAL ASSET PRICING MODEL—CAPM

Three researchers, William Sharpe, John Lintner, and Jan Mossin, working independently, simplified Markowitz's calculations. They developed the standard form of the capital asset pricing model, often referred to as the Sharpe-Lintner-Mossin form of CAPM. Their major contribution was to replace Markowitz's complex calculation of risk with beta.[†] The researchers stated that each security's movements could

---

* The riskiness of a portfolio depends upon its covariance, or the extent to which asset prices move together, and not upon the average of each investment held. Thus, several risky bets may prove to be low risk as an aggregate so long as prices do not move together in the same direction.

[†] Sharpe, Lintner and Mossin break risk down into two distinct elements. The first is the systematic risk, or market risk (beta) outlined previously. The second element of risk is that portion of risk or volatility unique to the specific stock or other investment. This is called nonsystematic or diversifiable risk. Alpha represents the amount of return produced by a stock on average independent of the return of the market. It measures the specific component of a stock's return. Suppose, for example, the alpha is 1% and the beta is 1.5. If the market's return in a month was 2%, the most likely return on the stock would be 4%. The 4% is derived as follows: a 2% market return with a beta of 1.5 translates into a stock return of 3% (2% × 1.5). In addition, and independent of the market, the stock tends to produce a return of 1%. Alphas can be positive, negative or zero. These correlations, the theorists tell us, are what occur on average. In any short period of time, they can diverge from this relationship.

be related by its beta to a broad-based stock index such as the S&P 500, thus establishing a practical way to use the Markowitz model, while eliminating the tortuous calculations that came with it.

Chart A–1 demonstrates MPT risk and return measurements. The vertical axis is expected return,[1] while the horizontal axis indicates the risk. A key tenet of capital asset pricing theory is represented by point E. This is the expected return and the risk of the market as a whole.*

The important concept is that the market or its surrogate stock price index is seen as the optimal risk portfolio. No other combination of securities can produce a better trade-off between risk and reward. The point R_T on the capital market line is the expected rate of return on Treasury-bills, the risk-free asset, during the period under consideration.[†]

The segment of the line from R_T to E indicates the various returns available through the combination of Treasury-bills and risky assets, most often stocks. The range varies from investing your portfolio entirely in 91-day T-bills, or their equivalent, to increasing the equity risk by moving right along the line to E, which is the risk of owning the S&P 500 or its equity equivalent.

In order to receive an above market return, according to the theorists, the investor is assumed to be able to borrow at the T-bill rate (the risk free rate), and then leverage the portfolio, reinvesting the borrowed funds into the market. He can thus move along the capital market line from point E to point A. The more one borrows, of course, the greater the risk, but if the market behaves itself, the larger the return. The concept of the capital market line has played a crucial role in the development of modern portfolio theory (MPT).

ASSUMPTIONS UNDERLYING THE CAPITAL ASSET PRICING MODEL

The researchers base the standard capital asset pricing model on some very dubious assumptions. Here are the top nine.[‡]

---

* This is theoretically defined as the complete universe of risky investments available for purchase, with each weighted for its share of the total market value. Since it is impossible to calculate precisely the universe of risky investments at a given point of time, it is necessary to use a proxy for this universe. As noted, the S&P 500 is frequently used, although there are certainly other choices.

† The risk-free asset in the sense of assured rate of return is usually the 91-day treasury bill. Other important risks, such as loss of purchasing power because of inflation, are not considered.

‡ These assumptions and their shortfalls are also discussed in chapter 17.

Figure A–1

The Capital Market Line

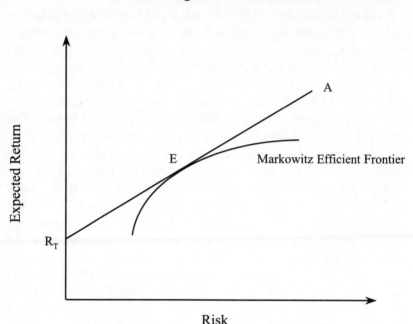

1. There are no transaction costs in buying or selling stocks or other investments. This includes not only commissions, but also the spread that exists between the bid and asking price. Specialists who make their money on the eighth or quarter spreads between the bid-ask spread, Nasdaq market-makers whose spreads are far higher, and, oh, yes, the entire brokerage industry, simply disappear, or become philanthropic organizations. Not bad for starters, but wait—the assumptions get better.

2. An investor can take any position in a stock that he wishes, re-gardless of its size, without affecting the market price. He can, for ex-ample, buy a dollar's worth of Intel or a billion dollars of it. Robert Stansky, the manager of the $63 billion Fidelity Magellan Fund, would cheer at the news, as it would make his life a heck of a lot easier. I have trouble, at times, buying or selling positions for my clients whose assets total only several billions of dollars, so if this academic pronouncement were true, my hat would also be in the air.

While no single investor's actions affect prices, the theorists con-tinue, investors, in total, determine prices by their combined actions.

3. The investor does not consider taxes in making decisions and is indifferent to receiving dividends or capital gains.

4. Investors are risk averse; they will demand greater return for a higher level of volatility.

5. Investors seek to control risk through diversification of their holdings.

6. Investors, as a group, look at risk-return relationships over similar time horizons. In other words, a speculator and a long-term investor allow almost identical time periods for their investments to work out. If I am a day trader, trying to make a quick buck by buying and selling, and you are a long-term investor, the professors say, the amount of time we give an investment to work out is exactly the same.

7. Investors, as a group, have similar views on how they measure risk. This assumes all investors have identical expectations with respect to the necessary inputs for a stock or portfolio decision.

If you can live with the initial five, these last two assumptions are doozies. Assumptions 6 and 7 suggest that each and every individual has the same time horizon and analyzes the outlook for every stock, or the market as a whole, in a similar manner. We need only look at First Call, a service that reports analyst recommendations, or the brokerage house reports themselves, to see major differences in opinion among various brokerage research departments. There is no evidence of homogeneity of investor expectations about stocks. This also brings up the question of why we buy or sell securities at all, since we all have the same analytical framework. But bear with me—there's more.

8. All assets, including human capital, can be bought and sold on the market.

9. Investors, as seen, can lend or borrow at the 91-day T-bill rate—the risk-free rate—and can also sell short without restriction.

You can see at a glance that most of the assumptions behind the CAPM model do not come close to reality—at least on this planet. First of all, nobody but Uncle Sam gets the risk-free rate of return. If Microsoft or General Motors can't get it, how can you or I? Everyone else pays slightly to significantly higher interest costs. Second, most institutional investors are restricted in their ability to borrow, while most individual investors are reluctant to borrow at all. The assumption that the investor does not consider taxes in making decisions is far-fetched. In the real world, capital gains are such a "minor issue" that virtually every Presidential election in the last 40 years has seen major pressure by Republican candidates to lower capital gains taxes. If investors do not mind paying regular income taxes, one might ask, why do we have a trillion-dollar tax-free municipal bond industry?

Large investors certainly affect the prices of stocks with their buy and sell decisions, and it is certainly not reasonable to assume the trader who thinks in terms of hours or days will have the same expectation of future value as an investor looking years ahead. The above sampling of academic reasoning, choice as it may be, is only the hors d'oeuvre; the risk assumptions of Markowitz, Sharpe, Lintner, Mossin, et al., may be even more difficult to accept, as we saw in chapter 14.

But it is precisely this complicated statistical formulation, built upon a logical briar patch, that allowed a theory like this to be formulated at all. If the assumptions were looked at on their own, separated from the formidable equations, the theorists might have a hard time maintaining credibility. In fact, the assumptions were so removed from reality that it took less than 20 years for the theory to be discredited by some of its strongest original proponents.

For the researchers, faith reigns supreme. Most theorists argue that these assumptions are close enough to reality to make important inferences about the behavior of stocks. They draw the conclusion that individual securities and the market as a whole are fairly priced according to the risks associated with owning them. The theorists advise, therefore, that investors focus their main attention on the "risk profiles" of their portfolios. That is, they should not expect to earn higher returns without taking on additional risk, as Sharpe, et al., have defined it, and if they want a lower risk profile, they will have to accept lower returns.

The theorists will counter critics of their assumptions by asking, "How much is reality distorted by making these assumptions? What conclusions about investment markets do they lead to, and do these conclusions seem to describe the actual performance of these markets?"

In conclusion, they emphatically state, "The final test of a model is not how reasonable the assumptions behind it appear to be, but how well the model actually works." Elton and Gruber, two well-regarded researchers, state that "despite the stringent assumptions and the simplicity of the model, it does an amazingly good job of describing prices in capital markets."[2] This is the major defense, not only of modern portfolio theory, but also of efficient markets themselves. At this point the reader should be able to assess how accurate the last statement might be.

APPENDIX B

Contrarian Investment Rules

CHAPTER 2

RULE 1

Do not use market-timing or technical analysis. *These techniques can only cost you money.*

CHAPTER 4

RULE 2

Respect the difficulty of working with a mass of information. Few of us can use it successfully. In-depth information does not translate into in-depth profits.

RULE 3

Do not make an investment decision based on correlations. All correlations in the market, whether real or illusory, will shift and soon disappear.

RULE 4

Tread carefully with current investment methods. Our limitations in processing complex information correctly prevent their successful use by most of us.

CHAPTER 5

RULE 5

There are no highly predictable industries in which you can count on analysts' forecasts. Relying on these estimates will lead to trouble.

RULE 6

Analysts' forecasts are usually optimistic. Make the appropriate downward adjustment to your earnings estimate.

RULE 7

Most current security analysis requires a precision in analysts' estimates that is impossible to provide. Avoid methods that demand this level of accuracy.

RULE 8

It is impossible, in a dynamic economy with constantly changing political, economic, industrial, and competitive conditions, to use the past to estimate the future.

RULE 9

Be realistic about the downside of an investment, recognizing our human tendency to be both overly optimistic and overly confident. Expect the worst to be much more severe than your initial projection.

CHAPTER 6

RULE 10

Take advantage of the high rate of analyst forecast error by simply investing in out-of-favor stocks.

RULE 11

Positive and negative surprises affect "best" and "worst" stocks in a diametrically opposite manner.

RULE 12

(A) Surprises, as a group, improve the performance of out-of-favor stocks, while impairing the performance of favorites.
(B) Positive surprises result in major appreciation for out-of-favor stocks, while having minimal impact on favorites.
(C) Negative surprises result in major drops in the price of favorites, while having virtually no impact on out-of-favor stocks.
(D) The effect of an earnings surprise continues for an extended period of time.

CHAPTER 7

RULE 13

Favored stocks underperform the market, while out-of-favor companies outperform the market, but the reappraisal often happens slowly, even glacially.

RULE 14

Buy solid companies currently out of market favor, as measured by their low price-to-earnings, price-to-cash flow or price-to-book value ratios, or by their high yields.

CHAPTER 8

RULE 15

Don't speculate on highly priced concept stocks to make above-average returns. The blue chip stocks that widows and orphans traditionally choose are equally valuable for the more aggressive businessman or woman.

RULE 16

Avoid unnecessary trading. The costs can significantly lower your returns over time. Low price-to-value strategies provide well above market returns for years, and are an excellent means of eliminating excessive transaction costs.

RULE 17

Buy only contrarian stocks because of their superior performance characteristics.

RULE 18

Invest equally in 20 to 30 stocks, diversified among 15 or more industries (if your assets are of sufficient size).

RULE 19

Buy medium- or large-sized stocks listed on the New York Stock Exchange, or only larger companies on Nasdaq or the American Stock Exchange.

CHAPTER 9

RULE 20

Buy the least expensive stocks within an industry, as determined by the four contrarian strategies, regardless of how high or low the general price of the industry group.

RULE 21

Sell a stock when its P/E ratio (or other contrarian indicator) approaches that of the overall market, regardless of how favorable prospects may appear. Replace it with another contrarian stock.

CHAPTER 10

RULE 22

Look beyond obvious similarities between a current investment situation and one that appears equivalent in the past. Consider other important factors that may result in a markedly different outcome.

RULE 23

Don't be influenced by the short-term record of a money manager, broker, analyst, or advisor, no matter how impressive; don't accept cursory economic or investment news without significant substantiation.

RULE 24

Don't rely solely on the "case rate." Take into account the "base rate"— the prior probabilities of profit or loss.

RULE 25

Don't be seduced by recent rates of return for individual stocks or the market when they deviate sharply from past norms (the "case rate"). Long term returns of stocks (the "base rate") are far more likely to be established again. If returns are particularly high or low, they are likely to be abnormal.

RULE 26

Don't expect the strategy you adopt will prove a quick success in the market; give it a reasonable time to work out.

CHAPTER 11

RULE 27

The push toward an average rate of return is a fundamental principle of competitive markets.

RULE 28

It is far safer to project a continuation of the psychological reactions of investors than it is to project the visibility of the companies themselves.

CHAPTER 12

RULE 29

Political and financial crises lead investors to sell stocks. This is precisely the wrong reaction. Buy during a panic, don't sell.

RULE 30

In a crisis, carefully analyze the reasons put forward to support lower stock prices—more often than not they will disintegrate under scrutiny.

RULE 31

(A) Diversify extensively. No matter how cheap a group of stocks looks, you never know for sure that you aren't getting a clinker.

(B) Use the value lifelines as explained. In a crisis, these criteria get dramatically better as prices plummet, markedly improving your chances of a big score.

CHAPTER 14

RULE 32

Volatility is not risk. Avoid investment advice based on volatility.

CHAPTER 15

RULE 33

Small-cap investing: Buy companies that are strong financially (normally no more than 60% debt in the capital structure for a manufacturing firm).

RULE 34

Small-cap investing: Buy companies with increasing and well-protected dividends that also provide an above-market yield.

RULE 35

Small-cap investing: Pick companies with above-average earnings growth rates.

RULE 36

Small-cap investing: Diversify widely, particularly in small companies, because these issues have far less liquidity. A good portfolio should contain about twice as many stocks as an equivalent large-cap one.

RULE 37

Small-cap investing: Be patient. Nothing works every year, but when smaller caps click, returns are often tremendous.

RULE 38

Small-company trading (e.g., Nasdaq): Don't trade thin issues with large spreads unless you are almost certain you have a big winner.

RULE 39

When making a trade in small, illiquid stocks, consider not only commissions, but also the bid/ask spread to see how large your total cost will be.

RULE 40

Avoid the small, fast-track mutual funds. The track often ends at the bottom of a cliff.

CHAPTER 16

RULE 41

A given in markets is that perceptions change rapidly.

APPENDIX C

Glossary of Terms

Bold type within a definition denotes a term also defined in the glossary.

American Depository Receipts (ADR)—Foreign securities traded in the U.S. markets. ADRs represent a stated number of shares of a foreign stock. Many of the larger ADRs are listed on the New York Stock Exchange and most have detailed financial information available in English.

Anchoring Bias—The failure to make sufficient adjustments from an original earnings or other estimate. Especially problematic in complex decision-making environments where the original estimate is far off the mark.

Anomaly—An empirical observation that contradicts the prevailing theory.

Availability—A mental rule of thumb, or **heuristic**, by which people "assess the frequency of a class or the probability of an event by the ease with which instances or occurrences can be brought to mind."* For example, most people would say that shark attacks are more probable than being hit by falling airplane parts, since shark attacks receive far more publicity. Yet being killed by falling airplane parts is 30 times more likely than being killed by a shark attack.

Base Rate—The prior probability that some event will occur. An example would be the average return on the stock market over a period of many years. Not to be confused with the **case rate**. See also **availability, heuristics, regression to the mean, representativeness**.

Behavioral Finance—The integration of psychology and economics into a new study of financial markets. It seeks to replace **efficient markets** with a new **paradigm** that explains **anomalies** inconsistent with the old paradigm.

---

* Amos Tversky & Daniel Kahneman, *Judgments Under Uncertainty: Heuristics and Biases* (Cambridge: Cambridge University Press, 1982).

Beta—The standard academic measure of **systematic risk**, or market risk. It is a measure of how much a stock or portfolio moves up and down as the market moves up and down. A stock or portfolio that fluctuates more than the market is considered to be more risky and has a higher beta. One that fluctuates less is less risky and has a lower beta. Mathematically, beta is the **covariance** of a stock's or portfolio's return with the market return divided by the **variance** of the market return.

Bid/Ask Spread—The difference between the price an investor is willing to pay for a stock (the bid) and the price a seller is willing to sell it for (the ask, or offer). It can be expressed as a percentage of the bid price.

Big Board—Trade lingo for the New York Stock Exchange.

Book Value, or **Net Asset Value**—The value of all common stock after deducting all liabilities and **preferred shares**.

Bubble—A mass speculation in which prices rise out of all proportion to intrinsic worth, only to crash (or "burst") as investors finally come to their senses.

Buy-and-Hold Strategy—Buying a portfolio and then holding it without any further buying or selling for a specified period of time.

Capital Asset Pricing Model (CAPM)—A model for the pricing of securities that assumes that a security's return is related to the market return through **volatility** as measured by **beta**.

Capital Structure—The proportion of debt, preferred stock, and equity in the total capital a company employs. The S&P 500 had a 55% debt-to-equity ratio as its capital structure in the mid-nineties.

Case Rate—The probability of an event occurring based on a relatively short recent history. An example would be predicting a high rate of return on technology stocks in the next few years based on their high return in the past few. The likelihood of such returns repeating is usually given by the **base rate**, not the case rate. See also **availability, heuristics, regression to the mean, representativeness**.

Cash Flow—After-tax earnings, adding back depreciation and other noncash charges. It is a measure of a company's real earnings power, as well as an indicator of its financial viability.

Closed-End Fund, or **Closed-End Investment Company**—Similar to mutual funds except that they do not continuously issue and redeem shares: their number of shares outstanding is fixed. Hence shares of closed-end funds must be bought and sold on the open market rather than directly from the issuing company. Many large closed-end funds trade on the New York Stock Exchange.

Cognitive Bias—The tendency to make logical errors when applying intuitive rules of thumb. See also **heuristics**.

Concept Stock—A company that may or may not have a financial record, but definitely has a good story to tell. Such stocks usually have high price/earnings ratios, if they have any earnings at all.

Confidence Level—One hundred percent minus the **statistical significance** level. A 95% level of confidence is the lowest level considered acceptable for claiming a finding is meaningful rather than simply random chance.

Configural Reasoning—Interpretation of a piece of information depending on its interaction with other inputs. Also called interactive reasoning, it contrasts with linear reasoning, in which inputs are evaluated sequentially, without considering their mutual interactions.

Covariance—The extent to which asset prices move together. If two stocks have similar reactions to investment news, their covariance is positive, if they have opposite reactions to events their covariance is negative, and if they are uncorrelated with each other their covariance is zero. See also **beta**.

Current Assets versus Current Liabilities—Same as **current ratio**.

Current Ratio—A ratio of current assets to current liabilities. This ratio determines how able the company is to pay its near-term debts—those due in a year or less. For most nonfinancial companies, a current ratio of 2 to 1 or better is considered sound, although this varies from industry to industry.

Debentures—Debt securities that are backed only by the "faith and credit" of the issuer (as opposed to first or second mortgage bonds, etc., that are backed by specific assets of the corporation).

Debt-Equity Ratio—The ratio of debt outstanding to equity (the value of all preferred stock, common stock, earned and capital surplus).

Debt Security—Any security issued by a firm that has the payment of income and/or principal to the holders set by legal contract (compare **equities**).

Discount Broker—A **broker** who offers lower commission rates in exchange for fewer of the additional services offered by traditional ("full service") brokers.

Dow Jones Industrial Average—An index originated over a century ago that consists of 30 of the largest "blue-chip" companies in the country. It is the most commonly followed stock index, though not the most comprehensive.

Earnings Surprise—The difference between a company's quarterly earnings and the analysts' consensus forecast, usually expressed as a percentage of actual earnings.

Efficient Market Hypothesis (EMH)—The notion that all securities are priced "rationally" in the market, that is, that all prices "fully reflect" all available information. Proponents of EMH claim that because all information is contained in stock prices it is impossible to "beat the market" without taking on excess risk.

Equally Weighted Return—The return on a portfolio in which each stock begins with an equal amount of money invested in it. See also **value-weighted return**.

Equities—Trade jargon for common stocks. The term "equity" refers to the fact that the holder has a share in the equity of the issuing company (compare **debt securities**).

Event Trigger—An event that initiates a change in investors' perceptions of a company, an industry, or the market itself, such a positive **earnings surprise** on an unfavored stock, or a negative surprise on a favored stock. Event triggers cause large changes in stock price (compare **reinforcing events**).

Expense Ratio—The expense ratio of a mutual fund is the annual charges the fund deducts for expenses, including management fees, expressed as a percentage of total investment. This comes right out of the investors' pockets. The lower the expense ratio for a fund the more favorable it is to the investor.

Fundamental Analysis—The practice of valuing stocks based on their underlying "fundamentals": balance sheet and financial measures such as earnings, **cash flow**, **capital structure**, etc.

Fundamentalist—One who believes in and practices **fundamental analysis**.

GARP (Growth At a Reasonable Price)—A relatively low **P/E ratio**, in respect to a company's above-average sales and earnings growth prospects. This is expected to result in the stock outperforming the market even if the P/E remains constant, as well as the possibility of significant additional appreciation if the P/E multiple expands.

Growth Stock—A stock whose price reflects the market's expectation of better-than-average future growth prospects; normally a higher P/E stock.

Heuristics, or **Judgmental Heuristics**—Mental shortcuts, or learning and simplifying strategies people use to manage large amounts of information. Most of these judgmental shortcuts normally work well in allowing - people to process large amounts of data that would otherwise overwhelm them. However, these simplifying processes that are usually efficient time- savers often lead to systematic mistakes in investment decisions, because of their shortfalls in processing statistical and market information.

Hindsight Bias—People's mistaken belief that past errors could have been seen much more clearly, if only they hadn't been wearing dark or rose-colored glasses. This heuristic seriously impairs proper assessment of past errors and significantly limits what can be learned from experience.

Holding Period Return (HPR)—The return on a portfolio (appreciation and dividends) that is bought and held for a specified period of time without any additional trading or rebalancing.

Hyperinflation—A spell of inflation that is so high, ranging well above normal levels (sometimes in excess of 100% per year), that it results in the total erosion of a country's currency.

Index Fund—A mutual fund that is not actively managed but instead mirrors the same holdings as one of the major market indices (most commonly the **S&P 500**) in order to match its return.

Indexing—The practice of managing a portfolio as an **index fund**. Also known as "passive management."

Inflation Risk—The risk that a **debt security** may lose a significant portion of its value due to inflation eroding the underlying principal.

Initial Public Offering (IPO)—Stock in a company being sold to the public for the first time.

Junk Bonds—High-yield bonds rated BB or lower by the major credit agencies. These bonds provide higher returns than "investment quality" bonds.

Large Cap—Short for large capitalization, the market value of the shares of a large company. Large cap stocks are generally considered to have market values above $5 billion. See also **market capitalization**.

Law of Small Numbers—Not an actual law, but a tongue-in-cheek reference to the tendency to overstate the importance of findings taken from small samples, which often leads to erroneous conclusions. This fallacy contrasts with the statistically valid, true law of *large* numbers.

Leveraged Buyout—In a leveraged buy-out, the buyer borrows from banks and/or other third parties (for example, by issuing **junk bonds**) to raise cash to purchase the common stock of a target company. The target company's resources are often utilized (divisions sold off, cash reserves used, etc.) to finance the takeover.

Liquidity—The ease with which a reasonable number of shares of a stock can be bought or sold with only a minor change to the market price. Stocks trading with large **bid/ask spreads** and at low **volume** are said to be "illiquid."

Load—The sales charge on a mutual fund, usually 1% to 8½% of the initial investment.

Long-Term Bond—A **Treasury bond** with a maturity of 10 years or more. "The long bond" usually refers to the 30-year Treasury bond.

Margin—Money deposited with a broker in partial payment of a stock's purchase. Typically, margin requirements are 50%, that is, the investor must put up at least 50% of the purchase price of stocks bought "on margin." The Great Crash of 1929 was blamed in part on the speculative bubble caused by investors buying on margins as low as 10%.

Market Capitalization—The total dollar value of all of a company's outstanding shares of common stock. It is equal to the price per share times the number of shares outstanding. Also called the "market value," or simply "market cap."

Market Timing—The attempt to time purchases and sales to the phases of the market. If this could be done successfully, money would grow on trees.

Market Value—Same as **market capitalization**.

Mean—Also known as the average, the mean is simply the sum of a series of numbers divided by the number of numbers in the series. For example, the mean of the three numbers 2, 3, and 10 is $(2+3+10)/3 = 15/3 = 5$.

Median—The middle value in a list of numbers. By definition, half of the numbers in the remainder of the list are greater than the median and half are less than the median. (If there is an even number in the list the average of the two middle numbers is used.) For example, the median of 2, 3, and 10 is 3. The median can differ significantly from the **mean**, or average.

Modern Portfolio Theory (MPT)—A large body of academic financial research, within the **paradigm** of **efficient markets**. MPT posits that returns on "risky" assets can be fully explained by **volatility**. The **capital asset pricing model (CAPM)** is a subset of modern portfolio theory.

Momentum Investing—Buying stocks with rapid earnings growth or companies or industries that are outperforming the market in the expectation that current trends will continue, and selling them when they lag.

Mortgage Bonds—Debt securities that are secured by real collateral (such as property, buildings, machinery, etc.), as opposed to debentures, which are backed by the issuer's credit rating. These are distinct from mortgage-backed securities, which are normally secured by pools of home mortgages.

Multiple—Short for P/E multiple, or **P/E ratio**.

Net Worth—The value of all common stock and retained earnings.

No-Load Fund—A mutual fund with no sales charges.

Nominal Return—A return that has not been adjusted for inflation.

P/BV Ratio—The ratio of a stock's current price to the latest fiscal year's **book value**.

P/CF Ratio—The ratio of a stock's current price to the latest fiscal year's **cash flow**.

P/D Ratio—The ratio of a stock's current price to the current annual dividend; the reciprocal of the dividend **yield**.

P/E Ratio—The ratio of a stock's current price to the latest 12 months' earnings (before nonrecurring gains or losses).

Paradigm—The working beliefs underlying all theory and research in a particular science. As the paradigm becomes widely accepted, its tools and methods become more deeply rooted in the solution of problems. **Anomalies** that contradict the basic tenets of the paradigm are a serious challenge to it. A paradigm must be able to explain the anomalies or it will eventually be abandoned for a new one that does provide explanations which the first one cannot.

Preferred Stock—As opposed to common stock, stock in a company that pays a dividend but does not endow the holder with ownership or normally with voting rights in the company. In the event of bankruptcy or liquidation, preferred shareholders are fully repaid before common shareholders receive a penny. Preferred shares are often convertible into common shares.

Profit Margin—Income as a percentage of net sales.

Quant—Short for "quantitative analyst," a Wall Street or academic statistician.

Quintile—One of five equally-sized groups making up a full sample. The items are first ranked by some measure, such as **P/E ratio**, and then grouped by the highest 20%, the next highest 20%, and so on down to the lowest 20%.

Random Walk—A process in which each event or measurement is uncorrelated with, and cannot be predicted from, any past events or measurements of the same process.

Real Return—A return that has been adjusted for inflation.

Recency and Saliency—Two aspects of events—how recent they are and how much of an emotional impact they have (often establishing a **case rate**)—that contribute to their being given greater weight than prior probabilities (i.e., the **base rate**). See also **availability, heuristics, representativeness.**

Regression to the Mean—The tendency of extreme events to discontinue, and for processes to revert to their mean values. For example, a study of the height of men found that the tallest men usually had shorter sons, while the shortest men usually had taller sons.

Reinforcing Event—An event that reinforces perceptions, such as a positive **earnings surprise** on a favored stock, or a negative surprise on an unfavored stock. In contrast to **event triggers**, reinforcing events generally have little or no impact on stock price.

Representativeness—A subjective judgment of the extent to which the event in question "is similar in essential properties to its parent population" or "reflects the salient features of the process by which it is generated."*

Return on Equity—After-tax profit divided by **net worth.**

Return on Sales—Same as **profit margin**.

Risk Aversion—The academic expectation that investors will demand greater return in exchange for taking on greater risk, usually defined as **volatility**.

Russell 2000 Index—The most widely followed **small cap** index.

S&P 500 Index—A **value-weighted** index of 500 large cap stocks specifically selected to represent all major industry groups. It is the most commonly used market index in statistical studies.

Sharpe-Treynor Index—A measurement of return that takes into account the amount of **volatility** in a stock or portfolio; essentially a "risk-adjusted" return.

Small Cap—Short for small capitalization. Small-cap stocks are generally considered to have **market capitalizations** roughly between $100 million and $1 to $2 billion (although stocks in the $500 million to $1 to $2 billion range are often called "midcaps"). Stocks smaller than about $100 million are often called "microcaps."

Standard Deviation—A statistical measure of the amount of spread, or scatter, of a collection of measurements about the average. Standard deviation answers the question, are the measurements packed closely together, or spread far apart? Standard deviation of returns is widely used as a risk measurement. Generally, the larger the standard deviation the greater the

---

* Daniel Kahneman & Amos Tversky, " Subjective Probability: A Judgment of Representativeness," *Cognitive Psychology* 3 (1972): pp. 430–54.

uncertainty (or risk) in the measurement. About two-thirds of the measurements normally lie within one standard deviation of the **mean**.

Statistical Significance—The probability that a statistical measurement has a causal relationship between the factors measured rather than simply being random chance. In economics, and many other social sciences, a 5% level of significance (5% chance that the measurement was random) is considered the standard threshold for accepting or rejecting a hypothesis.

Survivorship Bias—The failure to use all stocks in studies of past returns that would have been available to investors at that time. Stocks that did poorly and disappeared due to bankruptcies and reorganizations are sometimes not picked up in databases.

Systematic Risk—Risk that is endemic to the market, i.e., that cannot be reduced through diversification. Also called market risk.

T-test—A common test that uses **mean** and **standard deviation** to measure **statistical significance** levels.

Tactical Asset Allocation (TAA)—The attempt to move into and out of various markets at the right time. TAA shifts the portfolio mix (normally stocks, bonds, and cash) as conditions change. Most TAA signals are based on both economic and market indicators.

Technical Analysis—The practice of studying past patterns in price movements to determine future price movements (compare **fundamental analysis**).

Technician—One who believes in and practices **technical analysis**.

Thin Market—A market exhibiting low **liquidity**.

Transaction Costs—The costs of trading due to brokers' commissions and **bid/ask spreads**, as well as any additional fees (usually very small) imposed by the exchange or by regulatory agencies.

Treasury Bills (T-Bills)—Notes issued by the U.S. Government usually weekly and usually payable after 90 days (and in some cases up to 12 months). T-bills do not pay interest. Rather, they are sold at auction and the buying price is discounted by the market to the face value of the bill to reflect an equivalent interest rate. See also **zero-coupon bonds**.

Treasury Bonds—Bonds issued by the U.S. Government that pay regular interest (with the exception of **zero-coupon bonds**). U.S. Treasury bonds are a standard benchmark for bond return.

Turnover—The rate at which a portfolio changes its stock or bond holdings, usually stated as a percentage of assets each year.

Two-Tier Market—A market, such as the stock market of the early 1970s, in which a select segment of favored stocks were priced much higher (i.e., had much higher **P/E ratios**) than other stocks in the market.

Value Stock—A low P/E, low price-to-book or other stock, that is believed to be good value for the money.

Value-Weighted Return—The return on a portfolio in which each stock begins with an amount of money invested in it that is proportional to its market value. Also called a market-weighted return. See also **market capitalization, equally weighted return**.

Variance—A statistical measure of the amount of variation in a series of returns, very similar to the **standard deviation**. Academics often use variance in combination with the **mean** to describe the theoretical relationship between risk (as measured by variance) and return (as measured by the mean).

Visibility—Clearly definable prospects, such as projected earnings growth, for a company or an industry.

Volatility—A measure of the amount a stock or portfolio moves up and down relative to some average. Usually measured by **standard deviation, covariance, beta**, etc.

Wealth Relative—Academic jargon for the value of a portfolio per dollar initially invested over a specified period of time. It is calculated by dividing the (total, not annualized) percentage return by 100 and adding 1. For example, if the 10-year return to a portfolio is 250%, its wealth relative is 3.50, which means that for every dollar invested ten years previously, the investor now has $3.50.

Yield—Normally the dividend paid annually on a stock divided by its price. For a bond, current yield would be the identical calculation, i.e., the annual interest payment divided by the current price, while yield to maturity would measure all interest payments to maturity over the current price.

Zero-Coupon Bond—A security that pays no interest, but instead is sold at discounts large enough to include the interest rate over the life of the bond. The zero-coupon bond allows investors to lock in the interest rate for long periods, if rates are high. Thus if yields rose to 10%, the investor would receive not only the 10% on the principal of the bond, but also would have all the interest to maturity reinvested at this rate. For a long-term bond the difference in reinvesting the interest at higher rates can be considerable.

NOTES

CHAPTER 1   *The Sure Thing Almost Nobody Plays*

1. "Special Report: Money Managers," *Pension and Investments,* May 13, 1996, p. 23.
2. Burton Malkiel, "Returns From Investing in Equity Mutual Funds 1971 to 1991," *Journal of Finance* 50 (June, 1995), pp. 549–73.
3. Equity mutual funds were most bearish at the market bottoms of 1966, 1970, 1974, 1987, and 1990 (cash reserves rose to 9.7, 11.8, 13.5, 11.2, and 12.9% respectively) and were fully invested near the market tops of 1967, 1972, and 1987 (when these reserves dropped to 5.7, 3.9, and 8.8% respectively). *See* Investment Company Institute, *1995 Factbook,* 35th Edition (1995); Robert McGough, "How Much Cash is Enough?," *Wall Street Journal,* January 9, 1997, p. R1; and Martin Zweig, *Investor Expectations* (New York: Martin Zweig, n.d.). Ordinarily, common stock mutual funds keep about 7% of assets in cash or its equivalent and do not change these reserves markedly. The high and low figures presented are thus quite extreme.
4. But not quite as strong, only 65% of the letter-writers were bearish.
5. *See* the Sentiment Index of the Leading Services produced by Investors Intelligence of New Rochelle, New York.
6. Paul Samuelson, another Nobel laureate and perhaps the most influential economist of our time, was another important contributor to the efficient market hypothesis.
7. Gregg A. Jarrell, "En-Nobeling Financial Economics," *Wall Street Journal,* November 17, 1990, p. A14.
8. *See* George Anders, Cynthia Crossen, Scott McMurray & Robert Rose, "Big Board Curb on Electronic Trading Results in Halt at Stock-Index Markets," *Wall Street Journal,* October 21, 1987 (describing the New York

Stock Exchange's unilateral move "to restore stability to its own market by handcuffing institutional traders whose [index] strategies have exaggerated swings in stock prices"); Julia M. Flynn, "Officials Halt Trading in Several Futures Pits," *New York Times,* October 21, 1987 (describing 11:15 A.M. halt to trading on Merc's S&P 500 pit as "an unprecedented move"); Julia M. Flynn, "Merc Puts Daily Limits on Stock Exchange Futures," *New York Times,* October, 24, 1987 (intending the trading restrictions "to calm violent price swings"); James Sterngold, "Top Merc Official Defends Stock Futures," *New York Times,* October 28, 1987 (interviewing Leo Melamed, then Chairman of the Executive Committee of the Chicago Mercantile Exchange, who stated John Phelan of the New York Stock Exchange requested the Merc's S&P 500 pit be closed to relieve the pressure of sell orders).

9. George Melloan, "The Market Meltdown Makes Phelan a Prophet," *Wall Street Journal,* October 27, 1987.

10. David Dreman, "Doomsday Machine," *Forbes,* March 23, 1987.

CHAPTER 2   *From Technical Analysis to Astrology*

1. Mark Hulbert, "Long Term Performance Ratings," *Hulbert Financial Digest,* July 31, 1996. Mark Hulber5t's *Financial Digest* tracked the performance of 12 asset allocators who write market letters from January 1, 1987 to August 31, 1995. He notes that performance records are scanty on asset allocators before this time. His portfolios returned 8.38% versus 11.4% for the S&P 500 and 10.7% for a balanced portfolio of stocks and bonds (60–40).

2. David N. Dreman, *New Contrarian Investment Strategy* (New York: Random House, 1982), p. 23.

3. Lewis Knox, "A not-so-random walk on the Quant Frontier," *Institutional Investor,* April, 1991, p. 33.

4. Jason Zweig and James M. Cash, "Show Your Hand," *Forbes,* June 21, 1993, p. 240.

5. "The Stars Say Sell," *Evening Standard,* November 17, 1995, p. 36.

6. Anne Mathews, "Markets Rise and Fall, but He's Always Looking Up," *New York Times,* March 12, 1995, p. C12.

7. *Ibid.*

8. Harry V. Roberts, "Stock Market Patterns and Financial Analysis: Methodological Suggestions," *Journal of Finance* 14 (March, 1959), pp. 1–10.

9. M.F.M. Osborne, "Brownian Motion in the Stock Market," *Operations Research* 7 (March–April, 1959), pp. 145–173.

10. Arnold B. Moore, "Some Characteristics of Changes in Common Stock Prices," in Paul H. Cootner, ed., *The Random Character of Stock Market Prices,* (Cambridge: MIT Presss, 1964) pp. 139–161.

11. Clive W.J. Granger and Oskar Morganstern, "Spectral Analysis of New York Stock Market Prices," *Kyklos* 16 (1963), pp. 1–27.

12. Eugene F. Fama, "The Behavior of Stock Market Prices," *Journal of Business* 38 (January, 1965), pp. 34–105.

13. Eugene F. Fama, "Efficient Capital Markets: II," *Journal of Finance* 46 (December, 1991), pp. 1575–1617.

CHAPTER 3   *Bigger Game Ahead*

1. Chet Currier, "Value Managers on a Roll," *Associated Press,* March 22, 1994.
2. Sidney Cottle, Roger F. Murray, Frank E. Block, *Graham and Dodd's Security Analysis*, 5th ed. (New York: McGraw-Hill, 1988).
3. The capital structure is defined as the proportion of debt, preferred stock, and equity in the total capital a company employs. A number of other important ratios deal with financial strength. The current ratio, a ratio of current assets to current liabilities, is one of the most commonly followed. This ratio determines how able the company is to pay its near-term debts—those due in a year or less. For most nonfinancial companies, a current ratio of 2 to 1 or better is considered sound, although this too will vary from industry to industry.
4. Julie Rohr, "Has value investing lost its value?," *Institutional Investor* (June, 1991), p. 49.
5. William F. Sharpe, "Likely Gains from Market Timing," *Financial Analysts Journal* 31 (March–April, 1975), pp. 60–69.
6. Arthur E. Gooding and Edward T. Owens, "Peeling away mythical perceptions of TAA," *Pensions & Investments,* March 8, 1993, p. 28.
7. *See* The Morningstar Mutual Fund Survey.
8. One new academic study by Louis Chan, Narasimhan Jegadeesh, and Josef Lakonishok, forthcoming in *Journal of Finance,* claims momentum provides well above average returns for up to a year, but it does not take account of the high transaction costs. After these costs, the excess returns might be canceled out entirely.
9. Michael Jensen, for example, measured the record of 155 mutual funds between 1945 and 1964, adjusting for risk as the academics defined it, and found that only 43 of 115 funds outperformed the market after commissions. In 1970, Friend, Blume, and Crockett, of the Wharton School, made the most comprehensive study of mutual funds to that time. They measured 136 funds between January 1, 1960, and June 30, 1968, and found that the funds returned an average of 10.7% annually. During the same time span, shares on the New York Stock Exchange averaged 12.4% annually. Value-weighting for the number of outstanding shares of each company (which gave far more emphasis to the changes of the larger companies), the increase was 9.9%. *See* Michael C. Jensen, "The Performance of Mutual Funds in the Period 1945–1964," *Journal of Finance* 23 (May, 1968), pp. 389–416; and Irwin Friend, Marshall Blume, and Jean Crockett, *Mutual Funds and Other Institutional Investors: A New Perspective,* a Twentieth Century Fund Study (New York: McGraw-Hill, 1971).
10. No-load funds and funds with low sales charges perform marginally better.
11. Eugene F. Fama, Lawrence Fisher, Michael Jensen, and Richard Roll, "The Adjustment of Stock Prices to New Information," *International Eco-*

nomic Review 10 (February, 1969), pp. 1–21; James H. Lorie and Mary T. Hamilton, *The Stock Market: Theories and Evidence* (Homewood, Illinois: Dow Jones-Irwin, 1973), pp. 171ff.

12. Ray Ball and Phillip Brown, "An Empirical Evaluation of Accounting Income Numbers," *Journal of Accounting Research* 6 (Fall, 1968), pp. 159–178.

13. Here the efficient market theorists acknowledge a paradox. Since it is fundamental analysis that is largely responsible for keeping markets efficient, if enough practitioners believed the efficient market hypothesis and stopped their analytic efforts, markets might well become inefficient.

14. Daniel Seligman, "Can you beat the stock market?," *Fortune*, December 26, 1983, p. 82.

15. James H. Lorie and Victor Niederhoffer, "Predictive and Statistical Properties of Insider Trading," *Journal of Law and Economics* 11 (April, 1968), pp. 35–53.

16. Eugene F. Fama, "Efficient Capital Markets: A Review of the Theory and Empirical Work," *Journal of Finance* 25 (May, 1970), pp. 383–417.

17. Eugene F. Fama, "Efficient Markets: II," *Journal of Finance* 46 (December, 1991), pp. 1575–1617.

18. *Ibid.*

19. *Ibid.*

20. There are a number of precise ratios to determine risk. The most commonly used is the Sharpe-Treynor Index. If a portfolio outperformed the market or provided an equal return with lower risk, it is deemed to have displayed superior performance. The capital asset pricing model (Markowitz-Sharpe-Lintner-Mossin theory) has become predominant on Wall Street today. The theory or parts of it are used in most important aspects of investing; the average reader may be only vaguely aware of it, if at all.

21. Daniel Seligman, "Can You Beat the Stock Market?," *Fortune,* December 26, 1983, p. 82.

CHAPTER 4 *Dangerous Forecasts*

1. Christopher Cerf and Walter Navasky, *The Experts Speak* (New York: Pantheon, 1984), p. 203.

2. *Ibid.*, p. 116.

3. *Ibid.*, p. 115.

4. *Ibid.*, p. 152.

5. *Ibid.*

6. *Ibid.*, p. 155.

7. *Ibid.*

8. *Ibid.*, p. 157.

9. *Ibid.*, p. 159.

10. *Ibid.*, p. 175.

11. *Ibid.*

12. *Ibid.*, p. 167.
13. *Ibid.*
14. *Ibid.*, p. 183.
15. *Ibid.*, p. 182.
16. *Ibid.*
17. *Ibid.*, p. 186.
18. *Ibid.*
19. *Ibid.*, p. 206.
20. *Ibid.*
21. *Ibid.*, p. 228.
22. *Ibid.*, p. 207.
23. *Ibid.*, p. 208.
24. *Ibid.*, p. 215.
25. *Ibid.*
26. *Ibid.*, p. 52.
27. "Here Comes 1970," *Wall Street Journal,* September 30, 1969, p. 1.
28. Floyd Norris, "The Fed Will Act, But Does It Matter?," *New York Times,* September 22, 1996, section 3, p. 1.
29. Herbert Simon, *Models of Man: Social and Rational* (New York: Wiley, 1970).
30. *Ibid.*
31. P. E. Meehl, *Clinical Versus Statistical Predictions: A Theoretical Analysis and Review of the Literature* (Minneapolis: University of Minnesota Press, 1954); Robyn Dawes and Bernard Corrigan, "Linear Models in Decision Making," *Psychological Bulletin* 81, (1974), pp. 95–106.
32. Stewart Oskamp, "Overconfidence in Case Study Judgments," *Journal of Consulting Psychology* 29 (1965), pp. 261, 265.
33. L. S. Garland, "The Problem of Observable Error," *Bulletin of the New York Academy of Medicine* 36 (1960); Hans Elias, "Three-Dimensional Structure Identified from Single Sections," *Science* 174 (December, 1971), pp. 993–1000.
34. Harry Bakwin, "Pseudodoxia Pediatricia," *New England Journal of Medicine* 232 (1945), pp. 691–697.
35. P. J. Hoffman, P. Slovic, and L. G. Rorer, "An Analysis of Variance Model for the Assessment of Configural Cue Utilization in Clinical Judgment," *Psychological Bulletin* 69 (1968), pp. 338–49.
36. These can combine into 15 possible two-way interactions, 20 possible three-way interactions, 15 possible four-way interactions, 6 possible five-way interactions, and 1 six-way interaction.
37. L. G. Rorer, P. J. Hoffman, B. D. Dickman, and P. Slovic, "Configural Judgments Revealed," *Proceedings of the 75th Annual Convention of the American Psychological Association* 2 (Washington, D.C.: American Psychological Association, 1967), pp. 195–196.
38. Lewis Goldberg, "Simple Models or Simple Processes? Some Research on Clinical Judgments," *American Psychologist* 23 (1968), pp. 338–349.

39. Paul Slovic, "Analyzing the Expert Judge: A Descriptive Study of a Stockbroker's Decision Processes," *Journal of Applied Psychology* 53 (August, 1969), pp. 225–263; P. Slovic, D. Fleissner and W. S. Bauman, "Analyzing the Use of Information in Investment Decision Making: A Methodological Proposal," *Journal of Business* 45, no. 2 (1972), pp. 283–301.

40. Lewis Goldberg, *op. cit.*

41. Paul Slovic, "Behavioral Problems Adhering to a Decision Policy," IGRF Speech, May 1973.

42. Dale Griffin and Amos Tversky, "The Weighing of Evidence and the Determinants of Confidence," *Cognitive Psychology* 24 (1992), pp. 411–435; and S. Lichtenstein and B. Fischhoff, "Do Those Who Know More Also Know More About How Much They Know?, The Calibration of Probability Judgments," *Organizational Behavior and Human Performance* 20 (1977), pp. 159–183.

43. W. Wagenaar and G. Keren, "Does the Expert Know? The Reliability of Predictions and Confidence Ratings of Experts," in E. Hollnagel, G. Maneini, and D. Woods (eds.), *Intelligent Decision Support in Process Environments* (Berlin: Springer, 1986), pp. 87–107.

44. Stewart Oskamp, *op. cit.*

45. L. B. Lusted, *A Study of the Efficacy of Diagnostic Radiology Procedures: Final Report on Diagnostic Efficacy* (Chicago: Efficacy Study Committee of the American College of Radiology, 1977).

46. J. B. Kidd, "The Utilization of Subjective Probabilities in Production Planning," *Acta Psychologica* 34 (1970), pp. 338–347.

47. M. Neal and M. Bazerman, *Cognition and Rationality in Negotiation* (New York: The Free Press, 1990).

48. C.A.S. Stael von Holstein, "Probabilistic Forecasting: An Experiment Related to the Stock Market," *Organizational Behavior and Human Performance* 8 (1972), pp.139–58.

49. S. Lichtenstein, B. Fischhoff, and L. Phillips, "Calibration of Probabilities: The State of the Art to 1980," in K. Kahneman, P. Slovic, and A. Tversky (eds.), *Judgment Under Uncertainty: Heuristics and Biases* (Cambridge: Cambridge University Press, 1982).

50. G. Keren, "Facing Uncertainty in the Game of Bridge: A Calibration Study," *Organizational Behavior and Human Decision Processes* 39 (1987), pp. 98–114; and D. Hausch, W. Ziemba, and M. Rubenstein, "Efficiency of the Market for Racetrack Betting," *Management Sciences* 27 (1981), pp. 1435–52.

51. J. Frank Yates, *Judgment and Decision Making* (Englewood Cliffs, NJ: Prentice-Hall, 1990).

52. *Wall Street Transcript,* September 23, 1974.

53. The belief that all paranoid patients accentuate certain characteristics in their drawings belongs in the category of psychologists' old wives' tales.

54. L. Chapman and J. P. Chapman, "Genesis of Popular but Erroneous Psychodiagnostic Observations," *Journal of Abnormal Psychology* (1967), pp.

193–204; Chapman and Chapman, "Illusory Correlations As an Obstacle to the Use of Valid Psychodiagnostic Signs," *Journal of Abnormal Psychology* (1974), pp. 271–280.

55. *For details,* please see David N. Dreman, *The New Contrarian Investment Strategy* (New York: Random House, 1982), Appendix I, pp. 303–307.

56. "Vanderheiden Choices Top Other Pickers," *Wall Street Journal,* January 3, 1994, p. R34; John R. Dorfman, "'Value' Still Has Value, Says This Quartet of Stock Pickers," *Wall Street Journal,* January 4, 1993, p. R8; John R. Dorfman, "Cyclicals Could be the Right Way to Ride to New Highs in 1992," *Wall Street Journal,* January 2, 1992, p. R24; John R. Dorfman, "New Year's Stock Advice in an Icy Economy: Insulate," *Wall Street Journal,* January 2, 1991, p. R22; John R. Dorfman, "The Sweet Smell of Success Might Be One of Caution," *Wall Street Journal,* January 2, 1990, p. R6; John R. Dorfman, "Champion Stock-Picker Is Facing 3 Challengers for Title," *Wall Street Journal,* January 3, 1989, p. R6; John R. Dorfman, "Four Investment Advisors Share Their Favorite Stock Picks for 1988," *Wall Street Journal,* January 4, 1988, p. 6B; John R. Dorfman, "Stock Pickers Nominate Big Gainers for 1987," *Wall Street Journal,* January 2, 1987, p. 4B; Rhonda L. Rundle, "Stock Pickers Make Their Picks Public, Betting on Low Inflation, Falling Rates," *Wall Street Journal,* January 2, 1986, p. R4.

57. Just as the theory holds that even professionals cannot outdo the market over time, it also holds that they cannot do substantially worse. After all, it is their very decision-making that keeps prices at their proper level in the first place. The surveys, however, give us a different picture from the one assumed by the theorists. The massive underperformance in both up and down markets indicates that their most crucial assumption is inconsistent with a significant body of evidence. The hypothesis is made of straw.

CHAPTER 5   *Would You Play a 1 in 50 Billion Shot?*

1. Michael Siconolfi and Anita Raghavan, "Brokers Launch Bidding War for Top Analyst," *Wall Street Journal,* August 4, 1995, p. C1.

2. *Ibid.*

3. "The Superstar Analysts," *Financial World,* November, 1980, p. 16.

4. *Ibid.*

5. David Dreman, "Cloudy Crystal Balls," *Forbes,* October 10, 1994; David Dreman, "Chronically Cloudy Crystal Balls," *Forbes,* October 11, 1993; David Dreman, "Flawed Forecasts," *Forbes,* December 9, 1991; David Dreman, "Hard to Forecast," *Barron's,* March 4, 1980; David Dreman, "Tricky Forecasts," *Barron's,* July 24, 1978; "The Value of Financial Forecasting: A Contrarian's Approach," Fortieth Annual Meeting of the American Financial Association, 12/29/1981. Recently [6/1996], the study was updated again in collaboration with Eric Lufkin of the Dreman Foundation.

6. David Dreman and Michael Berry, "Analyst Forecasting Errors and Their Implications for Security Analysis," *Financial Analysts Journal* 51 (May/June 1995), pp. 30–41.
7. The average of the forecasts of the analysts covering the company. Studies have shown these estimates are reasonably closely bunched.
8. Before the early 1980s, the database used the forecasts of analysts in the Value Line Investment Survey, which normally were very close to consensus forecasts.
9. We used the database of A-N Research Corporation (formerly the research department of Abel Noser Corp.), which contains estimates from the leading forecast services: Value Line prior to 1981, Zacks Investment service beginning in 1981, and I/B/E/S beginning in 1984, and also First Call. The utilized portion of the database includes approximately 500,000 individual estimates. Eric Lufkin of the Dreman Foundation updated the findings for the 1991–1996 period using A-N data through 1993Q3 and I/B/E/S estimates thereafter.
10. The four separate error metrics:
    SURPE = (Actual Earnings – Forecast) / | Actual Earnings |
    SURPF = (Actual Earnings – Forecast) / | Forecast |
    SURP8 = (Actual Earnings – Forecast) / standard deviation of
        Actual Earnings, 8 quarters trailing
    SURPC7 = (Actual Earnings – Forecast) / standard deviation of
        change in Actual Earnings, 7 quarters trailing.
    All the results in the book are for SURPE—Forecast error divided by actual earnings.
11. With signs removed. We recorded a total of 79,182 surprises in expansions (34,072 positive and 35,181 negative) and 14,769 surprises in recessions (5,872 positive and 7,107 negative). Note that negative surprises outnumbered positive surprises in both expansions and recessions. Surprises of zero, although not true surprises, have been retained in calculations of all surprises, because they count in assessing analysts' overall accuracy.
12. Fried and Givoly, "Financial analysts' forecasts of earnings: a better surrogate for market expectations," *Journal of Accounting and Economics,* 4 (1982), pp. 85–107; O'Brien, "Analysts' forecasts as earnings expectations," *Journal of Accounting and Economics* 10 (1988) pp. 53–83; Butler & Lang, "The Forecast accuracy of individual analysts: evidence of systematic optimism and pessimism," *Journal of Accounting Research,* 29 (1991), pp. 150–156; M. R. Clayman and R. A. Schwartz, "Falling in love again—Analysts' Estimates and Reality," *Financial Analysts Journal* (September–October, 1994), pp. 66–68; A. Ali, A. Klein, and J. Rosenfeld, "Analysts' Use of Information about Permanent and Transitory Earnings Components in Forecasting Annual EPS," *The Accounting Review* 87 (1992), pp. 183–198; L. Brown, "Analysts' Forecasting Errors and Their Implications for Security Analysis: An Alternative Perspective," *Financial Analysts Journal,* January–February 1996, pp. 40–47.

13. Jennifer Francis and Donna Philbrick, "Analysts' Decisions as Products of a Multi-Task Environment," *Journal of Accounting Research* 31 (Autumn, 1993), pp. 216–230.

14. A Ph.D. in astrophysics who works for the Dreman Foundation.

15. *Forbes,* January 26, 1998.

16. Managements' estimates taken from *The Wall Street Journal.*

17. Minus signs removed so errors do not tend to cancel each other out. The last six analysts' studies use the S&P Earnings Forecaster exclusively or as major source of estimates.

18. David Green, Jr. and Joel Segall, "The Predictive Power of First Quarter Earnings Reports," *Journal of Business* 40 (January, 1967), pp. 44–55.

19. Ronald M. Copeland and Robert J. Marioni, "Executives' Forecasts of Earnings per Share Versus Forecasts of Naive Models," *Journal of Business* 45 (October, 1972), pp. 497–512.

20. McDonald, "An Empirical Examination of the Reliability of Published Predictions of Future Earnings," *Accounting Review* 48 (1973), p. 502.

21. Bart A. Basi, Kenneth J. Carey, and Richard D. Twark, "Comparison of the Accuracy of Corporate and Security Analysts' Forecasts of Earnings," *Accounting Review* 51 (1976), 244–254.

22. Samuel S. Stewart, Jr., "Research Report on Corporate Forecasts," *Financial Analysts Journal,* January–February, 1973, pp. 77–85.

23. R. M. Barefield and E. E. Cominsky, "The Accuracy of Analysts' Forecasts of Earnings per Share," *Journal of Business Research* 3 (July, 1975), pp. 241–252.

24. R. Malcolm Richards, "Analysts' Performance and the Accuracy of Corporate Earnings Forecasts," *Journal of Business* 49 (July, 1976), pp. 350–357.

25. R. M. Richards and D. R. Frazer, "Further Evidence on the Accuracy of Analysts' Earnings Forecasts: A Comparison Among Analysts," *Journal of Economics and Business* 29 (Spring–Summer, 1977), pp. 193–197.

26. R. Malcolm Richards, James J. Benjamin, and Robert W. Strawser, "An Examination of the Accuracy of Earnings Forecasts," *Financial Management,* Fall 1977.

27. J. G. Cragg and Burton Malkiel, "The Consensus and Accuracy of Some Predictions of the Growth of Corporate Earnings," *Journal of Finance* 23 (March, 1968), pp. 67–84.

28. *Ibid.* You may recall the Meehl studies of clinical psychologists, where it was shown that simple mechanical techniques performed as well as or better than the complex analytical diagnoses in 20 separate studies of trained psychologists. In fact, mechanical prediction formulas have been suggested in a number of fields, primarily psychology, as a direct result of these problems, and they will be a part of the strategies proposed in the following chapters.

29. I.M.D. Little, "Higgledy Piggledy Growth," *Bulletin of the Oxford University Institute of Economics and Statistics,* November, 1962.

30. I.M.D. Little and A. C. Rayner, *Higgledy Piggledy Growth Again* (Oxford, Eng.: Basil Blackwell, 1966).

31. *See,* for example, Joseph Murray, Jr., "Relative Growth in Earnings per Share—Past and Future," *Financial Analysts Journal* 22 (November–December, 1966), pp. 73–76.

32. Richard A. Brealey, *An Introduction to Risk and Return from Common Stocks* (Cambridge, Mass.: MIT Press, 1968).

33. François Degeorge, Jayendu Patel and Richard Zeckhauser, "Earnings Manipulation to Exceeds Thresholds," Working Paper, 1997.

34. John Dorfman, "Analysts Devote More Time to Selling As Firms Keep Scorecard on Performance," *Wall Street Journal*, October 29, 1991, p. C1.

35. *Ibid.* See also Amitabh Dugar and Siva Nathan, "Analysts' Research Reports: Caveat Emptor," *Journal of Investing* 5, (Winter, 1996), pp. 13–22.

36. Michael Siconolfi, "Incredible Buys: Many Companies Press Analysts to Steer Clear of Negative Ratings," *Wall Street Journal,* July 19, 1995, p. A1.

37. *Ibid.*, p. 3; and Debbie Gallant, "The Hazards of Negative Research Reports," *Institutional Investor,* July 1990.

38. *Ibid.*

39. E. S. Browning, "Please Don't Talk to the Bearish Analyst," *Wall Street Journal,* May 2, 1995, p. C1.

40. Dugar and Nathan, op. cit.

41. Siconolfi, "Incredible Buys: Many Companies Press Analysts to Steer Clear of Negative Ratings," p. A1.

42. Debbie Gallant, "The Technology Trap," *Institutional Investor,* May 1994, p. 122.

43. *Ibid.*

44. Amos Tversky, "The Psychology of Decision Making," in A. Wood (ed.), *Behavioral Finance and Decision Theory in Investment Management,* ICFA Continuing Education series, 1995, pp. 2–6.

45. *Ibid.*

46. *Ibid.,* p. 6.

47. *Ibid.*

48. Baruch Fischhoff, "Debiasing," in *Judgment Under Uncertainty: Heuristics and Biases,* D. Kahneman, P. Slovic, and A. Tversky (eds.) (New York: Cambridge University Press, 1982).

49. D. Kahneman and A. Tversky, "On the Psychology of Prediction, *Psychological Review* 80 (1973), pp. 237–251.

50. D. Kahneman and D. Lovallo, "Timid Choices and Bold Forecasts: A Cognitive Perspective on Risk Taking," *Management Science* 39 (January, 1993), pp. 1–16.

51. Jeff Cole, "10–9–8 . . . Privatized Space Program Is Near," *Wall Street Journal,* July 7, 1996, p. B1.

52. A. Cooper, C. Woo, and W. Dunkleberg, "Entrepreneurs' Perceived Chances for Success," *Journal of Business Venturing* 3 (1988), pp. 97–108.

53. E. Merrow, K. Phillips, and C. Myers, *Understanding Cost Growth and Performance Shortfalls in Pioneer Process Plants* (Santa Barbara, Calif.: Rand Corp., 1981).

54. J. Arnold, "Assessing Capital Risk: You Can't Be Too Conservative," *Harvard Business Review* 64 (1986), pp. 113–121.

55. S. Taylor & J. Brown, "Illusion and Well-Being: A Social Psychological Perspective on Mental Health," *Psychological Bulletin* 103 (1988), 193–210.

CHAPTER 6   *Nasty Surprises*

1. For the definitions and a discussion of these measurements see chapter 3.

2. For greater detail, see David Dreman and Michael Berry, "Overreaction, Underreaction, and the Low-P/E Effect," *Financial Analysts Journal* 51 (July–August 1995), 21–30; David Dreman, "Nasty Surprises," *Forbes,* July 19, 1993, p. 246.

3. We formed the portfolios at the end of the first quarter, and measured earnings surprises thereafter.

4. Compustat, provided by Standard & Poor's, is one of the largest stock data bases available providing price, earnings and other information on nearly 19,000 stocks. The studies reported here use the largest 1,500 companies in the Compustat database, traded on the NYSE, AMEX, and NASDAQ exchanges, as measured by the total market value of all shares outstanding at the beginning of each calendar year. (This sample is referred to here as the "Compustat 1500.") We use the Compustat tapes for all price and accounting information. Annual items, such as cash flows, are available in a 20-year moving window. We also used the "back data annual" tapes, which provide an additional 20 years of coverage extending back well before the earliest date in these studies. The Monthly file, which contains all the necessary price, dividend and earnings data, begins in 1962. We have also included all companies that were subsequently deleted from the Compustat files due to mergers, acquisitions, bankruptcies, liquidations, etc.

5. To control for negative earnings, we delete companies with no earnings or negative earnings. We also delete P/E multiples above 45, to control for stocks with nominal earnings, as a result of poor quarters. In doing so we also unfortunately lose some of the most highly favored issues.

6. Jennifer Francis and Donna Philbrick, "Analysts' Decisions as Products of a Multi-Task Environment," *Journal of Accounting Research* 31 (Autumn, 1993), pp. 216–30.

7. The t-statistics show that the probability is less than 1 in 1,000, often much less, that these results are just chance.

8. Jeffrey Abarbanell and Victor Bernard, "Tests of Analysts' Overreaction/Underreaction to Earnings Information as an Explanation for Anomalous Stock Price Behavior," *Journal of Finance* 47 (July, 1992), pp. 1181–1208; and V. Bernard and J. K. Thomas, "Evidence that Stock Prices

Do Not Fully Reflect the Implications of Current Earnings for Future Earnings," *Journal of Accounting and Economics* 13 (1990), pp. 305–340.

9. Eric Lufkin and I came up with findings similar to those of Abarbanell and Bernard. We also discovered that after the surprise quarter, stocks in the high, low, and middle P/E groupings (with positive surprises in that quarter) outperformed those stocks in the same groups without positive surprises, for the next three quarters. (The same was also true with price-to-book value and price-to-cash flow measures.) This seems to be caused by additional positive surprises, if the initial surprise was positive—or negative surprises if the initial surprise was negative—in the three succeeding quarters. Again indicating that analysts' forecasts do not adjust to changing conditions quickly.

CHAPTER 7 *Contrarian Investment Strategies*

1. Francis Nicholson, "Price-Earnings Ratios in Relation to Investment Results," *Financial Analysts Journal,* January/February 1968, pp. 105–109.

2. All fiscal years in the study were between September 30 and January 31. All companies studied had positive earnings. The number of such companies increased from 110 in the former year to 334 in the latter. (Paul F. Miller, Jr., Drexel Harriman, and Ripley, Inc., Report, October, 1966.)

3. Francis Nicholson, in an earlier test that eliminated companies with nominal earnings, measured the performance of high and low P/E stocks in the chemicals industry between 1937 and 1954. The results strongly favored the low P/E stocks. James McWilliams used a sample of 900 stocks from the S&P Compustat tapes in the 1953 to 1964 period and found strong corroboration of the better performance of low P/E stocks. McWilliams further discovered that while stocks having the highest individual appreciation in any given year appeared to be randomly distributed, those with the greatest declines were in the high P/E group. William Breen used the 1,400 companies on the Compustat tapes for the 1953 to 1966 period. He eliminated all stocks with less than 10% earnings growth and then set up portfolios of 10 stocks with the lowest P/Es relative to the market, comparing them with a series of randomly selected portfolios of 10 stocks in each year. See Francis Nicholson, "Price/Earnings Ratios," *Financial Analysts Journal* 16 (July–August, 1960), pp. 43–45; James D. McWilliams, "Prices and Price-Earnings Ratios," *Financial Analysts Journal* 22 (May–June 1966), pp. 137–142; and William Breen, "Low Price/Earnings Ratios and Industry Relatives," *Financial Analysts Journal* 24 (July–August, 1968), pp. 125–127.

4. For details, see footnote, *The New Contrarian Investment Strategy,* p. 149.

5. All companies with five-year records and with fiscal years ending in March, June, September, or December were included. In the high P/E group, a maximum multiple of 75 was used to filter out companies with only nominal earnings, which were put into an eleventh group and included in the calculation of the overall sample return. Results of this group

were erratic, partly because the sample size varied markedly in the different holding periods.

6. The stocks were arranged by computer into five equal groups strictly according to P/Es. The subsequent performance of each quintile was measured. To determine P/E rankings, most-recent 12-month earnings were used to the end of each period, along with the price on the last day of trading two months later. In effect, the earnings information was fully public at the time, and the P/E ratios were the ones currently available in the financial section of any newspaper.

7. David Dreman, "A Strategy for All Seasons," *Forbes,* July 14, 1986, p. 118.

8. David Dreman, "Getting Ready for the Rebound," *Forbes,* July 23, 1990, p. 376.

9. We used the same methodology in all my studies as was outlined in chapter 6.

10. David Dreman, "Cashing In," *Forbes,* June 16, 1986, p. 184.

11. Within the experimental design, we adjusted for methodological criticisms of previous studies, such as hindsight bias—selecting stocks, as Nicholson did, that had survived to 1962, something an investor of 1937 could not have known; and not using year-end earnings and prices, as previous studies did, when investors could not know earnings until several months later. I did not think these would markedly change results, and our findings indicate they didn't.

12. Sanjoy Basu, "Investment Performance of Common Stocks in Relation to Their Price-Earnings Ratios: A Test of the Efficient Markets Hypothesis," *Journal of Finance* 32 (June, 1977), pp. 663–682; Sanjoy Basu, "The Effect of Earnings Yield on Assessments of the Association Between Annual Accounting Income Numbers and Security Prices," *Accounting Review* 53 (July, 1978), pp. 599–625; and Sanjoy Basu, "The Relationship Between Earnings' Yield, Market Value and Return for NYSE Common Stocks: Further Evidence," *Journal of Financial Economics* 12 (June, 1983), pp. 129–156.

13. Sanjoy Basu, "Investment Performance of Common Stocks in Relation to Their Price-Earnings Ratios: A Test of the Efficient Markets Hypothesis," *op. cit.*

14. B. Rosenberg, K. Reid, and R. Lanstein, "Persuasive Evidence of Market Inefficiency," *Journal of Portfolio Management* 13 (1985), pp. 9–17; Dennis Stattman, "Book Values and Stock Returns," *Chicago MBA: A Journal of Selected Papers* 4 (1980), pp. 25–45.

15. Ray Ball, "Anomalies in Relationships between Securities' Yields and Yield-Surrogates," *Journal of Financial Economics* 6 (1978), pp. 103–126.

16. Eugene Fama and Kenneth French, "The Cross-Section of Expected Stock Returns," *Journal of Finance* 47 (June, 1992), pp. 427–465.

17. Terence Pare, "The Solomon of Stocks Finds a Better Way to Pick Them," *Fortune*, June 1, 1992, p. 23.

18. J. Lakonishok, A. Shleifer, and R. Vishny, "Contrarian Investment, Extrapolation, and Risk," *Journal of Finance* 49 (December, 1994), pp. 1541– 1578.

19. "Look ahead" bias—a problem resulting from dramatically increasing the number of stocks on Compustat tapes in 1978.

20. D. G. MacGregor, P. Slovic, D. Dreman, and M. Berry, "Imagery, Affect and Financial Judgment," Decision Research Report 97–11, Eugene, Ore., (1997).

CHAPTER 8   *Boosting Portfolio Profits*

1. The Compustat tapes comprise most of the major companies traded in this country. For details see chapter 6.

2. The methodology is identical to that described in our study in chapter 7, page 155.

3. As discussed in chapter 3, back in Graham's time, investors used actual book value to price, while today most contemporary investors use relative book value—the book value of the company relative to its industry or the market. The reason is that with inflation putting prices up manyfold in the postwar period, the replacement costs of land, plant, and equipment are substantially higher than the value shown on most corporate balance sheets. The average company in the S&P 500 currently trades at 5½ times its book value.

4. Although not shown in the chart, all three strategies continue to outperform for up to 10 years. For those of a statistical bent, the T-tests are also high. For example, low P/E and low price-to-cash flow have only a 1 in 200 possibility of being pure chance, while low price-to-book has 1 in 100. With the best stocks by each value measurement, the probabilities are 1/20. The t-tests are generally weaker on the high P/E side, but 1/20 (the "95% level") is generally considered the basic threshold for significance.

5. Financial studies have indicated that well-diversified portfolios of as few as 16 stocks have an excellent chance of replicating approximately 85% to 90% of the return of the group from which they are selected, even if the group is the stock market as a whole.

6. The large company rule is not etched in stone, however. As chapter 15 will demonstrate, small contrarian companies provide somewhat higher returns over time than their larger siblings. But the small cap strategy is entirely different and requires substantial resources to implement properly. It should normally be used for only a relatively small portion of your stock portfolio.

7. The second time was on June 21, at $14. Our firm was also a large holder of the stock.

8. The price is adjusted for two 2 for 1 stock splits.

9. Keefe Bruyette is a brokerage house specializing in bank research.

10. See page 205 (chapter 9) for the record of the Kemper-Dreman High Return Fund, which I manage using this strategy. In *The New Contrarian Investment Strategy,* I gave a similar record of performance from the 1976 to

1982 period, one of moderate market decline. The approach significantly outperformed the S&P 500 during this earlier period too.

11. The results are taken from the 27-year study from 1970 to 1996 that I did in collaboration with Eric Lufkin, which we reviewed in the last chapter.

12. And other studies over 60 years come up with similar results.

13. This is for one quarter. For one year there would be 25 draws with the card returned to the deck (from 105 possible cards because in holding our portfolios annually we would have three fewer quarters of data to use).

14. The numbers are startling but true. To follow up, we did a Monte Carlo simulation with 100,000 trials. Low P/E won 99,994 times.

CHAPTER 9   *A New, Powerful Contrarian Approach*

1. Some, like overconfidence and expert error, were viewed earlier, while others like cognitive biases and group and peer pressures are examined in chapter 10 and in chapter 16.

2. This work is based in part on an exchange of ideas between Sanjoy Basu and myself. Basu produced preliminary results, which, unfortunately, were lost after his untimely death in 1983.

3. The previous literature on whether contrarian strategies worked included Breen, 1966, who analyzed low P/E stocks for 1-year periods between 1953 and 1966. He found that stocks with low absolute P/E did only slightly better than stocks with the lowest P/E in an industry. See William Breen, "Low Price-Earnings Ratios and Industry Relatives," *Financial Analysts Journal,* July–August, 1968, pp. 125–127. However, the test used extremely small samples of 10 stocks each. R. Fuller, L. Huberts, and M. Levinson, "Returns to E/P Strategies, Higgledy-Piggledy Growth, Analysts' Forecast Errors, and Omitted Risk Factors," *Journal of Portfolio Management,* Winter, 1993, pp. 13–24, found that low P/Es within industries outperform the market.

4. All other methodology was identical to that described in our work in the last two chapters.

5. The industries that had the largest numbers of the cheapest stocks absolutely only marginally outperformed the averages, with returns well below those gained by the relative industry strategy.

6. Since I use large-cap companies in this strategy, the reader would be shielded from the frenetic small-cap concept stocks and IPOs, which were not a part of our study, and which I doubt would come close to these results.

7. In April 1979, for example, with widespread market disillusionment, the discounts on many of the leading closed-end funds ran well over 20 percent, making them appear particularly attractive relative to equity mutual funds at that time.

8. The record of these mutual funds can be found in the *Forbes* Annual Mutual Fund Guide (August 25, 1997). Similar information on no-load funds can be found in Lipper, Morningstar, or *Barron's.*

CHAPTER 10   *Knowing Your Market Odds*

1. Victor Niederhoffer, *The Education of a Speculator* (New York: John Wiley & Sons, 1997), p. 37.
2. Daniel Kahneman & Amos Tversky, "Subjective Probability: A Judgment of Representativeness," *Cognitive Psychology* 3 (1972), pp. 430–454.
3. A. Tversky and D. Kahneman, "Judgment Under Uncertainty: Heuristics and Biases," *Science* 185 (1974), pp. 1124–1130.
4. David Dreman, "Beware of False Parallels," *Forbes,* September 17, 1990.
5. Reed Abelson, "From Bulls to Bears and Back Again," *New York Times,* July 28, 1996, p. D1.
6. Robert McGough and Patrick McGeehan, "Garzarelli Proves She Can Still Roil the Market," *Wall Street Journal,* July 24, 1996, p. C1.
7. Reed Abelson, "From Bulls to Bears and Back Again."
8. Amos Tversky and Daniel Kahneman, "Belief in the Law of Small Numbers," *Psychological Bulletin* 76 (No. 2, 1971), pp. 105–110.
9. Tversky and Kahneman, "Judgment Under Uncertainty: Heuristics and Biases"; Amos Tversky and Daniel Kahneman, "Intuitive Predictions: Biases and Corrective Procedures," *Management Science,* Spring, 1981.
10. Amos Tversky and Daniel Kahneman, "Causal Schemata in Judgments Under Uncertainty," in *Progress in Social Psychology,* M. Fishbein (ed.) (Hillsdale, N.J.: Lawrence Erlbaum Associates, 1973); Daniel Kahneman and Amos Tversky, "On the Psychology of Prediction," *Psychological Review* 80 (1973), pp. 237–251.
11. Daniel Kahneman and Amos Tversky, "On the Psychology of Prediction," *op. cit.*
12. The reader may observe that this is the same course of action recommended in the discussion of the "inside view" versus the "outside view" in chapter 5.
13. Tversky and Kahneman, "Judgment Under Uncertainty: Heuristics and Biases," *op. cit.*; Tversky and Kahneman, "Intuitive Predictions: Biases and Corrective Procedures," *op. cit.*
14. Daniel Kahneman and Amos Tversky, "On the Psychology of Prediction," *op. cit.*
15. Roger G. Ibbotson and Rex A. Sinquefield, *Stocks, Bonds, Bills and Inflation 1996 Yearbook, Market Results for 1925–1995* (Chicago: Ibbotson Associates, 1996). Roger G. Ibbotson and Rex A. Sinquefield, *Stocks, Bonds, Bills, and Inflation: The Past (1926–1976) and the Future (1977–2000)* (Charlottesville, Va.: Financial Analysts Research Foundation, 1977).
16. *Business Week,* August 13, 1979.
17. Tversky and Kahneman, "Intuitive Predictions: Biases and Corrective Procedures" *op.cit.*
18. Kahneman and Tversky, "On the Psychology of Prediction," *op. cit.*
19. Tversky and Kahneman, "Judgment Under Uncertainty: Heuristics and Biases," *op. cit.*
20. Benjamin Graham, David Dodd, Sidney Cottle, and Charles Tatham, *Security Analysis,* 4th ed. (New York: McGraw-Hill, 1962), p. 424.

21. *See,* for example, George Katona, *Psychological Economics* (New York: American Elsevier, 1975).

22. Scott Plous, *Psychology of Judgment and Decision-Making* (McGraw-Hill, 1993).

23. "Death Odds," *Newsweek.* September 24, 1990, p. 10.

24. Tversky and Kahneman, "Judgment Under Uncertainty: Heuristics and Biases," *op. cit.*

25. Amos Tversky and Daniel Kahneman, "Availability: A Heuristic for Judging Frequency and Probability," *Cognitive Psychology* 5 (1973), pp. 207–232.

26. Tversky and Kahneman, "Intuitive Predictions: Biases and Corrective Procedures"; Tversky and Kahneman, "Causal Schemata in Judgments Under Uncertainty"; Don Lyon and Paul Slovic, "Dominance of Accuracy Information and Neglect of Base Rates in Probability Estimation," *Acta Psychologica* 40 (No. 4, August 1976), pp. 287–298.

27. Amos Tversky and Daniel Kahneman, "Belief in the Law of Small Numbers."

28. S. C. Lichtenstein and Paul Slovic, "Reversals of Preference Between Bids and Choices in Gambling Decisions," *Journal of Experimental Psychology* 89 (1971), 46–55; S. C. Lichtenstein, B. Fischhoff, and L. Phillips, "Calibration of Probabilities: The State of the Art," in *Decision Making and Change in Human Affairs,* H. Jungermann and G. de Zeeuw (eds.) (Amsterdam: D. Reidel, 1977).

29. Baruch Fischhoff, "Hindsight Does Not Equal Foresight: The Effect of Outcome Knowledge on Judgment Under Uncertainty," *Journal of Experimental Psychology: Human Perception and Performance* 1 (August, 1975), pp. 288–299; Fischhoff, "Hindsight: Thinking Backward?" *Psychology Today,* April 1975, p. 8; Fischhoff, "Perceived Informativeness of Facts," *Journal of Experimental Psychology: Human Perception and Performance* 3 (1977), pp. 349–358; Baruch Fischhoff and Ruth Beyth, "I Knew It Would Happen: Remembered Probabilities of Once-Future Things," *Organizational Behavior and Human Performance* 13 (No. 1, 1975), pp. 1–16; Paul Slovic and Baruch Fischhoff, "On the Psychology of Experimental Surprises," *Journal of Experimental Psychology: Human Perception and Performance* 3 (1977), pp. 511–551.

30. Paul Slovic, Baruch Fischhoff, and Sarah Lichtenstein, "Behavioral Decision Theory," *Annual Review of Psychology* 28 (1977), pp. 1–39.

31. Baruch Fischhoff, "Debiasing," in D. Kahneman, P. Slovic & A. Tversky (eds.), *Judgments Under Uncertainty: Heuristics and Biases* (New York: Cambridge University Press, 1982).

GENERAL REFERENCES, CHAPTER 10

Bar-Hillel, Maya, "The Base-Rate Fallacy in Probability Judgments," *Acta Psychologica* 44 (No. 3, 1980), pp. 211–233.

Dawes, Robyn M., and Bernard Corrigan, "Linear Models in Decision Making," *Psychological Bulletin* 81 (No. 2, 1974), pp. 95–106.

Fischhoff, Baruch, Paul Slovic, and Sarah Lichtenstein, "Knowing with Certainty: The Appropriateness of Extreme Confidence," *Journal of Experimental Psychology: Human Perception and Performance* 3 (1977), pp. 552–564.

Kahneman, Daniel, and Amos Tversky, "Subjective Probability: A Judgment of Representativeness," *Cognitive Psychology* 3 (No. 3, July 1972), pp. 43–454.

Payne, J. W., "Alternative Approaches to Decision Making Under Risk: Moments Versus Risk Dimensions," *Psychological Bulletin* 80 (1973), pp. 439–453.

Plous, Scott, *Psychology of Judgment and Decision Making* (McGraw-Hill, 1993).

Shaklee, Harriet, "Limited Minds and Multiple Causes: Discounting in Multicausal Attribution," Ph.D. dissertation, University of Oregon.

Slovic, Paul, "Choice Between Equally Valued Alternatives," *Journal of Experimental Psychology: Human Perception and Performance* 1 (No. 3, 1975), 280–87; "Psychological Study of Human Judgment: Implications for Investment Decision Making," *Journal of Finance* 27 (September, 1972), pp. 779–799. I think this is a particularly interesting article and one easily understood by the lay financial reader.

_____, "From Shakespeare to Simon: Speculations—and Some Evidence—About Man's Ability to Process Information," Oregon Research Institute Research Monograph 12 (No. 2, April 1972).

_____, and Baruch Fischhoff, "On the Psychology of Experimental Surprises," *Journal of Experimental Psychology: Human Perception and Performance* 3 (1977), pp. 544–551, and Sarah Lichtenstein, "Behavioral Decision Theory," *Annual Review of Psychology* 28 (1977), pp. 1–39. A thorough review of the literature in the field. Bernard Corrigan and Barbara Combs, "Preferences for Insuring Against Probable Small Losses: Insurance Implications," *Journal of Risk and Insurance* 44 (No. 2, June 1977), pp. 237–258.

Slovic, Paul, Howard Kunreuther, and Gilbert F. White, "Decision Processes, Rationality, and Adjustment to Natural Hazards," in *Natural Hazards, Local, National and Global,* Gilbert F. White (ed.) (New York: Oxford University Press, 1974, pp. 187–205.

Tversky, Amos, and Daniel Kahneman, "Availability: A Heuristic for Judging Frequency and Probability," *Cognitive Psychology* 5 (1973), pp. 207–232.

_____, "On the Psychology of Prediction," *Psychological Review* 80 (No. 4, 1973), pp. 237–251.

von Holstein, C. S., "Probabilistic Forecasting in Experiments Relating to the Stock Market," *Organizational Behavior and Human Performance* 8 (1972), pp. 139–158.

Yates, J. Frank, *Judgment and Decision Making* (Englewood Cliffs, N.J.: Prentice Hall, 1990).

CHAPTER 11 *Profiting from Investor Overreaction*

1. David Dreman, "A Bernard Baruch Kind of Market," *Forbes,* August 30, 1982.
2. David Dreman, "The Buy of a Lifetime?" *Forbes,* June 7, 1982.
3. David Dreman, "The Setting Sun," *Forbes,* August 24, 1987.
4. W. Braddock Hickman, *Corporate Bond Quality and Investor Experience* (Princeton, N.J.: Princeton University Press for NBER, 1958).
5. Atkinson, Thomas R., *Trends in Corporate Bond Quality,* NBER (New York: Columbia University Press, 1967).
6. The original Investor Overraction Hypothesis was updated in David Dreman and Michael Berry, "Overreaction, Underreaction and the Low P/E Effect," *Financial Analysts Journal* (July/August 1995), pp. 21–30.
7. David Dreman, Eric Lufkin, and Nelson Woodard, "The Dark Side of the Moon," Dreman Foundation Working Paper, 1998.
8. The study also uses 10 years of prior data, so the statistical measurements commence in 1963, because 1963 is the first year data are available on the Compustat Monthly file.
9. We use medians rather than averages for profit margins, return on equity, and the three growth rates within each quarter to avoid the problem of distorted numbers resulting from outliers or negative numbers. The medians for each quarter, however, are averaged over each 5-year timespan.
10. We use 77 five-year periods between 1973 and 1996. A five-year portfolio is formed in each quarter between 1973Q1 and 1992Q1. We start in 1973 to allow for 10 years of back data to 1963, the first year data are available on the Compustat Monthly file.
11. As noted, we ran the same tests for price-to-earnings, price-to-cash flow, and price-to-dividends with reasonably similar results.
12. David Dreman and Michael Berry, *op. cit.*
13. Statistically these figures are significant at the 0.1% level, which means there is less than a 1 in a thousand possibility they are chance.
14. R. Fuller, L. Huberts, and M. Levinson, "Returns to E/P Strategies, Higgledy-Piggledy Growth, Analysts' Forecast Errors, and Omitted Risk Factors," *Journal of Portfolio Management,* Winter 1993, pp. 13–24.
15. This is not the same thing as fine-tuning earnings estimates quarter to quarter. Growth will not be in a straight line. A company growing at 15% over 5 years will have quarters of 5% growth and others of 25% growth. The heuristic biases we looked at in the last chapter, however—the inputs matching outputs, the failure to understand regression to the mean, etc.—make us unable to accept the unpredictability of analysts' quarterly estimates. This is the reason I recommended in chapter 8 to look only at an approximate growth rate rather than attempting to fine-tune forecasts, because of the disastrous consequences of incorrect forecasts.
16. Academics have, I believe, unintentionally muddled the issue by confusing the fact that regression to the mean as contrarian stocks rise and fa-

vorites drop doesn't occur instantaneously, but over a time period of as much as 9 years, as was shown in chapters 8 and 9.

17. The information comes from a working paper I am currently completing in collaboration with Nelson Woodard (formerly of James Madison University) and Dr. Eric Lufkin.

18. We used all four contrarian measures to see if this effect worked in all cases—which it did.

19. Werner F.M. DeBondt and Richard H. Thaler, "Does the Stock Market Overreact?," *Journal of Finance* 40 (1985), pp. 793–805. Werner F.M. DeBondt and Richard H. Thaler, "Further Evidence on Investor Overreaction and Stock Market Seasonality," *Journal of Finance* 42 (1987), pp. 557–580.

20. Benjamin Graham, David Dodd, Sidney Cottle, and Charles Tatham, *Security Analysis,* 4th ed. (New York: McGraw-Hill, 1962), p. 179.

CHAPTER 12 *Crisis Investing*

1. As measured by the Keefe Bruyette Bank Index, a major research house specializing in banking and other financial stocks.

2. Money center banks seemed to us to have too many other unquantifiable bad loans in addition to those of real estate. We played it safe—perhaps too safe—because on the recovery many of the money centers, including Citibank and Chemical, went up as much as tenfold or more.

3. Prices are adjusted for the merger with National Bank of Detroit in 1995.

4. Duane P. Schultz, *Panic Behavior* (New York: Random House, 1964), p. 49.

5. The treasuries are redeemed at face value thus ensuring the interest payments were reinvested at the same abnormally high rates in the future. The longer the period the greater the discount. As an example, a 30-year Treasury yielding 15% would be discounted by 15% for each year the bonds are outstanding. In this case the bonds would be redeemed at $100 but only cost the investor $1.51.

6. The inflation rate at the beginning of each quarter is based upon the latest reported inflation figures (Consumer Price Index) for the previous 12 months.

7. M. Rothbart and B. Park, *Journal of Personality and Social Psychology* 50 (1986), p. 131. Paul Slovic, James H. Flynn, and Mark Layman, "Perceived Risk, Trust, and the Politics of Nuclear Waste," *Science* 254 (Dec. 13, 1991), pp. 1603–1607.

8. Paul Slovic, "Perceived Risk, Trust, and Democracy," *Risk Analysis* 13 (1993), pp. 675–682.

CHAPTER 13 *An Investment for All Seasons*

1. The book is currently being updated. Siegel took the returns from 3 sources: 1802 to 1870 from William Schwert, "Indexes of United States Stock Prices from 1802 to 1987," *Journal of Business* 63 (1990), pp.

399–426; 1871 to 1996 from the Cowles Indexes as reprinted in Robert Shiller, "Market Volatility" (M.I.T. Press, 1989); and the 1926 to 1995 period from the CRSP value-weighted indexes of all New York, American, and Nasdaq stocks. *See* Jeremy J. Siegel, *Stocks for the Long Run* (New York: Irwin, 1994), pp. 3–4.

2. Edgar L. Smith, *Common Stocks as Long-Term Investments* (New York: Macmillan, 1925).
3. Jeremy J. Siegel, *op. cit.,* pp. 3–4.
4. Irving Fisher, Foreward to Kenneth F. Van Strum, "Investing in Purchasing Power," *Barron's* (1925), p. vii.
5. *Forbes,* November 15, 1976.
6. William D. Nordhaus, "The Flexibility of Wages and Prices," *Inflation Theory and Policy* issue, *American Economic Review* 66 (May, 1976), pp. 59–64.
7. A 50% tax bracket is used, which was the bracket on $70,000 in taxable income in 1965. Tax rates ranged as high as 90% for much of the postwar period, only dropping with the Tax Reform Act of 1985. Tax adjustment assumes the following: stock dividends and T-bill and bond returns are taxed as income at the 50% rate until 1988, and at the 35% rate thereafter. Stock appreciation is taxed at an assumed capital gains rate of 25%. Stocks are assumed to have a turnover rate similar to the major market averages, roughly 100% every 33 years. This is implemented by calculating the average gain over the previous 30 years (or retrospective to 1946, whichever is shorter) and taking 3% of that amount as the taxable appreciation each year. The capital gains part of the calculation is far smaller than the income tax. Inflation adjustment is calculated after adjusting for taxes.

CHAPTER 14 *What Is Risk?*

1. Standard deviation measures the ups and downs of an asset's returns, irrespective of what the market is doing. Either way, beta and standard deviation measure past returns and *nothing* else.
2. J. Michael Murphy, "Efficient Markets, Index Funds, Illusion, and Reality," *Journal of Portfolio Management* (Fall 1977), pp. 5–20.
3. *Ibid. See also* Shannon Pratt, "Relationship Between Variability of Past Returns and Levels of Future Returns for Common Stocks, 1926–60," in *Frontiers of Investment Analysis,* 2nd edition (Scranton, PA: International Textbook Company, 1971); Fischer Black, Michael Jensen, & Myron Scholes, "The Capital Asset Pricing Model: Some Empirical Tests," in *Studies in the Theory of Capital Markets* (New York: Praeger, 1972); R. Richardson Pettit & Randolph Westerfield, "Using the Capital Asset Pricing Model and the Market Model to Predict Securities Returns," *Journal of Financial and Quantitative Analysis* (Sept. 1974), pp. 579–605; Merton Miller and Myron Scholes, "Rates of Return in Relation to Risk: A Re-Examination of Some Recent Findings," in *Studies in the Theory of Capital Markets* (New York: Praeger, 1972); Nancy Jacob, "The Measure-

ment of Systematic Risk for Securities and Portfolios: Some Empirical Results," *Journal of Financial and Quantitative Analysis* (March, 1971), pp. 815–34.

4. Dale F. Max, "An Empirical Examination of Risk-Premium Curves for Long-Term Securities, 1910–1969," unpublished Ph.D thesis (University of Iowa, 1972), Microfilm Order No. 73-13575.

5. Marshall Blume & Irwin Friend, "A New Look at the Capital Asset Pricing Model," in James L. Bicksler (ed.), *Methodology in Finance-Investments* (Lexington, MA: Heath-Lexington, 1972), pp. 97–114.

6. Albert Russell & Basil Taylor, "Investment Uncertainty and British Equities," *The Investment Analyst,* Dec. 1968, pp. 13–22.

7. Quoting J. Michael Murphy, op. cit. (the foregoing three citations are references made by Murphy within the quoted passage).

8. Robert A. Haugen and James A. Heins, "Risk and the Rate of Return on Financial Assets: Some Old Wine in New Bottles," *Journal of Financial and Quantitative Analysis* (December, 1975), pp. 775–84.

9. Eugene Fama and James MacBeth, "Risk, Return, and Equilibrium: Empirical Tests," *Journal of Political Economy* 81 (1973), pp. 607–636; Eugene Fama, "Efficient Capital Markets: A Review of Theory and Empirical Works," *Journal of Finance* 25 (1970), pp. 383–417.

10. *See* Eugene Fama and Kenneth French, "The Cross-Section of Expected Stock Returns," *Journal of Finance* 67 (1992), pp. 427–465.

11. *See* Eric N. Berg, "Market Place: A Study Shakes Confidence in the Volatile-Stock Theory," *New York Times,* Feb. 18, 1992, p. D1.

12. Bill Barnhart, "Professors Say Beta Too Iffy to Trust: A Substitute Stock Scorecard is Proposed," *Chicago Tribune,* July 27, 1992, p. 3.

13. Terence P. Pare, "The Solomon of Stocks Finds a Better Way to Pick Them," *Fortune*, June 1, 1992, p. 23.

14. Bill Barnhart, op. cit.

15. Mary Beth Grover, "Slow Growth," *Forbes,* Oct. 12, 1992, p. 163.

16. David Dreman, "Bye-bye to Beta," *Forbes,* March 30, 1992, p. 148.

17. Bill Barnhart, op. cit.

18. *Ibid.*

19. George M. Frankfurter, "The End of Modern Finance," *The Journal of Investing* (Winter, 1993), p. 9.

20. The impact of beta went far beyond the market itself. The Capital Asset Pricing Model had long been used by corporate managers to determine the attractiveness of new ventures. Because the accepted wisdom holds that companies with higher betas must pay commensurately higher returns, chief financial officers of high beta companies might be loath to invest in new plants unless they feel they can earn the extra dollop of return. Said a business consultant, "Dethroning the model may have been the best thing that has happened to American business." (Terence Pare, op cit.) MPT, it seems, resulted in bad business decisions in corporate America for a long time.

CHAPTER 15 *Small Stocks, Nasdaq, and Other Market Pitfalls*

1. E. F. Ehrbar, "Giant Payoffs From Midget Stocks," *Fortune,* June 30, 1980.
2. Rolf W. Banz, "The Relation between Return and Market Value of Common Stocks," *Journal of Financial Economics* 9 (March 1981), pp. 3–18.
3. *Pension and Investments Age,* February 2, 1981.
4. Trading for each stock in the Banz sample is only reported on the last day of the quarter. The 58% figure is an average of the last day of the 20 quarters in the 1931 to 1935 period. From spot checks with the original stock pages, the pattern looks consistent.
5. Marc R. Reinganum, "Misspecification of Capital Asset Pricing: Empirical Anomalies Based on Earnings' Yields and market Values," Ph.D. Thesis, University of Chicago, 1979; Marc R. Reinganum, "Misspecification of Capital Asset Pricing: Empirical Anomalies Based on Earnings' Yields and market Values," *Journal of Financial Economics* (March, 1981), pp. 19–46.
6. E. F. Ehrbar, op. cit.
7. John Cunnif, "A Profitable Crack in the Efficient Market," *Associated Press,* February 16, 1984.
8. Tim Loughran and Jay Ritter, "The New Issues Puzzle," *Journal of Finance* 50 (March, 1995), pp. 23–51.
9. *Pension and Investments,* February 15, 1982, p. 34.
10. Maurice Barnfather, "We Have a Tie-in to Mecca," *Forbes,* December 21, 1981.
11. *Ibid.*
12. Marc Reinganum, "Revival of the Small Firm Effect," *Journal of Portfolio Management,* Spring 1992.
13. The market value of each firm was measured at the beginning of each year. The breakpoints are given here in 1995 dollars. In each year, the assignments to market-cap quintiles were based on information that would have been available to investors at the time.
14. Transaction costs will likely wipe out any marginally greater return of the middle or second highest quintiles in the two smallest market cap groups.
15. Sanjoy Basu, "The Relationship Between Earnings' Yield, Market Value and Return for NYSE Common Stocks: Further Evidence," *Journal of Financial Economics* 12 (June, 1983), pp. 129–156.
16. Jay Ritter, "The Long-Run Performance of Initial Public Offerings," *Journal of Finance* 46, March 1991.
17. The National Association of Securities Dealers (N.A.S.D.) dates from 1939, when all firms that sold securities were required to join. It now has 5,400 securities firms as members, the vast majority of them tiny. Most trade in bonds or mutual funds, not stocks. Nasdaq is owned by the N.A.S.D. The Nasdaq stock market was started a quarter of a century ago as the National Association of Securities Dealers Automated Quotation System. Though a subsidiary of the N.A.S.D., it had its own board of di-

rectors. Until recently there was little representation by anyone but brokerage firms, although presumably its main responsibility was to investors.

18. Jeffrey Taylor, "A Fairer Nasdaq:," *Wall Street Journal,* August 29, 1996, p. C1.
19. Scott Paltrow, *Los Angeles Times,* October 23, 1994, p. D1.
20. *New York Times,* Dec. 12, 1997, p. D8.
21. Anita Raghaven and Jeffrey Taylor, " Will NASD Accords Transform Nasdaq Markets?," *Wall Street Journal,* August 8, 1996, p. C1.
22. *New York Times,* June 7, 1997, p. 31.
23. Anita Ragharen and Jeffrey Taylor, *op. cit.*

CHAPTER 16   *The Zany World of Rationality*

1. Lee Hockstader, "Russians Blame Leaders for Stock Fund's Crash; Government Becomes Scapegoat When Dreams of Capitalist Riches Run into Reality," *Washington Post,* July 31, 1994, p. A27.
2. Adi Ignatius, "As 'Pyramid Scheme' in Russia Begins to Collapse, Rubble May Trap Many," *Wall Street Journal,* July 27, 1994, p. A6.
3. Fred Hiatt, "The Russian Equivalent of Swampland in Florida," *Washington Post,* November 5, 1994, p. A1.
4. Lee Hockstader, "Stock Fund Collapses in Russia: At Least 1 Million Lose Savings in Crash," *Washington Post,* July 30, 1994, p. A11.
5. Steven Erlanger, "Russian Tied to Stock Scheme Gains Election to Parliament," *New York Times,* November 1, 1994, p. A14.
6. The Sharpe-Treynor index calculates risk-adjusted returns, considering a high return with low beta much higher than one with normal beta.
7. Christopher Farrell, Robert Neff, Igor Reichlin, Richard A. Melcher, Charles Hoots, and Pete Engardio, "Those Empty Spaces Won't Fill Up Anytime Soon," *Business Week,* August 31, 1992, p. 72.
8. Carol J. Loomis, "Victims of the Real Estate Crash," *Fortune*, May 18, 1992, p. 70.
9. *Ibid.*; and Bill McConnell, "GAO puts Bailout Tab at Nearly $500 Billion," *American Banker,* July 15, 1996, p. 3.
10. Charles Mackay, *Extraordinary Popular Delusions and the Madness of Crowds* (New York: The Noonday Press, 1974), pp. xix–xx. Originally published in London in 1841 by Richard Bentley.
11. Gustave Le Bon, *The Crowd* (New York: Viking Press, 1960), pp. 41–61.
12. *Ibid.,* p. 70
13. Carl Sandburg, *Abraham Lincoln: Volume 2, 1861–1864* (New York: Dell, 1970), p. 410.
14. Leon Festinger, "A Theory of Social Comparison Processes," *Human Relations* 7 (1954), pp. 117–140.
15. Muzafer Sherif and Carolyn W. Sherif, *Social Psychology* (New York: Harper & Row, 1969), pp. 208–209.
16. William Samuels, *Contemporary Social Psychology* (New York: Random House, 1969).

17. Joseph Alper, "What's New in Biotechnology," *New York Times,* November 18, 1984, p. D13.
18. Robert J. Shiller, "Initial Public Offerings: Investor Behavior and Underpricing," photocopied, Yale University, September 24, 1989.
19. Tim Loughran and Jay Ritter, "The New Issues Puzzle," *Journal of Finance* 50 (1994), pp. 23–51.
20. Jay R. Ritter, "The Long Run Performance of IPOs," *Journal of Finance* 46 (March 1991), pp. 3–28.
21. Nejat Seyhun, "Information Asymmetry and Price Performance of IPOs," Working Paper, University of Michigan, 1992.
22. Mario Levis, "The Long-Run Performance of Initial Public Offerings: The UK Experience 1980–88," *Financial Management* 22 (1993), pp. 28–41.
23. Bharat Jain and Omesh Kini, "The Post-Issue Operating Performance of IPO Firms," *Journal of Finance* 49 (1994), pp. 1699–1726.
24. Tim Loughran and Jay Ritter, "The New Issues Puzzle," *Journal of Finance* 50, no. 1 (1995), p. 46.
25. Richard Stern & Paul Bornstein, "Why New Issues Are Lousy Investments," *Forbes*, December 2, 1985, p. 152.
26. John Curran, "New Life in New Issues," *Fortune*, June 24, 1985, p. 119.
27. Scott Reeves, "From Sizzle to Fizzle," *Barron's*, March 31, 1997, p. 21.
28. Christopher Farrell, "The Boom in IPOs," *Business Week,* December 18, 1995, p. 64.
29. Browning, "Aggressive Growth Stocks Churn the Market," *Wall Street Journal,* June 13, 1996, p. C1.
30. Julie Schmit, "Fast Track to Riches: High-Tech Payoff: 'Boom! You Are Rich,'" *USA Today,* December, 26, 1995, p. 1A.
31. Steve Kaufman, "Investing in Internet Stocks Can Pose a Big Risk," *Dayton Daily News,* August 14, 1995, p. 18.
32. Gary Weiss, "Sidestepping Danger Before You Hear the Rattle," *Business Week,* December 25, 1995, p. 90.
33. *Ibid.*
34. Edward Wyatt, "Market Watch: A Lesson. This Time We've Got It on Tape," *New York Times,* December 10, 1995, p. D1.
35. *Ibid.*
36. *Ibid.*
37. In chapter 10, we looked at some relatively new psychological research that at least partially accounts for the behavior witnessed above.

CHAPTER 17   *Beyond Efficient Markets*

1. George Santayana, "Flux and Constancy in Human Nature," *The Life of Reason* I (1905–1906), chapter 12.
2. Milton Friedman, " The Methodology of Positive Economics," in *Essays on Positive Economics* (Chicago: University of Chicago Press, 1953).
3. Paul A. Cootner, *Industrial Management Review,* Spring 1962, p. 25.

4. Eugene Fama and Kenneth French, "Size and Book-to-Market Factors in Earnings and Returns," *Journal of Finance* 50, No. 1 (March 1995), pp.131–155.

5. John Cassidy, "The Decline of Economics," *The New Yorker,* December 2, 1996, pp. 50–60.

6. *Ibid.*

7. *Ibid.*

8. *Ibid.*

9. *See* Eugene Fama, "Efficient Capital Markets: A Review of Theory and Empirical Works," *Journal of Finance* 25 (1970), pp. 383–417.

10. EMH thus creates something of a paradox, for if the professionals are important to the operation of the efficient market, if they do help to keep price synonymous with value, they must also, according to EMH, be dismal failures in the primary goal of their profession—helping their clients outperform the market.

11. J. Michael Murphy, "Efficient Markets, Index Funds, Illusion, and Reality," *Journal of Portfolio Management* (Fall 1977), pp. 8–9.

12. *Ibid.,* p. 10.

13. *Ibid.*

14. *Ibid.*

15. Michael C. Jensen, "The Performance of Mutual Funds in the Period 1945–1964," *Journal of Finance* 23 (May 1968), pp. 389–416.

16. As indicated, this would exclude a minute number of extraordinarily skilled professionals, using extensive resources only for their own use.

17. "The Best Record Around: They Call It the Value Line Enigma, and It Is a Stumper," *Inc.,* Sept. 1983, p. 168.

18. Tim Loughran and Jay Ritter, "The New Issues Puzzle," *Journal of Finance* 50, No. 1 (1995) pp. 23–51.

19. Eugene Fama, Lawrence Fisher, Michael Jensen, and Richard Roll, "The Adjustment of Stock Prices to New Information," *International Economic Review* 10 (1969), pp. 1–21.

20. Ray Ball and Philip Brown, "An Empirical Evaluation of Accounting Numbers," *Journal of Accounting Research* 6 (1968), pp. 159–178.

21. Myron S. Scholes, "The Market for Securities: Substitution Versus Price Pressure and the Effects of Information on Share Prices," *Journal of Business* 45 (1972), pp. 179–211.

22. Eugene Fama, "Efficient Capital Markets: II," *Journal of Finance* 46 (1991), p. 1601

23. Roni Michaely, Richard H. Thaler and Kent Womack, "Price Reactions to Dividend Initiations and Omissions: Overreaction or Drift?," Working Paper, Cornell University, 1994.

24. *Ibid.,* p. 14.

25. *See* Victor Bernard & Jacob Thomas, "Evidence That Stock Prices Do Not Fully Reflect the Implications of Current Earnings for Future Earnings," *Journal of Accounting & Economics* 13 (1990), pp. 305–340; Victor

Bernard & Jacob Thomas, "Post-Earnings-Announcement Drift: Delayed Price Response or Risk Premium?," *Journal of Accounting Research* 27 (S) (1989), pp. 1–36; George Foster, C. Olson & Shevlin, "Earnings Releases, Anomalies, and the Behavior of Security Returns," *The Accounting Review* 59 (1984), pp. 574–603.

26. Jeffery Abarbanell and Victor Bernard, "Tests of Analysts' Overreaction/ Underreaction to Earnings Information as an Explanation for Anomalous Stock Price Behavior," *Journal of Finance* 47 (1992), pp. 1181–1206.

27. *See*, for example, Tables 8–1 and 9–1.

28. Robert J. Shiller, "Do Stock Prices Move Too Much to Be Justified by Subsequent Changes in Dividends?" *American Economic Review* 71 (1981), pp. 421–436.

29. *Ibid.*, pp. 432–33.

30. *See* David N. Dreman, *Psychology and the Stock Market* (New York: AMACOM, 1977), p. 221.

31. Edward M. Saunders, Jr., "Testing the Efficient Market Hypothesis without Assumptions," *Journal of Portfolio Management,* Summer 1994, p. 28.

32. Karl R. Popper, *The Logic of Scientific Discovery* (New York: Basic Books, 1959).

33. Thomas S. Kuhn, *The Structure of Scientific Revolutions* (Chicago: University of Chicago Press, 1970).

34. *Ibid.*, p. 23.

35. *Ibid.*, p. 52.

APPENDIX A

1. J. B. Cohen, E. D. Zinbarg, and A. Zeikel, *Investment Analysis and Portfolio Management* (Homewood, Ill.: Richard D. Irwin, 1987), p. 152.

2. Edwin J. Elton and Martin J. Gruber, *Modern Portfolio Theory and Investment Analysis,* 5th Edition (New York: Wiley, 1995), pp. 294–295.

INDEX